D1453833

North

THE JOHN HOPE FRANKLIN
SERIES IN AFRICAN AMERICAN
HISTORY AND CULTURE

*Waldo E. Martin Jr. and
Patricia Sullivan, editors*

The University of
North Carolina Press
Chapel Hill

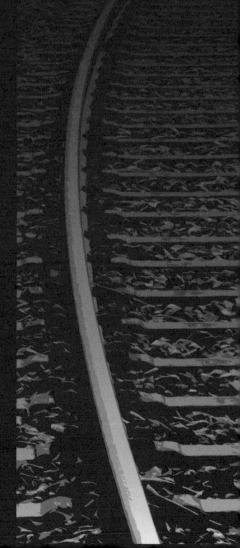

SARAH-JANE MATHIEU

of the Color Line

Migration and Black Resistance
in Canada, 1870–1955

Designed by Jacquline Johnson
Set in Minion
by Keystone Typesetting, Inc.
Manufactured in the United States of America

The paper in this book meets the guidelines for
permanence and durability of the Committee on
Production Guidelines for Book Longevity of the
Council on Library Resources.

The University of North Carolina Press has been a
member of the Green Press Initiative since 2003.

Library of Congress Cataloging-in-Publication Data
Mathieu, Sarah-Jane.
    North of the color line : migration and Black
resistance in Canada, 1870–1955 / Sarah-Jane Mathieu.
    p. cm. — (The John Hope Franklin series in African
American history and culture)
    Includes bibliographical references and index.
ISBN 978-0-8078-3429-9 (cloth: alk. paper)
ISBN 978-0-8078-7166-9 (pbk.: alk. paper)
1. Blacks—Canada—History. 2. African Americans—
Canada—History. 3. West Indians—Canada—History.
4. Canada—Race relations. 5. Immigrants—Canada.
6. Blacks—Canada—Social conditions. 7. African
Americans—Canada—Social conditions. 8. West
Indians—Canada—Social conditions. I. Title.
    F1035.N3M318 2010
    305.800971—dc22
    2010018364

Portions of this work appeared earlier, in somewhat
different form, as "North of the Colour Line: Race,
Migration, and Transnational Resistance in Canada,
1870–1955," *Labour/Le Travail* 47 (Spring 2001), and
are reprinted here by permission.

cloth   14 13 12 11 10   5 4 3 2 1
paper   14 13 12 11 10   5 4 3 2 1

To MIA AVERY *and* HÉLÈNE LOCHARD
for teaching me the magic of telling stories

I don't know if you've ever noticed, or perhaps would care very much if you did, that the sweater numbers of all the dominant hockey players of an earlier age . . . were single digits. Think about it, Richard, 9 and Howe the same, and later on Bobby Hull. Bobby Orr was 4, of course but so was Jean Béliveau and Red Kelly, even after he switched from defence to centre. Tim Horton, 7. Doug Harvey, 2. This list could go on. . . . But even if you noticed all the low numbers, you may not know why so many of the better players wore them. It all had to do with sleeping cars. When teams travelled only by overnight train, someone had to rule on who got the lower bunks. The solution, well you've guessed it by now, they were allotted by sweater number, and of course, you didn't want to have your stars having to clamber awkwardly up those silly but necessary ladders. Ergo, good player, low sweater number, lower berth. . . . It's surprising how much social history is reflected in the history of train travel and nowhere more so, I'd say, than in the story of those old sleeping cars.

PETER GZOWSKI, CBC RADIO
"Some of the Best Minds of Our Times"
2 July 2000

Contents

Figures

Acknowledgments

The Haitian adage "cé zye ki pè travay" admonishes that " 'tis the eyes that fear the work." Facing hundreds of archival files and seemingly endless microfilm reels—none of them reassuringly labeled "black/Negroes/colored"—made these eyes fear indeed. So too did staring at the computer screen wondering how and when I would make this story come to life, how I would do justice to the many families who handed over their memories and photographs to me, then a graduate student hitchhiking across Canada scouting for surviving sleeping car porters. I am not sure when I stopped fearing in favor of writing, but I do know to whom I am beholden for committing my thoughts to page and delighting in the process.

This story about sleeping car porters, the forgotten black men who slipped in and out of Canada's famed railway stations during the first half of the twentieth century, first took shape in the kitchen of Mrs. Frances Atwell. Born in Winnipeg in 1923, Mrs. Atwell grew up with many of the key figures in this story and remembered them with infectious enthusiasm and enviable clarity. During our first interview—which lasted nine hours!—Frances and her husband, George, told of the impressive measures taken by porters intent on protecting their workers' rights and defending African Canadians' social, political, cultural, and economic interests. Most important, Mrs. Atwell played a critical role in helping me meet other Winnipeg railway families—Lee and Alice Williams, Helen and Eddie Bailey, Eddie Blackman, and Lawrence and Ethel Lewsey—who also graciously shared their experiences with me. To all the black Winnipeggers who entrusted their stories to me, who drove me around town, and who fed me, I thank you.

I also owe tremendous thanks to the Blanchette family—Yvonne Blanchette, Diane Chambers, and Dr. Howard Blanchette—for sharing their memories of the man I would most have liked to meet: the indefatigable railway activist Arthur R. Blanchette. Dr. Blanchette was especially generous with his time and even invited me to join his family for a reunion in St. Kitts. Arthur R. Blanchette's joie de vivre lived on in his son's baritone laughter and in the many stories he recounted. I hope that this book honors Arthur R.

Blanchette's legacy and all the black men who worked the rails. This book is for them.

North of the Color Line received assistance from several sources who believed in this project and proved it: the National Endowment for the Humanities, the Schomburg Center for Research in Black Culture, the Social Science and Humanities Research Council of Canada, the Canadian Pacific Archives, the Library and Archives of Canada, the Archives of Manitoba, the Paul Mellon Foundation, the American Historical Association, and the Organization of American Historians, as well as Yale, Harvard, and Princeton universities.

Innumerable others deserve thanks for helping with my research, reading my work in its various incarnations, and patiently listening to my many stories about sleeping car porters. I am deeply indebted to Robin Winks for insisting that I think broadly and argue boldly. I am so very grateful to Glenda Gilmore, whose insight, wisdom, counsel, support, and friendship carried this book to completion. David Montgomery, Patricia Pessar, Nell Painter, and Colin Palmer invested time and care in this manuscript, and for this I sincerely thank them. I also shamefully exploited the patience and kindness of my family, friends, and colleagues in order to get this book finished. Gerry Atwell, Jennifer Baszile, Kelly Davis, Jhieny Fabre, Kirsten Fischer, Lance Herrington, Matthew Joseph, Michelle Wittcoff Kuhl, Ferentz Lafargue, Annick and Meiz Majdoub, MJ Maynes, Alicia Pittard, Hildegard Quevedo, Jim Walker, and Barbara Welke made sure that I laughed, ate, slept, and purged this book of many of its imperfections. Mila and Mahalia Majdoub and Vanessa Constant spent incalculable hours pouring over microfilm material, newspaper articles, employee rosters, border entry records, and census data. Mille merci mes soeurs!

And finally, thanks to Mia Avery for sleeping through her nights from her first night home so that I could work into the morning.

Abbreviations

The following abbreviations are used in the text. For abbreviations used in the notes, see p. 219.

AFL   American Federation of Labor
BSCP   Brotherhood of Sleeping Car Porters
CBRE   Canadian Brotherhood of Railway Employees
CLACP   Canadian League for the Advancement of Coloured People
CNR   Canadian National Railways
CPR   Canadian Pacific Railway
DISCO   Dominion Iron and Steel Company
GTR   Grand Trunk Railway
ICR   Intercolonial Railway
IDIA   Industrial Disputes Investigation Act
NAACP   National Association for the Advancement of Colored People
OSCP   Order of Sleeping Car Porters
UNIA   Universal Negro Improvement Association

North of the Color Line

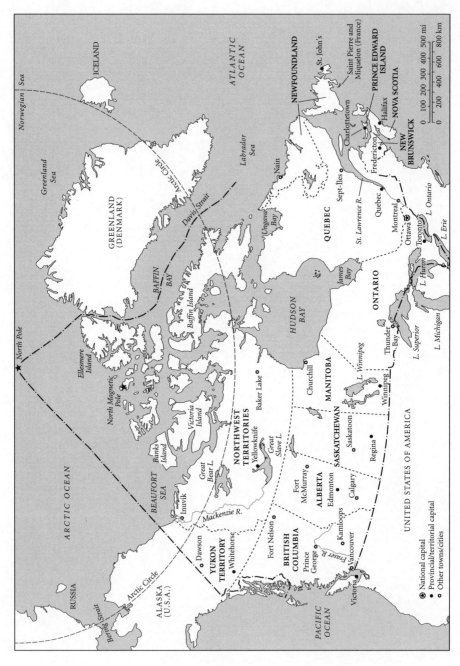

Fig. 1. Canada

Birth of a Nation

Race, Empire, and Nationalism during Canada's Railway Age

Smoke belched from the *Pacific Express*'s engine as it slowly snaked into Winnipeg the morning of 1 July 1886—just in time for Canada Day celebrations. Three thousand excited spectators and an artillery salvo heralded the arrival of Canada's first transcontinental train, now halfway through its maiden voyage.[1] It was, just as the Canadian Pacific Railway (CPR) company had promised, a red-letter day. The procession of train cars spanned seven hundred feet end to end and included a wood-burning locomotive, two first-class cars, two baggage cars, the "Holyrood" dining car, and the "Honolulu" and "Yokohama" sleeping cars.[2] Enthusiasts quickly besieged the opulent sleepers and marveled at their awesome appointments. W. F. Salisbury, a passenger and CPR executive, described the pandemonium over the sleepers in a letter to his wife: "Our car the *Honolulu* was thronged with admiring visitors during our stay," and added, "I dare say a hundred or more people passed through it—in fact, I may say we were treated with this kind consideration at almost every place we stopped during daylight. Modesty, I presume, forbade them [from] disturbing us during the night."[3]

Canadians had much cause for celebrating the completion of their national railway line. Their first through train signaled the rebirth of Canada as a modern nation and pointed to the country's maturation into the new industrial era. Accordingly, they made powerful emotional connections between railroad technology and the rise of their new nation-state. Canadian statesmen and railway barons alike looked to the railway as the nation's guaranteed path to modernity and prosperity, explicitly wedding technology, race, nationalism, and empire. The railway linked the nation—even becoming Canada's national icon—and promised stability, wealth, and power into the twentieth century. More important, the CPR helped Canadians lay claim to their place as guardians of the British Empire's North American interests. Measured against the Caribbean, imagined as a source of black brawn and raw goods, decidedly modern white Canadians crafted their national image as one of Anglo-Saxon industry.

Canada's enrapture with modernity—overwhelmingly defined as railway technology during the late nineteenth century—was predicated upon the racialized and gendered constructions that enabled that technology in the first place. But if Canadians welcomed technological advancement, wagering their nation's very future on it in fact, they often held competing views about the racial and gender baggage the railway age brought with it. In other words, just as Canadians celebrated their newfound status as an Anglo-Saxon modern nation-state, they made deliberate racialized and gendered decisions—codified into law and institutional practices—about what that nation-state would be, who would belong to it, and who would not. Protestant Europeans and white American migrants could fit into Canada's national vision; Jews, Catholics, Asians, Native peoples, and blacks should not. Consequently, as of the mid-nineteenth century most white Canadians immediately pointed to the arrival of Chinese and black railway workers—Canadian or foreign-born—as the quintessential embodiment of that conflict.

Even as Canadians fêted their new railway line and the prosperity that it promised, questions of race lurked beneath the surface. The crowds gathered in Winnipeg for the occasion listened as Mayor H. S. Wesbrook waxed poetic about Canada's new prominence within the British Empire: "by placing an iron girdle round the continent," the Canadian Pacific Railway brought a vast territory "under the beneficent influence of civilization and commerce, thereby maintaining in British hands that supremacy, which would appear to be the heritage of the Anglo-Saxon and Celtic races." Wesbrook then proclaimed that "we have no doubt as to the influence this stupendous work will have upon the commercial progress of the grand old Empire . . . [and] that the consummation of the work will unite and consolidate an extensive British Colonial Empire in America."[4] In other words, the *Pacific Express*'s grunting caravan epitomized the country's preeminence and captured the new nation's imperial ambitions.

Once rousing cheers subsided, Mayor Wesbrook presented the CPR directors and president with a special gift from the people of Winnipeg: a statue of a "little negro whose iron hand is to carry the city's greeting to the Pacific shores." The cherubic negroid figurine, welded prominently to the front of the train, shouldered a blue flag and red satin banner pronouncing "Winnipeg's Greetings."[5] As with all other events marking the through train that day, Winnipeg's gift of a black infant statuette embodied the nation's optimism and faith in the CPR's omnipotence. The black baby, much like the newborn country, became the city's symbolic offering to the mighty railroad, serving double duty by asserting the city's existence and its expectant stead on the iron horse's ride to eminence.

Yet the sight of a powerless ebon babe fettered to a fiery engine must have represented something very different to black spectators taking part in the day's festivities.[6] The *Pacific Express*'s adornment stood for their station in the railway age: strapped in isolation to Canada's destiny, seemingly without voice or venue. In truth, blacks viewed the advent of the railway era with a mixture of both hope and frustration. In some ways, the railroad had almost taken on mythical proportions for blacks in North America, as evidenced by the many songs, Negro spirituals, and poems written in its homage. For many, the train symbolized freedom, escape, movement, security. It did not represent the nation so much as it afforded an escape route out of a nation committed to slavery. Theirs was an underground railroad, with secret connections, invisible passage, and a stealthy movement of aspirations, ideas, and dreams.

Whereas the rails had once stood for a future within their control, during the railway age it seemed that white passengers, railway managers, and white workers would insist on having black men act out an antiquated racialized and gendered performance as servants, entertainers, sleeping car porters. Working against that expectation, African American, West Indian, and African Canadian railwaymen utilized the rails and the mobility that it afforded them, forging transnational social and political alliances—unions, Freemason temples, churches, and the press—that redefined the railroad's place in the black imagination.

In truth, black life in Canada has always been inextricably linked to the railroads. African Canadian men first found work laying down tracks; they later cut across the country in sleeping cars much like the ones causing a sensation in Winnipeg that Canada Day in 1886. This project examines how railway life shaped and defined the black experience in Canada since the nineteenth century, with the railroads serving as an instrument for tremendous social and political advancement. By the same token, the rails also became the site of much racialized conflict, where white passengers demanded antiquated depictions of blackness, where white union men eyed black railroaders with suspicion and at times outright hostility, and where white bosses hedged their profits on exploiting black railwaymen. As of the late nineteenth century, union leaders, railway managers, and white Canadians systematically rallied around the discourse of race and supported each other's efforts at codifying clear demarcations—whether social, political, or economic—between black and white Canadians. Despite their insistence to the contrary, there developed a distinct Canadian color line by the twentieth century that shared important similarities with the one taking shape in the United States.

To be sure, Canadians crafted their own Jim Crow model, producing their own distinct language and rationalizations when propping up white suprem-acist ideology and practices. Where Americans pointed to African Ameri-cans' alleged criminality, Canadians said that blacks were "climatically un-suitable" for the full responsibilities of citizenship. When accused of bigotry, Canadians consistently countered that, in actuality, their "negrophobia" was a concern over American expansionist zeal. They explained away Canada's color line as a form of protection against American invasion, tapping into well-worn anti-American fears and resentments and adding a transnational dimension to white supremacist discourse.

Latching on to strained Canada-U.S. relations proved particularly effec-tive in Western Canada, where anxiety over American annexation became steeped in white supremacist rhetoric. White westerners panicked over "Ne-groes Swarm[ing] into Canada," or those grabbing up their jobs, neighbor-hoods, or worse still their white daughters, playing up the dual angle of race and American aggression.[7] After World War I, many white Canadian judges, journalists, and juries concurred that jazz, drugs, and alcohol, presumably peddled by black porters and entertainers, jeopardized white Canadians' morality and white womanhood in particular.[8] They exploited these racial-ized red herrings, stressing that Canadian civility, modernity, and democracy were at stake.

But what ultimately distinguishes Canada's record on race from its Carib-bean or American neighbors? In 1922, Canada's leading news periodical, *Maclean's*, ran a special exposé on immigration and conceded, "If our history is one of immigration our problems have been, are, and will continue to be problems of race."[9] Consequently, throughout the Jim Crow era (1877–1954) Canadians—bureaucrats, employers, and citizens alike—saw blacks as an im-migrant problem, conveniently ignoring that blacks had been in Canada since the early seventeenth century; in 1931, 80 percent of the nearly twenty thousand blacks in Canada were in fact born there.[10] As a result of always positioning blacks as an invading foreign force, Canadian imagination and historiography persistently framed African Canadians through the lens of recent immigration, erasing their investment in the formation of the Canadian nation-state, even when it had meant working against a rising tide of xenophobia.

Canadians justified their race-based exclusion policies—be they in federal law, employment practices, or social services—by narrowly discussing blackness as an alien problem. As of the nineteenth century, Canadians began wrestling with what to make of their heterogeneous society, especially when what they wanted most was to be the "last white man's land." This study provides an alternative arena for evaluating the evolution of Jim Crow thinking and practices in North America, particularly given that white Canadians insisted that they never traded in racism in the first place. And as scholars Thomas Borstelmann, W. E. B. Du Bois, Brent Edwards, Glenda Gilmore, Paul Gilroy, and Robin Kelly remind us, Jim Crow did not respect nation-state boundaries, taking on progressively broader transnational dimensions throughout the twentieth century.

During the Jim Crow era, Canadians maintained that African Americans, whom they viewed as Uncle Sam's problem,[11] should be avoided at all cost. They framed their stance on race as one of self-protection, as though blacks who came to Canada carried the contagion of racism that would infect the burgeoning nation, thereby robbing it of its full modern promise. Alarmed by the threat posed to their modernity, white Canadians increasingly turned to American southerners for clear cues on how to handle blacks, adopting and adapting Jim Crow to fit into Canada's own political archetype. Consequently, analyzing the role of race in state-building processes during the Jim Crow era becomes extremely instructive on how race—in particular blackness—became a crucial catalyst for advancing debates about national identity, citizenship, empire, and law in Canada.

THE DISCOURSE OF EMPIRE and Anglo-Saxon superiority permeated inaugurations of Canada's new transcontinental railway service. Throughout its nearly twenty years of construction, the Canadian Pacific Railway wrestled with pessimistic forecasts, pecuniary entanglements, and political calumny. At last completed, the grand enterprise stood as an emblem of engineering mastery, corporate steadfastness, national success, and great pride in the British Empire. Canadian politicians and industrialists reimagined the British Empire by placing the dominion at its center, exposing their preoccupation with the nation's status as a modern Anglo-Saxon state. Reporting on the *Pacific Express*'s inaugural voyage, the *Manitoba Daily Free Press* presaged that "in war time, the Suez Canal could be rendered useless for weeks by sinking ships in it, and if England had no other way of reaching India except the Cape of Good Hope the delay might lose her an empire and her position as a power of the first rank." It seemed that the British Empire's destiny now rested on Canada's CPR line "because it solidifies the empire by bringing its distant dependencies into nearer connection with the mother land."[12] Indeed, with passage *a mari usque ad mare*—from sea to sea—now feasible via the CPR, Canadians trusted that their nation would serve as the empire's coupling link, safely bridging England to Australia and India continually through British sea and soil.

The completion of the transcontinental railway thrust Canada into the industrial age. Despite ridicule from its southern neighbor and skepticism from London bankers, Canadian railway barons proved that they too could build a technological empire—the world's longest railroad under a single corporate umbrella. Canada's first prime minister, Sir John A. Macdonald, stressed that the nation's very viability depended on this national highway: "The prime purpose of Canada was to achieve a separate political existence on the North American continent. The prime function of the Canadian Pacific Railway was to assist in this effort—to help in the building of a national economy and the national society."[13] As a result, British North Americans embraced that corporate paragon as their national icon, and as they did so, the CPR's iron braces bound the Dominion of Canada into a technological nationalist compact.

Victorian conceptions of empire pitted divinely inspired human ingenuity against untamed nature. Thus Canadians romanticized and co-opted the arduous construction of their transcontinental line into an ethos of survival and national identity, fashioning it into Canada's "national dream."[14] While hurriedly chiseling a path to the Pacific shore, the Canadian Pacific Railway domesticated the Prairies and its people, beat back American encroachment, and asserted Canada's expansionist might. Historian Pierre Berton insisted that Canadians relished the CPR's "powerful icons, its mighty locomotives, soaring bridges, and piercing tunnels; they gladly ascribed to it the capacity to legitimize" the nation-state's "purpose and its policies."[15] Yet Canada's triumph of technology begat a fragile national identity rooted in a seductive myth of modernity.

Canada's vision of a transcontinental dominion functioned as the young nation's constitutive modern motif.[16] Advocates of Confederation in the East argued that a national railway line would be a powerful homogenizing national force. They maintained that if the line reached British Columbia, the

Prairies would remain under the Union Jack. Though always masked as an urgent nationalist preemptive strike against the threat of American manifest destiny, the CPR eagerly shackled the West under the guise of a confederative agreement and a covenant with the British Empire. The country and railway industrialists rationalized their westward expansionist zeal as a quest for national survival and the key to upholding the integrity of the Anglo-Saxon Empire. Yet at the same time, Canada's transcontinental rhetoric gives evidence of its own thinly veiled expansionist design—the nation's own concoction of manifest destiny.

Paradoxically, Canadian imperialism and nationalism depended on foreign capital and technology given that British bankers funded early Canadian forays into railroading. London financiers invested more than ten million pounds sterling in Canada's two largest trunk lines in the mid-nineteenth century—the Grand Trunk Railway (GTR) and the Maritimes' Intercolonial Railway (ICR).[17] Railroad promoters in Canada lobbied British support by arguing that "if this aid was rendered, the Queen's name would become a tower of strength on the continent, but if we had to borrow largely from America, a revulsion of feeling dangerous to British interests would be created."[18] Joseph Howe, chairman of the Nova Scotia Railway Board, augured that should Britain fall short of its obligation to its Canadian colonies, it would subject British North Americans to republican domination. Howe offered what he saw as a simple solution: "Commence the road, and the drooping spirit of the colonists would revive."[19]

The British government authorized capital earmarked for Canadian railway construction and encouraged connections with American lines, despite Howe's calamitous warnings. Consequently, the earliest railway lines built in Canada strategically targeted American seaports such as Portland, Boston, and New York. Throughout the rest of the nineteenth century, Canada's railway elite aggressively propelled railroad construction confident in the ascendancy of railway technology, trusting that the mileage of tracks laid and the proliferation of railway companies certified Canadian technological advancement. By 1901, more than eighteen thousand miles of railway track sheathed British North America.[20]

Americans also bankrolled Canada's fervent railway development. Nineteenth-century Canadian railway schemes fostered trade with the United States, targeted American technological expertise, and embraced Americans' industrial culture. Canadian railway industrialists arrogated American railway technology and culture as Canada's assured path to modernity. They measured the nation's progress by its ability to adapt that technology into a national agenda—the completion of the Canadian Pacific Railway. Consequently Canadian railway barons like George Stephen, William Van Horne, Thomas Shaughnessy, and Charles M. Hays obsessed over creating an industry that rivaled their American railway competitors.[21]

In order to reshape itself as a modern technological contender, Canada required a premodern measuring stick: its menacing wild West.[22] Anglo-Saxon ingenuity would therefore serve as a powerful civilizing salve on the West. The railroad's "civilizing mission" transformed Canada into a modern state by exporting technology to a presumably culturally destitute territory. Canada's modernizing artery—the new railway line—promised to populate the vast western provinces with sound European stock, save British Columbia from its perilous proximity to Asia, rescue the Prairies from its rebellious Native peoples, and centralize British-style political power in the East.

If the railroad itself connoted Anglo-Saxon omnipotence, the Pullman Palace Car Company permanently fixed the image of black men to the railroads with the introduction of its opulent sleeping cars in 1865. Pullman advertised African American porters much in the same way he did his sleeping cars: both, he promised, would provide comfort, luxury, and great service. In August 1870, the Pullman Palace Car Company and Grand Trunk Railway introduced sleeping cars to Canada and built the first Canadian sleepers—the "Portland," "Montréal," "Toronto," and "Québec"—in Montreal's Pointe St. Charles shop.[23] The GTR's eight new sleepers dazzled Canadians. The *Canadian Illustrated News* announced that Canada's first sleeping cars were "an object of much interest and admiration." It warned enthusiasts that "one is at a loss which most to admire, the elegant black walnut cabinet work, the splendid mirrors, the warm crimson velvet upholstery, or the snug convenient tables, lit as they are, so as to take from night traveling all its gloom."[24]

From the beginning, Pullman exported African American railwaymen to Canada along with his palace cars. Pursuant to article 3 of Pullman's standard contract, sleeping car porters were licensed along with the elegant liners for a period of five years; their "business it shall be . . . generally to wait upon passengers therein and provide for their comfort." The contract also declared that "it is hereby mutually agreed that the said employees . . . shall be governed by and subject to the rules and regulations" of the company leasing Pullman's sleepers. With article 5, Pullman completely disavowed all liability in the event of "injury, death, or otherwise" to African Americans contracted out to Canada, stripping these men of their humanity, listing them instead as commodities.[25] By 1900, regular runs from Montreal to New York and from

Toronto to Chicago featured sleeping and dining cars staffed exclusively by black railroaders.

George Pullman profited from the use of African Americans in his sleeping cars after the Civil War because their presence reminded rich white American passengers of a bygone antebellum era. Canadian railway promoters trusted Pullman's racialized recipe for success and imported his liners—as well as the archaic cultural archetype they upheld—as an infallible prescription for prosperity. A seasoned railwayman, William Van Horne was well acquainted with Pullman's service from his days as general manager of the Chicago and Alton Railroad. When he took up management of the Canadian Pacific Railway in 1881, he insisted on importing Pullman's signature service.[26] Each summer, the CPR culled porters from historically black colleges and universities, with Morris Brown College, Fisk, and Howard their schools of choice.[27] Van Horne, who demanded flawless service from his black porters, reportedly reminded his workers frequently, "You belong to the company while you are on duty."[28]

Why did Canadian companies so want to mirror deeply polemical racialized American symbols? Van Horne and other Canadian railway tycoons quickly realized that racialized images of black men were equally attractive to white passengers traveling on Canadian lines. That appeal to superior white manhood also proved highly profitable. As of its earliest days, the Canadian railroad industry exploited blacks—especially young men—for their powerful reminder of a racialized antebellum social order that affirmed, at least in the minds of white men, that Canadians' ascendancy to civilization had neared completion.[29] In contrast, Pullman's sleeping cars encapsulated a gendered and racialized mobile beau ideal in which rich, civilized white men were served by black men doing women's work, thereby reinforcing black manhood's incompleteness. Sleeping car porters made beds, cleaned house, tended to white children, shined shoes, served food, and catered to passengers' caprices. Within Pullman's sleepers, black manhood posed no threat to white civilization, since porters, uniformly called "George," were most often stripped of their individual identities.[30]

Even if the rules were clear, some white passengers still resented the presence of black men in their privileged fantasy world, as revealed in Douglas Sladen's travel account *On the Cars and Off*. Sladen, an English tourist who journeyed across Canada during the 1890s at the invitation of the Canadian Pacific Railway, griped that the "real autocrat of the sleeping car is, however, the negro, apparently selected for the lightness of his colour, for other qualifications are rare." Crass and boastful by nature, the porter, Sladen groused, "talks of his ladies, and makes himself generally objectionable until the last day when he takes up most of your morning brushing you and other genial patronage. You give him a dollar, if you have not seen too much of him." Sladen added that while porters on "other lines [were] maddening," the CPR's black railroaders were "pretty well behaved, because if there is one man in the world who stands no nonsense, it is the President of the Canadian Pacific Railway," William Van Horne.[31]

Some white passengers, annoyed by their proximity to black men in sleeping cars, albeit as workers, brutally reinforced white supremacy. Sladen described an English officer who, offended by a porter's request for his ticket, taught the worker "his position in the scale [by] taking the porter by the scruff of his neck, [and] kick[ing] him off the car." Shocked by the assault on their co-worker, other porters came to his rescue and met with more of the officer's scorn. Sladen recalled that when the "major saw them coming [he] called out, 'Get as many as you can, I've been longing to kick the whole lot of you.'"[32]

Against the background of Victorian conceptions of civilization, the domestic nature of the porter's work, his dependence on handouts from wealthy whites, and the violent enforcement of "his position in the scale" confirmed for many that blacks were not civilized modern men.[33] In fact, Sladen refers to black railwaymen only as "niggers" or "mud-coloured porters."[34] Segregated workforces, racialized wage disparities, denial of promotions in the Canadian railway industry, and exclusion from membership in burgeoning railway unions reaffirmed the inadequacy of black manliness.

The deficiencies of blackness, whether male or female, remained a core concern in late nineteenth-century North America, with Canadians, like Americans, worrying about the impact of emancipated blacks on their modern nation-state. Whereas Americans trained their attention on keeping African Americans out of voting booths, Canadians focused their strength on locking blacks out of the dominion, even though the country was desperate for new immigrants. Between 1870 and 1914, Canada's aggressive immigration campaign attracted more than 1.8 million new denizens, including more than 5,000 African Americans and West Indians who came to the dominion with clearly defined visions of modernity and citizenship. Throughout that period, the Canadian press predicted huge waves of black migration that never materialized, though we will never know how many more African Americans and West Indians eased their entry into Canada by passing as whites. Some may also have emphasized their Indianness given that those coming from the Oklahoma basin were leaving Indian Territory and often lived a dual identity as what historian William Katz has called "black Indians."[35] Whatever their cultural identity, African Americans who migrated to Canada after 1870 were driven by Reconstruction ideals about civil rights and meaningful citizenship; they repeatedly declared their desire for "British fair play" in matters of civil rights, reminding white Canadians—as Anglo-Saxons—of their hand in nineteenth-century abolitionist movements.

What is more, these African American émigrés, overwhelmingly from the southern United States, came to Canada confirmed in the belief that the spread of Jim Crow had taken their country backward, away from equality, prosperity, and industry. Those who petitioned the Canadian Department of Immigration for homestead lands pointed to their industry as a most valuable resource, no doubt acutely aware of their import as newly waged labor, especially given anxieties in the South over the mass exodus of that class of workers.

In this sense, then, Reconstruction—and its emphasis on controlling the value of one's labor—is absolutely central to these African Americans' political strategies and their vision of racial utopias. Among those black migrants who took up farming in Canada were Reconstruction statesmen like Rev. Henry Sneed of Oklahoma, who eyed the dominion as a Canaan, a second chance at making Reconstruction work without white supremacists cutting short what he saw as God's work. That work included setting up successful racial utopias in foreign lands, a common political strategy advanced by other black emigrationists like Martin Delaney and Alexander Crummell, who by the late nineteenth century called for African Americans to abandon all hope of meaningful citizenship in the United States. Accordingly, African Americans who set their sights on Canada voted with their feet, renouncing their confidence in post-Reconstruction American democracy. They reclaimed some control over their destinies by setting the terms and value of their labor, including offering that labor to a country willing to embrace them. With Canada's railway age in full swing precisely when African Americans needed political asylum, the Canadian railroads became the chief employer of many of these black migrants and their descendants.

Although the official number of black migrants admitted into Canada from the last decades of the nineteenth century to World War I hovered around five thousand, the mere idea or rumor of a black immigrant movement to Canada generated hysteria comparable to that over Chinese immigrants in the United States during the same time. Historian Erika Lee compellingly reveals that the very year that Chinese exclusion became federal law, only ten Chinese migrants had actually crossed into the United States.[36]

Consequently, the real point of interest here is not so much who among African American and West Indian migrants successfully got past Canada's gates but rather how their objectively negligible numbers roused legal and provincial bureaucracies, exposing deeply entrenched racialized anxieties among Canadians in the process. In this way, the reaction to blacks in Canada parallels that to Chinese migrants to the United States, given that both were affected by the same xenophobic knee-jerk responses, especially legislative ones. And while most white Canadians outside Toronto, Montreal, and Halifax would rarely have seen a black person before the Great Depression, Canadian racial paranoia had already leached into popular culture by the nineteenth century, as evidenced by Canadian parents who kept their children in line with grisly tales of how the boogeyman, "Nigger Dan," would surely get them.[37]

Between 1870 and 1940, every prime minister, whether running on the Liberal or the Conservative ticket, insisted that the Dominion of Canada would be a white man's land toiled by brawny Europeans and Americans, without elbow room for people of color. They adopted restrictive immigration regulations—and an outright ban on all black migrants in 1911—that deterred all but the most persistent African American and West Indian immigrants. Even so, a cluster of African American and West Indian migrants successfully skirted Canada's restrictive immigration policies, setting roots across the West by World War I and forming the bedrock of future black Canadian leadership.

Because of its dependence on black railroaders for its sleeping and dining car department, the Canadian Pacific Railway played a pivotal role in helping African Americans and West Indians circumvent immigration restrictions. Throughout the first half of the twentieth century, CPR managers clandestinely shuttled their own black immigrant workforce into Canada, cloaked in porters' uniforms, safely stowed in Pullman cars. During this time, Canadian railway companies secured uninterrupted access to low-wage black porters by delving into the American South and the Caribbean for their ideal prototype of servility; between 1900 and 1945, they imported several hundred porters each year as guest workers on short-term contracts. Railway executives continually ignored public outcry over black immigration and focused instead on maximizing profit, thwarting unionization, and keeping black workers where they needed them most—shining shoes, mixing drinks, making beds, and cadging for loose change from satiated passengers.

Whether driven by dread or greed, white Canadians choreographed their world along rigidly defined racial lines. They spent the first half of the century erecting barriers that reinforced white supremacy in every sector of Canadian life, moving ever closer to an institutionalized system resembling American Jim Crow, especially the de facto segregation model favored throughout the northern and midwestern United States. Heated debates over immigration, education, employment, entertainment, housing, lynching, unionization, and mobilization inspired responses from virtually every segment of Canadian society. Some white women's groups argued that black men imperiled their virtue, while white workers and farmers claimed that black immigrants stole their jobs and their land. Business owners, who by the 1920s began posting "white-only" trade signs in greater earnest, explained away their discriminatory policies as a requirement for staying in good standing with white customers. For its part, the federal government resolved that nature had not equipped blacks for Canada's winters, thereby justifying more exclusionary federal immigration legislation.

Even though they persistently buttressed a color line during the Jim Crow era, most white Canadians were unwilling to concede to racism's salience in their society. Fear of blackness, "negrophobia" Canadians called it, gripped white Canadians just as white southerners panicked over their insurgent black population. It is imperative that historians remember that by the mid-nineteenth century, Canada and the southern United States had a lot in common: both regions were largely agrarian economies eager for transition to industrial ones; both had a history of removing their Indian populations in order to make those agrarian economies possible; both struggled with harsh farming terrain—too hot or cold for too much of the year; and both were caught up in major railway-building projects also meant to unify and solidify the regions' identities.

Most important, by the 1870s, both regions were held together by tenuous, nascent governmental structures. After 1865 the South grappled with a post–Civil War identity and makeup, while Canadians wrestled with making sense of a fragile Confederation forged in 1867. The greater point is that both societies approached the fin de siècle as a promising period when they could be remade into modernized states. This study positions the American South and Canada as regions connected by black immigration and the discourse of white supremacy as a tool for responding to an insurgent black presence. With the movement of ever more African Americans from the South to Canada after 1870, a logical connection developed between those two zones of North America. To be sure, while the regions made substantively different investments in violent white supremacy, both turned to white supremacy as a rational model of modernity and civility.

Throughout the first half of the twentieth century, white Canadians and American southerners crafted their own explanations for segregation and other Jim Crow practices. Moreover, both demonstrated an insatiable appetite for degrading depictions of black men, as evidenced by the popularity of minstrel shows and *The Birth of a Nation*'s uninterrupted run in many Canadian cities.[38] Like their southern neighbors, white Canadians shared contempt for blacks, especially men intent on equitable citizenship. While some white southerners took matters in their own hands, exacting violent retribution against alleged racial and sexual transgressions, white Canadians hid behind an outward civility, harboring, as countless mainstream newspaper headlines affirm, seething resentment meted out in fits of brutality, as during Canada's World War I race riots.

Canadians quickly point out that no lynching has ever been reported in Canada, but it is not for want of trying. As early as 1891, five hundred white Canadians threatened to lynch George Freeman, a black man from Chatham, a city best known as a destination on the Underground Railroad and home to thousands of formerly enslaved African Americans.[39] As of World War I, some white Canadians advocated lynching with an arresting ease and frequency as a means of controlling blacks within their borders. In August 1920, the *Montreal Gazette* and *New York Times* reported: "Canadians Burn Jail to Lynch Ex-Soldier." The noose had already been fastened to the man's throat before tempers cooled, sparing the victim's life and protecting Canada's reputation as a nation of levelheaded Anglo-Saxon racial restraint.[40]

In that regard, then, whites in Canada and the United States codified racialized hysteria—southerners into lynch law, northerners into sweeping social segregation, and Canadians as thinly cloaked Jim Crow—exposing a continental preoccupation with race during the industrial age. Whereas white southerners turned to state legislatures and sheeted marauders to enforce their model of white supremacy, white Canadians did their bidding with federal bureaucrats and in the mainstream press. Consequently, by World War I Jim Crow had become ingrained into federal practices in the departments of Immigration, Labor, and Militia and Defence. To be sure, white Canadians did not indiscriminately replicate American segregation, though they borrowed freely from their American counterparts when Canadian imagination ran short.

White Americans and white Canadians locked horns with blacks intent on living out the full meaning of their citizenship. Southern African American migrants, well versed in white supremacist ways, unmasked their practice in the dominion, debunking white Canadian lip service to a prized abolitionist legacy. West Indians, known for their political savoir faire, docked in Canada and immediately demanded their full entitlement as British citizens, not backing down until their demands were met, appealing to the governor-general, the queen's representative, when they were not. And African Canadians, citizens by birthright, overwhelmingly rural, and sometimes less forward than Americans and West Indians, were grounded in institutions whose roots ran deep—the church, education, Masonic lodges, small businesses. Together, and at times individually, these three ethnicities rounded out what emerged as organized, galvanized, and politically active African Canadian communities throughout the twentieth century.

Black men who migrated from the United States or the Caribbean, and those who left Nova Scotian farms for Canadian cities, landed in Canadian railway yards soon after their arrival, bound for sleeping car portering. According to the Canadian census of 1921, 92 percent of porters were either Canadian, West Indian, or American.[41] They came from Antigua, St. Kitts, Jamaica, Barbuda, and St. Vincent, countries whose young men were seasoned intraregional migrants by force or choice. They came from Mississippi, Georgia, Kansas, Oklahoma, and Minnesota, dodging the draft, outrunning Jim Crow, or chasing promises of easy money in Canada. They came from New York, Detroit, and Chicago, seeing Montreal and Toronto as painless jaunts, made more palatable by the prospect of extra income running bootleg liquor during Prohibition. Finally, they came from Nova Scotia and Alberta, abandoning generations of farming for a new line of work on the railroad.

Black men glided along the rails, cutting across the dominion, connecting black neighborhoods with their music, food, politics, hope, and political visions. They made the most of meager wages, particularly during the Great Depression, understanding that they were also their communities' spokespersons, since through their work, they regularly rubbed up against powerful politicians, wide-eyed new immigrants, and wealthy whites. They saw the country—witnessed its very development through fogged-up sleeping car windows—like few Canadians could ever afford, and they felt bound to its destiny in ways most never understood.

Whereas many whites saw the sleeping car porter as a servile Uncle Tom, he had a very different image within his own community. Most African Americans and African Canadians held the porter—uniformed and gainfully employed in the most powerful industry of the day—in high esteem. Schooled and very well traveled, porters were viewed by many black women as ideal husbands. Sleeping car porters were cosmopolites comfortable in urban settings, be it New York or Montreal. Moreover, as a result of the transnational lifestyle fostered by their work on the rails, sleeping car porters developed an awareness of social and political problems facing their race across North America, producing a powerful diasporic consciousness by the interwar years. Accordingly, sleeping car porters were the vanguard of social and political reform prior to the civil rights movement, confirming their leadership just as white Canadians questioned its merit. After World War II, African Canadian porters teamed up with other civil rights activists throughout North America, becoming political agitators striking down unfair labor practices and separate and unequal doctrines in the United States, as well as colonial rule in the West Indies. As such, sleeping car porters serve as an excellent looking glass into black life in Canada during the first half of the twentieth century, since so many were drawn to the country by work on the rails and then used that foothold for carving out a place as citizens.

Canada's railways, so often recognized as a unifying Canadian icon, solidified a national sense of belonging and "Canadianness" for blacks in the dominion as well. Every major Canadian city bragged of its majestic railway station—Windsor Station, Union Station, Bonaventure—and within a few steps of those doors a black community was placed there to service the rails, such as Montreal's St. Antoine and Winnipeg's Point Douglas.[42] And while most white Canadians might not have known of their existence or grumbled about them as centers of swing and sin, for the thousands of blacks who made their lives there, cut through between train shifts, these neighborhoods' black barbers, tailors, grocers, and news agents represented an instantly recognizable community. For so many African Canadian men and women, black churches and Freemason temples conferred membership and fraternity when white trade unionists and landlords held the line on black exclusion. The black-owned boardinghouse or late night diner, Rockhead's Paradise or the Rex Café, affirmed blacks' sense of belonging precisely when their work robbed them of any sense of place. As Eddie Blackman, a former sleeping car porter and lifelong Winnipeg resident, so eloquently put it, "We weren't from the right side or the wrong side of the tracks. We were *from* the tracks."[43]

North of the Color Line is a study of life "from the tracks" for blacks in Canada from 1870 to 1955. It examines how, thanks to the development of the Canadian railway industry and Canada's aggressive immigration campaigns in the late nineteenth century, African Americans and West Indians fought their way into the dominion, circumventing laws and gatekeepers intent on keeping them out. Chapter 1 charts the newly formed Department of Immigration's response to black migrants who sought refuge in Canada in the wake of Reconstruction's collapse. Elected statesmen and federal bureaucrats increasingly adopted surreptitious measures to keep Canada "for the white race only," with the goal of effectively banning black immigration completely. I demonstrate that the arrival of African Americans—but very specifically black southerners—forced Canadians to come to terms with their own negrophobia, which they quickly and deliberately framed into law, making Jim Crow a national federal legal practice before World War I.

Since those African Americans who successfully entered Canada between 1870 and 1919 became overwhelmingly employed on the rails, sometimes landing there after fruitless attempts at farming in the West, chapter 2 analyses the experiences of black railwaymen prior to the Great War. I contend that while blacks in Canada had enjoyed a broad range of employment options, by World War I the Canadian workforce would become firmly racially stratified, with black men locked into lower-wage service positions. The application of Jim Crow labor practices in Canada came at the demand of the Canadian Brotherhood of Railway Employees (CBRE), the nascent white-only nationalist railway union. In fact, during his forty-four-year tenure as president of the CBRE and the Canadian Congress of Labour, Aaron Mosher set much of the tone for race relations in Canada's labor movement, lending his union's full-throated support to white supremacist dogma. Working in concert with the Department of Labour, white railroaders and railway executives banded together around the notions of white manhood and white supremacy, ultimately embracing Jim Crow as an easier concession than higher wages or safer working conditions. More important, by the outbreak of the Great War, the Department of Labour became the second branch of the federal government to make segregation official national practice.

World War I radically transformed the social and political climate in Canada, perhaps no more so than within the ranks of labor and the military. Chapter 3 looks at how blacks in Canada approached the Great War as an opportunity to make the case for their meaningful partnership in the British Empire. Within the early days of the conflict, blacks in Canada volunteered for military service, only to be told that the Department of Militia and Defence would not accept black recruits, as "the prejudice against negross [*sic*] in this country is extremely bitter."[44] Just as they had protested segregation in immigration and labor, African Canadians took on the federal government's de facto ban on black enlistment, using their newly formed press to call international attention to Jim Crow in the military and Canada more broadly. Most strikingly, by 1919, the three most powerful branches of the

Canadian federal government—the departments of Immigration, Labour, and Militia and Defence—had all instituted a clearly defined and firmly entrenched policy of white supremacy. And while African Canadians successfully made their case for service in the Great War, this after an embattled Canadian government reluctantly conceded to conscription in 1918, they were pooled in an all-black battalion and put to work hauling waste and dismembered remains in European battlefields known to be peppered with land mines. Those fortunate enough to see the war's end then met with violent racial clashes in Canada's military camps and on its city streets in the summer of 1919.

Chapter 4 examines how blacks in Canada responded to the strained postwar years by utilizing labor organizing as a tool for winning economic and citizenship rights. Canada's first generation of black civil rights leaders were veterans of the Great War, men and women who had believed that their contributions to the war effort would produce more equality but now understood the import of defining and exercising racial democracy for themselves. As founder of the nationally recognized Order of Sleeping Car Porters (oscp), one of the earliest black railway unions in North America, John Arthur Robinson quickly emerged as the preeminent example of this postwar leadership. Robinson would represent the oscp before the Department of Labour and demand a living wage as well as safe working conditions for his men. Though he did not always win over his bosses, he secured the support of African Canadians, who subscribed in greater zeal to the New Negro model of leadership he advanced—one that promoted melding the best principles from various existing racial uplift organizations. While many African American political leaders wrestled over constituencies, limited resources, and differing approaches, African Canadian racial uplift ideology bridged groups who most likely would not have worked together in the United States. It would have been completely common for a 1920s Canadian race man to simultaneously be a preacher, a Freemason, a Universal Negro Improvement Association (unia) member, and the head of the Canadian League for the Advancement of Coloured People (clacp). John A. Robinson was indeed one such man. Thus, this chapter is principally interested in how black Canadian labor, social, and political organizations emerged during the 1920s, especially as a response to an intensification of social segregation in Canada.

The final chapter explores African Canadian life from the 1930s to the 1950s. The Great Depression brought to the fore even more white Canadian resentment over the presence of blacks in Canada and required coordinated responses by African Canadian social and political organizations. Held responsible for the nation's economic demise and for the frustrations of urban life, African Canadians invented creative ways of keeping their communities and their spirits afloat. Though working with limited funds and resources during the Great Depression, blacks in Canada took their fight against Jim Crow all the way to the supreme court, challenging new social conventions denying them public services or forcing them into "monkey cages," the dehumanizing term Canadians reserved for black-only theater and arena seats.

By the 1930s, blacks in Canada were keenly aware that their plight was inextricably linked to that of African Americans. The two groups joined forces when possible and shared resources and strategies for social advancement; most important, both adopted transnational alliances as their assured path to success. The arrival of the New York–based Brotherhood of Sleeping Car Porters (BSCP) in Canada serves as the best example of this new transnational approach to civil rights activism. The American A. Philip Randolph and Canada's leading black labor activist, Arthur Robinson Blanchette, the retired John A. Robinson's protégé, met during the 1929 American Federation of Labor convention in Toronto and resolved to meld their unions into the largest black union in the world, one that included every black railroader (and several Mexican, Filipino, and white ones as well) from Montreal to Mexico City. Each camp would apply pressure on their bosses, working in tandem as a check and balance across the border. After World War II, this work increasingly involved transnational civil rights and human rights advocacy. Randolph and Blanchette shared a lifelong friendship, forged in large part by their deep-seated commitment to labor and civil rights activism. They also created a transnational and international model of black labor activism that made a campaign for black civil rights possible in both Canada and the United States by continually linking both regions' legacies to each other, just as they always had in fact been throughout slavery, emancipation, and emigration and on the rails.

CHAPTER ONE

Drawing the Line

Race and Canadian Immigration Policy

On the morning of 22 March 1911, a reporter for the *Manitoba Free Press* paced nervously in Winnipeg's CPR station as he awaited the arrival of the Great Northern No. 7, now infamous for the cargo it carried north from the U.S. border. For the past two days, Canadian immigration officials had held up the train and its 194 black passengers as they hastily searched for cause to bar their entry.[1] For months, Canadian newspapers had warned of an impending "Black Peril" from an "Invasion of Negroes."[2] Western Canadian newspapers took particular interest in these migrants from Oklahoma, "the advance guard," they claimed, "of at least 5,000 people of mixed Cree Indian and negro blood" forced out of the South by white supremacists turned elected statesmen.[3] The *Manitoba Free Press* reporter hoped that he would be first to witness "Negro Settlers Troop into [the] West."[4]

Rev. Henry Sneed, a Baptist minister of "considerable executive ability, and comfortable means," shepherded the group of "Negroes Swarm[ing] into Canada."[5] "Old Daddy" Sneed had culled his flock of southern migrants from his church and Masonic lodges back in Oklahoma, Arkansas, and Texas.[6] He then carefully plotted their immigration to Canada over the next two years. After canvassing the Canadian Plains for future homesteads in August 1910, Sneed selected northern Alberta as their future home.[7] In March 1911, determined migrants loaded up seven freight cars with horses, mules, cattle, and farming equipment and boarded the special train commissioned for the trek north.[8] It was the last time most of them ever saw the South.

Aware of growing unrest over black immigration into Canada, the Sneed party anticipated harassment from Canadian immigration officials and headed for the Canadian border armed with doctors and lawyers—"the former to certify to their physical fitness, and the latter to argue the legal side of the matter."[9] The politically shrewd Sneed added an extra measure of precaution. His attorneys summoned the U.S. consul general stationed in Winnipeg, Dr. John Jones, "to the border to see that the negroes receive fair treatment," declared the *Ottawa Free Press*.[10]

The *Manitoba Free Press* journalist meeting the Sneed party faced a savvy set of settlers, describing the migrants as "quiet and well-behaved" and "cleanly . . . especially after so long a trip." The reporter explained that Sneed's choice of healthy, experienced farmers "fitted for the strenuous work of pioneer life" would ensure success for this group of migrants in Canada. One such would-be settler, Reddick Carruthers, born into slavery in Texas, joined the Sneed gang "at the age of 70 aspiring after a free home." After examining the Oklahoma immigrants, the reporter drew the sobering conclusion that "apart from race, they were a very promising lot of settlers."[11]

The question of race colored Canadian debates over immigration throughout the first half of the twentieth century. An Englishwoman who had lived in Oklahoma before immigrating to Manitoba offered a view shared by many white Canadians in the West: "It is with regret that I have read the account of the invasion of thousands of negroes from Oklahoma to the fair land of Canada. As there is in my heart a desire for the welfare of the Dominion, . . . I feel sorry that this country should be saddled with those that the Southern States are all too glad to be rid of." She countered the *Manitoba Free Press*'s claim that the Sneed group's wealth and farming know-how suited them for Canadian citizenship, proclaiming that for "those who have never lived in districts inhabited by negroes, and who have only come in contact with certain well-disposed persons of that race, the disgust felt towards the tribe is perhaps unintelligible or at any rate misunderstood." She warned that "those acquainted with the habits of them can only take the negative side as to the desirability of the negro as a resident, a colonist, a settler. As negroes flourish in a hot country and do as little work as possible, it is to be hoped that Jack Frost will accomplish what the authorities apparently cannot."[12]

By 1911, Canadian hostility to black migration gave African American would-be homesteaders ample cause for concern. Yet with the spread of Jim Crow in the South and the de facto exercise of segregation in most northern and western states, many African Americans increasingly sought political asylum from white supremacist demagogues. In a letter to the Department of Immigration, a potential black migrant, Rev. Will Hurt, captured the frustrations shared by countless African Americans, succinctly listing his reasons for coming to Canada: "I want too change government. I am tyird of this one. . . . I want too live in peace if I can for god sake."[13]

Canada's western homesteading program enticed African Americans to head north, as did its legacy as a haven for freedom seekers prior to the Civil War. But if during the 1850s Canada had ushered in African Americans on the run from slavery, by the turn of the century most white Canadians strove for an impenetrable border. Canadian governments throughout the first half of the twentieth century averred that the Dominion of Canada should remain "for the white race only."[14] William D. Scott, the superintendent of immigration from 1903 to 1924 and Canada's most influential gatekeeper prior to the Great Depression, adamantly insisted that the "negro problem, which faces the United States, and which Abraham Lincoln said should be settled only by shipping one and all [blacks] back to a tract of land in Africa, is one in which Canadians have no desire to share."[15] Many white westerners concurred with their government's position, as evidenced by the *Edmonton Evening Journal*'s declaration "We Want No Dark Spots in Alberta."[16] Immigration officials and Canadian nativists rallied to ensure that this time white Canadians would not inherit Uncle Sam's "problem."

According to the Canadian Department of Immigration and white nativists, crime, miscegenation, and lynch law accounted for much of Uncle Sam's problems. So "long as negroes are in this country . . . crime will continue and increase, in proportion as the negro population increases," explained an editorial in the *Edmonton Evening Journal*. A "black cloud is looming up from the south which is dangerous enough," warned the writer, because southern African Americans "are a menace to the welfare of the country." He urged the Canadian government to "close out the yellow man, the red man, and the black man," lumping together Asians, Natives, and people of African descent as undesirable citizens.[17] Many white Canadians also posited that admitting African American migrants would result in moral turpitude and a decline in Canadian prosperity. For example, the Edmonton Police Department claimed that within three years of their arrival "20% of them [African Americans] were undesirables, either prostitutes or men living upon the avails of prostitution."[18]

Canadian hysteria over black immigration was specifically rooted in language, stereotypes, and anxieties with powerful purchase during the nascent age of segregation. The arrival of black men in particular sparked groundless white paranoia, especially among some white women's groups. The Daughters of the Empire, an organization affiliated with the Guild of Loyal Women of South Africa, exhorted, "We do not wish that the fair fame of Western Canada should be sullied with the shadow of Lynch Law but have no guarantee that our women will be safer in their scattered homesteads than white women in other countries with a Negro population."[19] Canadians opposed to black migration persistently conjured up images of the black rapist, made popular in D. W. Griffith's internationally celebrated film *The Birth of a Nation*, when making the case for blocking passage of blacks into Canada. Fritz Freidrichs of Alberta alerted the minister of the interior that "these negroes have misused young girls and women and killed them. They will do the same in our country too."[20] Even before any confirmed cases of crime, violence, or rape occurred, white Canadians against black migration invoked the "finger of hate pointing at lynch law" as an unimpeachable outcome of interracial coexistence. The simple solution, according to Dr. Ely Synge, was to cut off southern black migration at its source: "Now is the time to prevent," he forewarned, "later on it will be too late."[21]

Even when visions of black criminals floated in their head, white Canadians panicked at the sight of actual organized, affluent, and determined African American migrants—like the Sneed party—arriving in the Canadian Prairies. Destitute enslaved fugitives had stroked Canadian egos, but galvanized black migrants raised the alarm over the possibility of inheriting a caste of black insurgents stirred up by visions of independence, democracy, entrepreneurial spirit, and populist ideology. Canadians cooked up a rationale for black exclusion that danced around white supremacist convictions of the day, pointing instead to nature as the root cause of their concern over African Americans. The *Edmonton Evening Journal* proclaimed that the "extensive immigration of negroes is causing considerable uneasiness. That it should is not at all surprising." Its editorial explained that nature—rather than racism—accounted for Canadian nativist anxiety. "Whether well-founded or not, we have to face the fact that a great deal of prejudice exists against the colored man and that his presence in large numbers creates problems from which we naturally shrink."[22] Prime Minister Wilfrid Laurier's administration reasoned that black migrants should be barred from the dominion as "the Negro race . . . is deemed unsuitable to the climate and requirements of Canada."[23] Unable to stop determined black migrants by the spring of 1911, the minister of immigration, Frank Oliver, finally admitted that Canada's "Negro Problem is a difficult one."[24]

Yet white Canadians constantly discussed that "Negro Problem" as though it were a virus carried north by black migrants themselves. In effect, from the 1890s to the 1950s, white Canadians quite effectively produced their own "negrophobia."[25] They rationalized their xenophobia and white supremacist propaganda by blaming nature—what they called "climatic unsuitability"—and black settlers themselves. Both the Canadian government and white nativists dreamed up hyperbolic tales, advocated racialized federal laws, and proposed segregation and lynch law as measures for controlling Canada's own troublesome "Negro Problem." Their actions demonstrate that white Canadians in fact shared many white Americans' racial tenets. While white southerners fought an insurgent black citizenry, white Canadians struggled with what to do about blacks in their dominion. They would spend the first half of the century wrestling with that question as African Canadians made increasingly effective use of their voice and their vote.

Insofar as white Canadians opposed black immigration, they worried most about "Southern Negroes still coming to [the] Canadian West."[26] After all, these were the same people who, within one generation, had fought for their freedom, savored their new citizenship, believed in its promise, flexed their political muscle during Reconstruction, and then were stripped of their citizenship rights during what white southerners quixotically called "Redemption." Instead of facing the dehumanizing effects of Jim Crow, millions of African Americans cast down their buckets and hopped a train out of the South.[27] Those bound for Canada, like the Sneed party, plotted their immigration, braved the long journey north, outwitted Canadian immigration officials, flashed fists full of dollars, and declared upon entry, "We came to this Sunny Alberta . . . not as peons, not as a subject race. . . . We feel that our gentlemen and ladies are able to compete with the white ladies and gentlemen of this country. . . . We crossed the boundary not asking for anything but loyal citizenship."[28]

The Sneed case demonstrates how African American migrants came to Canada in search of meaningful citizenship and refused to let nativists dictate the quality of that citizenship. It should be remembered that for southern African Americans, white resistance was neither new nor a compelling reason to forsake their citizenship claims. These same southern African American settlers brought with them decades of experience fighting white supremacy, with some even remembering life under slavery.[29] White Canadians immediately encountered that defiant spirit, as evidenced by Sneed's comments to awaiting journalists. "There ain't nothin' the matter with us mister. Sick! Ah'd like youh to show me whar we got any sick peoples. . . . We're goin' in for farmin' [as] all of our men have farmed all their lives."[30] He added, "We are going to take up our homesteads . . . as soon as our effects arrive." The Sneed party's self-sufficiency, resourcefulness, and assertiveness alarmed white Canadians and fueled much of the hysteria engulfing the West from the 1890s to World War I.

IMMIGRATION ISSUES DOMINATED CANADIAN politics during the first two decades of the twentieth century. On 23 June 1896, Sir Wilfrid Laurier, a Liberal, ended twenty-two years of Conservative rule and won control of the House of Commons of Canada. Only the second Liberal prime minister ever elected since Confederation in 1867, Laurier immediately implemented bold new plans for his government. Within his first decade in office, Laurier brokered the Alaska boundary negotiations with Russia, authorized the construction of two more transcontinental railway lines, added two new provinces, Saskatchewan and Alberta, to the dominion, and wooed almost two million immigrants to Canada's western provinces.[31] Prime Minister Laurier also modernized and broadened the federal bureaucracy, thanks in large part to his cabinet, known as the "ministry of all talent."

Laurier assembled some of the most forward-thinking politicians of his time and entrusted his newly formed Ministry of the Interior to Clifford Sifton, the former attorney general of Manitoba. Born in Ontario, Sifton moved in 1875 to Manitoba, where he and his brother Arthur Lewis Sifton, future premier of Alberta, practiced law.[32] As minister of the interior, Clifford Sifton oversaw both the Department of Indian Affairs and the Department of Immigration. A migrant to the Canadian Prairies himself, Sifton seemed perfect for the task at hand. He inherited the daunting job of advertising Canada's vast Plains to the world and convincing millions of immigrants that Canada promised more to new citizens than did the United States, Australia, or South Africa.[33]

Clifford Sifton's Department of Immigration adopted a twofold approach to the immigration question. As of 1896, Sifton lured immigrants west with an offer of free land: 160 acres of free farmland awaited a would-be settler from Europe or the United States willing to homestead on the Canadian Prairies. Sifton then stationed throughout Europe and the United States salaried immigration agents who enticed immigrants to the dominion with tales of pioneering adventures and lucrative farming. By 1902, 15 agents, and 236 subagents hired on commission, combed the American West and South for farmers willing to relocate to Western Canada.[34] Strategically assigned to posts in states where demand for land was high and free land sparse, Canadian government agents capitalized on local discontent and became effective salesmen of the Canadian Northwest.

The Liberal government's immigration program became an immediate success. Within years of Sifton's plan, European and American migrants poured into Canada in record numbers. Between 1896 and 1911, more than 1.88 million migrants streamed into Canada, with 47 percent heading directly for Manitoba, Saskatchewan, or Alberta.[35] Canada's new prosperity even attracted some expatriates. During Laurier's administration, returning Canadians, most of whom were French Canadians, accounted for 9 percent of migrants received at ocean ports.[36] Norwegians, Swedes, Austro-Hungarians, Russians, and Italians also made up an impressive number of migrants accepted into the dominion.[37] Canada's most sought-after immigrants, British and American immigrants, outstripped all other newcomers from 1900 to World War I. Initially, it certainly seemed that so long as settlers were willing to take up farming, few restrictions would prevent their entry into Canada.

Canadians aggressively courted white American immigrants because they brought needed capital and technology when migrating north. According to the official estimate, Canada-bound Americans migrated with an average of $1,000.[38] In contrast, European migrants arrived with average capital ranging from $41.51 for Scots to $7.96 for Lithuanians.[39] In his report on operations in the United States, a senior department bureaucrat in charge of U.S. operations, William J. White, proudly divulged that "the wealth of these people [Americans] into the country . . . might approximately be placed at 133 million dollars."[40] In the end, Canadians considered Americans ideal immigrants because of their substantial financial investments. Americans also shared the same continent, language, and religions as Canadians, if not the same allegiance to the British Crown.

Since the Laurier government persistently maintained that what Canada needed most were farmers, especially in the West, mechanics, laborers, and merchants bound for cities met with a cold welcome from Canadian immigration officials. In his address to the House of Commons on 17 April 1902, Clifford Sifton underscored his government's position: "It has not, for many years, been the policy . . . to make any attempts to induce mechanics or wage earners to Canada." Sifton added, "The test we have tried to apply is this: Does the person intending to come to Canada intend to become an agriculturist? If he does, we encourage him to come and give him every assistance."[41]

Homesteaders of color found little of the "assistance" Sifton promised to the House of Commons. Instead, Chinese, Japanese, Indian, West Indian, and African American migrants ran headlong into Department of Immigration officials and white Canadians determined to prevent their entry. Canada, argued white businessmen in the West, should be "the last country open to the white race."[42] William D. Scott, the federal bureaucrat most responsible for keeping immigrants of color out of the dominion, insisted that "the fertile lands of the West will be left to be cultivated by the white race only."[43]

Consequently, African American farmers headed for the Canadian Prairies —especially after Reconstruction—found that wealth and American citizenship did not automatically expedite their admission into Canada. Requests for information about Canada's homesteading program from black would-be migrants soared once Jim Crow began taking hold of the American South. Throughout the 1890s, race riots, mob rule, disfranchisement, and lynchings across the American South added to African Americans' urgent need for political asylum in Africa, Mexico, and Canada. Conditions in northern and midwestern cities were not always better, as unemployment, housing discrimination, and racial violence made clear that African Americans were not safer there either. After the grisly lynching and mutilation of Will James in Cairo, Illinois, in 1909, many African Americans looked farther north for sanctuary from white supremacists. In fact, lynching peaked between 1889 and 1899, with an average of nearly 190 lynchings reported annually, causing many African Americans to wonder what the new century would bear. Further intensifying tensions, throughout the 1890s southern state governments systematically attacked African Americans' newly acquired civil and constitutional rights, including their most prized right—suffrage.[44] During these same years, southern legislatures enacted segregation statutes for public services and facilities, entrenching segregation into virtually all aspects of southern life.

When in 1896 the Supreme Court conferred definitive legal sanction to Jim Crow segregation with its support of the separate but equal doctrine in *Plessy v. Ferguson*, Canada felt the immediate impact of the American high court's ruling.[45] The perfect timing of Canada's homesteading campaign in 1896, in the wake of the *Plessy* decision, seemed like a godsend for many southern African Americans. In addition to the promise of meaningful citizenship rights, the Laurier government's free land program offered disheartened African Americans respite from the prospect of America's oppressive racial regime. Moreover, land ownership, the bedrock of Reconstruction ideology, upheld the promise of meaningful citizenship for those southern African Americans facing the collapse of Reconstruction. Thus, soon after Jim Crow engulfed the South, the Canadian Department of Immigration noted a marked increase in African Americans requesting information on immigration to the dominion. Prospective black settlers wrote from a total of thirty-one states, including every southern and midwestern state.[46]

Freedom, peace, franchise, citizenship, and social equality appealed to

African Americans as much as Canada's promise of free land. On 27 October 1901, Barney McKay of the Afro-American Literary Bureau in Washington, D.C., offered to provide Canada with five thousand "thrifty, hardy, agriculturalists who will be good, substantial loyal citizens" because "every Colored man has a warm spot in his heart for all that is English." Astutely aware of their agrarian know-how and their value as waged labor, McKay pledged to help "my people to a land free from prejudice, caste, and social and political slavery" and explained that "now is the time for England to strike in order to secure a class of people who will build up the waste places in Canada and make barren fields and primitive forests blossom like the rose."[47] In July 1902, James A. Strachan of Atlanta informed the Ministry of the Interior that a "movement is being inaugurated to induce the best element of negroes of Georgia to emigrate to Canada and take up homesteads." Strachan planned to organize a colony of one thousand "of the most industrious negroes [who] can be inlisted."[48]

As white supremacy intensified in the United States, Canadian immigration agents seemingly could not convince black migrants to remain in the South. African American newspapers and letters from potential black migrants cited racial violence, Jim Crow coach and depot laws, grandfather clause acts, disfranchisement, and separate school laws as the primary causes for black immigration to the Canadian West. One would-be settler from Oklahoma wrote the Department of Immigration explaining his reasons for coming to Canada: "My intention for goin too Canada well I will tell you the truth the first, I am deprive of life liberty." Alluding to the rise of gendered and racialized violence, he added, "Our women is not treated rite at all." The sharecropper pointed to the exploitative impact of sharecropping and debt peonage schemes as yet another urgent reason for abandoning the South: "We have no schools [and] I am tyird raising cotton and the other man get it all and 'd get nothing." Finally, he concluded, "I like your law better they are good. . . . I can't owen no land here" and want "too Become a Setlar or a British Subject."[49]

Though they were technically British citizens, West Indians found no warmer welcome in Canada than did African Americans. As of 1903, the Department of Immigration received a steady flow of requests for information from West Indians wishing to homestead in the West or work as domestic servants throughout Canada. In mid-August 1908, J. Bruce Walker, the commissioner of immigration in charge of the West, alerted his supervisors in Ottawa that the arrival of forty-six Barbadian farmworkers in Manitoba and Saskatchewan caused vociferous protests in the *Regina Leader*.[50] George

Clingan, the mayor of Virden, Manitoba, a small farming community bordering North Dakota, informed the Department of Immigration that "they certainly were not asked for nor wanted. . . . These men cannot find work as farmers' wives are afraid of them."[51]

Back in the Maritimes, immigration branch officer W. L. Barnstead also notified Ottawa of an increase in West Indian arrivals at his ports. Canadian immigration agents in Nova Scotia and New Brunswick had been monitoring a stealthy marine traffic of West Indians for some time. British and American cargo ships illegally transported West Indian passengers and dropped off their human cargo at various ports in the Maritime provinces. J. B. Williams, the Department of Immigration's investigator in Halifax, reported that at least seventy-five West Indians had unlawfully landed in Canada between April 1909 and May 1910.[52] West Indian migrants so unnerved the Canadian Department of Immigration that agents in Halifax advocated drastic and illegal tactics. In a confidential memorandum sent to the secretary of the interior, a Department of Immigration agent avowed, "I think that it is the opinion of the Department that we don't want the West Indian nigger," and the agent insisted that "every obstacle is to be put in their way."[53]

Prime Minister Laurier's government moved swiftly to shield Canada from African American and West Indian newcomers. Immigration branch officials concocted various reasons for keeping black migrants out of Canada, arguing, for example, that black settlers quickly became public charges upon entry into the dominion. African Americans and West Indians were often criminally inclined or diseased, insisted Department of Immigration bureaucrats. When those arguments failed, the Canadian government claimed that black migrants could not withstand Canada's cold climate, making them fundamentally inassimilable. Just three years into Laurier's homesteading program, the Canadian Department of Immigration instructed all its agents that "it is not desired that any negro immigrants should arrive in Western Canada, under the auspices of our Department, or that such immigration be promoted."[54]

More than fifty years of black experience in the Canadian West had already given the lie to the Canadian government's prejudicial claims. Black westerners had proven themselves capable farmers, ranchers, interpreters, and scouts since the early 1850s, a fact disproving the Department of Immigration's contention that black migrants failed to secure gainful employment and were therefore predisposed to becoming public charges.[55] Given that in 1901, 63 percent of blacks in Western Canada lived and thrived in the Yukon, attracted there by "Gold Fever," it seemed that Canadian xenophobia posed a greater threat than the frigid climate.[56] Although the Laurier administration declared black settlers inassimilable, African Americans and West Indians shared the same language and religions as most Canadians, while the same could not be said of Scandinavian, Ukrainian, and Russian immigrants also coming to Canada in record numbers during those years. Paradoxically, in 1858 Canadians had viewed African Americans as ideal new citizens and welcomed black Californians to British Columbia specifically because of their loyalty, industriousness, entrepreneurial zeal, and assimilability.[57]

By the turn of the twentieth century, however, the Canadian government did a complete about-face on the question of black immigration. Frank Oliver, the new minister of the interior as of 1905, implemented rigorous immigration restrictions distinguishing the best migrants from purportedly undesirable ones. Oliver's Immigration Act of 1906 introduced several new principles to Canadian immigration law, including mandatory medical and character examinations and race-based exclusion clauses.[58] Section 20 of the act weeded out possible public charges by imposing racial and monetary requirements as a condition for entry. The Immigration Act's section 30, perhaps the most devastating clause to nonwhite immigrants, empowered the minister to dictate Canadian immigration policy without scrutiny from the House of Commons. The minister could introduce orders in council to "prohibit the landing in Canada of any specified class of immigrants"—a privilege utilized by Oliver against African Americans before the end of the decade. An amendment of the Canadian Immigration Act in April 1908 introduced the continuous journey clause, which required that immigrants come to Canada via uninterrupted passage from their country of origin. While this new clause later impeded the immigration of black Britons and West Indians, its primary aim was to make passage from India, China, and Japan virtually impossible, since steam liners made frequent stops en route to North America.[59]

Despite the Canadian government's more rigorous 1908 immigration provisions, determined black migrants skillfully circumvented the various obstacles to crossing the border. Much to the minister of immigration's frustration, his department noted that black immigration had in fact increased between 1907 and 1910.[60] Moreover, Canadian newspapers continually published reports of more African Americans coming to Canada. In April 1908, the *Ottawa Free Press* announced that seven black families from Oklahoma had purchased 100- to 300-acre farms west of Edmonton.[61] One month later, the *Manitoba Free Press* reported that fifteen hundred "colored people have come to Alberta during the past year, and there promises to be a big immigration in the future."[62] In March 1910, forty African American families from Pennsylvania, Oklahoma, Illinois, Minnesota, Wisconsin, Iowa, and Nebraska entered via Manitoba with an average handsome sum of $360.25 per family.[63] In May of that same year, W. Saunders, his wife, and six children left Kansas for Alberta with $2,000 in hand for life on their new Canadian homestead.[64]

Frustrated with its Immigration Act's ineffectiveness against persistent African American and West Indian migrants, the Laurier government advocated more stringent measures. Frank Oliver believed that his new Immigration Act of 1910 would definitively end black immigration from the United States and the West Indies by blatantly targeting black immigrants and making race an indisputable part of Canadian immigration policy.[65] Pursuant to section 37, the Laurier government set fiscal requirements for immigrants and tourists according to race, occupation, or destination. Quite simply, with this new standard in hand, border agents could, for example, arbitrarily require that black migrants possess $500 at the time of entry but wave in a white American migrant with only $25. A further clause, section 38, authorized the minister of immigration to exclude whole classes of migrants for an indefinite period of time. The revised Immigration Act empowered the minister to "prohibit for a stated period or permanently, the landing in Canada . . . [of] immigrants belonging to any race deemed unsuited to the climate or requirements of Canada."[66] The Department of Immigration hoped that with such provisions sealing off the border to blacks would be far more successful.

African Americans, particularly those from the South, still forced their way north despite Canada's new law. Political events in Oklahoma and Kansas after 1907 gave thousands of African Americans compelling new reasons for emigration. Oklahoma's transition to statehood in 1907 emboldened hostile Democrats like William "Alfalfa Bill" Murray, Charles N. Haskell, and Roy E. Stafford, who ruled the new state with a white supremacist fist.[67] Then, southern white migrants, disappointed with segregation politics elsewhere, flooded Oklahoma and Kansas. Their arrival in Oklahoma signaled a palpable shift in race relations in contested Indian Territory. Lynching, mob violence, disfranchisement, and Jim Crow laws soared during statehood negotiations. Democratic Party rhetoric in Oklahoma made clear for African Americans there that so long as they remained in the United States, Jim Crow would jeopardize their civil rights and indeed their very lives.

In response to mounting racial violence and Reconstruction's failed promises, there developed an emigrationist movement among African Americans fueled by utopian visions of racial democracies in other parts of North America and in Africa. While some African Americans considered emigration to Liberia and Mexico, others turned northward for the Canadian Plains.[68] Blacks in Kansas and Oklahoma were a generation well acquainted with migratory lifestyles. Henry Adams and Benjamin "Pap" Singleton had shepherded the largest flocks of black migrants out of Louisiana, Mississippi, and Texas during "Kansas Fever" in the spring of 1879.[69] That generation of African Americans, commonly known as Exodusters, had gone west decades before Oklahoma statehood driven by the belief that land ownership, civil liberties, and meaningful citizenship were inextricably linked.[70] Democratic Party encroachment on their land and civil rights—particularly in education —confirmed many Exodusters' resolve to resettle once again.[71]

The Canadian West had all the makings for twentieth-century "Prairie Fever." Canada's Plains seemed a logical choice given that Exodusters were seasoned prairie farmers capable of adapting northern agriculture. Railway lines out of St. Louis, Chicago, and Minneapolis gave would-be black settlers easy access to Winnipeg and other Western Canadian destinations (see Figure 2). If black Oklahomans were losing their land to white Democrats, Canada's homesteading program immediately remedied their displacement. Canadians were white but thankfully not southerners. Finally, Canada's ethos as a "Promised Land" prior to the Civil War left an indelible mark on African Americans who remembered the Dominion of Canada as a Canaan for political asylum seekers during the 1850s.[72] That reputation beckoned southern black migrants like the Sneed party north.

Black emigrationists who abandoned the South for Liberia, Mexico, and Canada gave evidence of the transnational dimension affecting the Great Migration movement from its earliest phase during the Progressive Era. Those migrants revealed that St. Louis, Chicago, Detroit, and New York were not the only northern options considered by southern African Americans. In fact, since the end of Reconstruction, black emigrationist movements had spread quickly, particularly in the South. While several studies emphasize the popularity of back-to-Africa programs during the late nineteenth century, Mexico and Canada were more expedient options for most African Americans, who could, in haste, swim, walk, or run to either border. In fact, several predominantly African American expatriate communities existed along the Rio Grande and the Great Lakes, with the latter region becoming a more attractive option after the outbreak of war during the Mexican Revolution in 1910.[73]

A new generation of black emigrationists, namely, attorneys, doctors, and

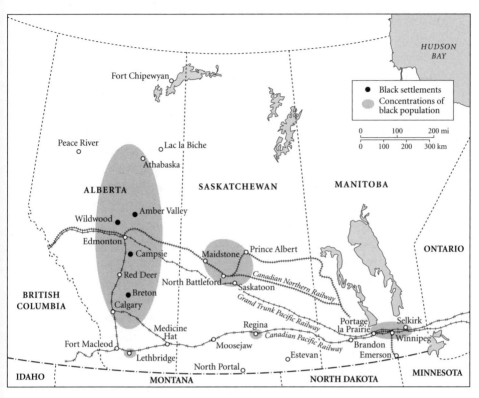

Fig. 2. Black settlement in the Canadian West, 1911

clergymen like Rev. Henry Sneed, orchestrated and led groups of migrants out of the South and onto Canadian homesteads in the years between the end of Reconstruction in 1877 and World War I. They envisioned a progressive or chain migration whereby a first wave of settlers would clear Canadian immigration, establish homesteads, and help others do the same in subsequent months.[74] Two organizations, the Loyal Legion Co-Operative Educational System and the Alberta Negro Colonization and Settlement Society assisted with this sequential migration, even "financing impecunious negroes during the[ir] first season" in Canada.[75] C. W. Mitchell, "a highly educated negro [and] founder" of the Loyal Legion, explained his organization's straightforward objectives to Western Canadian newsmen and stressed that African Americans "desire to be under the freedom of Canadian law, which affords better treatment to negroes than do those of the United States."[76] Because African American migrants were escaping regions where Jim Crow rule completely unhinged civil rights secured during Reconstruction, they frequently cited the appeal and stability of Canadian law as a reason for coming to the dominion.

Mitchell, Sneed, and other men spearheading this calculated southern African American emigration understood its long-term impact on the South. An Oklahoman reporter noted, "It develops that the Canadian colonization work among the negroes has been in progress for several months, the intention being to move 1,000 families or about 7,000 negroes." The Oklahoma newsman ominously informed readers that African Americans willingly "sold all their property in this state, intending to homestead quarter section claims in Canada. Many . . . indications are there will be a general exodus."[77] Unnerved by that possibility, the *Calgary Herald* charged that " 'Old Daddy Snaid' . . . the bearded patriarch of the party and the bunch of blacks that he is leading into the promised land" were a worrisome vanguard.[78]

African American immigrants from Oklahoma and other parts of the South saw Canada's homesteading program as a new chance at Reconstruction politics and exported that vision with them when they came to the dominion. Education, suffrage, and equal protection before the law had remained at the forefront for African Americans during the Reconstruction era, as it did for those considering migration to Canada years later. Rev. W. A. Lamb-Campbell of Galveston, Texas, warned the Laurier government that "the American of African descent likes much to handle his affairs. He must be put on the same footing with his neighbor, and, where he settles in large numbers would require representation in the local and general parliament by men of his own people." He added that "whatever franchise is enjoyed by his neighbor must be one and the same with him. He would not think of making a change to the Dominion under other circumstances."[79] Rev. Henry Sneed, also a Reconstruction statesman, told the *Edmonton Daily Capital*, "I have been . . . from sheriff to representative in the state legislature of my state. I stand before you clear to show that I have a record as a gentleman not only in one but in several countries and states."[80]

Just as southern blacks brought their fight for full citizenship north, some white Canadians, especially those experienced with southern segregation, were determined to import the South's racialized social order. Frank Powell, a white Albertan who had lived for a time in the South, shared his insight with the Department of Immigration. "The average Canadian does not seem aware that the darky may be vicious, and is apt at first to look upon him as an amusing and harmless character." Canada, proposed Powell, should take heed from the South. "In the States where Negroes are numerous they give the Police Force and Criminal Court three times more work and trouble than an equal number of white people living near them." Powell reasoned that Reconstruction had emboldened African American southerners who no longer worked compliantly for white overseers, with many "of those born since the war . . . inclined to be indolent and troublesome."[81]

Powell outlined why African American southerners threatened Canadian peace and civility. "If all Negroes were good, I would still consider it unwise for Canada to receive any of them, for the simple reason that they cannot be assimilated." He reassured the Canadian government that no "fair minded white man in the United States would blame Canada for keeping them out, and I am, of course, in favor of letting the Negro problem stay in that country where it belongs." Should southern African Americans continue homesteading in the West, Powell foreshadowed that "it will only lead to trouble." He offered the Laurier government a simple solution: "I hope that Canada is not bound in any manner to admit the Negroes and give them land, and having the future welfare of our country at heart, I would certainly like to see this kind of immigration stopped . . . now and forever by the imposition of a sufficient capitation tax, at least $1000."[82]

If white Canadians took notice of African Americans defecting to the Prairies, so too did American newsmen in the South. "General Exodus of Negroes into Canada: Movement Follows Colonizing Campaign by Canadian Representatives during Winter Months," proclaimed an Oklahoma newspaper. The reporter accused the "final action of the Canadian government in admitting to that country negro families from Oklahoma" of "having the effect of further colonization movement among the negroes, especially in Okfuskee, Muskogee and Creek counties, where there is a heavy negro population and several negro towns." He confirmed that black southerners were "leaving Oklahoma because of adverse legislation, 'Jim Crow' coach and depot laws, the 'grandfather clause' act that prohibits them from voting, separate school laws and others." Such emigrants, declared the article, "as a rule are educated negroes, many of whom were taught in the government schools for Indians in old Indian Territory."[83] In effect, the departure of this particular class of African American migrants often signaled the loss of Oklahoma's educated black middle class—those who owned the land and businesses that afforded black Oklahomans a level of prosperity unparalleled in most other parts of the South.

Exodusters, Reconstruction politicians, and "educated negroes" in the South knew that without sophisticated manipulation of their own government, their emigration plans to Canada might just fail. Canada's antiblack immigration sentiment threatened their vision of utopian agrarian communities as well as their quest for meaningful citizenship outside the United States. Consequently, black settlers petitioned the State Department for support of their cause, hoping that news of maltreatment of American citizens would spur the United States to diplomatic action, especially during key free-trade negotiations scheduled for 1911.[84] Ultimately, they gambled that both countries would avoid calling attention to this burgeoning immigration crisis.

Aware of Canada's antiblack xenophobia, African American would-be settlers came prepared for stonewalling at the border. One Canadian immigration agent advised his supervisors that "many of them [African Americans] are getting wise. They are getting advice as to what they can claim as American citizens and to that extent are becoming more insistent, more incredulous, and less apprehensive." He counseled, "Several have recently declared they would have the matter brought to the attention of the U.S. Congress through their representatives. Others who have been debarred from entering Canada are determined to seek legal redress."[85] By 1910, Dr. John Jones, the U.S. consul general stationed in Winnipeg, made regular trips to the border in defense of African Americans stalled by Canadian immigration officials and negotiated the peaceful admission of several African Americans intent on homesteading in the Prairies.

Determined to avoid tensions with the Laurier government, however, the U.S. State Department tried rerouting African American immigrants to the Northwest or to Central America. A group of Oklahoma settlers bound for Alberta admitted that the "United States Government would like to see us go to Washington, Montana, or even to Mexico, and at the last minute tried to get us to change our minds" about going to Canada.[86] The *Manitoba Free Press* posited that "should it appear that the dominion government decided against the whole class because of their color the state department would probably feel called upon to protest such action as clear violation of the treaty rights of Americans."[87] For its part, the *New York Times* pointedly resolved that, on balance, it "is very difficult to take any high view regarding the inhospitality of Canadians, both citizens and officials, toward 'nationals' [African Americans] who are fleeing from equal intolerance at home, and ill-treatment at the hands of both neighbors and legislators."[88]

The Laurier government solved its problem with the State Department by appealing directly to President William Taft's administration. In a secret memorandum to Minister Frank Oliver, the supervisor of immigration in Winnipeg, J. Bruce Walker, disclosed the details of his conversation with U.S. consul general Jones. "Dr. Jones informs me in the most confidential manner that he has just returned from Washington, where he had an opportunity of discussing this matter with Mr. Secretary of State," Philander C. Knox. According to U.S. consul general Jones, the Taft administration gave assurances that no "one could very well blame the Canadian[s]" for not wanting African American denizens and that "the United States Authorities . . . would not look upon the enactment of" further restrictions "as an unfriendly or discourteous act on the part of the Dominion Government."[89] Indeed, the *Chicago Record Herald* confirmed reports that Canadian and American bureaucrats were busy negotiating "a line of procedure" for black migration, with "Canadian immigration officials giving grounds upon which the American negro might be barred from the Dominion."[90]

Just as the U.S. government covertly abandoned its black citizens, W. E. B. Du Bois came to their defense with his usual candor. Du Bois unveiled Prime Minister Laurier's shifty stance on black migrants and exposed the Canadian government's racist immigration practices in the African American press. During this era, the black press became a salient platform for exchanging political ideas and legal strategies. As America's leading black scholar-activist, Du Bois oversaw publication of the *Crisis*, the official publication of the National Association for the Advancement of Colored People (NAACP). In March 1911, he wrote the Department of Immigration asking for clarification on Canada's immigration laws. "It is reported in the American Press that the Dominion Government has issued a decision barring colored people from entrance into Canada as settlers. Will you kindly let me know the exact text of this decision?"[91] F. C. Blair, a senior department bureaucrat, simply dismissed Du Bois's inquiry, citing that "the climate and other conditions of this country are not . . . congenial to coloured people."[92]

The Laurier government never imagined that its curt response to Du Bois's letter would ignite into a politically explosive issue. The exchange of letters between the Department of Immigration and W. E. B. Du Bois—and their subsequent appearance in the New York–based the *Crisis*—revealed that immigration to Canada appealed to northern as well as southern African Americans.[93] Even so, by outlining the Canadian government's plot to keep black immigrants out, Du Bois inadvertently aided the Canadian government's cause. Instead of reassuring African Americans that no legal barriers prevented them from seeking land in Canada, the *Crisis*'s exposés confirmed that Canada's only intention was to keep blacks out. As a result of those reports, the immigration branch began receiving letters of protest from African Americans who decided against emigrating to Canada after learning of the country's racist policies.[94]

In Du Bois's opinion, Canadian immigration policy stood as indisputable proof that a color line existed in the Dominion of Canada, with the Immigration Act of 1910 demarcating the country's color line at the international boundary. In addition, Du Bois's *Crisis* editorials fundamentally challenged Canada's claim that the color line was singularly an American social and political dilemma. He acknowledged that African Canadians and African Americans shared a similar plight and informed his readers that "this episode in Canada is indeed a disquieting, yet not a hopeless, 'symptom.'" For Du Bois, it proved "that the Negro problem is not merely a local affair of our own, but a great moral question for whose solution the whole white race is responsible." Thus, Du Bois concluded that white Canadians were no more immune to racism than other whites in North America. Rather, he stressed that the "United States has now become simply one laboratory in which the necessary experiments may be tried."[95]

Du Bois's critique of Canadian "colorphobia" struck a chord with many African Canadians. For example, in his letter to the minister of immigration, a black man from New Brunswick, John T. Richards, described Canada's immigration policy as "downright southern-cracker tactics or hidebound *colorphobia*." He argued that the Canadian government "is certainly drawing the *color line* when the United States Consul General has to be on the *Border* to aid men enter Canada, [and that] it is certainly a crying shame for a British speaking Govt, to attempt to allow a *color line* to be drawn by any of its servants." Threatening to exact vengeance at the polls, Richards advocated political action from African Canadian voters, reminding Prime Minister Laurier, "The Coloured people here feel this matter keenly and if this *color bar* is not lowered speedily [we] will without doubt join with the coloured voters in Nova Scotia and Ontario in registering [our] verdict against the Government at the next Federal Election."[96] The Department of Immigration scoffed at Richards's threat to withdraw his support from the Liberal government, stressing that white westerners were the prime minister's chief concern. Yet at the same time, the Canadian government persistently denied upholding the color line in its immigration policy. When pressed in the House of Commons about the exclusion of African American migrants in the winter of 1911, Minister of Immigration Oliver denied any knowledge of such actions. Seemingly unaware of how this undid his earlier pretense, Oliver vowed, "I can assure my honorable friend that there are no instructions issued by the Immigration Branch of my department which will exclude any man on account of his race or colour."[97]

Frank Oliver deceitfully denied allegations that "the Dominion government has issued orders through its officials to prevent the entry of negroes into Canada" as "absolutely and entirely incorrect."[98] Minister Oliver rationalized that in the case of desired immigrants "the restrictive provisions of the law are administered laxly." Other immigrants, "of the presumably less desirable class . . . are administered more restrictedly."[99] He disingenuously insisted, however, that the Liberal government evaluated would-be settlers "without any distinction of race, colour, or previous condition of servitude."[100]

Minister Frank Oliver's orders "to prevent the entry of negroes into Canada" were long-standing and well known to immigration officials, especially those manning the western border. In fact, on the same day that Oliver lied to the House of Commons, the minister examined the first draft of a new law advocating a complete ban on black immigrants. On that day, William D. Scott, the superintendent of immigration, counseled the minister, "I fail to see wherein negroes are more desirable than the yellow races," and he suggested "some drastic action to prevent the threatened influx." Scott recommended that Oliver use his powers under the Immigration Act to introduce an order in council prohibiting "the admission of negroes." Should the minister ignore this proposal, Scott warned, the Liberals would "receive . . . reprimand from portions of Alberta and Saskatchewan" in the coming election.[101]

Frank Oliver tabled Scott's legislative plan as too drastic, opting instead for a new four-stage attack on African American immigrants. With sanction of its racist immigration policies from the U.S. State Department, the Laurier government disregarded Du Bois's outcry and African Canadian protest in favor of bolder campaigns against African American and West Indian immigrants. First, the Department of Immigration wanted the movement of black people choked off at its source in the South. William J. White, a senior department bureaucrat in charge of U.S. operations, insisted that so long as African Americans could obtain excursion fares and Canadian Land Seeker's certificates entitling them to rail rates for as low as one cent per mile, Canada would not break the tide of northbound black migrants. "Notwithstanding our very best efforts to guard carefully the class of people who go to Central Canada, we find the case of the Negro probably most difficult to deal with. If given a free hand and the privilege to absolutely refuse to give a certificate entitling him to the settler's rate, we could meet it."[102]

William J. White then instructed American railroad companies to block ticket sales to black passengers headed for Canada. In a letter to the general traffic manager for the Soo Line serving Winnipeg via Minneapolis, White wrote, "There seems to be an inclination on the part of a number of coloured persons of the south to go northward this spring, and many of them are undesirable as settlers on land in Canada." He contended that since southern African American immigrants were "suffering from disease of one kind or another and in many ways are unfitted," the Canadian government wished "to check the movement of undesirables." White asked for the Soo Line's cooperation in the matter and emphasized that with "this end in view I am writing to you, hoping that I may be able to get your influence with the railroads operating in the south to discourage as much as you can the starting off of this coloured movement."[103] White also secured the collaboration of traffic managers on the Great Northern, the Northern Pacific, the Santa Fe, the Rock Island Railroad, the Missouri, Kansas and Texas, the Frisco Lines, and the Union Pacific; all agreed not to sell special reduced fare tickets to black immigrants bound for Canada, increasing the average cost of rail passage to the Canadian border for African Americans up from approximately $20.00 to $200.00.

Next, the Department of Immigration demanded that border guards apply strict scrutiny when examining black and other undesirable immigrants at entry ports. Despite no outright legal ban locking blacks out of Canada at the time, the Department of Immigration's most powerful bureaucrat, William D. Scott, counseled medical examiners that "there are certain nationalities who are required to pass more stringent regulations than other[s]."[104] Dr. Peter H. Bryce, the department's chief medical officer and one of Canada's leading eugenicists of the day, supervised all doctors in the department's employ.[105] The Canadian government rewarded meticulous medical examiners with a $5.00 bonus for each black migrant rejected at the border.[106] Dr. Maxwell Wallace, the examiner at the Emerson, Manitoba, border post, capitalized on Canada's racial paranoia, earning $1,710.50 in twenty-five months, forcing the Department of Immigration to remind its agents that "it was never intended to keep medical inspectors at these ports for the examination of ordinary immigrants." The minister of immigration reiterated that the Canadian government had hired Wallace and other doctors like him at boundary stations principally "because of the movement of coloured people."[107]

Given that the Immigration Act of 1910 did not specifically spell out medical bases disqualifying potential immigrants, medical officers enjoyed great leverage when revoking would-be settlers. For instance, between 1910 and 1912, Canadian immigration officials refused entry to almost five thousand immigrants for a plethora of reasons including poverty, criminality, vagrancy, immorality, prostitution, insanity, and physical disability.[108] In their zeal to keep Canada lily white, medical inspectors rejected immigrants on the wildest of pretenses. Medical examiners cited arthritis, asthma, cellulitis, curvature of the spine, diabetes, defective sight, eczema, hookworm, goiter, gout, hare lip, lameness, melancholia, opium habit, poor physique, varicose veins, and pregnancy as causes for rejection.[109] It is surprising that any black immigrants passed Canada's medical examination at all, yet 1,234 African Americans and 3,577 West Indians officially passed border inspections between 1900 and 1916.[110]

Unfortunately, passing medical examination did not safeguard new immigrants from further harassment from medical and immigration officials. Canadian immigration law authorized the immigration branch to deport immigrants who strayed from the law or developed medical complications within two years of their landing. Furthermore, during that same period, medical officers ordered more than twelve thousand immigrants deported for a host of ambiguous reasons. William D. Scott, the overseer of black migration in the immigration branch, regularly recommended that field agents maximize existing restrictions when dealing with black immigrants. When Scott learned that thirty-four black Oklahomans cleared border inspections and entered Canada via White Rock, British Columbia, he urgently telegraphed the immigration agent in Edmonton demanding that he take decisive action against the newcomers. Scott ordered, "If you can find any reason why any of the thirty-four from Oklahoma should be deported, take action. If you are suspicious that there are any who would not come up to the physical qualification, call in [the] City Health officer to examine [them]."[111]

Word of Canada's gruesome medical examinations provoked the ire of many African American settlers. M. C. Baltrip of Oklahoma lodged a complaint with the Laurier government after his family's humiliating experience at the hands of medical border guards in Saskatchewan. When every hotel near the border refused him a room, Baltrip and his family spent their first night in the dominion quite literally on Canadian soil. The Baltrips found shelter in a barn, where they slept "in the cold with Frost on the ground." The dehumanizing encounter infuriated Baltrip, who told the Department of Immigration, "My wife has become dissatisfied over our treatment here without any cause and we are so discouraged over it [that] we have decided we would not live where we are not wanted simply because of our color."[112] His letter so pleased William D. Scott that he smugly informed his supervisors, "We are not disappointed at this man's decision to go back as it will probably result in deterring a number of others from coming . . . [since he was] not met with a very kind reception."[113]

Minister Frank Oliver's next plan of action against black immigrants involved recruiting prominent southern African Americans opposed to emi-

gration. Suspecting that certain African Americans opposed the massive departure of their compatriots, immigration branch bureaucrat William D.
Scott reasoned that if the Canadian government secured the partnership
of key African American leaders, these men could successfully intercept
the movement of even more black migrants. To that end, Scott dispatched
federal special agent Charles Speers to Oklahoma and Kansas to find such
collaborators.[114]

Speers quickly located supporters among African American doctors, clergymen, and news editors in Muskogee and Okfuskee counties, home to
Oklahoma's largest African American populations. Within days of his arrival
in the South, Agent Speers proudly reported to the Department of Immigration, "I have, in most places, secured I think, the co-operation of the leading
Clergymen . . . [who] are using their influence to assist us in this special
propaganda." Speers confidently declared that clergymen's "influences will be
more important and [will have] more potential than anything else in bringing about the desired results" of stopping southern African American immigration to Canada.[115]

Two doctors, G. W. Miller and J. B. Puckett, and clergymen I. Bland, W. H.
Jernegin, S. S. Jones, L. J. Haywood, and D. A. Lee, seven prominent black
southerners anxious about losing their constituencies to Canada, carried on
the Laurier government's "special propaganda." Immigration agent Speers
emphasized the importance of their alliance and sold the men on Canada's
Faustian pact by reasoning that discouraging black emigration amounted to
civil rights activism. Speers instructed Rev. W. H. Jernegin, pastor of Oklahoma City's "Colored Church," "Advise your people to remain just where
they are until they had sufficient strength to demand through the Courts a
restoration of their rights taken from them" since Oklahoma statehood and
the adoption of grandfather clauses. Speers stroked Jernegin's ego, stressing,
"I must compliment you upon this . . . wise decision, which is not only in the
interest of your people, but will reflect credit upon yourself."[116]

Agent Speers even suggested that southern African American clergymen
make the most of challenges to grandfather clause acts and other anti–Jim
Crow rulings headed for the Supreme Court in order to advance the percep-
tion that conditions were in fact improving for black Oklahomans. The
Laurier government's greatest ecclesiastic ally, Rev. Dr. S. S. Jones, then president of the Oklahoma Baptist Conference and chief editor of the African
American newspaper *Baptist Informer*, commanded a monthly salary of fifty
dollars for his work on behalf of the Canadian government.[117] Given that
Jones ministered to a congregation of more than a thousand parishioners,

Speers proposed that the reverend mention the Supreme Court decision when proselytizing against immigration to Canada, as "I am persuaded you will be able to continue vigorously the cause you have been advocating."[118] Jones also capitalized on his control of a large press to remind black southerners that "the Negro that cannot make a living in Oklahoma cannot make it in Canada or Mexico; hence, he is as well off here as" anywhere else.[119]

The Laurier government understood the importance of the African American press and astutely utilized it for its campaign against southern black migrants. The Department of Immigration commissioned articles and advertisements from African American journalists, favoring reports exaggerating Canada's cold climate and downplaying the country's appeal to black southerners. In 1911, William D. Scott drafted C. W. Miller, an alleged black Chicago doctor, for the department's special crusade in Oklahoma and Kansas. Miller proved an excellent choice, since his outrageous "tales from the northside" drew large crowds and full-page coverage in the southern black press.

Dr. Miller's exposés on the Canadian West terrified southern audiences unfamiliar with northern climates. Miller claimed that during visits to Canada he witnessed "coloured people frozen along the roadside, just like fenceposts and that they would remain in that position until the spring thaw."[120] In another article published in the *Oklahoma Guide*, Miller recommended that prospective black migrants consider the full ramifications of migrating to Canada and described the Canadian Northwest as a "desolate, frigid, unsettled" region to which African Americans were "climatically and financially unfit."[121] Far from a welcoming promised land, Miller's Canada seemed more like frigid Elysian Fields.

Miller claimed that inimical Canadian border guards and arctic cold hampered access to that Elysium. He laced his entire description of a "typical" passage to Canada with sensational hyperbole and used powerful imagery reminiscent of slave auctions, knowing what resonance this would have with black audiences, particularly southern ones. Miller explained how would-be settlers faced their first obstacle at the Canadian border. He told readers that when "the Government Inspector meets you, . . . you and your family are sent to a physician to be examined, where your wife and daughters are stripped of their clothes before your very eyes and are examined by a board of men." Against the background of the endemic sexual exploitation of black women with black men often feeling powerless to stop it, this description of women and girls being publicly undressed by white men surely struck a raw nerve with southern African Americans. Miller appealed directly to black migrants' pride and manhood, asking, "What man of you would desire his family undressed and humiliated in such a manner?" Even if black women and children were spared such humiliation, Miller stressed that "you yourself cannot stand the cold. You were bred and born here in the south and it will cost you your life to live one winter in Canada." According to Miller, livestock were no safer in Canada than black women. "Another thing, your chickens cannot go out and get food, . . . if they try they are sure to freeze up and die. . . . Your cattle can not go out and graze for the ground is covered with snow. . . . Your horses and mules cannot stand the cold and they curl up and die."[122] Thus Canada's cold climate imperiled black families as well as their livelihood.

In the event that Miller's ill-omened reports did not entirely persuade African Americans to stay in the South, he informed readers of another Canadian tragedy. "You can get no watermelons, sugarcane or sweet potatoes. These you know as well as I do that you are instantly fond of." The doctor offered prudent final advice to southern African Americans still flirting with thoughts of emigration to the dominion. "Why not stay here," he beseeched, for in Canada "you will simply catch cold and die of consumption or pneumonia or freeze to death."[123]

Dr. Miller's "authentic" reports likely convinced many African Americans that Canada was one big frozen cemetery not worth the apocalyptic long trek.[124] Though Miller's tales appear obviously absurd, they successfully deterred southern black immigration to Canada. The Department of Immigration noted a dramatic decline in African American migration even before Miller completed his four-week tour of Oklahoma. In addition, the immigration branch agent in Kansas City reported that fewer black Oklahomans inquired about homesteading in Western Canada after hearing or reading Miller's fanciful stories.[125]

The Department of Immigration placed great faith in its partnership with southern African American leaders and journalists. Immigration branch bureaucrats even hatched a plot to recruit Booker T. Washington, the most influential African American leader at the time. Born into slavery in Virginia in 1856, Washington rose to prominence in the South as founder of the Tuskegee Institute, a college renowned for producing seasoned farmers and domestic workers. By the turn of the twentieth century, Booker T. Washington had brokered a precarious balance of backing from both white southern Democrats committed to Jim Crow and northern philanthropists. Most important, and the chief reason for the Canadian government's interest in winning his support, Washington enjoyed the greatest eminence among African Americans in the South, where he preached against abandoning Dixie for emigration elsewhere. A Canadian immigration agent combing the South for black allies advised his superiors in Ottawa, "It has since occurred to me it might be good policy for the Department to send the right kind of man here—collect such evidence as can be used in this way, and then lay the matter before Booker T. Washington." The Laurier administration confidently believed that Washington, "a wise and level-headed man, who strongly feels that his people should remain in the south," would readily support their cause, turning his influence into a "material advantage to us in this matter."[126] Though evidence does not suggest that Department of Immigration bureaucrats moved ahead with their Washington plot, the proposed plan exposes the desperation felt by the Laurier government by 1911.

The "Washington plot" certainly presents an alternative interpretation of Booker T. Washington's now famous 1895 Atlanta Compromise address—"to those of my race who depend on bettering their condition in a foreign land . . . I would say: 'Cast down your bucket where you are'"—reminding us of the international scope of African American immigration by the end of the nineteenth century.[127] More important, the Canadian government's cabal with other southern African American clergymen, doctors, and newsmen reveals the full extent of Prime Minister Laurier's determination to keep Canada "for the white race only." Likewise, it demonstrates how the Department of Immigration upheld and protected its own white supremacist beau ideal by shrewdly tapping into southern racial anxiety. In so doing, zealous white Canadian bureaucrats unveiled their own mastery of Jim Crow ideology and practice. Moreover, by sending agents to the South, hindering the sale of railway fares, subjecting African American settlers to grueling medical examinations, harassing black immigrants after their entry, co-opting celebrated southern African American leaders, and polluting African American newspapers with falsified accounts, the Laurier administration, just as Du Bois aptly presaged, gave contour to Canada's own color line.

British and American journalists confronted this Canadian Jim Crow rhetoric head-on. A special correspondent for the *Times* of London reported on Canada's unsettling tactics, acknowledging that "Canada and Negro Immigration" had become "A Growing Problem." The reporter observed, "One rarely meets a coloured person in Canada except on the dining and Pullman cars of the great through trains. The truth is that the severity of the Canadian climate either kills the negro or drives him back to the South." He resolved that "possibly our boasted toleration for negroes in Canada is explained by their scarcity."[128]

The American national press also scrutinized Canadian immigration policy and debunked the Laurier government's two-faced swagger on the color question. In 1911 alone, Portland's *Advertiser*; Boston's *Globe*, *Post*, and *Transcript*; New York's *Commercial*; Augusta's *Chronicle*; New Orleans's *Picayune*; and Chicago's *Record Herald* and *Tribune* all ran articles on African American emigration and Canadian immigration policy. They did not contest Canada's right to legislate against any class of immigrants so much as they took issue with Canada's premise that African Americans were somehow unsuited for its northern climate. A *Chicago Tribune* article entitled "The Negro in the Arctic Zone" adamantly rejected Canada's claim that its frigid climate presented insurmountable obstacles for African American would-be homesteaders. The author lambasted Canada's "cold argument," declaring, "That does not hold good of negroes whose ancestors were brought to this country 200 years ago or more. They are by this time pretty well acclimated." While two centuries of cohabitation with white Americans had not secured civil rights for African Americans, it seemed that slavery had somehow outfitted blacks with a climatic robustness shared by their white American compatriots. "They have become so thoroughly acclimated that when they go to tropical Africa, . . . they suffer much as a white man does," insisted the *Tribune*. The article concluded by discouraging black immigration to Canada as African Americans "would encounter prejudice which would be a more formidable enemy than the bitter cold."[129]

Back in Western Canada, where no one knew of the Department of Immigration's southern scheme, white Canadians still raged against "Negro Colonists in the West."[130] The greatest outcry against black immigration came from Edmonton, a city with a black population of less than 1 percent. By far the most outspoken opponents of black migration, Edmonton businessmen called for an apartheid-style homesteading system in the Canadian Plains. Led by F. D. Fisher, the Edmonton Board of Trade presented Prime Minister Laurier with a resolution demanding that Canada "take such steps as will effectually prevent the advent of negroes to western Canada; and that such negroes as are now on homestead lands in the country be segregated in a certain defined area or acres from which white settlers should be removed."[131]

Fisher warned Minister of Immigration Frank Oliver that "public agitation" over black immigration and negrophobia had become so strong that if black immigration remained unchecked, Western Canada would witness a "natural backlash" to their presence. Fisher cautioned the Canadian government that blacks in Canada would produce the same social chaos witnessed south of the border, as "it is a matter of common knowledge that it has been proven in the United States that negroes and whites cannot live in proximity without the occurrence of revolting lawlessness, and the development of bitter race hatred."[132]

Like W. E. B. Du Bois, Fisher invoked the American Jim Crow model but with a very different purpose. While Fisher and Du Bois concurred that "the most serious question facing the United States to-day is the negro problem," the Edmontonian businessman held, "We are anxious that such a problem should not be introduced into this fair land at present enjoying a reputation for freedom from such lawlessness as has developed in all sections in the United States where there is any considerable negro settlement." Fisher predicted a terrible outcome should the Canadian government discount his warning. "There is no reason to believe that we have here a higher order of civilization, or that the introduction of a negro problem here would have different results" from conditions in the American South.[133]

Fired up by Fisher's forewarning, the Edmonton Board of Trade lobbied for total exclusion of African American migrants from Canada. Members circulated a petition urging the Canadian government to take decisive action against "the serious menace to the future welfare of a large portion of Western Canada, by reason of the 'alarming' influx of negro settlers."[134] The *Edmonton Evening Journal* joined the board's protest and encouraged all Edmontonians to sign the petition posted at various banks, hotels, and Board of Trade offices.[135] Within weeks, Fisher proudly proclaimed that thirty-five hundred Edmontonians had endorsed his organization's campaign to keep black immigrants out of Alberta and the rest of Canada.[136]

Despite its overtly racist comments, the Edmonton Board of Trade persistently denied that white supremacy fueled its actions. Fisher alleged that "the sentiment of the public generally . . . is one largely without prejudice. The position taken by this Board of Trade, for instance, is based purely on broad general lines of public welfare and entirely apart from anything approaching race prejudice." He adamantly maintained that his sole interest remained protecting Canada from the social turmoil wreaking havoc in the United States. Fisher and Edmonton's Board of Trade declared themselves the watchdog of the Prairies and insisted that greater numbers of African Americans would discourage more favorable white settlement in Alberta and the Canadian West more generally. Fisher reasoned that "if the free land is taken away from them they will not come, or at least, not to any considerable extent."[137] Accordingly, he proposed that the Laurier administration consider an immediate amendment to existing dominion land laws disqualifying future black migrants from free homesteads. The Athabasca Landing Board of Trade went even one step further and advocated the "absolute prohibition of negroes into Canada."[138]

Yet all westerners did not share white nativists' views. Some black settlers and white westerners joined forces against the antiblack petitions creeping across the Plains. Rev. J. E. Hughson of Edmonton's predominantly white Methodist Church urged his congregation to boycott the Board of Trade's crusade. Edmonton's *Bulletin* and *Capital* reported that "one canvasser's steps were dogged by several negroes who introduced into the conversation . . . and sought to dissuade [white Edmontonians] from signing" the petition.[139] In his letter to the editor in the *Lethbridge Daily Herald*, L. D. Brower, a southern African American settler, accused white nativists in the West of "appealing to the lowest passions of man to hate his fellow man, and instituting an era of agitation and abuse." He deplored white Canadians' "adoption of those cowardly, slimy tactics of dragging the cesspools of moral depravity [and] . . . then holding it out to the nostrils of public sentiment shrieking behold!" Brower concluded that "there has never been a race problem here, and never will there be. So what is the use of opening that old sore on this side."[140]

The Canadian press ripped open "that old sore" and fanned white supremacist dogma in Western Canada, despite Brower's injunction. For more than a decade, Canadian newsmen aggravated tensions in the Prairies and stirred many white westerners into frenzy with sensational and often outlandish reports. For instance, the *Edmonton Bulletin* claimed that a black Oklahoman threatened to "pilot 5000 niggers into British-American soil before summah goes, suh. Ah'll put a niggah and a team of hosses on every quarter section of land [160 acres] I can get my hands on in Alberta, British Columbia and Saskatchewan."[141] Canadian newsmen's use of minstrel jargon served to reinforce the inadequacy and latent threat posed by unchecked black immigration.

Canadian news articles always depicted black migrants as either inarticulate simpletons, daring denizens, or smiling servants. Two Alberta newspapers allegedly quoted Rev. Henry Sneed within days of his group's arrival in Canada in 1911, with one reporter saddling him with fragmented speech— "there ain't nothin' the matter with us"—and the other presenting him as a calculating bellwether: "We are but the advanced guard . . . and if the new country is up to the representations of the agents, several thousands more will follow us this summer and fall."[142]

Conversely, other newsmen presented certain types of black immigrants as a tolerable alternative to African Americans roused by Reconstruction ideals and dreams of free land. An editorial defending black immigration in the *Edmonton Evening Journal* posited that "if he follows out the ideas set forth for his guidance by Booker Washington . . . who ha[s] done so much in stimulating self-respect among the members of his race . . . there is every reason to believe that he will become a useful citizen."[143] Likewise, many white Canadians fancied blacks like Charles H. Smiley, a Canadian-born descendant of freedom seekers who became a caterer to the wealthy white elite. The *Lethbridge Daily Herald*, a plainspoken opponent of African American immigration, lauded Ol' Smiley as the "Perfect Servant . . . a type of old-fashioned southern negro that tales of the 'Old Dominion' have immortalized."[144]

The *Lethbridge Daily Herald*'s full-page homage to this African Canadian transfigured into an "old-fashioned southern negro" exposed white Canadians' shifting stance on race matters. Though nativist white Canadians fumed when organized southern African American immigrant groups came north, Booker T. Washington and Ol' Smiley types made for endearing potential compatriots. Instead of dealing with the reality of the African American migrants at hand, white westerners nurtured warm images of servile black manliness. Independently minded black immigrants endangered Canada's social fabric, whereas compliant black men befitted a romanticized bygone "old dominion." Just as white southerners mourned the passing of their "Old South," white Canadians and their press also fabricated an old-dominion reverie threatened by African American southerners touched by Reconstruction ideology. The *Daily Herald* no longer conjured up tales emphasizing the indelible spirit of freedom seekers. Instead, its "old dominion" legacy, like that of the "Old South," mused about how "Smiley Served" and entertained "presidents and princes."[145]

Whether dumb, docile, or demanding, black immigrants posed a dilemma too titillating and controversial for white Canadian newsmen to ignore. Falsified accounts and dramatic headlines like "Black Settlers Invade the West," "Invasion of Negroes," "Negro Settlers Troop into the West," and "Negroes Ousting Whites in Canada" made sport of spreading antiblack sentiment. Many of Canada's leading newspapers, including the *Toronto Globe*, *Ottawa Free Press*, and *Montreal Gazette*, openly stated their objections to uncontrolled black immigration and supported white westerners' calls for further Canadian immigration restrictions, making clear that antiblack sentiment was shared nationwide.

Just like the American press, Canadian newsmen adopted and adapted rape scare tactics to call further attention to black migrants' undesirability.

For instance, in April 1911, the Canadian press pounced on the Hazel Huff affair, producing "wild excitement" and unequaled outrage in Western Canada.[146] The *Winnipeg Tribune* announced that a "Fiendish Attack by A Colored Man" had left a "Little Edmonton Girl" shaken by the ordeal.[147] On the evening of 4 April 1911, neighbors discovered Hazel Huff gagged and unconscious on the kitchen floor of her parents' home. The fifteen-year-old white Edmontonian appeared dazed from chloroform poisoning; worried neighbors immediately summoned a doctor and the police. Huff testified that when she answered a knock at the door earlier that day, "a big, black, burly nigger" forced his way into the house.[148] Though she resisted, the black assailant overpowered the young woman, bound her eyes, and forcibly drugged her. Left for dead, Hazel said that she could remember nothing more. A search of the home revealed that money and a diamond ring were missing: the attack, they concluded, had been a robbery. Enraged by a black man's assault on his innocent white teenaged daughter, Hazel's father loaded his gun and went hunting for her aggressor. Snow rolled off his shoulders and talk of violent retribution his lips as he set off in the cold spring night.

News of the attack on Hazel spread swiftly across the West. Newsmen quickly blamed unrestricted black immigration for the misdeed against a young white woman and foreshadowed "a Black Peril."[149] Despite the lack of any concrete evidence, coverage of the Huff affair linked her attack to the recent arrival of a group of black Oklahoman homesteaders. The *Calgary Albertan* prophesied that "the assault made by a colored man upon a little girl in Edmonton should open the eyes of the authorities in Ottawa as to what may be expected regularly if Canada is to open the door to all the colored people of the republic and not bar their way from open entry here."[150] The *Lethbridge Daily News* warned that white women isolated on rural homesteads lived in fear of black lechery and urged immediate action from the federal government because "almost simultaneously with the arrival in the West of a band of negroes from the South comes reports of a brutal assault on a white girl." The *Daily News* editor admonished that southern African American men "will constitute an ever-present horror to their neighbors, particularly . . . where the [white] women of the house are often left alone." He demanded that steps be taken to "keep the black demon out of Canada."[151] Western outcry over Hazel Huff's assault made clear that in white men's minds, guarding the Canadian border equated defending white women's chastity from irrepressible black lust.

The Edmonton police decided that two black men must have pulled off the heist. Chief R. W. Ensor, a stout and cantankerous Irish immigrant, informed the press that officers posted at railway yards were watching outgoing freight trains for black fugitives.[152] Within two days of the attack, Edmonton constables arrested J. F. Witsue and continued their hunt for another assailant. Chief Ensor charged Witsue with larceny, though he had not arrived with the Oklahoma party and could not be linked to the Huff home. The *Edmonton Daily Bulletin* augured that the Huff "incident," or another like it, "would push the rowdy element to the lynching point."[153]

Never before had lynching black men so preoccupied white Canadians. White nativists contended that African Americans who insisted on migrating to and farming in Canada brought vigilante persecution on themselves. These white westerners presented murderous death as a rational management of perceived racial problems in Canada. In the years leading up to World War II, white Canadians repeatedly presented lynching as an inevitable way of policing blacks in Canada, as though homicidal mob rule were a natural course of race relations.[154]

Nine days after initial reports of Hazel's maltreatment at the hands of a black intruder, the young white woman confessed that her entire story had been a racial red herring. Huff admitted that, fearing punishment for losing her mother's ring, she fabricated the attack by a "big, burly nigger," specifically because of the outcry over black immigration. The hysteria caused by her tale, the arrest of an innocent man, and the risk of inciting a lynching finally forced her confession. Edmontonians eventually learned that the city's chief of police had known of Huff's hoax a week before her public admission and had sworn her family to secrecy. Instead of releasing the innocently jailed Witsue, Chief Ensor demanded that the family let the story snowball, hoping to shock the federal legislature into action.[155] Presumably, the chief of police felt that swelling nativist sentiment outweighed the defamation of Witsue's character or even his possible lynching.[156]

When news of Hazel Huff's canard hit the press, infuriated black westerners attacked both the white girl's insidious tale and white westerners' racialized knee-jerk responses. Splintered southern Reconstruction politics, white supremacist firebrands, Prairie-bound Exodusters, and the virtue of white women forced an interesting debate on race relations in Canada before World War I. L. D. Brower, a black homesteader originally from Arkansas, denounced white supremacist rabble-rousers and the mischief they produced in both the U.S. South and Western Canada. Brower debunked white supremacists as "moral lepers" seeking post–Civil War retribution as far north as the Canadian Prairies. "But why do we hear so much about rape today? It is because the nature of the crime arouses the indignation of every self-respecting man and offers a plausible excuse for the murder of from one to one thousand negroes who were not slaughtered so liberally before the Civil War because they sold for from five hundred dollars up."[157]

Brower rejected the bewitching depiction of black men as "big, burly, niggers" who preyed on young white girls. "During the Civil War, when every able bodied white man was . . . engaged in a life and death struggle to maintain the institution of slavery, their women and children were left at home entirely to the mercy of these 'black brutes.' . . . If they were a vicious race by nature, would they not have avenged their long suffering on those thus unprotected?" White Canadians now claimed that these same southern African Americans "should be kept out of Canada" because of a presumptive danger to white girls and women, with Brower adding that, quite to the contrary, "suffice it to say, ten millions of negroes of mixed blood are the indisputable evidence of the depth of depravity" displayed by white men against black women during slavery.[158]

Daily News editors undermined Brower's protests by once again appealing to Jim Crow iconography. The newspaper sliced up Brower's editorial, "Defence of the Negro," with an advertisement featuring a blackfaced, buxom-lipped buffoon entreating, "Have a laugh on me—all the fun of a real minstrel right in your home on a Victor gramophone" (see Figure 3).[159] Such passive-aggressive actions by white journalists affirmed their contempt for blacks. Mockery of Brower and other black protesters signaled that unless their voices crooned old minstrel favorites, white Western Canadian newsmen dismissed African Canadians' political opinions.

L. D. Brower's numerous letters to the Laurier government and Western Canadian newspapers laid bare the broad impact of southern racial politics across North America. On the one hand, white Canadians insisted that with southern African American migrants came Uncle Sam's problems. Yet on the other hand, white nativists nostalgically embraced Dixie daydreams like Ol' Smiley content with his station. Inasmuch as white supremacist Canadians repudiated intrepid black southerners, they felt entitled to southern-style punishments meted out against African Americans who coveted white women or defied the entrenched racialized social order.

The arrival of astute southern black migrants tested and proved lacking white Canadians' hollow convictions in white supremacy. Experienced southern African American farmers who established viable farming communities in the West debunked the idea that only white farmers held the know-how for coaxing crops from the Plains. Affluent, autonomous black homesteaders, aware of their franchise and willing to wield it as a weapon,

Fig. 3. Canadian newspaper headlines, 1911

challenged the very bedrock of Canada's carefully crafted immigration plan, since their potential success signaled that Canada's path to modernity and prosperity need not be paved solely by brawny Europeans. If dispossessed and disfranchised former slaves could come north, punch their way through a seemingly impenetrable border, stake their land claims, and flourish despite white hostility, perhaps the white supremacist paradise Canadians envisioned for themselves was not so supremely unattainable after all.

White westerners needed to believe that black migrants could not adapt to life in the dominion because if they could assimilate Canadian agriculture, democracy, and citizenship, maybe African Americans and West Indians were not so "naturally" inferior after all. What would Canadians make of white farmers who could not do the same, whether Canadian or foreign-born? Blacks' prosperity uprooted the notion that their presumed inferiority was a natural outcome. If Jim Crow—rather than nature—reduced southern African Americans to second-class citizenship, white Canadians had cause for concern. Hence, white westerners resolved that something had to be done quickly and definitively. They put two options before Sir Wilfrid Laurier's administration: enact a decisive law against black immigration or step aside for a new government.

By late spring of 1911, the Laurier government forcibly came to terms with its "Negro Problem." Western discontent over black immigration dogged the Liberal government throughout its election campaign that year. Prime Minister Laurier feared for his party's standing in the West given the clamor over black immigration and U.S. tariff negotiations. Minister of Immigration Frank Oliver toured the West that spring and faced town halls packed with angry white westerners demanding resolutions on those two key matters, though by no means were tariffs and black immigration equally weighted.[160] Oliver tried to soothe his audiences by conceding that Canada's "Negro Problem Is a Difficult One."[161]

Conservative candidates were already exploiting western antiblack sentiment and promised thorough reform of Canadian immigration laws if elected to office. In an interview with the *Edmonton Evening Journal*, C. E. Simmonds, a Conservative candidate up for reelection, proclaimed, "Like the province of British Columbia being called 'Yellow British Columbia,' our own province might be called 'Black Alberta.' . . . We do not want to have this name attached to us, nor do we want to have the province black in spots." Simmonds offered the Conservative Party's solution to the problem: "I can only see one way out of this difficulty and this is to put the present government out of power and bring in one who will listen to our pleas." Conservative candidates maintained that the Liberals had consistently failed to protect the dominion from an "invasion of colored people," be they Chinese, Japanese, East Indian, or black.[162] Another Conservative candidate plainly asked the Laurier government, "Would it not be preferable to preserve for the sons of Canada the lands they [Liberals] propose to give to niggers?"[163] Speaking for the Liberals, immigration minister Frank Oliver explained that "until parliament had made provision in the law that some other action should be taken," his office could do little more against the "negro colonization" so worrying to white westerners.[164]

In a last-ditch effort to save his government's electoral support in the West, Oliver gave white westerners what they wanted most: new and definitive immigration regulation against African American and West Indian migrants. Fearing stonewalling in the House of Commons, Oliver presented Prime Minister Laurier with an order in council requiring that, for a period of one year, "the landing in Canada shall be . . . prohibited of any immigrants belonging to the Negro race, which race is deemed unsuitable to the climate and requirements of Canada."[165] The order in council could become federal law without consent from elected members in the House so long as members of the Privy Council voted in its favor. During the next Privy Council meeting, on 12 August 1911, Sir Wilfrid Laurier signed into law the order in council prohibiting black immigration.[166] The new edict, the first ever of its kind adopted in Canada singling out a racial group for unqualified exclusion, codified white paranoia into federal law and earned the Department of Immigration the dubious distinction of being the first federal government branch to institute a nationally implemented Jim Crow law in Canada.[167] Never before had the Canadian government imposed a complete ban of any group of migrants based on their race; neither had any division of the federal government enacted segregation legislation with a national application.

The Laurier government's adoption of an overtly racist immigration law confirmed that appeasing white supremacist Canadians outweighed the cost of violating Canada's treaty agreements with the United States and insulting African Canadian voters. Likewise, Laurier's actions gave compelling force to Du Bois's earlier assertion that the color line was indeed extant in Canada. Most important, the order's deleterious tenets would dictate immigration policy with respect to blacks for the next fifty years. Although the order in council fell through the cracks of a federal government turnover in the fall of 1911, the white supremacist federal rationale fueling it haunted black would-be settlers for another half century.

Laurier's desperate move against African American and West Indian immigrants could not save his government. His Liberal Party lost the 1911 election to Sir Robert Borden's Conservatives. Borden, who only months before the election had professed to the House of Commons that "it would be very unfortunate if any impression got abroad that any person, coming as an immigrant, was to be excluded simply because of his colour," hummed a very different tune once in office. By 1912, Prime Minister Borden's government, fearing that blacks would enter "under the guise of tourists or visitors," discouraged them from crossing the border altogether, proving once again that those who did bumped up against a line that would most often not bend.[168]

Canadian xenophobia thrived during Borden's nine-year term. Debates over immigration of blacks and the question of purposeful citizenship for those already in the dominion nagged Borden's government just as it had Laurier's. With career bureaucrat William D. Scott still commanding the Department of Immigration, Borden trusted in an unyielding continuity of Canada's position on African American and West Indian migrants. African Canadians, meanwhile, intensified their fight against the suffusion of Jim Crow ideology in federal decision making, employment practice, and foreign policy, not backing down from Borden any more than they had during Laurier's heyday.

The Borden government introduced two paradoxical dimensions to the black immigration debate in Canada in the years leading up to World War I. While Laurier had plotted to keep blacks out altogether, Borden admitted what he hoped would be subservient African Americans and West Indians into the Canadian workforce. So long as southern African Americans and West Indians were coming to the dominion to serve and entertain white Canadians as domestics, musicians, minstrel troupes, and sleeping car porters, Borden reluctantly conceded to their entry in limited numbers. Consequently, thanks to aggressive courtship by Canadian railway companies, young black male workers—especially sleeping car porters—constituted the largest class of black immigrants admitted into Canada between 1911 and the early 1960s. As such, sleeping car porters will logically become this study's chief focus. Prime Minister Borden also fancied confederation with the West Indies and believed that "the sense of responsibility [white] Canadians should gain from administering lands 'largely inhabited by backward races'" would greatly benefit the nation, proving once again that white Canadians relished control over black people, even as they beat back those seeking equal standing within the dominion.[169]

FEW ISSUES HAUNTED Sir Wilfrid Laurier's administration as much as the question of race and immigration. From his election in 1896 to his defeat in 1911, southern African American and West Indian immigration bogged down the Department of Immigration, inspiring increasingly repressive regulations. In effect, black migrants never accounted for more than 0.04 percent of the total immigrant pool heading to Canada between 1900 and 1916, at most totaling approximately five thousand identifiable African American and West Indian newcomers. Even so, their arrival during the first two decades of the twentieth century produced unparalleled hysteria. Mandatory medical examinations, monetary requirements, harassment from immigration agents, and exclusion based on dubious "climatic unsuitability" proved ineffective barriers to black immigration when Jim Crow and colonial rule presented a far greater threat to their well-being. That black homesteaders—and later railroaders—journeyed north despite proscriptions against their entry makes evident that African Americans included Canada in their imagination of a Great Migration, complicating existing understanding of African American movement out of the South. That West Indians also moved north during this time suggests that the risk of unemployment in the Caribbean forced an early great migration of its own, with Canada appealing to some West Indians because of its status as a British outpost in North America. In spite of restrictive federal legislation and panicked white westerners, African American and West Indian immigrants defiantly peppered every corner of Canada by World War I.

The demise of Reconstruction politics and the rise of white supremacy in the American South, especially in Oklahoma, forced millions of African Americans out of their homeland. Many looked to Canada because of its abolitionist legacy and generous homesteading program. Southern African American immigrants came to the Dominion of Canada hoping for a second chance at Reconstruction politics and citizenship based on fair play. Instead, they encountered white Canadians enraptured with white supremacist ideals of their own. Accustomed to white resistance and racialized rhetoric yet determined not to have it limit their new citizenship, southern African American immigrants demanded evenhanded civil rights from their new Canadian government and would not back down until they received it.

American and Canadian historians have argued that the border did not matter to American migrants who crossed it painlessly, almost becoming an invisible majority in the West during Canada's homesteading program.[170] But black immigrants never experienced that invisibility, feeling instead awed by the hateful frenzy sparked by their arrival. For black Americans, the border had always mattered. Those who fled a deadly South in the 1890s did so remembering how during the 1850s that same border had demarcated the line between slavery and freedom, bondage and the promise of citizenship. At the turn of the twentieth century, African Americans wagered that crossing the border would ensure asylum from Jim Crow and the white supremacist legislators elected to enforce it.

Southern racial politics colored relations between blacks and whites throughout North America, even seeping into Canadian consciousness and political debates prior to World War I. White Canadians, who might not have expressed their thoughts on blacks so long as they remained south of the line, found that the prospect of sharing land, citizenship, jobs, and quite possibly their daughters with black men warranted immediate action. That action, articulated in the press, letters to the government, and Parliament, included segregation, exclusion, and at times even reckless talk of lynching. Most important, white Canadians rallying against inheriting Uncle Sam's "Negro Problem" created one of their very own in the process.

At its core, the dispute over black immigration to Canada before the Great War revealed how white Canadians and their government adopted, adapted, and advocated white supremacist ideology. They did so at the same time that white southerners crafted their distinct racial social order—Jim Crow—and white northerners cast a thin veil over their color line. W. E. B. Du Bois had accused Prime Minister Laurier's government of also fostering a Canadian color line. Paranoid white Canadian businessmen, irresponsible journalists, elected statesmen, federal bureaucrats, women's organizations, and private citizens gave contour to that line in ways that even Du Bois could not have foreshadowed.

Whether natives or newcomers, blacks in Canada fought against white Canadians' racialized reveries. They denounced the Laurier government's hypocrisy and vowed to register their discontent at the polls. Southern African American migrants were disarmingly candid when articulating their complaints against white Canadian nativists and made unapologetic claims to their new Canadian citizenship rights. African Canadians also defended black settlers' rights and demanded that their members in Parliament give voice to their cause in the halls of power. Such bold actions by Reconstruction veterans or empowered African Canadians confirmed that they would not passively witness the shadow of Jim Crow creep into their dominion.

CHAPTER TWO

Jim Crow Rides This Train

Segregation in the Canadian Workforce

In April 1854, the Great Western Railway declared that it urgently needed eight hundred workers to guard its tracks against stray cattle and hog crossings. Its advertisement, strategically placed in Canada's most important black newspaper of the day, the *Provincial Freeman*, sought African Canadians for the task.[1] Before the turn of the twentieth century, African Canadian men laid down tracks for the transcontinental railroad and worked as cooks and dining car attendants for the Grand Trunk Railway.[2] Black workers earned a more prominent place on the rails by the 1880s with the introduction of the Pullman Palace Car Company's sleeping car service. Canadian railway companies modeled their sleeping and dining car departments after Pullman's plan, favoring black men for the task of serving affluent white passengers. By 1910, however, they feared that the growing paranoia over black immigration witnessed in Western Canada would jeopardize their continued access to black railwaymen.

Canadian railway companies experienced rapid growth between the 1880s and World War I thanks to the completion of the transcontinental line. They spent the period bemoaning persistent labor shortages, blaming restrictive immigration and labor laws for their troubles. William Van Horne, general manager of the Canadian Pacific Railway, fumed over Prime Minister Wilfrid Laurier's opposition to foreign industrial workers, insisting that Canadian prosperity depended on unencumbered immigration. Van Horne, who normally remained tight lipped on federal matters, denounced Canada's restrictive immigration policy, claiming that "what we want is population. Labour is required . . . throughout North and South America." He stressed that the "governments of other lands are not such idiots as we are in the matter of restricting immigration."[3]

Annoyed with chronic workforce shortages, Canadian railway and steel companies experimented with Canadian and foreign-born black labor before the Great War. They initially envisioned black workers for treacherous work—like hauling hog and cattle roadkill from railway tracks—believing, as did many of their contemporaries in other industries, that workers of African descent were well suited for those positions. Because demand for workers soared when able hands were few, African Canadian railwaymen eventually enjoyed a wider range of employment options during the early days of railroading. For instance, the Intercolonial Railway tapped into existing black communities in the Maritimes and Quebec and found a ready-made pool of experienced transportation workers.

Other Canadian companies, namely, the Dominion Iron and Steel Company (DISCO) of Nova Scotia and the Canadian Pacific Railway, turned a gleaming eye to southern African Americans and West Indians as an underutilized source of cheap labor. As of the 1890s, DISCO managers culled African American steelworkers from the Deep South, exporting them to Nova Scotia as needed. Meanwhile, the CPR and the Pullman Palace Car Company funneled thousands of black railroaders into Canadian urban centers for work in their new sleeping and dining car departments. By the turn of the century, Canadian industrialists also strategically positioned black workers as a useful weapon against white workers clamoring for unionization.

White workers recognized management's heavy-handed tactics and protested the introduction of black workers in Canadian industries as demeaning to their profession, their manhood, and their whiteness. Black laborers were, in their minds, scabs imported for the sole purpose of undermining unionization. The Canadian Brotherhood of Railway Employees, the most powerful railway union of its day in Canada, codified its contempt for black railwaymen at its inaugural meeting in 1908 by extending membership to white men only. Locked out of partnerships with white railwaymen by constitutional decree, black railroaders witnessed white supremacy as an integral part of Canadian trade unionism.

Although excluded from white unions, black workers viewed the rails as a viable career path and defended their right to work and their newly found place in Canadian industry. They understood that companies saw them as a disposable workforce, easily dismissed during economic recession. In spite of this, black railroaders protested their displacement and capitalized on the national press and the House of Commons when making their grievances known. Though often migrant workers, they asserted their right to a livelihood as well. Unable to gain the respect of their white co-workers, they formed a union of their own in 1917, the Order of Sleeping Car Porters—one of the first black railway unions in North America. John Arthur Robinson, who emerged as the chief defender of black workers during this era, cut his young union's teeth fighting Jim Crow trade unionism and segregationist employment policies on Canadian rails in the pre–World War I era. He and other sleeping car porters used existing labor law and publicized the discrimination they faced in the Canadian workforce. By World War I, these politically savvy actors forced a place for themselves in the Canadian House of Labor and unmasked white supremacy in every aspect of their lives as working men and Canadian denizens.

The rapid expansion of Canadian railway companies, the emergence of trade unionism, and the institutionalization of segregation across North America gave way to Jim Crow employment practices on Canadian rails between the 1880s and the Great War. White supremacy, institutionalized in separate and unequal practices governing both black and white workers, dictated labor-management relations as well as railway trade unionism. Quite simply, both white workers and railway managers acted out their frustrations on black workers. Canadian companies imported black workers, even considering for a time the annexation of a Caribbean island as a source of cheap labor, because they viewed black men as a malleable class of workers softened by southern Jim Crow and colonial rule, ignoring at times how these two models of white supremacy differed substantially from each other. In the end, railway executives exploited racialized divisions in their workforce by pitting railroaders against each other and displacing white union men with illegally imported black labor.

White railway workers created, fostered, and profited from a racially stratified workforce in Canada. By 1915, white railwaymen demanded and won a color line on Canadian rails. Separate and unequal guidelines prescribed the roles and privileges of black railroaders and severely hindered their career options in the process. White railroaders fought vehemently against the introduction of black workers, targeting them as the sole reason for their failed unionization efforts. Yet if Canadian industrialists and white trade unionists held conflicting positions on black labor, both readily conceded to a racialized division of the workforce. Consequently, the period from 1880 to

World War I saw Jim Crow institutionalized as an ideal rationale for labor-management relations in the Canadian railway industry.

CANADIAN RAILWAYS EXPERIENCED UNPRECEDENTED growth after the completion of the Canadian Pacific Railway transcontinental line in 1885. The Grand Trunk Railway, in conjunction with the Intercolonial Railway and the Canadian Northern Railway, completed another transcontinental line and joined the rapacious competition for passenger traffic.[4] Steam railway revenues soared at the turn of the twentieth century, thanks to William Van Horne's and Charles M. Hays's enterprising expansion of railway service, especially in sleeping, dining, and parlor car departments.[5] A four-hundred-pound bon vivant, Van Horne decided that he would make Canadian sleeping cars the most palatial liners in North America. The ambitious president tripled investments in the CPR's parlor and sleeping car department between 1885 and 1895.[6] He commissioned artists and interior designers who improved on Pullman's designs: they broadened berths to accommodate Van Horne's girth, installed bathrooms on first-class sleepers, and served generous gourmet portions in dining cars.[7]

Van Horne's tactics proved most lucrative. The Canadian Pacific annual shareholders reports boasted that revenue from the parlor and sleeping car department swelled from $24,071 in 1884 to $721,006 in 1904, with a profit margin for the latter year of more than a half million dollars.[8] Even smaller lines like the Canada Atlantic Railway joined the excitement over sleeping cars. In November 1898, it ordered four new cars from the Pullman Palace Car Company at a total cost of $31,740: two first-class sleeping cars with mahogany interiors and two second-class sleepers "finished in oak with double thick glass . . . [and] seats of leather."[9] That same year, the Intercolonial Railway spent $159,526.40 on eight sleeping cars built by Pullman's chief competitor, the Wagner Palace Car Company of New York.[10]

Corporate enthusiasm over sleeping car service produced a prodigious demand for other symbols of Pullman's signature service: black railway workers. Soon after the Civil War, George Pullman singled out newly emancipated African American men for his service, regarding them as paragons of docile diligence. Historian Brailsford Brazeal contends that Pullman also solicited black porters because they were a "plentiful source of labor [and] societal caste distinctions between Negro and white people created a 'social distance' which had become an accepted fact in the mores of American society."[11] Quite simply, Canadian railway companies avidly sought black railroaders for their sleeping car service because the image of broad-smiling, white-gloved, crisply uniformed black men proved a moneymaking triumph with Canada's wealthy white railway clientele as well. Initially, the CPR, GTR, and ICR recruited black railwaymen from Canadian cities with sizable African Canadian populations, namely, Halifax, Montreal, and Toronto.[12] In later years, still craving more black railroaders, Canadian railway companies increasingly turned to the southern United States and the West Indies.

The Intercolonial Railway found a ready supply of seasoned black service workers in Halifax, a vibrant port city teeming with black transportation workers.[13] Black Haligonians' lives were steeped in maritime culture. Hundreds of African American and West Indian seafarers docked in Halifax on their transatlantic steamship routes, with many establishing permanent residence in the city after careers at sea.[14] Already accustomed to transnational lifestyles, mariners were well suited to life on the rails. Many seafarers welcomed railway work as relief from long, dangerous sojourns at sea. Charles Pinheiro, a Barbadian steward on the SS *Acadia*, joined the ICR sleeping car department in 1888 and remained in its employ until his retirement.[15] Other black mariners wedded railroading with seafaring in order to ensure full employment, offset boredom, and shield themselves from seasonal layoffs. In some cases, mariners retired from sea employment for work on the rails after marrying into Halifax families. According to historian Judith Fingard, Demararan seaman James Knight married Annie Joseph, a Halifax mariner's daughter, in 1880; thereafter, he worked intermittently for the ICR and sailed on the *Orion*.[16]

Black Haligonians enthusiastically joined the rails during the ICR's heyday. The railroad promised steady employment and a respectable wage for those fortunate enough to land full-time employment, such as W. H. Blair, John Collins, Thomas Corbett, Joseph H. Daley, P. Driscoll, and P. Grannan, each of whom portered more than 340 days during 1898.[17] In fact, black railroaders readily found work across Canada. Company records confirm that by the turn of the twentieth century, many African Canadians migrated westward for promotions or better opportunities with the Pullman Palace Car Company, the Canadian Pacific Railway, and the Grand Trunk Railway headquartered in Montreal. Payroll rosters indicate that forty-nine men in Montreal, one hundred in Toronto, and thirty-nine in London portered for the GTR in 1902.[18] Full-time porters drew monthly salaries ranging from $20–35 per month to $300–450 a year.[19] Experienced porters were rewarded with higher-wage runs on private government cars. David Hawes and John B. Cameron, who manned the sleepers "Cumberland," "Montreal," and "Ottawa" exclusively reserved for prominent members of Parliament, earned annual salaries of $420.[20] Even Winnipeg offered work for men willing to bear its bitter winters and long runs to the Pacific coast. Canadian Northern Railway payrolls show that seventy-six men portered out of Winnipeg during the summer of 1909, with wages varying from $1.75 per day to $50 per month for seasoned railwaymen.[21]

Black railroaders in Canada enjoyed a broad range of employment options not readily available to most black transportation workers in the United States at the turn of the century, where Jim Crow and the Big Four brotherhoods restricted their occupational choices.[22] Variable wages, uncertain demand, and exclusion from white unions taught black railroaders in Canada the importance of diversifying their experience on the rails, as evidenced by employment patterns on the Intercolonial Railway. R. J. Murray was a brakeman for 51¾ days, worked as a baggagemaster for 2 days, and portered for 12¾ days, while L. Scothorn worked as a brakeman for 67 days, then as a shunter for 14 days, and finally as a porter for 5 days.[23] B. Dickie, R. Elliott, J. R. Fraser, J. P. Gough, and B. F. McKinnon supplemented their portering wages with work as brakemen, car checkers, shunters, and baggagemasters.[24]

During the early years of railroading, working the rails in any capacity meant flirting with danger. Brakemen had the death-defying task of running on top of moving railway cars, made icy during winter months, and turning the brake wheel while also maintaining their balance. Those who failed, as no doubt many did, met with sudden death along the tracks. The shunter's work proved no less perilous. Switchmen, as they were also known, dropped a levy to stop the cars and switched often poorly lit tracks so that trains going in the opposite direction could gain safe passage. Facing less hazardous conditions, though much fewer in number, were black nightwatchmen who moonlighted when on leave from the sleeping car service.[25] Other black railroaders like Peter Bushenpin and David Jones worked as coopers for the ICR after years of portering.[26] Before World War I, African Canadian men worked as waiters and cooks on the ICR and GTR, higher-paying positions otherwise solely reserved for white men working for most other railway companies in North America.[27]

Black railwaymen in Canada held a virtual monopoly over sleeping car service as early as the 1880s. Caring for passengers in first-class sleeping cars remained the porter's primary function, though the company also expected that he render various other services without additional compensation. The porter was responsible for all aspects of the sleeping car ride, except for collecting tickets, which the conductor performed. Although they did not pay for this time-consuming dead work, railway companies required that porters report to their cars at least two hours prior to a scheduled run in order to prepare their sleepers. Once assigned to a car, porters ensured that it was clean and fully equipped; in case it was not, they hurriedly buffed and polished before passengers boarded (see Figures 4–7).

Wood- or coal-burning ovens heated early sleepers not yet equipped with central heating at the turn of the century. Before leaving the station on a run, porters had to load their sleepers with enough fuel for the journey. They constantly struggled to keep soot from soiling the car or flying cinders from starting unruly fires. During the summer, huge blocks of ice cooled down the sleepers. Loading these slabs was clumsy, dangerous work, as it required that porters crawl onto the sleeper's roof and drop the heavy cube down into its cooling mechanism compartment. Controlling the temperature, an ongoing annoyance to both passengers and workers, often made early sleeping cars unbearably hot or cold, depending on the season.

Once on the road, the sleeping car porter catered to his passengers' every whim. The porter greeted travelers, stowed luggage, pulled down berths in the evening, and hurriedly converted them back into seats in the morning. Responsible for remembering passengers' schedules, he was severely reprimanded when someone missed his or her stop. The porter, whom passengers condescendingly called "George" or "boy," served food, mixed drinks, shined shoes, cared for small children, sick passengers, and drunken ones too.[28] Herb Carvery, who portered during the 1950s, remembered, "We were babysitters, not only for little kids but for adults. . . . Someone would get drunk on the train and many times you would have to stay up all night just to watch them so they wouldn't aggravate somebody else." He added that when "someone would get sick, you would have to attend to them."[29] Viewing the sleeping car porter as a historian on wheels, passengers expected him to know the landscape and history of areas along his trek. A confidant and armchair therapist, the porter feigned interest in travelers' tales and told a few of his own.

Sleeping car porters tended smoggy smoking cars, swept up cigarette and cigar ashes, washed out cuspidors, and inhaled stale, smoky air for hours on end. In the days before automated washrooms, they did their best to maintain sanitary conditions in crudely equipped lavatories. Porters frequently suffered from chronic sleep deprivation, since the company worked them on seventy-two-hour-shifts without providing them with sleeping quarters; whenever possible, porters stole catnaps in the smoking car. They endured other health hazards on the road as well. Derailments, common in the early days of rail travel, cost many railroaders their lives, particularly

Fig. 4. Dining car attendant, late 1930s (Canadian Pacific Archives, CPA# A-28551)

Fig. 5. Sleeping car porter helping women passengers off the train, late 1940s (Canadian Pacific Archives, cpa# 25637)

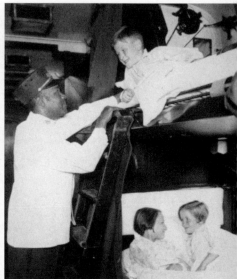

Fig. 6. Porter preparing sleeping berths and caring for children, 1950s (Canadian Pacific Archives, CPA# B-5793-1 and NS-20171)

when traveling through the Rockies' slippery slopes.[30] Policing gamblers, thieves, and rambunctious passengers also posed a constant danger for black railwaymen.

The consummate diplomat, the porter walked a social tight rope in Pullman's romanticized mobile time capsule. In 1930, journalist Murray Kempton reflected that, for many white travelers, porters seemed like "a domestic apparently unaltered by the passage of time or the Emancipation Proclamation." Yet alluding to the film *The Emperor Jones* featuring famed actor Paul Robeson, Kempton proposed that "there was a certain thrill to the notion that he might be a Communist or a murderer or even an emperor."[31]

Sleeping car porters understood that these racialized fantasies were inseparable from their passengers' other expectations. They enabled white passengers to cling to an antebellum racial beau ideal, understanding that their livelihood—and at times their very lives—depended on acting out the part of this offensively racialized construction. Challenges to this charade and perceived social transgressions, especially against white women, carried heavy penalties: a porter could be fired or subjected to a worse fate—lynching. As Stanley Grizzle, a former porter, so eloquently recalled, "Some porters were a study in controlled anger during their work shifts, always angry. And they

Fig. 7. Sleeping car porters at work, late 1930s. *Clockwise from top left*: Canadian Pacific parlor car, interior of a sleeping car, porter preparing berths in standard sleeping car, and porter in summer uniform. (Canadian Pacific Archives, CPA# A-28542, A-8560, A-8664, and A-28554)

would simmer during those shifts—for this was a job where, every day, you were made to feel that you were beneath the passengers."[32] Required to smile and act submissively, black railwaymen did so, hiding their thoughts, their dreams, and sometimes their rage.[33]

Despite the work's emotionally and physically taxing nature, black Canadians embraced railway employment because other industrial jobs presented a different set of hazards without the reward of lasting employment. Likewise, working for Canadian railway companies afforded enterprising black transportation workers the freedom to pursue other professional interests. For instance, John D. Curl portered for a time before opening a cigar shop in Halifax.[34] B. A. Husbands operated a West Indian import goods store with money obtained from seafaring and portering, while Jamaican-born Rufus Rockhead financed his famous Montreal jazz club, Rockhead's Paradise, with income earned on the rails.[35]

Thus it seemed that by the end of the nineteenth century Canadian railway companies and African Canadians had struck a mutually beneficial covenant: the railroads needed workers when African Canadians needed stable employment. Canadian railway companies found an untapped pool of ready black workers among African Canadians who spoke English and adapted easily to railroading because of their experience in other transportation sectors. Most conveniently for employers, black railroaders did not belong to any unions. For African Canadians, the rails fulfilled the wanderlust of men accustomed to lives on the move and promised dependable work during a period of industrial transition.

But if African Canadian railroaders hoped for a secure place on the rails, they did not find it. During periods of high unemployment or economic recession, Canadian railway companies discharged black workers, replacing them with inexperienced white labor. The *Halifax Herald* exposed this practice in the spring of 1898 when it headlined "Colored Porters on the Intercolonial Railway Were All 'Fired' and Without Cause." J. S. Barbee, one of the dismissed ICR porters, told reporters that "our places have been filled by white officials" and accused railway managers of "drawing the color line with a vengeance." William Dixon, another fired ICR sleeping car porter and brother of the celebrated pugilist George Dixon, informed Halifax journalists that "the action of the government . . . is a shabby piece of business. Men with families have been turned out without notice or cause, and failing to find work in Halifax they must leave the city."[36]

All the Intercolonial Railway porters fired shared similar backgrounds. Experienced transportation workers, many had joined the ICR after careers at sea. A number of the men were West Indians married to white or biracial women. All the porters also belonged to Union Lodge, a black Freemasons' temple popular with seafarers, sleeping car porters, and prosperous black Haligonian businessmen. Members of Union Lodge, which was established in January 1856, controlled black commercial assets in Halifax and served as guardians of their community's interests.[37] Hence, the federally owned Intercolonial Railway's move against sleeping car porters roused black Haligonians who viewed these Union Lodge men as their most prominent denizens. Disillusioned, black Haligonians questioned whether the rails were indeed a wise investment in their future when white supremacy—more than industriousness—determined their fate.

"Righteously indignant," black Haligonians gathered to "consider the best means to be taken to remedy a most serious matter."[38] Rev. Dr. J. Francis Robinson, an African American Baptist minister stationed in Halifax, led the charge. Speaking before his predominantly black congregation at the Cornwallis Street Baptist Church only days after the firings, Robinson did not mince words when linking the experiences of African Americans with those of blacks in Canada. "The recent dismissal of the porters from the service of the I.C.R. brings us face to face again with the race, which in the United States and here remains an unsettled question." Robinson urged his congregation and all African Canadians to concede that race "is no longer a sectional question: it is a national question" and also an international one.[39]

Robinson and other black Haligonian protesters insisted that, in addition to race, the ICR's move against black workers underscored citizenship, right to work, and living wage issues of import to all Canadians. Robinson proclaimed, "Don't drive the poor white or the poor black man out of your country. Give him work and give him good pay. . . . A policy which would arm the strong and cast down the defenceless is unwise . . . and one fraught with disastrous consequences." Robinson admonished against white supremacist employment practices, reminding the Canadian government that "peace between the races is not to be secured by degrading one race and exalting another; by giving power and employment to one and withholding it from another." Alluding to the United States' strained race relations, Robinson alerted his congregation that "experience proves that those [who] are most abused can be abused with greatest impunity." He stressed that white Canadians should and could distinguish themselves from white Americans by "maintaining a state of equal justice between the classes."[40]

African Canadians hoped for due process and "equal justice between the classes" but knew that these would be obtained only through political mobilization. Peter Evander McKerrow, a West Indian sailor turned powerful black Haligonian businessman, maintained that since Reconstruction African Americans enjoyed certain citizenship rights still denied to blacks in the Maritimes, throwing into question whether blacks were indeed better off in Canada than in the U.S. South: "The United States with her faults . . . has done much for the elevation of the colored races. She has given to the race professors in colleges, senators, engineers, doctors, lawyers, mechanics of every description. Sad and sorry are we to say that is more than we can boast of here in Nova Scotia."[41]

For Rev. Robinson, the solution to black railwaymen's problems was a simple one. He insisted that if "the Negro porters and the race [were] as strongly organized into labor protective unions, etc., like their white brothers, the I.C.R. would not have succeeded so well and peaceably in displacing their colored labor and substituting white in their stead."[42] Without unionization, black railwaymen in Canada would never enjoy true job security and would continually be forced into unemployment or positions "at starvation wages," held Robinson. He berated the Canadian government and ICR managers for subjecting black men and their families to a life of further poverty and degradation, insisting that for "over 250 years, this race served in bondage, suffering the most poignant sensations of shame, immorality, demoralization and degradation. Its men have been victimized, . . . proscribed against and imposed upon by the dominant race both in the United States and here in Canada." Robinson warned against such white supremacist practices as violations of African Canadians' "civil rights [and] the human right to gain an honest livelihood for themselves and their families."[43]

Black Haligonians called immediate attention to Jim Crow in railway employment policy by notifying the national press.[44] "Have No Use for Them—Coloured Men on the Intercolonial Railway All Fired," exclaimed the Tory newspaper *Chatham Planet*. The Ontario newspaper accused the Liberal government of betraying its African Canadian constituents, charging that "Liberal leaders at Ottawa seem to have completely lost their heads. . . . While Premier Laurier speaks in the most flattering manner of the African race, his officials strike them down in a most brutal way, no complaint, no investigation—just kick them out."[45]

Blacks in the Maritimes also contacted their federal members of Parliament Benjamin Russell and future prime minister Sir Robert Borden. Rev. Dr. J. Francis Robinson emphasized that one thousand African Canadian voters in the Maritimes, "a sufficient number to give them the balance of power," would "get organized . . . so that their voices and vote would be respected."[46] Conservative Parliament members took Robinson's warning to heart and laid the case of "Coloured Intercolonial Porters" before the House of Commons in March 1898. George Foster, the member from New Brunswick, inquired whether newspaper reports that "all the porters on the Pullman cars had been dismissed from the service of the Intercolonial" were indeed true. If so, Foster demanded that the minister of railways and canals explain "whether they were dismissed for cause or whether the hon. gentleman is drawing the colour line in that service."[47]

Speaking for the Liberal government, Minister Andrew G. Blair rejected any notion that the color line fueled employment practices on the government-owned ICR, stressing, "I am quite sure that the colour line has not been drawn"; he assured Parliament that nothing had "been done in view of discriminating against the colour line in that service." Alphonse La Rivière of Quebec was not so easily persuaded, sardonically proposing instead that "perhaps the gentleman is colour-blind."[48] Paradoxically, while Blair denied any governmental wrongdoing with respect to ICR porters, the minister of railways and canals never actually disputed the existence of a color line in Canadian industries. Over the next two weeks, federal legislators debated the application of discriminatory employment policies, worrying less about its existence than its gentlemanly exercise.

Representatives from Ontario and Nova Scotia resuscitated the "color line" debate again during question period in early April, this time in defense of ICR managers. Ontario member Archibald Campbell motioned that the House retract "unfounded and unwarranted" charges of discrimination against black railroaders. In the end, the House of Commons resolved that the "report that the Government would at once draw the colour line and dismiss all the men, ought to have been rejected by . . . common sense," with George Fraser, a white member from Nova Scotia, insisting "that hereafter those who publish those statements will understand what the country understands, that there must be a terrific dearth of any ground of attack upon the Government, when they are compelled to fall back upon an attempt to raise the prejudices of the coloured population of Canada."[49]

Campbell's and Fraser's peculiar parade of circular reasoning branded African Canadians the racists for unveiling the specter of Jim Crow in a federal corporation and in Canadian railway policy. Yet African Canadians' swift mobilization of national advocates demonstrated their political sophistication and understanding of local and national institutions. Robinson and other advocates shrewdly argued for black railwaymen's entitlement to positions in the most powerful industry of the era, likely preventing greater unemployment among black railroaders. They did so by couching their protest in the language of citizenship entitlements, suffrage, and civil rights.

Black workers in other industries, though fewer in numbers, also experienced strained relations with management at the turn of the twentieth century. Several Canadian industries, namely, coal mining, iron, and steel, experimented with black labor beginning in the 1900s as a way of meeting labor needs and outwitting organized labor, confirming that corporate approaches to black labor were not singular to railway companies. While railway corporations initially selected their black workers from Canadian urban centers, other industries turned to African American and West Indian guest workers during periods of labor shortages. For instance, between 1901 and 1904 the Dominion Iron and Steel Company of Nova Scotia assuaged its labor needs with African American steelworkers imported from Alabama and Tennessee.[50]

Frustrated with the dearth of skilled industrial workers in Canada, DISCO foreman John H. Means recruited African American blast furnace men from Alabama, Pennsylvania, and Colorado. Means, a white southerner familiar with African American steelworkers from his days as a foreman in Birmingham's Means Fulton Iron Works, specified the quality of workmen he wanted for his Canadian plant. In a letter to Tom Goodwin, a white foreman in Birmingham's Woodward Iron Company, Means wrote, "I do not want anybody but first class men in every particular. Geo. Strong and Bill Bowling are now getting up men for me and I should not wonder if they can handle the situation among the niggers better than you, so . . . *allow them to be the movers in the whole thing*, keeping yourself in the background." Means believed that if he could persuade a first wave of African American steelworkers to come north, others would surely follow, as "these niggers are more apt to induce others to come than white people would be."[51]

Means valued "these niggers" as skilled steelworkers, if not as his social peers. He promised competitive wages, free transportation, and autonomous, peaceful working conditions to men willing to come to Canada, outlining his urgent labor needs and wage scheme in a letter to his former African American employee George Strong. "There is an opportunity here for about 50 real good men to do well and I should like to see you boys come and stay until next Fall. By that time, you should have saved a good bit of money." Means then spelled out his pressing need for skilled black workers, pointing out that "what I especially need to get right now is two good Keepers, about 10 or 12 good Sand Cutters and 10 or 12 first class iron carriers . . . for which I am willing to pay [the princely sum of] $3.00 a day." Means demanded loyalty and professionalism from his African American recruits and warned George Strong, "I dont want you and Bill to bring any men who are not first class in every way. Men that I can rely on at all times."[52]

Means enjoined black ironworkers and steelworkers to keep clear of union movements. Means, who was also trying to court black workers in Braddock, Pennsylvania, exhorted, "We have no labour trouble of any kind, but we need experienced hands and are willing to pay for them, but we do not want any but experienced men, and any man that comes up here with the idea that he can fool us will get left, but good men will be placed in a good position."[53] In exchange for their loyalty and compliance, he pledged, "I will put you in a furnace that is well-housed, and I do not see why you cannot stay in this country as well as I . . . so make up your mind to come with the intention of sticking by me for a year or 18 months."[54] Means also encouraged African American migrant workers to bring "their wives, . . . or any washerwoman or cook that they may prefer" so long as the men agreed to his terms.[55]

African American steelworkers accepted Means's offer of employment and began their journey north during the fall of 1901, attracting the curiosity of several journalists along their route. On 16 October 1901, the *Sydney Daily Post* announced that thirty "Coloured Furnace Men" from Pittsburgh would begin work at DISCO.[56] The successful arrival of this first wave of African American industrial migrants bolstered Means's plan. "Should I be able to satisfy them with the place," wrote the southern white foreman, "I am going south myself to move about 100" more African American steelworkers.[57]

Southern African American industrial workers came to the Maritimes, even without Means's heavy-handed herding. In January 1903, the *Bangor (Maine) Daily News* remembered that "a crowd of 250 colored people ranging in size from a baby in arms to old men barely able to walk" had cut through town nearly two years earlier en route to Nova Scotia. The reporter's jaundiced account described the travelers' demeanor: "They were dressed in all kinds of fantastic garb, none of which seemed sufficient to half warm a person. . . . But they didn't seem to mind it at all." Instead, he reported that the migrants "laughed and joked with one another. . . . Those who had musical instruments played upon them. Not sad and disheartening music, but the gayest of gay, rollicking jigs and that kind of stuff." The journalist enlivened his depiction of unsuspecting happy Sambos by giving them an authenticating southern vernacular: "Why, we're gwine to Sidney, Cape Breton, to work in the steel mill and we's gwine to get big wages is we uns. It's gwine to be mighty sight nicer'n working in the cotton fields, so tis honey."[58]

Means deliberately misled the African American steelworkers he brought to Canada by never informing the men enlisted that they were a substitute workforce until more suitable Austrian, German, and Italian workers could be found.[59] DISCO merely envisioned foreign black steelworkers as an interim workforce during labor shortages in its mills. Despite promising at least eighteen months of work, Means signed southern African American workers to only six-month contracts and repaid their transportation costs over that period. Means also withheld news of DISCO's racialized employment practices. Black workers, irrespective of their status as skilled workers, were sequestered in Cokaville, the company's sooty housing district north of the coke ovens. The company's dilapidated housing further humiliated African American skilled workers and their families, as evidenced by several local newspaper reports.[60]

The arduous work and unsanitary conditions in Cape Breton could not have surprised African American steelworkers well acquainted with working-class culture in steel mills. They were, however, soured by John H. Means's deceitful description of life and work in a Canadian steel town. By January 1903, conditions in DISCO's mills had so deteriorated that men and women who had enthusiastically abandoned Alabama cotton fields two years earlier were now trickling back south. Once again, the *Bangor Daily News* reported on the event, denouncing the Canadian experiment as a "Promised Land . . . of Dispair" and reproaching the African American migrant workers as "victims[s] of misplaced confidence, caused by a credulity that comes from ignorance." The *Daily News* explained that southern African American steelworkers "who had gone there [Canada] with such grand hopes . . . [and] the thought that they were to better their conditions . . . were now in a state of destitution, and were walking back to good old Alabama, without money and but scant clothing." Strained labor relations and "the rigors of a northern winter," rationalized the *Daily News* writer, certainly made conditions in Dixie seem more agreeable.[61]

Walter Griffin and his wife, veterans of the DISCO fiasco, drifted into a Bangor police station and recounted stories of their abuse at the hands of Canadian steel mill managers. They advised local authorities that "the other 248 were somewhere on the road . . . tramping through the snow and cold of a northern Maine winter." The group of African American steelworkers had left Cape Breton when "failure of the mill people to pay what they had promised" sparked "trouble and now the mill owners had refused to give any of them work." Local "overseers of the poor" cared for the couple and prepared for the arrival of more penniless shuttle migrants.[62]

The implications of the DISCO experiment with African American guest workers surpass its noted failure, which included labor recruiters' racism and deceptive reports of living and working conditions in Nova Scotia. First, southern African American laborers who came to Canada revealed the breadth of black industrial labor migration at the turn of the twentieth century. Seasoned employment-driven intraregional migrants, southern African Americans willingly extended their journeys northward in search of better working conditions and fair wages. When hundreds of skilled black migrants bypassed Pittsburgh, New York, Chicago, and Detroit for Canadian steel mills and railways, they affirmed that African American workers included Canada in their vision of a Great Migration.[63] These highly mobile skilled men formed a new class of transnational industrial workers who capitalized on employment opportunities without regard for regional or national borders.[64] Insofar as black workers left Birmingham, Memphis, and Philadelphia for positions in Canadian industries, they confirmed that African Americans belonged to a global industrial workforce affected by the same push-and-pull factors driving Italian and other European workers across the continent.[65]

Southern African American steelworkers and sleeping car porters who crossed into Canada on short-term contracts demonstrated that international migration did not depend on guaranteed long-term employment. Relief from segregationist politics compelled black migrant workers north just as much as the promise of better working and better living standards. In other words, these early African American industrial shuttle migrants followed the work when and where it became available, setting new roots in their host communities. They could not have known, however, that white supremacist employment policies circumscribed the lives of both white and black workers in Canada as well. For those who encountered Jim Crow at the hands of Canadian managers and union men, the experiment was in fact, as the *Bangor Daily News* proclaimed, "one of dispair." While some returned to a South they knew and understood, others dug in their heels determined to make life in Canada more meaningful than the life they had left behind.[66]

The problems faced by black railroaders and steelworkers, whether Canadian or foreign-born, mirrored growing tensions between management and employees in the early twentieth century. White workers also protested unfair labor practices, with miners and textile workers most vocal about their grievances. To complicate matters, at least in employers' minds, unions mushroomed particularly in Quebec and Ontario, where their numbers doubled between 1899 and 1903.[67] The International Ladies' Garment Workers' Union founded in 1905 brought working women into the fold of early Canadian trade unionism. Even the Industrial Workers of the World, also known as the Wobblies, trickled into Canada, setting up shop in coal mines, railway construction compounds, and lumbering camps throughout Alberta and British Columbia.[68]

The Laurier government and Canadian capitalists fought union expansion tooth and nail. The Canadian Pacific Railway controlled unruly workers with its private Pinkerton-inspired police force.[69] Other corporations not equipped with privately funded firepower called in federal guns. On order from the Laurier government, the North West Mounted Police and the Canadian militia regularly beat down men and women demanding fair working conditions and union recognition.[70] So terrorized were Canadian workers during the early years of trade unionism that historian Stuart Jamieson concluded that the state's coercion "had been felt with enough force to tip the scales of battle in hundreds of strikes and labour demonstrations . . . [and] in all probability has had a profound effect on the climate of industrial relations in this country." The federal government's and police forces' support of Canadian business owners' interests over workers rights produced a deep-seated distrust "in the eyes of so many in the ranks of organized labour," confirmed years later during the postwar upheaval of the Winnipeg General Strike.[71]

Violence only produced more violence, without crushing the surge of trade unionism in Canada. Prime Minister Laurier finally conceded that labor matters warranted more careful attention from the federal government. In 1900, Laurier created the Department of Labour and appointed William Lyon Mackenzie King its new deputy minister. A thirty-year-old ambitious Harvard graduate, King dove headlong into labor affairs, launching and editing the Department of Labour's monthly publication *Labour Gazette*. Initially conceived as a journal chronicling all matters related to labor in Canada, the *Labour Gazette* in later years kept pace with international labor news as well.

Believing that labor conflicts were best settled in mediation, King drafted new labor laws that he hoped would bring peace to volatile labor-management relations. He also authored the 1907 Industrial Disputes Investigation Act (IDIA) and envisioned the statute as a preemptive strike against further labor warfare in industries most important to the national economy, namely, mining, transportation, communications, and public utilities.[72] The Department of Labour explained that "obviously, the public interest, not less than the interests of employer and employed, lies in the settlement of such disputes in their initial stages and before they have assumed so serious a form as a lockout or a strike."[73]

The IDIA established three important labor policy principles. First, it recognized that workers had a right to represent themselves in a labor dispute. Second, insofar as the IDIA set up a board of conciliation, the Department of Labour implicitly endorsed workers' right to collective bargaining. Third, and most important, the IDIA instituted a course of action for trade unionists and workers contesting unfair employment practices. This last provision proved particularly useful for black workers exiled from burgeoning unionization among white railwaymen. By World War I, sleeping car porters operating in Canada would effectively utilize the IDIA when challenging Jim Crow corporate and federal employment policies.

Whatever the ambiguities and complexities of the relationship between organized workers and the state, many unionists took the rhetoric surrounding the IDIA at its word, believing that King's legislation signaled a new era for Canadian workers. One such unionist, Aaron Mosher, a twenty-eight-year-old freight handler on the ICR, advocated nationalist trade unionism "for the mutual protection and benefit of Railway Employees in Canada." Mosher argued that American brotherhoods, which dominated Canadian trade unionism until World War I, created "a humiliating type of dependence on foreign influence and authority . . . [and] an undesirable form of colonial servitude and subjection."[74]

Intent on shaping a distinctly Canadian union movement, Mosher and other white railway unionists on the Intercolonial Railway created the Canadian Brotherhood of Railway Employees and Other Transport Workers in 1908. He pledged that his union would be a "wholly-Canadian organization" for all railway workers.[75] Mosher's nationalist vision appealed to white railroaders who joined the CBRE en masse. Within its first two months, the CBRE recruited one thousand ICR running tradesmen, including freight and office clerks, freight handlers, car checkers, roundhousemen, station engineers, watchmen, day laborers, and "all classes of the Sleeping, Parlor and Dining Car employees, except Sleeping Car Porters."[76]

White supremacy formed the bedrock of Mosher's "wholly Canadian organization." The CBRE's explicit exclusion of sleeping car porters clearly implied black railroaders, given that cooks, waiters, and other railwaymen who were black were likewise denied membership. In contrast, the CBRE welcomed white sleeping car porters, though they were extremely rare and often recent immigrants.[77] Evidently, Mosher perceived white members' grievances —long hours, hazardous working conditions, low wages, workmen's compensation, lack of job security, and bargaining rights—as distinct from those of black railroaders. By adopting a motion ostracizing black running tradesmen from its brotherhood at its inaugural meeting, the nationalist CBRE gave its assent to racism in Canadian railway unionism.[78]

Like American brotherhoods, unionized white Canadian railroaders defined unionization along the lines of white manhood rights.[79] White unionists demanded that the most lucrative jobs on the rails be reserved for Anglo-Saxon Canadian men. The American Big Four brotherhoods of conductors, engineers, firemen, and trainmen had long argued that Anglo-Saxon superiority warranted segregating railway workforces, with immigrants and black railroaders occupying the least desirable positions.[80] Black engineers, brakemen, and conductors were a rarity on American lines, particularly in the North, where the Big Four reigned supreme.[81] The same, however, had not been true for black railwaymen on Canadian railroads before the advent of the CBRE.

Working against this diversity, the CBRE, just like the American Big Four, discouraged an interracial unionized railway workforce and pressured Canadian railway companies for a more recognizable color line among railroaders. During negotiations with the Intercolonial Railway, Aaron Mosher's new union called for separate negotiating schedules for white and black workers. In December 1909, the ICR agreed to a new contract that secured segregated collective bargaining rights, wage increases, and improved working conditions only for white running tradesmen.[82] Black railwaymen on the ICR, however, gained nothing from the 1909 contract.

Emboldened by its agreement with the government-owned Intercolonial Railway, Mosher celebrated the CBRE's triumph for Canadian trade unionism. He now represented the largest class of previously nonunionized white running tradesmen and proclaimed the CBRE the forerunner of twentieth-century nationalist industrial unionism. Yet by shutting out black workers, Mosher revealed that pioneering Canadian industrial unionists valued Jim Crow and white manhood rights as much as their American counterparts did.

White railwaymen extended their segregationist union vision westward throughout the second decade of the twentieth century. Mosher struck victory for Canadian segregationist railway unionism in April 1913 with a new ICR agreement. The CBRE's newest contract promised its members protection from harassment or discrimination by Canadian railway companies by establishing requisite due process for all dismissal claims, with back pay in the event of wrongful termination. The agreement recognized white railroaders' seniority rights after six months of permanent employment, secured two weeks' paid vacations, and payment for statutory holidays. White running tradesmen won a ten-hour workday, with time and a half for overtime. Conductors, chefs, waiters, pantrymen, and cooks enjoyed sizable raises. For their part, conductors secured two layoff days for every seven days worked, free uniforms, and subsidized meals while on the road. In sharp contrast, third cooks, who were most often black, were not awarded wage increases, even though they worked the same shifts as other dining car employees.[83]

Most important, the 1913 ICR contract instituted segregated contract negotiation schedules for black and white railway workers. All CBRE members' contracts were negotiated under Schedule 1, while separate terms set conditions of employment for black workers. The agreement between the federally owned ICR and the CBRE mandated that promotions to conductorships could come only from the parlor car staff with the implicit understanding that Canadian railway companies rarely employed black workers in that higher-wage sector. Consequently, the ICR agreement of 1913 institutionalized separate and unequal promotion scales for railway workers, reserving well-remunerated supervisory positions exclusively for white men and permanently locking black railroaders into competition for lower-wage service positions. Within two years, the Grand Trunk Railway, Canadian Northern Railway, and Canadian Pacific Railway followed the federal government railway's lead, also segregating their workforces by 1915. By the dawn of the Great War, then, white supremacy dictated employment policy on all Canadian railway lines. Whereas Americans eventually desegregated their sleeping and parlor car departments in 1945, Canadian railway corporations held true to their segregationist structure, not seriously considering African Canadians for supervisory positions until 1964.[84]

Canadian railway companies worried that with all other classes of white workers unionized and their benefits publicized, black railroaders would soon demand a contract of their own.[85] Without seniority rights, paid holidays, or workmen's compensation and in constant danger of harassment by company officials for vocalizing union ideals, black railwaymen had ample cause for dissatisfaction. Remembering the 1898 ICR affair yet expecting continued prosperity with their sleeping car service, Canadian railway companies could not chance that their latest rebuke would rekindle discontent among African Canadian railwaymen.

The decision to turn to southern African American and West Indian railroaders by Canadian railway companies mirrors employment patterns in other Canadian industries desperate for nonunionized workers and corresponds with the emergence of the CBRE. Soon after white running tradesmen organized into the CBRE and demanded segregated promotion schemes, Canadian companies began complaining that African Canadian railroaders were ill suited for their sleeping car service. They argued that since experienced black railwaymen were in short supply in Canada, additional workers would have to come from abroad. Since no other Canadian line matched the CPR company's aggressive pursuit of African American and West Indian railroaders, its practices offer cogent insight into approaches to foreign-born black labor by Canadian corporations of the day.[86]

Canadian railway companies dispatched recruitment agents to the United States who strategically combed American cities, black churches, and historically black colleges for prospective African American railwaymen. During such trips, S. A. Simpson, superintendent of the CPR sleeping car department, enlisted African American would-be porters in Harlem, Philadelphia, Washington, Detroit, Chicago, Minneapolis, and Seattle.[87] CPR officials deliberately targeted American cities affected by recent southern African American migration, believing that, having been raised in the Jim Crow South, southern black railwaymen would make for a pliant class of workers.[88]

A porter recruited for work on the CPR's western line described how Superintendent Simpson and Edward Williams, a sleeping car porter, handpicked one hundred men and arranged for their entry into Canada. The men were "furnished passes from St. Paul [Minnesota] . . . and just before arriving at Emerson [Manitoba] were awakened." Simpson provided each of the one hundred prospective porters with twenty-five dollars in order to meet their border entry requirements, this in clear violation of Canadian immigration and labor laws. Once all the men cleared customs, the porter explained that the "money . . . was again taken from each of them."[89]

Employment scouts even drafted would-be porters as far south as the West Indies. Caribbean workers appealed to Canadian railway companies, given that colonial rule and plantation economies had forced many black workers into service positions for the white ruling class.[90] Canadian corporate headhunters were particularly active in the Lesser Antilles, an archipelago stretching from the southeast of Puerto Rico to the northern tip of Trinidad. These little islands, too often reliant on single-crop economies, faced labor surpluses just as Canadian industries pined for workers. No longer finding employment in Panama, Costa Rica, Cuba, and Trinidad, key destinations for immigrant workers within the Caribbean basin especially during construction of the Panama Canal, some West Indian shuttle migrants therefore accepted work in Canada. Longstanding intraregional migration as skilled and semiskilled labor shaped a strong sense of being a transnational workforce among West Indian guest workers, possibly making the decision to go to Canada more tractable.

Canadian corporations encouraged West Indian immigration by reinforcing their interests in the Caribbean, appealing to the notion of empire, and downplaying Canada's hostility toward black migrants. As North American members of the British Empire, West Indians and Canadians supposedly shared a common bond. If Canadians worried about American annexation, so too did West Indians, especially after the Spanish-American War in 1898 and the U.S. takeover of Haiti in 1915. The West Indian press, such as the *St. Vincent Times*, *St. Kitts Daily Express Mail*, *Barbados Advocate*, and *Demerara Daily Chronicle*, fostered this ostensibly shared experience, carrying regular reports on Canadian business and politics that familiarized West Indians with economic and political conditions in Canada.[91] Since some West Indians also had family already living in various parts of Canada,

Fig. 8. Imperial dreams, *Saturday Magazine* section, *Globe*, 8 April 1911

immigrating to Halifax, Montreal, or Toronto might have seemed less alienating (see Figure 8).

Canadian corporations capitalized on these constructed connections, hoping to solve their pressing economic, military, and labor needs. They curried favor with West Indian regimes by promoting profitable trade relations and establishing banks, insurance companies, railroads, boards of trade, steamship lines, and import-export ventures.[92] Canadian businessmen felt particularly attracted to St. Kitts, a small island nestled between Puerto Rico and Guadeloupe. In 1912, Prime Minister Borden authorized reduced tariffs on West Indian sugar, sea island cotton, and other produce, making Canada the largest trading partner with islands like St. Kitts–Nevis, then known as St. Christopher. That same year, direct steamship service linked Basseterre with Montreal thanks to the Canadian Pacific steamship line, transforming St. Kitts into a major portal to Canada for northbound commodities and labor.[93] In March 1915, the Royal Bank of Canada introduced modern banking to the island.[94] Some Canadian industrialists even argued that Canada needed a permanent naval base in the Caribbean as a deterrent to American imperialist designs. Such a foothold would also conveniently provide Canadian ports for commercial freight liners doing business via the Panama Canal.[95]

Given that so many of those islands were also part of the British Empire, Canadian businesses like the Canadian Pacific Railway and the Dominion Iron and Steel Company trusted that the West Indies could supply Canada with cheap labor in ways that would not circumvent the Alien Labour Act, which explicitly outlawed courting foreign workers. In 1913, a CPR agent lured nine Antiguans to Canada—including Charles Este, future reverend of Montreal's influential Union United Church—with hollow promises of lucrative employment with the company.[96] DISCO, already acquainted with southern black workers since the turn of the century, also courted West Indian steelworkers for its Nova Scotian mills. In 1915, DISCO executive A. W. Macdonald petitioned the Department of Immigration for permission to import 150 West Indian steelworkers, but the federal government forestalled Macdonald's plan, citing long-standing resistance to black immigration. The immigration branch's chief administrator, William D. Scott, flatly denied DISCO's request, proposing instead that the company find more suitable white workers in Newfoundland.[97]

Canadian industrialists frustrated by immigration bureaucrats in Ottawa resolved that if the government insisted on barring foreign black labor, extending provincial status to a West Indian island would cancel out the immigration question. Likewise, incorporation would secure greater trading rights and find a permanent harbor for Canada's new navy.[98] If the Department of Immigration insisted on sealing off the border to West Indians, Canadian financiers would extend the frontier to the Caribbean. Chief among these corporate imperialists, and cofounders of the Canadian–West Indian League, were Thomas B. Macaulay, future president of Sun Life Insurance, the nation's leading insurance company, and Thomas G. Shaughnessy, first president of the Canadian Pacific Railway, then the country's largest company.

In the years leading up to World War I, Macaulay and Shaughnessy lobbied for political union with the West Indies, recommending provincial status for the Bahamas, Bermuda, Jamaica, Barbados, and other smaller islands. In the process, they inadvertently rekindled alarm over the growth of Canada's black population. Advocates for West Indian appropriation argued that, as the guardian of the British Empire in the Americas, Canada was the logical and "natural 'big brother' of the British West Indies."[99] Speaking for confederation with the Bahamas, Macaulay proclaimed, "Why should not Nassau become the Key West of Canada? I am an Imperialist. I am proud of our Empire, and jealous of its interests."[100]

Macaulay persistently courted Bahamian and Jamaican parliamentarians with promises of favorable trade agreements, bountiful Canadian markets, and bustling tourism. To Canadians, he pledged strategic access to the Panama Canal, emerging markets for Canadian goods, and glory for the empire. Just as the United States held Cuba, Haiti, the Dominican Republic, and Puerto Rico in its grasp, so too should Canada possess its own "great South," claimed members of the Canadian–West Indian League. Indeed, some explained that the dominion should adopt "imperial administrative tasks" over parts of the Caribbean just as "Australia was to be responsible in New Guinea."[101] Throughout the second decade of the century, Macaulay and other West Indian pro-union delegations shuttled between Toronto and Caribbean capitals negotiating favorable terms for confederation and trusted imminent unification.

If some Canadian industrialists readily envisioned gloriously upholding Anglo-Saxon imperialism in the Caribbean, the presence of blacks certainly soiled their reverie. In fact, the color question continually soured Macaulay's negotiations with the House of Commons. White Canadians' jaundiced view of blacks ignited protest in Parliament and in the press. Newspapers echoed admonitions that the presence of lascivious black men, whether from the West Indies or the United States, imperiled the morality of all white women in Canada. Historian Robin Winks contends that for many white Canadians "West Indians were aggressive, invariably urban, thought to be morally loose, and sufficiently hard working to constitute a threat."[102] In an interview about Bahamian confederation published in the *Toronto Globe*, the governor-general of the Bahamas, Sir William Grey-Wilson, confessed, "I had been specially requested to make a strong point of the absolute security enjoyed by the white woman in the midst of [our] negroes, because as I was informed a great many Canadians were under the impression that her position was as insecure as the American newspapers represent it to be in the Southern States."[103]

Canadians also worried that incorporation of predominantly black West Indian countries would upset political balance in Parliament. Extending provincial status to Canada's Caribbean possessions would entitle them to House of Commons and Senate representation. How would Canadian entrepreneurs allay nativist concerns about West Indian movement to other parts of the dominion? Since black migrants would come to Canada as laborers, the federal government anticipated opposition from labor leaders as well.

Those in favor of unification, including T. B. Macaulay, advocated various surreptitious ways of divesting West Indians of their franchise after a merger with Canada. Once again, Sir William Grey-Wilson of the Bahamas offered a crude solution. "Naturally no reference could be made to the question of color. I don't think it would be expedient that the representatives we sent to the Federal Parliament should be elected on anything like the suffrage for the present local House." Instead, he recommended "we could get over the suffrage difficulty by putting the qualification of an elector in the Bahamas so high that we should automatically shut out the ignorant blacks of the colony. This would also shut out some of the whites, but I do not think that would be a grievance."[104] Sir William Grey-Wilson's plot disquietingly resembled American segregationist tactics that gerrymandered voting laws with the explicit purpose of robbing blacks of their franchise. Its application, had it been successful, would have institutionalized Jim Crow in Canadian federal election law. Disheartened by his faltering campaign for Canada–British Guiana unification, Macaulay admitted that to permit British Guiana's "heterogeneous and unassimilated population equal votes with the [white] people of Ontario in controlling the destinies of Canada would strain our faith in democracy."[105]

By World War I, public debate over West Indian confederation depicted blacks as a threat not only to white women's chastity but also to Canada's very democracy. With so many white Canadians certain of black people's inherent racial inferiority, nativists also questioned their ability to assimilate complex democratic ideals. The *Manitoba Free Press* augured that extending the franchise to a "race of people . . . who have become indolent" would not only ensure the dominion's demise but might well sound the death knell of the British Empire's North American custodian.[106] The threat of blackening Canada with West Indian federation eradicated, at least for a time, Canadian imperialist designs in the Caribbean, though not corporate interest in cheap black labor.

Canadian railway companies carried on their recruitment of African American and West Indian workers, continually displaying blatant disregard for federal immigration and labor laws. Section 1 of the Alien Labour Act of 1897 specifically forbade "any person, company, partnership or corporation, in any manner to prepay the transportation, or in any way to assist or encourage the importation or immigration of any alien or foreigner into Canada, under contract or agreement . . . made previous to the importation or immigration of such alien or foreigner, to perform labour or service of any kind in Canada."[107] The act imposed a thousand-dollar fine on any person or company convicted of unlawfully soliciting foreign labor, with possible "separate suits . . . brought for each alien or foreigner . . . party to such contract or agreement." Section 8 penalized "the master of any vessel who knowingly . . . lands" contract foreign workers with fines of five hundred dollars or six months' imprisonment. The revised Alien Labour Act of 1906 intensified limitations on foreign labor by barring persons and companies from importing immigrants "by promise of employment through advertisements printed or published" in foreign countries.[108]

Canadian railway companies did not feel bound by the Alien Labour Act; neither were they concerned with restrictions under the Immigration Act. They intentionally wooed southern African American and West Indian immigrant workers, despite widespread press coverage of public agitation over black immigration. The Immigration Act of 1906 made violation of the law a costly expenditure, since all "railway or transportation companies or other persons bringing immigrants from any country into Canada" were made responsible for deportation costs for up to two years after entry.[109] Moreover, the act's section 38 expressly outlawed the solicitation, "either orally or by handbill or placard or in any other manner," of immigrants by unlicensed agents.

Not only did CPR agents publicize their recruitment of black workers, but sleeping and dining car department managers also brazenly handed out company cards to American would-be porters. In addition, they informed new employees that border guards presented with the CPR's business cards would overlook restrictions on black migrants. Ulysses Poston, Russell Rice, and Charles Brannon of Kentucky; Theodore Donaldson, Vernon Collins, and Maurice Lee of Texas; John Whittaker, George Harkness, and Leroy Bingham of South Carolina; and Thomas Wyche, Marcus Hargrave, and Charles Foushee of North Carolina painlessly coasted past Canadian border guards thanks to cards bearing the name of Mr. W. A. Cooper, the CPR's sleeping, dining, and parlor car department manager in Montreal.[110] The CPR boldly recruited foreign black railroaders, provided for their transportation, and paid their border taxes in order to ensure an uninterrupted flow of workers. Between 1916 and 1919 alone, the Canadian Pacific Railway imported more than five hundred African American sleeping car porters under this scheme.[111] The arrival of so many sleeping car porters peppered among trainloads of homestead-bound white immigrants confirmed that neither xenophobia nor the Canadian government's publicized ban effectively deterred determined black workers from immigrating to the dominion.

Canadian Pacific Railway executives blamed their insatiate demand for African American and West Indian railroaders on the Great War. With white men ripped from the rails for military service abroad, Canadian companies argued that the war aggravated existing labor shortages, forcing them into "bringing in colored help."[112] Since special troop trains hauled soldiers and implements of war to eastern ports, railway companies maintained that more sleeping and dining car personnel were urgently needed, especially on western lines.

The movement of Canadian armed forces generated enormous passenger traffic revenues for Canadian railway companies. Canadian Pacific Railway shareholders reports indicate that earnings from the sleeping and dining car service rose from $13 million in 1913 to more than $20 million in 1920.[113] The war promised such prosperity that the Canadian Northern Railway purchased one hundred sleepers from the Canadian Car and Foundry Company Limited for $325,000, the sum of which it hoped to quickly make back from moving returning veterans.[114]

Emboldened by the demands of the war, the CPR company became particularly audacious in its dealings with the Canadian Department of Immigration and the U.S. Department of Labor. CPR superintendents notified the local commissioner of immigration, who then informed Ottawa, that African American and West Indian railroaders were headed for the border and bound for Canadian rails. In turn, the Department of Immigration petitioned the U.S. Department of Labor for permission to export black railroaders on behalf of Canadian railway companies. A. Caminetti, the commissioner general of immigration in Washington, D.C., advised the Canadian government that "there will be no objection to the Canadian Pacific Railway's securing in this country the services of twenty or more colored waiters, cooks, etc. citizens of the United States, for dining car service . . . [and that] these men so engaged will experience no difficulty leaving."[115]

Once again, the CPR's aggressive pursuit of black workers outstripped rival corporations' strategies. The CPR's superintendent of the sleeping, dining, and parlor car department at Winnipeg, H. F. Matthews, shamelessly reminded the Department of Immigration of his company's long-standing defiance of labor and immigration laws. "You will recollect that for a number of years past, it has been necessary each Spring to bring in a large number of porters from south of the line to crew additional cars operated on summer train service."[116] Like the border guards who admitted black immigrant workers armed with CPR business cards, bureaucrats in the Department of Immigration abetted Canadian railway companies' traffic in black railway workers, actively undermining federal immigration and labor laws.

If the Department of Immigration obliged Canadian railway executives, trade unionists would not. World War I produced great wealth for Canadian railway corporations at great cost to workers. Desperate for peaceful class relations during the war, the Canadian government adopted special labor legislation, the Emergency War Measures Act of 1918, mandating arbitration of labor disputes and outlawing strikes and lockouts in all Canadian industries for the remainder of the war. The War Measures Act effectively gave Canadian employers free rein over their workers: they could, and often did, violate workers' rights with impunity. Whereas railroaders had worked long hours before, they were driven to near exhaustion during the war. Though railway companies' incomes soared, profits did not trickle down to overworked railroaders. Unable to strike, disgruntled white railway employees protested what they could: rampant inflation, exploitative working conditions, and the increased presence of black railwaymen on Canadian rails.

Canadian railway unionists filed several complaints with the minister of immigration and the minister of labour over the introduction of foreign black railway workers on Canadian lines. In June 1918, tensions between unionized white railwaymen and the CPR landed both parties before the Department of Labour's Industrial Disputes Investigation Board of Conciliation. It was the first of many disputes over foreign black railroaders taken to federal court over the next two decades. At issue was the CPR's "alleged dismissal of certain employees who were union members and their replacement by negroes, the number affected being given as 205 directly and 500 indirectly."[117]

The board, chaired by Justice W. A. Macdonald of Vancouver, heard evidence that white dining car workers operating between Vancouver and Calgary were being discharged and replaced by "negroes imported from the United States."[118] These white workers reasoned that they were being discriminated against because of their membership in the CBRE and that the CPR's decision to supplant them with black railroaders added insult to injury. The CBRE's George Hepburn averred that "the men wanted better conditions, and they didn't like being replaced by black labor as Canadians and white men."[119]

White CPR employees testified that when they notified company managers of their intention to become members of a union in April 1918, the CPR began ousting them from their runs. The superintendent at Winnipeg, H. F. Matthews, admitted to the Board of Conciliation that "the company did not want any such organization in the Dining Car Department and would discourage it all they could. Similar feelings of opposition to the Union were entertained or openly expressed" by other superintendents across western Canada. Instead of recognizing unionized dining car workers on its western lines, the Canadian Pacific Railway threatened that it would replace the men with "colored or Oriental help or employ women in their stead," stroking both gendered and racialized ire. CPR vice president Grant Hall confessed that the employment of women was "seriously considered" but the company ultimately abandoned its plot "for obvious reasons, namely [the] inability to provide proper sleeping quarters."[120]

If white women needed special provisions for work on the rails, black railwaymen did not, making it easier for CPR executives to follow through on their threat. The Canadian Brotherhood of Railway Employees charged that "before the company was called upon . . . to recognize this Union the situation changed and a large number of colored dining car employees were engaged and brought into Canada." The company's "discouragement" of unionization among its white running tradesmen was easily measurable. African American railroaders "practically took the place of all the white employees" on runs between Calgary and Vancouver while "50 per cent" of dining cars running out of Winnipeg were now manned by "colored crews" by the spring of 1918.[121]

Canadian Pacific Railway executives presented the Board of Conciliation with an alternative labor scenario on its western lines. Superintendents bemoaned the perennial workforce shortage occasioned by the war and explained that a policy formulated in February 1918 envisioned "introducing colored help" on Canadian rails. Superintendent Matthews, the CPR's advocate at the IDIA proceedings, could not supply any reliable evidence that his company's policy predated the CBRE's April union drive. Instead, Matthews produced a telegram, dated the day after interviewing white union men, proposing that his colleague in Vancouver "secure a satisfactory colored crew or more in Seattle." Matthews insisted that the company did not inform white workers of their new hiring policy until June because "such publicity might cause disruption amongst the dining car employees and . . . seriously effect, if not completely destroy, the service for a period."[122]

The board's majority report exposed a dizzying case of circular reasoning. Justice Macdonald argued that "it was not, and could not be contended, that there was any right or agreement on the part of the employees for continuous employment or that the company could not, without notice, discharge any, or all, of such employees at any time." Trade unionists certainly agreed. Lack of job security and due process in dismissals were long-standing union griev-ances. Justice Macdonald then argued that the CPR was justified in displacing white railroaders, since "dining car employees are migratory in their disposi-tion and frequent changes . . . militate against efficiency." Macdonald conve-niently disregarded that displacement by nonunionized foreign workers had caused white railroaders' recent unemployment; conscription also accounted for their high turnover rates on the rails. Ultimately, the board was left to decide whether to believe workers' allegations that, faced with a discrimina-tion suit, CPR executives fabricated a four-month-old change of employment policy. Alternatively, Justice Macdonald could side with the Canadian Pacific Railway, assuming "honesty of words and acts" on the part of its executives.[123]

Two Board of Conciliation members, Justice Macdonald and E. A. James, ruled in favor of the CPR, naively concluding that "it is not likely that persons would act in the reprehensible manner suggested" by the CBRE. They dis-missed the union's case, stating, "We believe that the presumptive case made by the employees, on whom the burden rested, has been rebuked by the sworn statements" of CPR representatives. The third board member, Victor Midgley, an outspoken member of the Socialist Party of Canada, a staunch union advocate, and the architect of the One Big Union movement in Can-ada, submitted a dissenting minority report. He averred that white workers had presented a "prima facie case of discrimination because of their mem-bership in a labor organization, and insisted that white union men be imme-diately reinstated and foreign dining car workers be deported by the Cana-dian government."[124]

Midgley strongly admonished the CPR for displacing white war veterans. "What will be the thoughts of these men when they learn that the jobs formerly held by them have been permanently filled with negroes, while they were shedding their blood and risking their lives in the defence of the Empire of which the Canadian Pacific Railway forms no small part?" He posited that CPR superintendents began their recruitment of African American railroaders in late April, well after learning of white unionization efforts. Midgley's dissenting opinion raised the obvious question: "If the company had definitely decided in February, 1918 to replace all the white men on the dining cars with colored [ones] before the end of the summer, why did [the CPR] go to the trouble of discouraging the organization of these men?"[125] In the end, both the CPR and Justice Macdonald actively ignored Midgley's inquiry.

The CBRE and the Board of Conciliation could not have known the extent of the CPR's duplicity. With a judgment in its favor and presumed support from the Department of Labour, CPR agents continued their hunt for more African American railroaders, this time for the railroad's sleeping car service. Aaron Mosher of the CBRE contested CPR recruitment of African American would-be porters in Chicago and Minneapolis, notifying the Department of Immigration: "My information is that Mr. Simpson, Superintendent of Sleeping Car Department, C.P.R., Winnipeg . . . went to St. Paul and had announcements made in the churches of the colored people there to the effect that the C.P.R., required 500 colored men for work in Canada." Mosher advised the immigration branch that black strikebreakers, more than one hundred men, were confined to CPR freight cars on the outskirt of town. In crushing heat, then the hottest June on record, these men lived, ate, and slept in the train cars, forbidden to interact with other railway workers, white or black.[126] Attorneys for the CBRE alleged that the CPR had clandestinely imported black railroaders from the United States in anticipation of postwar labor unrest in the West. Using the same warring language as white American workers offended by the introduction of black labor into their industries, Mosher warned the Department of Immigration that the continued importation of foreign labor—particularly African Americans—would "very possibly . . . lead to further industrial warfare and increased unrest among organized labor" in Canada.[127]

Though well aware of the CPR's recruitment program, having authorized the entry of African American railwaymen just months before, the Department of Immigration disavowed any knowledge of black labor migration to Canada. Instead, Mosher received a diplomatic denial of any wrongdoing from the department: "I assure you that the immigration regulations are being carefully enforced and we are not consenting to the entry of any labour unable to comply with the law, without first ascertaining from the Labour Department that there are no idle men of the particular class wanted, in Canada."[128]

Completely unaware that his letters were falling into the hands of William D. Scott, the CPR's greatest accomplice in the Department of Immigration, Aaron Mosher trusted swift government action. As the superintendent of immigration, Scott single-handedly dictated department policy on black migration and clearly favored the CPR, his former employer.[129] In every case between 1916 and 1945, the CPR obtained speedy approval for the importation of foreign black railwaymen, usually directly from Scott—the same man ordering border guards to reject black would-be homesteaders.[130]

Department of Immigration bureaucrats carefully monitored black immigration during the second decade of the century, documenting undesirable migrants in files earmarked "Immigration of Negroes from the United States to Western Canada" and "Dominion Immigration Agent . . . regarding vessels from the West Indies landing negroes."[131] Black workers bound for the rails, however, were tracked to another dossier—"Canadian Pacific Railway Requests Admission of Coloured Porters (Negros)."[132] On the one hand, the Department of Immigration castigated border inspectors for indulging black immigrants, deploring that more "colored persons are settling in the undesirable sections of our cities and towns." A department circular groused that "some Inspectors seem to be under the impression that if a colored person is an American citizen, and of money, he must be admitted." William D. Scott counseled more exacting defense of Canada's border: "Strict examination, however, will often reveal some statutory cause for rejection under section 3," while pursuant to section 33, ss. 13, the memo added, "A cash deposit may be taken from a non-immigrant, and Inspectors are requested to enforce this section."[133] Conversely, and without ever admitting to his department's compact with Canadian railway companies, Scott reasoned to Mosher that "when people comply with the law we cannot very well shut them out."[134]

Indeed, Scott's irresolute attempt to "shut them out" had completely failed by World War I, when more black railwaymen worked on Canadian rails than ever before. By 1920, Canadian railway companies had assembled a group of black railroaders representing a mélange of ethnicities, nationalities, and political cultures. Vexed by white men clamoring for unionization yet worried about African Canadian trade unionism, railway executives gambled that black railroaders harvested from abroad would yield a more malleable class of workers.

Canadian railway managers may have actively solicited a compliant immigrant black workforce, but it certainly was not what they got. Black railwaymen in Canada recognized that Canadian industrialists and white trade unionists viewed them as gullible pawns. Canadian railway companies upheld an antiquated racialized mirage in their Pullman car departments, exploiting black sleeping car porters in the process. When conditions deteriorated with white workers, Canadian railway administrators replaced them with African

Americans and West Indians herded into Canada by conniving managers. Since the beginning of the war, conditions on the rails worsened for all workers, even if the work itself became more readily available. Fearing greater unemployment and distracted by the rhetoric of war, white workers begrudgingly worked alongside black railroaders, all the while pressuring for a more rigorous racialized division of the Canadian railway workforce. Their nascent unions targeted black labor—Canadian and foreign-born—making them the scapegoats for unemployment, falling wages, and humiliation at the hands of company men.

Inasmuch as white workers and white managers thought little of black railroaders, West Indian, African American, and Canadian-born black railwaymen envisioned their position on the rails quite differently. Black railroaders understood white workers' growing hostility and sensed the nation's agitation over their presence. In the spring of 1917, Winnipeg-based porters John A. Robinson, J. W. Barber, B. F. Jones, and P. White began meeting secretly to discuss the possibility of unionization among black railroaders. Robinson, who came to Canada from St. Kitts to work on the CPR in 1909, led the charge. If black railwaymen were to survive the Great War, he resolved that they needed protection. The men carefully weighed their options. White union men had made clear that they would not accept black workers into their brotherhood. Their white-only membership clause and open animosity affirmed it daily. Though African American sleeping car porters were likely contemplating the value of railway unionization, no such organization yet existed at the time.[135]

Accordingly, Robinson and his allies discussed the possibility of forming a union for Canadian sleeping car porters. These clandestine meetings, held in an aging building just a stone's throw from Winnipeg's looming CPR station, changed the course of railway unionism in Canada.[136] In April 1917, John A. Robinson and his co-workers chartered the Order of Sleeping Car Porters—one of the earliest black railway unions in North America—and spread politicized trade union radicalism across Canada. Within two years of its inauguration, the OSCP negotiated successful contracts for all sleeping car porters —black as well as white—on the Canadian Northern and Grand Trunk railways.[137] By the end of the decade, Robinson emerged as the champion of black railway unionism in Canada. His two-fisted approach to Jim Crow on Canadian rails simultaneously fought segregation at work and in Canadian trade unionism.

Black railwaymen in the Order of Sleeping Car Porters targeted white trade unionists, holding union leaders to their rhetoric of working-class solidarity.

John A. Robinson began his campaign for national trade union recognition with the Trades and Labour Congress of Canada, a national coalition of trade and craft unions endowed with official collective bargaining recognition, and applied for a charter with the organization in 1917.[138] Though fully aware of the CBRE's white-only membership policy, Trades and Labour Congress of Canada president Tom Moore denied the OSCP's petition, ruling instead that Canadian sleeping car porters seek auxiliary endorsement in the existing national railway union—the Canadian Brotherhood of Railway Employees. In effect, Tom Moore's decision Jim Crowed black unionists into auxiliary status, a station otherwise exclusively reserved for women workers or trade unionists' wives and daughters.

Unwilling to concede such easy defeat, black railway unionists plotted their next move. The OSCP set its sights on the Canadian Brotherhood of Railway Employees' annual convention meeting in Port Arthur in September 1918. Sleeping car porters from across the country protested the CBRE's white-only membership policy, forcing the issue onto the convention floor. The question of black membership rocked the CBRE's 1918 assembly, developing into a tempestuous debate. White railroaders from Western Canada reminded delegates that throughout the spring of 1918 the "C.P.R. [had] imported a large number of coloured men from the States and promptly put into effect their threat" to replace "all the white cooks and waiters and putting negroes in their places." Black workers, stressed field organizer E. Robson, jeopardized white workers and their families, as evidenced by the fact that "white men are still off and the negroes are on the road."[139]

Black railroaders then presented their arguments for membership. George A. Fraser, president of Halifax's Canadian Grand Trunk Railway Sleeping Car Porters Association, seconded John A. Robinson's campaign against white supremacy in the Canadian Brotherhood of Railway Employees. Fraser addressed an open letter to CBRE members meeting in Port Arthur and imputed the organization for undermining national railway unionism with its racist policies. Fraser emphasized, "We wish to point out that we are working in the same capacity as all other railway men and in consequence we are asking for admission into the C.B.R.E." Moreover, the continued exclusion of black railroaders from the CBRE amounted to an egregious breach of African Canadians' citizenship rights, declared Fraser. "We feel that as British subjects and also Loyal Canadians, that there should be no discrimination shown . . . between different races." Dismantling racism in the CBRE, Fraser avowed, "will not only benefit us, but will greatly strengthen your Division No. 36, the [white] members of which are working hand in hand with us." Fraser requested that members of the Canadian Grand Trunk Railway Porters Association be admitted to the CBRE and hoped that African Canadian railroaders would "receive a square deal."[140]

White delegates meeting in Port Arthur were not moved by Fraser's appeal for a "square deal." Instead, members buried the matter in the Committee on Constitution and Laws and then boarded a specially commissioned bus for the Orpheum Vaudeville Theatre. There, the men feasted on a banquet, cooled their palates with drink, and washed down the day's events with a minstrel show, "The Boys from Memphis," featuring blackface singers Fox and Evans.[141] Whereas CBRE delegates could not fathom a meaningful partnership with black railwaymen, they cheerfully welcomed burlesqued images of black men. They could digest chuckling and jiving black buffoons but not equal status among workers as proposed by Fraser, Robinson, and other sleeping car porters.

Although the Order of Sleeping Car Porters lost in Port Arthur, black railroaders' initial bid for CBRE membership forced a debate on racial segregation among workers and unmasked the deep-seated resentments of many white railwaymen. In the process, they laid bare the hypocrisy of working-class rhetoric by a CBRE leadership wedded more to white supremacy than to working-class solidarity. Insofar as sleeping car porters from across Canada joined in the battle against Jim Crow unionization in the CBRE, it demonstrates that the OSCP's following was indeed national. John A. Robinson's crusade against the largest and most powerful railway trade union of its time gave bite to his young union, establishing black railroaders as principled and astute trade unionists who insisted that white supremacy disparaged the cause of organized labor for all workers.

The Great War served as a catalyst for black insurgency, especially among sleeping car porters. Emboldened by their union and with little else to lose having witnessed the slow encroachment of Jim Crow ideology in the federal bureaucracy, employment policy, and trade unionism, sleeping car porters in Canada became the chief political advocates for their communities. Together with the clergy and black press, black railwaymen protested violations of African Canadians' civil rights, particularly when Jim Crow fixed limitations on their citizenship.

Thus, the period between 1880 and World War I held great promise for black railroaders in Canada. After setting tracks and feeding work crews, black railwaymen moved from the fields to the freight yards, finally gaining footing in the industry poised to dominate the new century. They initially enjoyed a range of employment options and utilized railway work to ensure full employment, countervail ennui, and pursue other commercial enterprises. Wages were good, if the work itself gritty and always dangerous. Black railroaders in Canada soon learned, however, that their welcome on the rails was provisional.

White trade unionists and railway management, defining their new roles in an age of rapid industrialization, held conflicting positions on black labor. Against the threat of industrial strife, both adopted Jim Crow as a rational model for labor relations. Railway management, burdened by what it construed as uppity white railwaymen, manipulated its workforce by fueling racial tensions on their lines. When they wanted to appease disgruntled white railway workers, Canadian railway companies conceded to unionists' segregationist demands. The simple truth remains that white Canadian unionists won Jim Crow as one such compromise by 1915.

At other times, Canadian railway executives circumvented white unions by importing foreign-born black workers, confident in the knowledge that their race prevented membership in existing unions. Canadian railway companies creatively ignored immigration and labor laws and successfully engaged accomplices in the Canadian government. Consequently, twentieth-century immigration and labor restrictions never meaningfully hampered Canadian railway companies' insatiate appetite for African American and West Indian workers.

To be sure, the Great War strained labor-management relations on Canadian lines. If the war made Canadian railway companies rich, it also roused trade union activists. Radicalism among white unionized railwaymen intensified and moved west during the second decade of the century. They posited that the introduction of southern African American and West Indian railroaders demeaned their white manhood, citizenship, and rights as union men. Their resentment, so deep rooted, thwarted a bid for interracial unionization by sleeping car porters, favoring hollow white supremacy to equal status for all railway workers.

For their part, black railroaders took notice of the climate on the rails. As president of the oscp, John A. Robinson intensified his assault on Jim Crow in white Canadian unionism during the Great War years. The Order of Sleeping Car Porters targeted its first offensive on the Canadian Brotherhood of Railway Employees' white-only membership doctrine. Robinson challenged the CBRE's rank and file, arguing that if the CBRE were truly the beacon of Canadian trade unionism, it would set new industrial standards by striking racism out of its constitution. The time had come, Robinson contended, for black workers to get a permanent foothold in the Canadian House of Labor.

CHAPTER THREE

Fighting the Empire

Race, War, and Mobilization

The climate had dramatically changed for black railroaders in Canada by World War I and forced a more urgent appeal for the federal government to halt the advancement of Jim Crow in industry and public life. African Canadians feared that, if left to their devices, employers would capitalize on the distraction occasioned by the war and exploit their workers with even greater impunity. John A. Robinson, the OSCP's leader and its chief architect, rallied black railwaymen in defense of their rights, citing the critical import of labor-based radicalism. For Robinson and other black leaders, the Great War era made clear that Jim Crow practices could quickly expand beyond the realm of labor and immigration legislation. As a result, African Canadians joined forces in defiance of violations of their rights, marshaling the language of manhood and citizenship when making their case with federal bureaucrats, employers, and those blacks in Canada new to protest politics.

While John A. Robinson faced down the specter of Jim Crow in Winnipeg's stockyards, Toronto and Halifax sleeping car porters launched their attack on segregation in another sector of the federal government—the Department of Militia and Defence. J. R. Whitney formed the vanguard of that offensive with his African Canadian newspaper the *Canadian Observer*. Whitney and his supporters argued that the Great War presented African Canadians with an opportunity to prove that they were dedicated citizens capable of upholding the British Empire in its time of need; convincing Prime Minister Borden and the Department of Militia and Defence proved their first of many fights.

The Great War changed Canadian society and African Canadian communities in particular. Black Canadians immediately organized in defense of their country and their right to work. Because of their highly mobile lifestyles and their connections to Canadian urban centers, sleeping car porters quickly emerged as the logical agents of that political mobilization. Porters created various institutions—a railway union, a black Canadian press, various racial uplift associations—that became national organizations almost overnight by enabling rapid dissemination of information during the war era. These infrastructures, initially created to make military mobilization possible, also made postwar African Canadian radicalism viable. The Great War gave birth to a new radicalized transnational race consciousness and an infrastructure to make that radicalism manifest at home and abroad. Moreover, black railwaymen who joined the Canadian Expeditionary Force applied the defensive strategies they had learned on the rails to their military service overseas. Others who manned the rails in Canada throughout the Great War defended their communities from violent labor protest, xenophobic attacks, and postwar assaults on black civil rights.

AFRICAN CANADIANS DEFINED THEIR citizenship rights during the second decade of the twentieth century as the right to employment and the right to military service. For blacks in Canada, who by the dawn of the Great War had reached adulthood in record numbers, work and service in the most important conflict of the time quickly emerged as most pressing issues. As talk of war intensified in the early part of that decade and African Canadians joined that debate, rumors of Jim Crow practices in the militia surfaced with a frequency that resulted in the prime minister receiving scores of letters from black Canadians eager for a clarification on Canada's enlistment policy. As Arthur Alexander, a sleeping car porter, explained, "Prime Minister Borden, the coloured people of Canada want to know why they are not allowed to enlist in the Canadian militia" and why they were "refused for no other apparent reason than their color."[1] When that failed, African Canadians appealed directly to the governor-general, the queen's representative in Canada. John T. Richards, an outspoken opponent of Canada's antiblack immigration laws, wrote the governor-general threatening to expose Canada's Jim Crow policies to other Imperial Expeditionary Forces, stressing that it "is certainly highly insulting to the Colored people here . . . to not be allowed to serve their King simply because they faces are dark." Richards intimated that "some of my Colored friends have been suggesting that we ought to protest to the Allies" and expose Canadian segregation to the world.[2]

Another black Canadian, George Morton, informed the minister of militia and defence, Sam Hughes, that recruitment officers committed their racism to paper, as black volunteers "have been turned down and refused, [their race] being the reason given on the rejection or refusal cards issued." Morton explained that, as Canadians, black citizens felt that "in this so-called Land of the free, and the home of the brave, . . . there should be no colour line drawn." He warned the Borden government that African Canadians, being "humble, but loyal subjects of the King, trying to work out their own destiny should be permitted . . . to perform their part, and do their share in this great conflict."[3]

George Morton skillfully framed his challenge of Jim Crow in the military by conjuring up Canadian abolitionist tradition and British justice, reminding white Canadians that "gratitude leads [black Canadians] to remember that this country was their asylum and place of refuge in the dark days of American slavery, and that here on this consecrated soil, dedicated to equality, justice and freedom, that under the all-embracing and protecting folds of the Union Jack, that none dared to molest or make them afraid." Given white Canadians' generosity, Morton rationalized, "our people gratefully rembering [sic] their obligation in this respect are most anxious to serve their King and Country in this critical crisis and they do not think they should be prevented from doing so on the ground of the hue of their skin."[4] In other words, Morton insisted that racism should not thwart African Canadians' deep sense of indebtedness and duty to their nation.

Black Canadian clergymen and sleeping car porters mounted a three-year campaign against Jim Crow in the Canadian armed forces and spearheaded their crusade from their pulpits and their presses. Captain William White, an American-born, Canadian-ordained minister, and Albertan Rev. J. R. Butler pleaded with their congregations to register for a black battalion. Back in Toronto, journalist J. R. Whitney launched a tireless fight for a black battalion as early as 1915 when it became apparent that white men would not accept black soldiers within their ranks (see Figure 9). Whitney, who owned and operated the Toronto-based *Canadian Observer*, capitalized on his access to a national black readership. He presented African Canadians with compelling reasons for "assisting the Empire in fighting for justice and liberty," arguing, "Are we going to stand back and say let them fight and establish justice without taking a part? No! Most emphatically, No!" Whitney urged his readers to "be loyal to your God, Race and Country" and "in unity let us prove our worth to the country and the Empire." Convinced that the investment would pay off after the war, Whitney promised his readers

COLORED MEN!

Your KING and COUNTRY Need YOU!

NOW is the time to show your Patriotism ; Loyalty

Your Brothers of the Colonies have rallied to the Flag and are distinguishing themselves at the Front. ℚ Here also is your opportunity to be identified in the Greatest

LT. COL. D. H. SUTHERLAND
C. O. No. 2 Construction Battalion

Will you heed the call and do your share? ✄ ✄ ✄

War of History, where the Fate of Nations who stand for Liberty is at stake. Your fortunes are equally at stake as those of your white brethren

NO. 2 CONSTRUCTION BATTALION

Now being Organized All Over the Dominion
Summons You. WILL YOU SERVE?

The British and their Allies are now engaged in a great forward movement. Roads, Bridges and Railways must be made to carry the Victors forward. The need of the day is Pioneers, Construction Companies and Railway Construction Companies. No. 1 Construction Company has been recruited. No. 2 Construction Company is now called for.

Lt. Col. D. H. Sutherland is in charge of the Company's Headquarters at Pictou; at Halifax applications may be made at the Parade Recruiting Station; elsewhere to any Recruiting Officer, or by letter to—

MAJOR C. B. CUTTEN, *Chief Recruiting Officer, Halifax, N S.*

Royal Print & Litho Limited, Halifax N. S.

Fig. 9. "Your King and Country Need You!" *Atlantic Advocate*, January 1917

that "if we work together our united efforts will count for something, and whatever position we gain will prove a lasting credit to the progress of our race" in Canada.[5]

The Borden government responded to African Canadian protests over Canada's Jim Crow military policies by claiming that, while no outright ban on black enlistment existed, commanding officers controlled the selection and rejections of would-be soldiers without interference from headquarters.[6] African Canadians, however, would not let the matter rest so easily. Whitney and his colleagues forced the Canadian Department of Militia and Defence into publicly denying that a color line existed in its armed forces. Minister Sam Hughes disavowed the existence of segregation in Canada's armed forces in the press, professing instead that "there are scores of colored men in Canadian regiments today." He told reporters that while there existed "no Color Line in the Militia," he would "not, however, lend [him]self to the fad of giving them a regiment any more than I intend to have a regiment of one-eyed men, men with yellow moustaches or red hair."[7]

Whether deeply committed to the war effort or not, black Canadians steadfastly opposed a color line in the militia because white supremacy, particularly when it governed federal policy, posed a clear and present threat to their civil rights. To be sure, various black intellectual-activists throughout North America also questioned whether the Great War was indeed the black man's burden. Back in the United States, many black leaders exchanged heated words over the roles that African Americans should and would play in the European conflict. For his part, A. Philip Randolph challenged the value of defending freedom and democracy in Europe when disfranchisement, Jim Crow, and lynch law made democracy a lofty goal at home in the United States. Randolph's outspoken opposition to black involvement in World War I landed him in prison and earned him the dubious distinction of being denounced by J. Edgar Hoover as "the most dangerous Negro in America."[8] Harvard graduate and journalist Monroe Trotter confronted Woodrow Wilson's apathy toward African Americans in his newspaper the *Guardian*, pointing out with rapier resolve that until the federal government did its part to quash southern lynchers, African Americans should withhold their support for the war. Even W. E. B. Du Bois, who initially supported Wilson's war plans with guarded optimism, later wavered. In July 1917, he and New Negro men and women activists marched on New York, declaring that "Patriotism and Loyalty" demanded "Protection and Liberty."[9] Pressing domestic issues— segregation, fair access to education and employment, lynching, and Houston's recent race riots—seemed like more immediate risks to African Americans' lives than Kaiser Wilhelm II or Germany writ large.

African Canadians knew and respected Randolph, Trotter, and Du Bois. The *Crisis* and the *Messenger* circulated widely in Canada, thanks in large part to sleeping car porters who brought them back from runs to Boston, New York, Detroit, Chicago, and Minneapolis.[10] African American debates over black enlistment certainly resonated with African Canadian audiences concerned over similar obstacles in Canada. Yet if lynchings were a foreign horror, Jim Crow certainly was not. For years, African Canadians had been fighting the encroachment of Jim Crow ideology in Canadian federal law and in Canadian industries. Against the background of Canadian racial paranoia over black immigration and employment in industries like coal mining and railroading, some black Canadians questioned whether they indeed owed loyalty to a country determined to be the last white man's land.

As early as 1916 Captain A. G. Gayfer, canvassing for potential recruits in Alberta, witnessed an example of black opposition to serving in the Canadian military. In a memo to the minister of militia and defence, Gayfer warned that he "had four colored recruits lined up for Number two construction battalion [and] lost them through [a] crusade preached by [a] colored man against colored enlisting." He urgently telegrammed his superiors back in Ottawa that a black man had been dogging his steps, undermining his recruitment efforts at every turn. This antirecruitment proponent, an African American traveling with a minstrel troupe in Western Canada, irreverently threatened to "speak against recruiting in every town he visited." The Canadian government resolved its problem with the minstrel actor by notifying local police, arresting the man, and having him duly deported to the United States for violating Canada's War Measures Act.[11]

As Europe burned and white men mobilized in defense of its honor, African Canadians confronted white supremacy in the Canadian militia. They concluded that the Great War offered a chance to prove that they were meaningful citizens capable of upholding the British Empire. Perhaps the *Atlantic Advocate*, another African Canadian newspaper launched during the war era, said it best: "Colored Men! Your King and Country Need *You*! Your fortunes are equally at stake as those of your white brethren."[12] Thus, African Canadians believed that by saving democracy overseas they would safeguard it at home. If German bombs imperiled the British Empire—the very emblem of democracy and civilization—African Canadian men would come to its defense. This determination to play their role in Europe grew out of a burgeoning political agency made possible by a newly created black press and by race advocates—namely, sleeping car porters. Instead, riotous white Canadian servicemen taught African Canadians that their country repaid their lives and loyalty with brutality.

The Borden administration adopted a Janus-faced approach to African Canadian involvement in the Great War. On the one hand, the Canadian government urgently needed men on the front lines. On the other hand, remembering the clamor witnessed over black immigration in the years prior to the war, the Borden government feared objections to an integrated militia from white Canadians. In other words, the federal government suspected that the discontent registered in the Prairies over black migration was neither fixed in the West nor just a riposte to an influx of foreign-born blacks. Rather, the deep-seated resolve against black enlistees voiced by white commanding officers and soldiers alike clearly demonstrates that negrophobia had become a ruling concern for the federal government, this time in its armed forces.

In a 1916 poll of the Department of Militia and Defence, commanding officers repeatedly opposed black enlistment, insisting that black would-be soldiers were unsuitable for the mission. They posited that climatic unsuitability and a detrimental effect on white recruitment disqualified African Canadian men from service.[13] Time and again, commanding officers ridiculed the idea of blacks' service in the militia, as evidenced by the 173rd's commander, who resolved, "Sorry we cannot see our way to accept [Negroes] as these men would not look good in Kilts."[14] The commander of Toronto's 95th battalion wrote his superiors, "Thank goodness this batt. is over strength and does not therefore need a 'colored' platoon, nor even a colored drummajor!"[15] In truth, all but three of Canada's officers commanding recruitment zones vetoed the enlistment of blacks in the armed forces, citing that the "introduction of a coloured platoon into our Battalion would undoubtedly cause serious friction and discontent . . . [and] would be detrimental to recruiting throughout the Country."[16] In a rare instance of disarming candor, one lieutenant colonel prophetically remarked, "I would object very strongly to accepting the Platoon mentioned for the reason that the prejudice against the negross [*sic*] in this country is extremely bitter."[17]

Faced with a diminishing number of recruits yet in desperate need of more soldiers, the Canadian government passed the 1917 Military Service Act, a deeply unpopular law especially among French Canadians. The new law mandated conscription and as a consequence forced commanding officers to accept black enlistees, their objections notwithstanding.[18] After conferring with the British war office in London and being assured that "these niggers do well in a Forestry Corps and other Labour units," the Borden government resolved that "our authorities . . . might be induced to try the experiment" of pooling black conscripts into a segregated battalion.[19] Thus began the No. 2 Construction Battalion, Canada's experiment in Jim Crow military service.

In a strange twist of events, Canadian military commanders who had earlier resisted the introduction of blacks in the military now complained to headquarters that since the draft "a large number of coloured men" of military service age had absconded to Michigan and other American border states.[20] They alleged that within months of conscription as many as two hundred African Canadian draft dodgers had escaped to Detroit and New York.[21] By 1918, the Department of Militia and Defence further worried that "now that America has come into the war, most of these darkies, if they are doing any flocking at all, will flock where the better pay is, namely the American army."[22] Lieutenant Colonel Young, a commanding officer in Ontario, dreamed up a solution to Canada's new problem and explained, "In the ordinary way these men will not come in of their own accord . . . [as] the average negro is rather 'afraid of the Army.'" In language and reasoning reminiscent of antebellum slave catchers, Young stressed that "they have to be sought out," insisting that "if no effort is made to obtain these men that rightfully belong to us, they will be lost without hope of recovery."[23]

Then, in a real turnaround, some Canadian military officials even encouraged singling out African American and West Indian recruits for Canada's proposed black battalion. In May 1918, the British-Canadian Recruiting Mission in New York reported that "over two thousand black British subjects registered . . . at various depots as willing to serve" in the Canadian armed forces.[24] In July 1916, the Canadian government had selected Lieutenant Colonel Daniel Hugh Sutherland, a white railroad contractor from Nova Scotia, to head its segregated unit, the No. 2 Construction Battalion. Only months later, Sutherland petitioned his supervisors for permission to round up recruits in the West Indies, confident that he could return with several hundred men, demonstrating that like Canadian railway and steel companies, the Canadian military envisioned the Caribbean as a pool of readily accessible muscle easily herded north to serve Canadian interests.[25]

In the end, more than six hundred black servicemen defended the British Empire during World War I in Canada's segregated No. 2 Construction Battalion.[26] Though estimates place their number at about three hundred, the exact number of foreign-born black enlistees in the Canadian militia is unclear. It is known, however, that the majority of the African American men who fought under the Union Jack were southerners who immigrated to

Canada in the wake of the 1906 Brownsville, Texas, riots and Oklahoma statehood in 1907. They were also the men who had poured into Western Canada during "Prairie Fever," the 1906–12 homesteading movement. These turn-of-the-century southern African American migrants came of age in a Jim Crow South and learned the full meaning of citizenship upon immigrating to Canada. African American sleeping car porters working in Canada also accounted for many of the foreign-born black servicemen in the Canadian military. They came to the No. 2 Construction Battalion ripened by a decade of trade union insurgency—a fact that would prove central to their experiences as Canadian soldiers.

On 17 March 1917, just one month before Americans joined the war, the No. 2 Construction Battalion—a multinational company of African Canadians, West Indians, and African Americans dressed in Canadian military uniform—paraded through Dartmouth, a suburb of Halifax. Mabel Saunders, an African Canadian girl at the time, remembered, "I saw that parade on Prince Albert Road. I was standing by my gate when they came marching by with their chests stuck out and the Band playing. I can't tell you exactly how many [there were], but there was a large crowd of soldiers marching up the street." Saunders recalled that "everbody was watching: Black people and white people, waving their hands, cheering and clapping" as black soldiers "proudly march[ed] off to war," proving to their communities that "they were men the same as everybody else."[27] This sense of pride in manhood and community became extremely important to African Canadian communities, who bore the dysgenic cost of war just like their white counterparts without always winning the rewards for loyal service. On 28 March, the No. 2 Construction Battalion sailed to Liverpool on board the SS *Southland*, a segregated troop ship specially commissioned by the Department of Militia and Defence in order to avert "offending the susceptibility of other [white] troops."[28]

IF AFRICAN CANADIAN GREAT expectations for the war peaked on that March day in 1917, the dismal outcome of demobilization in Great Britain toppled hope that after the war life for blacks in Canada would improve. For Canadian servicemen stationed in Europe, 1919 was the winter of their discontent. The Ministry of Overseas Forces announced armistice on 11 November 1918, yet a quarter of a million Canadian soldiers still languished in Europe at year's end. War-worn Canadian servicemen had one wish: prompt return to their families and loved ones in Canada. The Great War took a great toll on Canadian lives. More than 200,000 men had fallen at Ypres, Festubert,

Givenchy, Amiens, Vimy Ridge, Passchendaele, and other such bloody battles since 1914. More than 3,500 men were still missing in action by 31 December 1918.[29]

Ominous conditions haunted those still living. Approximately 150,000 soldiers welcomed the new year in cold, rainy, putrescent military camps across the Welsh and English countryside while Canadian military commanders headquartered in London plotted their fate.[30] Canadian and British military administrators argued that the armistice might not hold; the Canadian Expeditionary Force would therefore remain in Europe.[31] In the meantime, Sir Edward Kemp, minister of overseas forces, and Major General Sydney Mewburn, minister of militia and defence, hurriedly devised a demobilization plan that would keep Canadian forces readied for combat while also allowing some soldiers to return to Canada.

British, Australian, New Zealand, American, and Canadian commanders compared demobilization schemes. They shared a common problem, since limited access to large ships complicated the safe return of hundreds of thousands of war veterans. The Canadians struggled with two additional concerns: inclement weather and postwar economic recession. With winter upon them, the frozen St. Lawrence River sealed off Montreal—Canada's largest port and railway hub—leaving Halifax as the country's last port of entry suitable for large carriers. To complicate matters, only two railway lines, the Intercolonial Railway and Canadian Pacific Railway, serviced that city. Company executives already warned the Borden government that they could not accommodate more than thirty thousand returning veterans monthly.[32] By December, the Canadian government's worst fears materialized. The coldest winter then on record locked Canadian soldiers in Europe until spring warmed the St. Lawrence back to life.

Race and class shaped Canadian military demobilization. The Borden government made the return of skilled white officers a priority, favoring them for higher-wage desirable veteran jobs in Canada.[33] A thankful nation bestowed its gratitude on this first wave of Great War veterans. Thus, white Canadians concluded that healthy, soldierly, professional white men had saved the British Empire. That image of Anglo-Saxon manliness fixed white Canadian conceptions of their armed forces. Conversely, working-class Canadians, many of whom were French Canadians, immigrants, or people of color, were the last men pulled out of European battlefields. Since many of these working-class soldiers manned labor platoons, they were still needed to feed, warm, and defend Canada's armed forces back in Europe.[34] Consequently, those soldiers were often the last units repatriated. Soured by a season of rioting, Canadians gave those soldiers a cooler welcome upon their return in late spring 1919.

Back in Europe, General Arthur Currie warned Prime Minister Borden of low morale in Canada's demobilization camps. Senseless bureaucracy, cramped housing in makeshift tents, poor nutrition, irregular disbursement of wages, outbreak of influenza, fuel shortages, biting cold, unyielding rain—and worse still, boredom—created an explosive climate in Canada's six military compounds surrounding Liverpool.[35] Just one fortnight after armistice, General Currie wrote the minister of overseas forces, "I cannot dwell too strongly on this matter of discipline. I know its value." The general cautioned that discipline had "been the foundation of our strength . . . and the source of our power." He stressed that this discipline "is worth preserving for the national life of Canada after the war" and beseeched Prime Minster Borden, "For God's sake do not play with it, for you are playing with fire."[36] The men were jumpy, and Canadian military commanders on the scene braced themselves for a difficult winter.

Gunfire broke out within a month of Currie's forewarning. A riotous mood descended on Canada's military camps much like the rain clouds that kept the region soaked and muddied. Just days after Christmas, Canadian soldiers ransacked "tin towns," overpriced shops encircling the Witley and Bramshott camps. On 2 January 1919, Canadian and British soldiers exchanged fire outside Ripon and shot 150 rounds at each other.[37] An investigation into the matter revealed that engineers and railway troops had led the brawl. Canadian military commanders had an even harder time controlling their younger soldiers. Kinmel Park, the largest military depot and last stop in Great Britain before boarding for Canada, housed railway troops, the Young Soldiers Battalion, and the Forestry Corps, including the No. 2 Construction Battalion made up entirely of black Canadian servicemen.

Kinmel Park proved a recipe for disaster. With shipments stopped by striking British mariners, dockers, and coal miners, demobilization had come to a virtual standstill by January 1919. Recruits kept pouring into Kinmel hoping that when ships moved again they would be well stationed for prompt return home. The Department of Militia and Defence also pursued an ill-advised policy of dismantling platoons at Kinmel and reorganizing the men into units based on regional Canadian military divisions.[38] Never before demobilization at Kinmel had the Canadian military peppered its white units with so many black soldiers. Sir Edward Kemp, minister of overseas forces, fought the plan in vain. He admonished Prime Minister Borden that when "you mix up all kinds of combatants and noncombatant troops into drafts to fit demobilization necessities in Canada and these men are held pending shipping arrangements, they become most difficult to control."[39]

The conflict, when it came on 7 January, exploded as a racial riot. When Edward Sealy, a black sergeant major, arrested an unruly white soldier and charged him to a "colored escort," fighting ensued.[40] A band of white officers went on a rampage, attacking any black serviceman unfortunate enough to cross their path. Then, enraged white soldiers assaulted a unit of Sealy's men en route to their baths. The race riot left soldiers on both sides of the color line nursing wounds that would not heal for some time. Disturbances at Kinmel had barely been quelled before a black soldier became the focus of another riot in nearby Witley.[41]

White Canadian servicemen rioted their way through the winter and spring of 1919, acting out their frustrations on black Canadian soldiers. Canceled shippings and beer shortages in March set off another three days of rioting at Kinmel in which eight to twenty-seven soldiers lost their lives and up to seventy-three landed in hospital.[42] The *Toronto Daily Star*'s front-page headline declared that Kinmel camp soldiers had exploded in rage when 4,800 "Colored Troops [were] Shipped to the States while Canadians Are Held" in England.[43] Canadian newsmen rationalized that white Canadian servicemen rampaged "due to preference being given to United States negro troops in returning home." The *Daily Star* interviewed a veteran who confirmed, "When I was at Rhyl the men knew about the big ships carrying Americans and were very sore. . . . There was a lot of discontent [and] men I know personally were about to riot." The same soldier warned, "Find the man who was responsible for taking the Olympic, Aquatania, and Mauretania off the Canadian transport route and you will find the man responsible for the Rhyl riots."[44] Frustrated with Americans for taking control of returning ships, this veteran's response demonstrates how black men became scapegoats for the perceived affront to white Canadians, a reaction that would become more prevalent during the interwar years.

The threat of ten years' imprisonment at a hard labor camp or death by firing squad did little to discourage future lawlessness.[45] Soon after Easter, three more battalions raided Witley canteens and surrounding small businesses.[46] In early May, fighting moved to Seaford, temporary home to engineers and machine gunners returning from France. The *Montreal Gazette* headlined that an "Outbreak Started over [the] Arrest of a Colored Soldier" on the evening of 10 May.[47] A white guard on picket duty harassed private George Beckford, a black conscript, and demanded that "he adopt a more soldierly demeanour in public."[48] Beckford, who worked as a sleeping car porter and chauffeur in Winnipeg before the war, disregarded the sentry's orders. Tensions mounted and fists flew before Beckford's eventual arrest. News of the fight quickly spread to the rest of the camp; before long, a crowd of one thousand servicemen gathered demanding Beckford's release. They eventually stormed the jail and stole the black soldier away to hospital, where he remained under examination overnight. Rioting continued well into the next day; seventy more men were arrested and fined for the outbreak before calm settled over Seaford.[49] Although soldiers publicly lamented the slow pace of demobilization, their frustrations, racialized once again, quickly turned on black soldiers. The Canadian commanding officer on the scene wired headquarters with news of the recent unrest, warning that "if our men get these wild ideas [here], they will carry them to Canada."[50] (See Figure 10.)

The winter's riots brought shame to the Canadian armed forces, especially since British and American newspaper reports drew attention to Canada's racial skirmishes.[51] Booze, boredom, and Bolshevism, reasoned the Canadian press, explained their soldiers' disgraceful behavior. It seemed as though querulous servicemen always turned to liquor during the revolts. During Kinmel's March affray, soldiers reportedly jumped a convoy of beer, busted open barrels, and sopped up the gushing brew in "firepails, saucepans, and mess tins."[52] Such reports scandalized British House member Sidney Robinson, who posited to then secretary of state for the imperial forces Winston Churchill "that had there been no liquor" in the camps, "there would have been no disturbance." Churchill defended the troops' time-honored right to grog, proposing instead that "far from proving a cause of disturbance, [alcohol] is believed to have had the contrary effect, as there was much discontent before [soldiers] were provided with regular supplies" of liquor.[53]

The true source of the problem, contended The *Halifax Morning Chronicle*, was boredom.[54] Canadian armed forces stockpiled in England without wages or diversions. The Canadian government had fallen behind on its daily stipend of a shilling, leaving the men unable to pay for local entertainment. The Khaki University, established during the war to help enlistees earn an education, the Salvation Army, and chaplain services provided options few soldiers found compelling on a Saturday night.[55] Without wages, even small-time gambling fell off, leaving the men without other forms of recreation. The riots, rationalized the *Morning Chronicle*, seduced otherwise law-abiding citizens "who simply indulged in a weakness for horseplay, while others were inflamed by liquor."[56] The Borden government and Canadian newsmen also maintained that foreign disease and ideas had spawned the riots. Acting Prime Minister Thomas White explained away the violence at Kinmel before

10 M. D. First Depot Battalion. Manitoba Regiment 6

Regtl. No.2378966

PARTICULARS OF RECRUIT DUPLICATE
DRAFTED UNDER MILITARY SERVICE ACT, 1917
(Class One)

1. Surname........Beckford

2. Christian name........George Hutchingson

3. Present address 100 McDonald Ave, Winnipeg Manitoba Canada,

4. Military Service Act letter and number........542785 JW

5. Date of birth ....March 10th, 1889

6. Place of birth........Jamacia, British West Indies
   (town, township or county and country)

7. Married, widower or single........Single

8. Religion........Church Of England

9. Trade or calling........Chauffer

10. Name of next-of-kin........Mrs Rebecca Beckford

11. Relationship of next-of-kin........Mother

12. Address of next-of-kin ....17 King Street Spanish Town, Jamacia,
    British West Indies

13. Whether at present a member of the Active Militia........No

14. Particulars of previous military or naval service, if any........No

15. Medical Examination under Military Service Act:—

(a) Place Winnipeg Canada. (b) Date.....14/11/17 (c) Category....A2

DECLARATION OF RECRUIT
I, George Beckford , do solemnly declare that the

above particulars refer to me, and are true.

George Beckford Signature of Recruit

DESCRIPTION ON CALLING UP

Apparent age ....28 yrs 9½ mths.			Distinctive marks, and marks indicating congential peculiarities or previous disease.
Height 5 ft 9 ins.			
Chest measurement { fully expanded 35 ins.			Nil.
range of expansion 2½ ins.			
Complexion Dark (Colored)			
Eyes Brown			
Hair Black			

O. C. First Depot Btn. Mnaitoba Regt.

Place Winnipeg Canada, Date....5/1/18

M. F. W. 101.

Fig. 10. World War I veterans and George Beckford's application

Left: Beckford's application. Beckford, a sleeping car porter, enlisted on 14 November 1917. He later served as OSCP president during World War II (Library and Archives of Canada, RG 150-1992-166-577-2). *Below*: World War I veterans from the No. 2 Construction Battalion. Private Cromwell (on the right) registered for the No. 2 Construction Battalion at the age of nineteen and died of tuberculosis in Europe. Private Brown (on the left) also signed up for this battalion. (Black Cultural Centre for Nova Scotia).

the House of Commons in March and justified the uproar as manifestations of "great privations, hardships and monotony."[57]

Canadian military commanders overseas flooded British newspapers with articles insisting that riot ringleaders were foreign-born servicemen taken into the Canadian militia.[58] An article in the *Times* of London entitled "Kinmel Camp Riot: Attack Led by a Russian" blamed the recent turmoil on a Bolshevist cluster contaminating Canadian troops.[59] Convinced that unrest could not have emanated from Canadians themselves, Canadian military officials overwhelmingly court-martialed white men with eastern European and French Canadian names.[60] Court-martial records of the Department of Militia and Defence also reveal that, of the black soldiers arrested during the riots, the overwhelming majority were African American and West Indian railroaders serving in the Canadian military.[61] This suggests that these railwaymen applied the agency that they had learned on the rails to their defensive strategies in Europe. Given the stern reprimand they were sure to receive, working-class military men understood the cost of their defiance.

Canada's demobilization debacle exposed the country's preoccupation with race and class to the British Empire and the world. The 1919 Canadian race riots in Liverpool and Wales revealed that, like Great Britain, Australia, South Africa, and the United States, white Canadians were not immune to racism. The Borden government's decision to favor white skilled workers for early return to Canada—leaving working-class white and nonwhite servicemen to live out their winter in weather-beaten diseased British military camps—made clear that the Great War had done little to equalize Canadian society. By singling out French Canadians, immigrants, and purported Bolshevists for its problems abroad, the Canadian government demonstrated that it too adopted knee-jerk red baiting as its solution to postwar social upheaval. Throughout the 1920s, eastern European Canadians, like African Canadians, became the country's convenient scapegoats for postwar labor unrest, peacetime economic recession, and urban demise.

A new rash of race riots in June presented Canadians with another rationale for insurrection in their armed forces. June proved a menacing month for blacks in Great Britain, particularly for those living in port cities. Throughout World War I, Liverpool and Cardiff experienced a large influx of black workers from Africa, the Americas, and the Caribbean.[62] Demobilization added West Indian, African American, and African Canadian soldiers to the fold. In early June, Britons responded to the presence of black soldiers and black mariners by besieging Arabs and blacks in Liverpool.[63] According to a confidential report produced by Liverpool's head constable, organized gangs of

2,000–10,000 young white men roved the city's streets "savagely attacking, beating, and stabbing every negro they could find."[64] For example, 300 white rioters hunted down a West Indian ship's fireman, Charles Wooton. Fearing for his life, Wooton jumped off a pier into blackened waters, despite being unable to swim. The mob then stoned the black mariner to his drowning death, ignoring his many pleas for help.[65]

White rioters targeted black soldiers and black workers during the Liverpool melee regardless of their citizenship. Witnessing this wanton violence against blacks, soldiers and mariners in the area quickly came to each other's defense. The *South Wales News* described how black denizens defended their families and properties by pointing out that the "coloured men, while calm and collected, were well prepared for any attack." The report claimed that "negroes [were] loading revolvers" all the while warning that "it will be hell let loose if the mob comes into our streets. If we are unprotected from hooligan rioters who can blame us for trying to protect ourselves?"[66]

Liverpool's racialized reign of terror paralyzed the city for more than a week before the mayor, head constable, and local labor officials met to reestablish order. The committee resolved that "coloured men should be removed quickly [from] the city and placed in an internment camp pending repatriation, which will be expedited."[67] The *Liverpool Echo* assured readers of hasty extradition as "over 700 [blacks were] rounded up" to deal with the "repatriation problem."[68] In truth, blacks in Liverpool and Wales did not so readily comply to banishment. A meeting called by black seamen in Cardiff adopted a resolution demanding that the British "Government afford them, as British subjects, adequate protection."[69]

By mid-June, rioting spread to South Wales, with Newport and the capital, Cardiff, now caught up in violence. London's *Times* informed readers that "racial riots of a grave character" had left one Irishman and one black man dead, and several "negroes beaten with frying pans," giving powerful imagery to the violence's frenzied pace. The *Times* confirmed that white rioters in Cardiff had destroyed black homes and attacked black men and women with sticks and bricks. The article described the white mob, many of whom were young men in Imperial Armed Forces uniform, charging into "Nigger Town," home to "a large colony of negroes many of whom have married white wives."[70]

White Britons condemned black foreigners for the turmoil in Liverpool and Cardiff.[71] Newspaper reports highlighted accounts of gun-toting black men firing down whites and even allegedly slashing one constable with a razor.[72] Adding fuel to the fire, the *Times* accused black mariners of stealing jobs and white women from otherwise deserving white British veterans. Ralph Williams, the former governor of Barbados, offered his assessment of the riots in an incendiary editorial defending the white rioters. "It is an undeniable fact," he asserted, that "to almost every man and woman who had lived a life among [the] coloured races, intimate association between black . . . men and white women is a thing of horror." Aversion to interracial unions, he insisted, "in no sense springs from hatred" nor did it "arise from any feeling of social superiority." Rather, Williams reminded readers that the cause was far more complex. "It is an instinctive certainty that sexual relations between white women and coloured men revolt our very nature." Williams's editorial warned readers that since black men were in England "without their women," their "passions [found] white women encouraging their attentions, and allowing themselves to be taken as paramours." He proposed that black soldiers be immediately returned to their countries of origin and prevented from further employment in port cities. Williams concluded his editorial by emphasizing, "I know that I am expressing the views of the vast majority of British white men and women. . . . This evil should be ended."[73]

The demobilization riots brought to the fore the debate concerning what to do about black denizens and the freedoms they enjoyed during wartime, including imagined greater access to white women. That such a debate raged in the British press just as white Canadian soldiers rioted over softening segregation becomes very pertinent, particularly since so many British and Canadian journalists clamored for a more stringent application of Jim Crow conventions. White Canadian soldiers and journalists openly speculated on whether, once back in Canada, black soldiers would dare to approach their wives, sisters, and daughters, having had license to socialize across the color line in Europe, in part because of the distraction of war. There, in the pages of London's *Times*, they found Williams, apparently well acquainted with blacks throughout the empire, warning of impending doom. If the metropole England could not manage this postwar riotous mood, how would Canadians? Thus, Williams effectively married the fear of black insurgency with white fears of unemployment and white women's burgeoning sexuality, setting off a most dangerous temper.

Many white American naval officers stationed near Cardiff felt vindicated by Williams's editorials. They used the Liverpool and Cardiff crises as a platform for denouncing "the laxity of the British law" on interracial sexual relations and ultimately marriage.[74] They intimated that had Great Britain taken note of the American South's model—Jim Crow and lynching as effective deterrents for black men set on white women—the postwar savagery in

Great Britain could have been averted. In the meantime, they and white South African soldiers took matters in their own hands, insisting that "rules relating to color . . . [were] necessary to preserve the superior white race." England's most potent black newspaper, the *African Telegraph*, and the United States' most influential black weekly, the *Chicago Defender*, warned readers that Americans and South Africans "in our midst as fighters of democracy" had been stirring up racialized rancor throughout the spring and dealing out "literature seeking to display racial prejudice," therefore placing at least some of the blame for the increased racial violence on non-British soldiers and showing the effect of Jim Crow and white supremacist ideology on international racial strife.[75]

Racialized violence meted out by white Canadians, Americans, South Africans, and Englishmen escalated in Great Britain once black workers were no longer needed for the war effort. The *Liverpool Courier* admitted "the Colour Bar—Race Prejudice on the Increase—Empire's Great Post War Problem," admonishing readers "both here and in the United States (where 63 negroes were lynched last year) race prejudice is growing," making a very pointed connection between conditions in Great Britain and those haunting the United States.[76] As in North America, British journalists were ambivalent about their regard for black denizens. On the one hand, British newsmen praised African, West Indian, and black North Americans for their valiant contributions during the war. On the other, the British press condemned blacks in Britain for demanding privileged citizenship rights like protection from wanton violence, fair access to employment, and the freedom to marry without persecution. Yet judging by the mayhem on Liverpool and Cardiff streets in 1919, perhaps war had not endangered British civility so much as the sight of white women locked in black men's arms.

World War I gave birth to a palpably more militant transnational race consciousness, as evidenced by a new crop of international and transnational organizations addressing black political concerns. The riotous winter of 1919 served as a chilling reminder that if democracy and the British Empire had been safeguarded, blacks' civil rights—on either side of the Atlantic—had not. If African Americans were facing down Jim Crow and lynching on their streets, black Canadian and West Indian veterans chased down Liverpool alleys to shouts of "lynch them" understood that white supremacy haunted them as well.[77] Accordingly, the Great War served as a cataclysmic moment for blacks both at home and abroad.

Abuses against West Indians in Great Britain in 1919 emboldened black British activist-journalist Eugene Hercules's Caribbean decolonization movement.[78] Marcus Garvey's emigrationist programs gained global appeal after the war as a result of black dissatisfaction with conditions in Great Britain, Canada, and the United States. For his part, W. E. B. Du Bois strategically planned the Pan-African Congress in Paris in 1919 to ensure that delegates meeting at the Peace Conference were reminded of black men's concerns.[79] If German bombs and segregated platoons had temporarily suppressed racial tensions in American and Canadian armed forces during the Great War, the riots in Great Britain served as a prophetic omen of what would follow during the summer of 1919.[80]

The black press—in Europe, the Caribbean, the United States, and Canada —sounded the alarm over the rise of racialized violence and made explicit connections between what happened to black soldiers on the streets of Cardiff and Chicago. Black journalists responded to the British riots with righteous discontent and galvanized readers to the importance of an international outlook on black civil rights, particularly when it involved racial violence. Throughout the spring and summer of 1919, news of the full extent of the Liverpool and Cardiff riots, as reported in the international black press, trickled into Canada by way of sleeping car porters' suitcases and black soldiers' satchels.[81] The newspapers were then sold and distributed in African Canadian eateries, barber shops, pool halls, and boardinghouses catering to sleeping car porters. These international black newspapers presented African Canadians with the racialized dimension of the riots missing from most mainstream Canadian newspapers. Conventional Canadian newspapers typically suppressed reports of Canadian military turmoil abroad, particularly when it involved racialized brutality. As the full scope of demobilization unrest reached home, many black Canadians finally realized that their gamble on the Great War had failed. Put simply, the 1919 demobilization riots shattered black Canadian servicemen's hopes that their support of the war effort would crystallize their status as Canadian citizens.

Black soldiers' defense of the empire had not translated into meaningful citizenship at home. Instead, they learned that for blacks Europe was a deadly place. In other words, if German bullets and warring Welshmen did not kill them, their white countrymen just might. Demobilization riots in Canadian military camps throughout the winter and spring of 1919 took on racial dimensions early on and exposed that disgruntled white Canadian servicemen exhibited their discontent with racial violence. If black Canadian veterans could neither fight, sleep, nor eat with their white compatriots abroad, could they really expect that they would live and work peacefully alongside them at home? Canadians had obsessed over the color line before the war and quickly resumed that preoccupation after demobilization.

World War I and the demobilization riots that followed in 1919 taught black Canadian servicemen important lessons. Through service abroad with the Canadian Expeditionary Force, African Canadians reaffirmed that they belonged to a black community that defied borders. For instance, West Indians and African Americans served in the Canadian militia; they were then joined in France and Great Britain by soldiers from Africa, the Caribbean, and the United States.[82] Black Canadians also learned that white Canadians repaid their loyalty and patriotism by disavowing their existence all together. When asked about the role of black servicemen during the Great War, the Borden administration's last words on the Liverpool and Welsh riots denied any notable black Canadian contributions to the Great War.[83] In the end, World War I taught Canada's black soldiers the futility of defending the British Empire and British civilization when white rage and rampaging Welshmen were their reward.

In contrast, World War I also instilled a new transnational race consciousness among black Canadian soldiers that, as the Borden administration had worried, they carried back with them. Within weeks of the No. 2 Construction Battalion's return to Canada, fighting migrated from European military camps to Canadian city streets when a rash of strikes erupted across the dominion. Black veterans witnessed what had happened to black workers in Great Britain and feared that the same fate awaited them at home. African Canadians concluded that they could not trust white benevolence as they had before the war. Besides, playing by the rules had not served them well. This time, they joined striking workers under the banner of the Order of Sleeping Car Porters and took to the streets. Likewise, they intensified their attack on Jim Crow in federal public policy and Canadian industries after the war. Black Canadian railwaymen and war veterans defended their right to work after the Great War by increasingly citing their rights as men, citizens, and now also as veterans.

Whether black or white, Canadian veterans returned to a country that they barely recognized. Rampant inflation, economic uncertainty, and looming labor unrest destabilized a country anxious for a peaceful transition to normalcy. The nation's agitation mirrored global unease, made all the more real by striking shipyard workers in Seattle, race rioters in Chicago, and news of additional turmoil back in Europe. Canadian workers had swallowed their ire during the war, forced in part by federal legislation outlawing strikes.[84] Emboldened by the armistice and a return to peace, organized labor stirred back to life, this time with vigor never before seen in Canada and a determination that alarmed both their employers and their government.[85]

The Borden administration braced itself for mayhem, hoping that its Royal Commission on Industrial Relations, modeled after the U.S. Commission on Industrial Relations of 1914 and the British Whitely Committee on Industrial Conciliation of 1917, would offer critical insight into labor's temper. Instead, Prime Minister Borden uncovered a nation of vocal workers fired up by socialist promises and readied for armed conflict. Thousands of workers, including Resina Asals of the Women's Labour League, denounced deteriorating working conditions before the Royal Commission. "There is only one thing that workers have to thank the capitalists for," she declared, "and that is that they have tightened the screw up so much that they are awakening the worker."[86]

The Great War did more than "awaken" Canada's working class; it changed its very makeup. World War I saw women, immigrants, and workers of color introduced in Canadian industry in record numbers. For instance, as of 1915 the Canadian Pacific Railway hired women in its Montreal Angus shops, where they worked in rolling stock maintenance keeping trains in running order.[87] Meanwhile, the Women's Labour League, made up of outspoken advocates for organized labor, especially in Toronto's textile industries, demonstrated that they too were willing to join picket lines in defense of their rights.[88]

Immigrants and workers of color, especially eastern Europeans, infused new radicalism and years of experience as rank-and-file operatives into Canada's trade union movement. Russian Jews Solomon Moishe Almazoff and Moses Charitonoff were two such immigrant unionists deported from Canada for their activities during the Winnipeg General Strike.[89] Black employees, sealed out of many employment sectors prior to 1914, gained a foothold in various Canadian industries during and after the war. Toronto's black-owned *Canadian Observer* reported that one of the country's leading meatpacking companies, Swift Packing, finally integrated its Edmonton plant in 1915.[90] The *Atlantic Advocate* announced that quite a number of black men had found employment with Cunard and Company as shovelers and teamsters, while another four hundred or more black Maritimers worked in munitions factories during the war years.[91] Black railroaders also saw their numbers swell as African Americans and West Indians joined Canadian rails, while Japanese Canadians worked as red caps, station luggage handlers, a position previously occupied by black men.[92]

If labor leaders had ostracized women, immigrants, and workers of color prior to the war, doing so after 1919 would quickly prove unwise. White trade unionists understood that if they overlooked this group of workers, company executives would not, perhaps even replacing a large number of white men with lower-wage, nonunionized labor. More important, though, women, immigrants, and workers of color spent the war establishing their commitment to rank-and-file interests, citing working-class and pro-union rhetoric in defense of their constituencies.[93] That too served as powerful persuasion for white union men facing striking women, immigrants, and workers of color on picket lines across the dominion. Consequently, immediately after the war, many Canadian labor leaders experimented, albeit briefly, with a more inclusive vision of trade unionism.

Black railwaymen, many of whom were returning veterans, found their own motivations for joining the nation's working-class movement. They now had a union of their own, the Order of Sleeping Car Porters, proving that they obviously believed in the principles of organized labor. With this union, however, came reprisals by employers. John A. Robinson, for example, slipped in and out of unemployment, eking out an existence as a stable hand for a time, after losing his job because of union activity among sleeping car porters.[94] Black railroaders also faced the same problems as other workers: intensified coercion from employers, postwar recession, and mounting costs of living, worsened by stagnant wages.

Black workers in Winnipeg had even greater cause for action. The seat of labor and the headquarters of the OSCP, Winnipeg attracted all sorts of labor radicals and would-be revolutionaries. Inasmuch as white Winnipeggers were jolted by the war, so too were Winnipeg's black veterans who had suffered losses on European battlefields, in demobilization camps, and returned to an equally uncertain future in Canada. Their time abroad emboldened their sense of entitlement after the Great War, especially with respect to work.

Whereas white railroaders had made their contempt for black workers clear in the years leading up to the war, labor leaders working Winnipeg's streets in the spring of 1919, many of whom were Socialists, had not yet registered their position on black labor. Instead, many welcomed foreigners, logically so since most were themselves immigrants from Great Britain, and appealed to working-class solidarity.[95] Hearing soapbox Socialists making daily visits to Victoria Park, located near the black and immigrant neighborhood known as the North End, many black workers and veterans likely concluded that they had little to lose. Whether Robinson ever belonged to or sympathized with the Socialist Party of Canada is not known, but he could not have missed the parade of white men heading over to Victoria Park to listen to a regular lineup of Western Canada's most famous labor leaders. In a city firmly divided along class lines—with Winnipeg's black community wedged at its center—black workers bordered by railway stations and freight yards lived out their social location on a daily basis.

A string of strikes paralyzed Canadian industry during the spring of 1919, giving blacks as well as whites the opportunity to back up rhetoric with action. Neither the Borden government, provincial legislatures, city officials, nor corporate managers were properly prepared for labor's tempestuous mood. That year alone, Canada experienced 298 strikes. The minister of labour, Gideon Robertson, announced that nearly 140,000 strikers had forced Canadian industries to a halt.[96] Ontario and Quebec accounted for almost 50 percent of the national strike action, with coal miners, metal shop workers, and civil servants the most persistent pro-union activists. It should be remembered that striking New Brunswick iron molders; Nova Scotia quarry workers and street railway operators; Montreal textile workers and shipbuilders; and Toronto garment workers, meatpackers, and metal tradesmen had caused great consternation in the nation's capital long before Winnipeg workers took to the streets.[97]

Prime Minister Borden's cabinet adopted a cautious approach to labor, leaving management of industrial disputes to municipal and provincial governments. With a federal election just months away, Borden walked a tightrope given that he did not want to be seen crushing labor or appeasing radicals. The House of Commons member for Winnipeg's North End best captured the government's misgivings and warned, "Sedition must be stamped out. It is all very well to talk of free speech, but to talk of Bolshevism and riots and overthrowing the Government is a different thing."[98]

Whereas the prime minister and the minister of labour shied away from agitated workers, the Canadian press made plain just how heavily strikers weighed on Canadian minds. Communist rhetoric espoused at pro-union rallies alarmed the mainstream press and management alike. In Montreal, *La Presse* charged that "Bolshevism has for certain planted its tent at Winnipeg" and issued a call to arms for all Winnipeggers, explaining that the "situation is so grave that all citizens of good will [should] take up arms in order to preserve law and order"; more than five thousand Winnipeg denizens allegedly heeded *La Presse*'s call.[99] Several Canadian and American newsmen denounced labor's demands as a call for the adoption of Communism. The *Regina Morning Leader* concurred with the *Toronto Globe*, positing that strikers were "out to destroy the whole industrial, financial, and governmental institutions of Canada to establish a system which prevails in Bolshevist Russia today."[100]

Canadian journalists' myopic obsession with a Communist threat blinded them to the broader and more compelling reality that workers in postwar Canada saw and understood their concerns globally rather than just regionally. Like workers protesting in the United States, for example, Canadian workers conceived of their strife with management as a conflict between the classes and employed warring language that revealed the full extent of that vision. Similarly, labor disturbance in Canada elicited responses from American newsmen. With Americans worried about a continentwide general strike and saddled with problems of their own with Seattle shipyard workers that winter, the *Chicago Tribune* counseled that the "strike in Canada is worthy of serious thought and more—of serious action in this country." The greater threat "in Winnipeg is not recognition of collective bargaining but of a Soviet control of industry . . . From that to a soviet form of government is but a [slippery] step."[101]

The Canadian press was right about the international scope of working-class consciousness in Canada, if not about its Communist subplot. Indeed, workers in postwar Canada envisioned their battles nationally and internationally. Speaking before a crowd of five thousand workers celebrating May Day, Max Armstrong, a white Toronto machinist, declared, "There is no greater barrier to the human race today than Anglo-Saxon democracy." I. Willshaw, a self-proclaimed "Bolsheviki," insisted that working-class Canadians "had to fight, not alone the Junkerdom of Germany, but the Junkerdom of the entire world."[102] Canadian workers repeatedly testified—in the press, before royal commissions, at rallies, and on the street—that "the way the fight in Winnipeg will be determined will very largely influence the attitude [of labor] throughout Canada."[103] Canadian labor was clearly poised for a radical clash in the spring of 1919, as evidenced by a fiery speech delivered by Robert Russell, one of Winnipeg's future strike leaders: "Blood is running in Russia, and blood will run in this country from the Atlantic to the Pacific, or we will get our rights."[104]

Blood, when it flowed, did so in Winnipeg when the Metal Trades Council and the Winnipeg Building Trades Council initiated a citywide general strike in May 1919. Both would-be unions worried that with a return to peace and reduced demand for munitions, massive layoffs would follow. Disgruntled metal and construction workers butted heads with the unyielding Builders' Exchange and Ironmasters, a conglomerate of industrialists and managers, over wages, hours of work, and collective bargaining rights. A standstill by early May forced a strike that many had talked about, few imagined would actually happen, and whose outcome no one could have predicted.

On the morning of 15 May 1919, Winnipeg industries came to a grinding halt. The Strike Committee had asked metal tradesmen and construction workers—as well as sympathy strikers in other industries across the nation—to walk off their jobs at eleven. As planned, streetcars stopped dead in their tracks. Telephones rang across the city, unanswered because telephone operators, mostly women, had left their posts and were not coming back. Bread and milk delivery men, waiters, barbers, and movie theater operators left customers coveting their goods and services. Garbage handlers, also responding to the call, ignored waste piling up along sidewalks and back alleys. The CPR's Transcona Shops fell silent as machinists joined their working-class brethren on the streets. Meanwhile, striking postal workers and telegraph operators ensured that within the initial phase of the strike Winnipeg remained sealed off from the outside world. By 20 May, running tradesmen on the Canadian Pacific Railway and the Canadian National Railways (CNR) unanimously voted in favor of joining other sympathy strikers. Even the city's police force threatened to put down their weapons; an eleventh-hour agreement with city council prevented a complete collapse of local law enforcement.[105]

The city, reported the North West Mounted Police, teemed with renegade Socialists, old-time Wobblies, and irascible veterans.[106] The Strike Committee claimed that more than twenty-seven thousand working men and women had voted with their feet the day the strike began. Unsure of what to do next, workers migrated to the center of working-class life, the North End, where they crowded Main Street from city hall to the black and immigrant quarter.

On the morning of 20 May 1919, John Arthur Robinson left the house he rented on Selkirk Avenue and headed for Winnipeg's Canadian Northern Railway station, where he worked as a sleeping car porter.[107] For ten years he walked the North End, making his way past Charles Browers's tailor shop, Busy Bee's diner, and the Rex Café on Main Street—all black-owned businesses in what amounted to Winnipeg's black and immigrant community.[108] Supplanted from his warm homeland, St. Kitts, the tall, svelte, and always dapper Robinson now called Winnipeg home.[109] That morning, he likely crossed several other black men donned in porters' uniforms. These men, most of whom were African American southerners imported by the Canadian Pacific Railway during the war, formed the backbone of Winnipeg's black working class. He also wove his way past scores of disgruntled white workers who clouded his streets with newspapers and banners in hand.

Among them were many white war veterans still cantankerous from their time abroad. Robinson studied these men's nervous parade wondering when their ire would engulf his neighborhood and his black co-workers. He would not have to wait long: all eyes were on Winnipeg.

Robinson witnessed how World War I had transformed Winnipeg and the nation. For five years, CPR trains carted off white men to war and replaced them with immigrant workers from the United States, Asia, and the West Indies.[110] He watched the company drive these new nonunionized workers to exhaustion during the war, only to earn the distrust of war veterans upon their return. He registered labor and management's strained ten-year tango and studied how that taut interplay had become increasingly racialized. On the one hand, the Canadian Brotherhood of Railway Employees' white-only membership policy locked black railwaymen out of its ranks. On the other, white workers blamed black railroaders, especially African Americans, for their failed unionization efforts. These white union men conveniently ignored that the country's economic depression, conscription, and the company's tenacious resistance to unionization accounted for much of their unemployment.[111]

Indeed, the rails had become a dangerous place for black railroaders during the war. Heightened xenophobia and white union action against the CPR's employment of black men gave many black Canadian railroaders serious cause for concern. For other black railroaders, patriotic duty drove them away from the rails and into Canadian military camps. Some had chosen enlistment in the Canadian Expeditionary Force as welcome relief from the menacing climate on the rails; but they met with a different set of hazards at the hands of white servicemen in Europe. Those, Robinson included, who stayed on the railways faced a fight of their own.

Robinson contemplated the implications of the Winnipeg General Strike. He concluded that black Canadian railroaders could not watch this showdown complacently; they were, after all, workers victimized by the same ruinous company policies. Furthermore, black workers' apathy would signal uncertain working-class solidarity with other striking men. Likewise, black workers could not remain indifferent given that white wrath could so easily turn on Winnipeg's small black community, just as it so quickly had during race riots in East St. Louis and Houston a few years earlier and as it did in Liverpool, Glasgow, and Cardiff in 1919. Besides, white veterans had already been terrorizing North End residents, particularly those of color.[112] (See Figure 11.)

John A. Robinson, walking cautiously down Main Street that morning,

Fig. 11. John Arthur Robinson, circa 1920s (Archives of Manitoba, Black Community in Manitoba Collection)

headed for Union Station to tell the bosses that his men had voted. They too were striking in support of labor and in defense of their own rights as workers. Years later, Robinson recalled that members of the Order of Sleeping Car Porters had "sacrificed their jobs in the 1919 Winnipeg General Strike." For black Canadian railroaders, that participation resoundingly affirmed that they were "men, knowing what we want, and capable of defending the benefits which should be obtained through Affiliation with other Unions working for the same objective."[113]

The OSCP's decision to join the Winnipeg General Strike gave meaning to their politicized race and working-class consciousness. White workers acknowledged that partnership in the *Western Labor News*, the Strike Committee's official newspaper. In a special edition of the *Western Labor News*, the editor Rev. William Ivens confirmed that Winnipeg-based sleeping car porters had overwhelmingly voted in favor of a sympathy strike, with only two porters opposing the motion.[114] Labor organizers also thanked the OSCP for its donation of fifty dollars to the strikers' fund.[115] When the OSCP advised the Strike Committee that railway executives had trucked in American scabs, white Winnipeg unionists defended black Canadian railroaders' rights to employment in their press, denouncing the company's tactics and promising to alert immigration authorities.[116]

Rhetoric of manhood, race, and citizenship permeated the Winnipeg General Strike. In an attack on the city council's mandatory no-strike pledge for police officers, *Western Labor News* editors declared, "Britons Never Shall Be Slaves." They claimed that "ONLY A SLAVE COULD SIGN" the city's no-strike pledge. "A FREE MAN, A WHITE MAN—NEVER."[117] The *Western Labor News* denounced attacks on immigrant workers, stressing that the plight of workers "is a worldwide upheaval, due to economic conditions." Labor leaders maintained that the Citizens' Committee's "anti-alien campaign . . . is deliberately waged to confuse the issue, to disrupt the ranks of organized labor, to deceive the public, and to distract attention from the misdeeds of the exploiting class."[118]

The Canadian press and the Citizens' Committee of One Thousand, made up of the antistrike business elite, further exacerbated matters by racializing the Winnipeg General Strike by hiring workers of color in the Chinese quarter and training in African American laborers.[119] Employers also targeted women and girls as strikebreakers, especially in the telephone and postal sectors, aggravating relations between striking workers.[120] For its part, the Canadian press made culprits of immigrants, especially eastern Europeans and Jews. The *Winnipeg Citizen*, the official journal of city residents opposed to strikers, declared that the "most obvious thing about the strike . . . is the way the alien—naturalized and otherwise—abounds." The real purpose of the Winnipeg General Strike, it alleged, "is to employ these masses of rough, uneducated foreigners, who know nothing of our customs and our civilization [and] to browbeat and override the intelligent and skilled craftsmen of the more technical trades."[121] Returned soldiers were seen plundering immigrant businesses and subjecting immigrants to humiliating public abuse. Reports surfaced that white veterans eager to lay their hands on immigrants found them readily in "New Jerusalem"—the North End.[122] The Royal North West Mounted Police also encouraged xenophobia and anti-Semitism, cautioning Prime Minister Borden that the "feeling against Jewery is becoming more bitter as people are realizing that the removal of Jews from responsible positions . . . will not only be the salvation of the country but a final victory over Bolshevism."[123]

By the end of May, sympathy strikers in Montreal, Toronto, Calgary, and Vancouver—particularly railway workers—threatened to escalate the walkout into a national work stoppage, testifying to the powerful status of national working-class consciousness in Canada after the war. Corporate executives, however, intensified their resolve against workers' demands for collective bargaining and closed shops by abruptly dismissing strikers who refused to return to work, further aggravating an already volatile situation.[124]

The Borden administration seemed less equipped to deal with war at home than it had been for the one overseas. Minister of Labour Gideon Robertson and Minister of the Interior Arthur Meighen traveled to Winnipeg during the second week of striking hoping to cool seething tensions. Instead, Robertson and Meighen threw their weight behind the business elite, agreeing to meet with them and shutting out labor leaders altogether.[125] Meanwhile, veterans both for and against the strike took matters into their own hands. The Returned Soldiers' Loyalist Association, veterans opposed to the strike and its alleged Bolshevist proclivities, faced off with the Great War Veterans Association's strike supporters, proving that both groups still hungered for combat. Demobilized soldiers roamed Winnipeg streets, some on the hunt for strikers, others convinced of the strike's objectives. Now out of work for more than two weeks, workers were noticeably jittery.[126]

Violence escalated rapidly after the third week of the strike and intensified both sides' resoluteness. A march by the Great War Veterans Association planned for 31 May dramatically changed the nature of the Winnipeg General Strike. Returned soldiers marched from the legislative building to city hall in support of workers' rights to collective bargaining. The event quickly developed into a shouting match between Manitoba premier T. C. Norris and riled up protesters. Daily marches would continue, warned the demonstrators, until employers met workers' demands.[127]

Fearing violence if veterans carried out their threat, Mayor Charles F. Gray turned to the federal government's most senior military commander in the region, Major General Herbert Ketchen, a Boer War and World War I veteran.[128] A career military man and graduate of the prestigious Royal Military College, Ketchen geared up for his new mission. His allegiance evident—he was, after all, an active member of the Citizens' Committee—Ketchen had been covertly preparing for Winnipeg's outbreak by recruiting unemployed police officers, armed guards, and demobilized soldiers, among them the Royal Canadian Horse Artillery.[129] Adding fuel to the fire, Prime Minister Borden authorized the relocation of a unit of North West Mounted Police officers, who reached Winnipeg just in time for the bloodshed.

Chaos erupted during a march scheduled for 10 June. Crowds both in favor of and against the Winnipeg General Strike came to a head at Portage Avenue and Main Street, the city's main throughway. That intersection marked the boundary between the business district and the working-class black and immigrant neighborhood to its north. Marchers rolled back their sleeves, outshouted each other, and, when fists and bricks flew, sought shelter. Members of the Order of Sleeping Car Porters peppered that crowd, siding with workers against corporate and governmental indifference to their plight.

The riot, now known by its grisly epithet Bloody Saturday, saw thousands of angry Winnipeggers armed with clubs, bats, and bottles. Some, accounts alleged, threateningly waved their revolvers at their adversaries. In truth, the North West Mounted Police, called to the region by Prime Minister Borden, outgunned protesters on both sides and were also the first to use their weapons.[130] Before calm came to the city that night, Mounties had shot down two strikers and injured countless others. While the riot was short lived, it served as an alarming display of a complete breakdown of law and order. The morning after Bloody Saturday, an antistrike demonstrator goose stepped into the North End and shot a striker dead. The murder took place in the heart of Winnipeg's black district—Main Street at Higgins.[131]

The Winnipeg General Strike quickly deteriorated after Bloody Saturday when strikers realized that their convictions could cost them their lives. It had already cost most of them their jobs. The Borden administration and city council swore out arrest warrants against the Strike Committee's leaders, hoping that with its leadership jailed the strike would fizzle out. Veterans in favor of the strike's principles continued their planned marches but only met with more violence at the hands of Mounties and bands of armed business-men. The Strike Committee finally called off the strike on 26 June, after winning assurances from the mayor that an investigative commission would review workers' demands, though talk of that commission eventually died down, just as workers' tempers did as well.[132]

The Winnipeg General Strike failed to win the right to collective bargain-ing and wage increases in the metal and building trades. It did, however, confirm that an indelible working-class spirit thrived across Canada after World War I. Workers—black and white, male and female, immigrant and Canadian—had banded together across the nation. Canadian workers regis-tered their discontent with existing employment and governmental policies by walking off their jobs in support of one another. The Winnipeg General Strike also fostered coalitions unimagined before the war. Women defended their access to work and bore the cost of company repression for doing so. Black railroaders, vilified by white running tradesmen before the war, stood shoulder to shoulder with other strikers and defended their neighborhood from rogue white veterans. The workers' Strike Committee repeatedly cred-ited those partnerships in its press.

The Winnipeg General Strike emboldened black railroaders and confirmed their racial and working-class consciousness. That affirmation, however, car-ried weighty penalties, especially for the OSCP's cadre of leaders. Throughout the interwar period, managers for the Canadian Pacific Railway and Cana-dian National Railways targeted black unionists, John A. Robinson in particu-lar, and tormented them for their union activities among other railroaders. In fact, most of the OSCP's leadership suffered from bouts of unemployment throughout the interwar period.[133] Despite continued browbeating by railway executives, Robinson's commitment to trade unionism and racial uplift never wavered.

African Canadian sleeping car porters, a unionized community of work-ers by 1919, capitalized on the momentum gained from Winnipeg's general strike. Robinson spared no time making black workers' needs known to the federal government and his fellow white unionists. In June 1919, the same month Winnipeg's six-week strike finally came to an end, Robinson repre-sented CPR porters before the federal Board of Conciliation to argue that the Canadian Pacific Railway underpaid its sleeping car porters, in violation of the rates set by the Department of Labour.[134] Robinson stressed that existing porters' salaries fell well below a living wage, especially since passengers' tips had also decreased during the war. Whereas Canadian sleeping car porters had received an average of sixty-five dollars in monthly tips in 1914, during the Great War gratuities dropped by more than 25 percent. Moreover, porters working for the CPR were the lowest paid on Canadian lines. Pullman and Canadian National Railways porters earned monthly salaries of eighty dollars in 1919, while the Canadian Pacific Railway paid its same class of workers nearly 15 percent less.[135]

The Board of Conciliation concurred with Robinson's charge that the CPR underpaid its black workers, making them victims of detrimental wage disparity, and ordered an immediate increase of porters' salaries to seventy-five dollars for standard cars and eighty-five dollars for special tourist and observation sleepers.[136] This wage hike represented a 60 percent leap from January 1918 wages—a meaningful gain given that Winnipeg metal and construction tradesmen's demand of a 10 percent raise had resulted in utter failure and set off a frenzied six-week strike that same month.

After World War I, Robinson's sleeping car porters union capitalized on the Industrial Disputes Investigation Act as an important federally sanctioned vehicle for improving and securing black railwaymen's rights. Robinson would appear before the IDIA Board of Conciliation several more times over the next decade. Building on the momentum from his successful CPR dispute, Robinson in the fall of 1919 took on the cause of CNR sleeping car porters and dining car attendants, who along with white railwaymen represented by the Canadian Brotherhood of Railway Employees, were negotiating new wage schedules with their employer. At issue was the company's plans to separate workers' negotiating schedules across regions. CNR executives hoped that this new scheme would prevent future national strike actions. CBRE representatives insisted that contractual bargaining be determined according to departments, with the contracts of engineers, running tradesmen, and shop workers negotiated separately from those of sleeping car porters.

By demanding separate racialized negotiating categories, white workers returned to a prewar method of managing tensions with employers, revealing that they had at best been fair-weather allies. In actuality, the negotiating tactics of both parties—management and white labor—unveiled just how much white supremacy still governed labor-management relations. If CNR executives and the CBRE's white union leadership disagreed on the terms of their contracts, both groups eagerly embraced Jim Crow. White workers expressly demanded that black parlor, sleeping, and dining car workers operate from separate wage scales.[137] In so doing, white trade unionists returned to a prewar segregationist contractual model, belying any claim that the Canadian labor revolts of 1919 had transformed Canadian trade unionists' racialized views. While the new agreement procured paid holidays and time and a half when working Sundays for white railroaders, article 14 Jim Crowed virtually all black railroaders out of these benefits. Since conductors, all of them white, had secured paid holidays since 1913, the CNR could not therefore claim that working holidays was a unique requirement of sleeping and dining car employees. The segregation of black railroaders—showcased in a separate contractual clause—further epitomized their marginalization in the railway workforce.[138]

White unionists' insistence on segregated wage schedules during the September 1919 IDIA proceedings exposed that race infected trade union ideology in Canada just as it had before the war and as it had for so long in the United States. By shutting out their fellow black union men before the Board of Conciliation, white railway unionists betrayed their black co-workers and, in so doing, also failed themselves. They confirmed that, just as white railway executives had for decades, they too wantonly used black workers as bargaining tools: railway managers strong-armed white workers with imported black labor; and for their part, white trade unionists insisted on Jim Crow as a condition for peaceful postwar labor relations. Yet white union men consistently played into corporate managers' hands by upholding white supremacy at the greater cost of stronger national trade unionism. To be precise, Jim Crow proved an easier and cheaper concession than higher wages, safer working conditions, and benefits for all railroaders. Paradoxically, white railway unionists' tenacious endorsement of white supremacy undermined national black railway unionism more than any railway corporation's actions prior to 1920.

For the Order of Sleeping Car Porters, a union founded by Canadian National Railways porters, this betrayal at the hands of white co-workers rubbed salt on old wounds. White CNR unionists' insistence on Jim Crow contractual terms reinforced the subordination of black railroaders by both corporate managers and white railwaymen. As Robinson watched these proceedings, he witnessed white trade unionists pairing up with railway executives, proving that white workers could neither be trusted nor counted on when white supremacy was at stake. Though railroaders shared a belief in collective bargaining and the right to unionization, white trade unionists confirmed that their vision unmistakably excluded black workers.

Against the background of the September 1919 Board of Conciliation debacle, John A. Robinson intensified his assault on Jim Crow in Canadian trade unionism by reviving his union's offensive on the Canadian Brotherhood of Railway Employees' white-only membership clause. Robinson set his sights on the CBRE's annual convention meeting in Ottawa in late September; this time, the OSCP resolved not to back down from its campaign to abolish white supremacy in Canadian railway unionism, especially given the CBRE's control over contract negotiations with railway companies.

Unable to shake off Robinson and his OSCP, CBRE president Aaron Mosher put the question of black membership before his delegation. Having proven their mettle during the Winnipeg General Strike, Mosher stressed in his opening address at the convention that the "O. S. C. P. made splendid progress and the officers of that organization have shown marked ability and a thorough knowledge of organizational work." He admitted that black railroaders' courageous involvement in the "general strike in Winnipeg in which many of the members of the O. S. C. P. engaged, [had] very seriously affected them." The CBRE president asked members to weigh the question of black membership carefully, concluding, "I have every confidence that they will survive and become a powerful branch of our organization."[139]

On 1 October 1919, delegates gathered in the capital Ottawa crammed into St. Patrick's Hall to deliver their vote on the union's ten-year white-only policy. Many of the members recalled that the debate over black membership at the previous convention in Port Arthur had developed into a tempestuous argument, and they hoped that this time the same would not be true.[140] Whereas no CBRE representatives had supported the OSCP's first bid for membership the year before, this time some white trade unionists from Toronto and Montreal seconded the motion for the admission of black railwaymen.[141]

Yet even those in favor of sharing the stage with black unionists stayed true to white supremacist tenets. The CBRE agreed to abolish its white-only membership clause but upheld a racialized hierarchy within the union's ranks. President Aaron Mosher delayed the inclusion of black workers for an additional year, appeasing, at least for a time, those members vehemently opposed to integrating the union.[142] Most important, white CBRE members conceded to black members with the proviso that they be segregated in auxiliaries. Insofar as auxiliary status was solely reserved for wives and other female relatives, the CBRE's marginalization of black men into a segregated, gendered, submembership framework plainly mapped out the conditions of black partnership. Despite continued pressure from black railwaymen, this racialized institutional structure remained the CBRE union vision and organizational structure until 1965—fully fifteen years longer than even southern white railway unionists were willing to uphold Jim Crow in their workforce.[143]

If Mosher imagined that auxiliary status would pacify black unionists, he was sorely mistaken. The Road Roamers, Toronto's local 175; Eureka, Montreal's local 128; the OSCP, Winnipeg's local 130; and the Sleeping Car Porters' Association, Halifax's local 36, sent outspoken members to every CBRE national convention every year as of 1921.[144] Additionally, sleeping car porters tirelessly served on the CBRE's various provincial and national grievance, negotiating, and regional committees.[145] Black unionists carried on their attack on the CBRE's segregated power structure, raising the issue at every national convention and in countless letters to the head office in Ottawa.[146] Every time they challenged the CBRE's racist organizational structure, African Canadian labor leaders gave meaning to their racialized working-class consciousness.

Mosher's Jim Crow compromise of 1919 made clear for John A. Robinson and other members of the Order of Sleeping Car Porters that white supremacy would continue to thrive in the Canadian Brotherhood of Railway Employees. William Greening, the CBRE's official historian, recalled that in Mosher's opinion extending membership to black railroaders had been a noteworthy enterprise. White trade union leaders were convinced that, once again, the CBRE had proven itself the vanguard of Canadian trade unionism by being "the first union in Canada to abolish membership restrictions based on racial grounds."[147] Mosher and Greening's flattering depiction of the CBRE membership conveniently ignored that the black railwaymen's union, the OSCP, had never excluded white workers. As Robinson pointedly reminded Mosher in later years, it had never been "our intention to have a 'color line' in the Order of Sleeping Car Porters."[148] Mosher and Greening's praise of white rank-and-file CBRE members similarly obscured that white supremacy remained the bedrock of Canadian railway unionism, even after admitting black members.

While Mosher applauded his members' valiant resolution, black trade unionists knew that they were the ones most intent on beheading Jim Crow in Canadian trade unionism. Always the politically savvy moderator, Robinson understood that by striking "white" from its organizational bylaws, the CBRE merely opened the floor for more purposeful debate about the role for black unionists. Years later, Robinson denounced Mosher's two-faced rhetoric, reminding him that "equal status in eligibility to membership is one thing which was accomplished when the word 'white' was struck out of your constitution. Equal status to schedule conditions—working conditions is the important concern of the Sleeping Car Porters." Robinson also accused CBRE executives of treating sleeping car porters as "infants" and "repeatedly giv[ing] away the[ir] rights . . . regardless of the contentions and protests of the Porters without using the means established . . . to protect said rights and to correct injustices."[149] Though Canadian sleeping car porters formally belonged to the CBRE, they remained frustrated with the union's indifference to their grievances, particularly with respect to wages, hours of work, seniority, promotions, and racial discrimination.

Conversely, Robinson's dedication to sleeping car porters' concerns never faltered. Having made his point at the CBRE convention and won the initial battle for admission, he moved on to his next round of fights with Canadian railway executives. CPR sleeping car porters fired for promoting unionization during the Winnipeg General Strike brought the company before the Department of Labour's Board of Conciliation in January 1920.[150] On this his second time before the board in less than a year, Robinson spoke on behalf of dismissed black railroaders, thereby solidifying his reputation as a dogged labor activist. He contended that the OSCP men, thirty-six in all, had lost their jobs for "claiming the right to their own organization and representatives."[151] Company managers, however, alleged that the porters' Grievance Committee turned otherwise compliant workers into rabble-rousers clamoring for collective bargaining rights. By exposing the CPR's systemic exploitation of black workers, Robinson hoped that the federally administered Board of Conciliation would hand down a scathing indictment of the CPR's segregationist employment policies.

In truth, railway managers did not object to collective bargaining, having recognized white workers' right to unionization as early as 1908. Rather, they took exception to dealing with black workers as men, as evidenced by the CPR's refusal to recognize the black union's petition before the Board of Conciliation. CPR porter R. O. Caines testified that company managers refused to acknowledge the porters' chosen committee or to hear their grievances, exposing the company's infantilization of black employees.[152] Instead, the CPR's sleeping car department manager stormed out of the negotiations, once again leaving the hearings without any corporate representation. CPR executives also declined giving any explanations for firing their black workers by claiming that under the terms of sleeping car porters' contracts, no rationale was required.

The Canadian Pacific Railway's willful sabotage of the IDIA's proceedings made clear its intention to preserve its racially segregated nonunionized black workforce, as it had since before the Great War. The full extent of Jim Crow employment practices in the Canadian railway industry, the board learned, included company coercion of black workers. For years, CPR managers had been strong-arming prospective sleeping car porters operating on Canadian Pacific lines into yellow dog contracts pledging that they would not join a union and could be fired without forewarning or reasons given. The CPR's manager admitted that "no other [CPR] workers" were subjected to such discriminatory contractual demands.[153] At issue, then, was whether the CPR could force black workers to sign away their rights or fire them at will.

The Board of Conciliation completely sidestepped the OSCP's protest of CPR yellow dog contracts for its black workforce. Judge Colin Snider ruled that, though the company's pledges were arguably irregular, they were certainly not illegal. Snider hoped to appease CPR porters with higher wages and seniority guidelines, ignoring the dismissed porters' petition altogether and not requiring their permanent reinstatement. His new wage schedule, however, codified alarming labor-management standards and set off two more decades of protest in federal court by steadfast black unionists.

First, Snider fragmented sleeping car porters into five divisional negotiating schedules, making it decidedly harder for black railwaymen to transfer to other areas of the country without losing a portion of their salaries or their accrued seniority. In so doing, the Board of Conciliation greatly enhanced the CPR's control over its black labor. Company managers could curtail the spread of trade unionism among sleeping car porters by confining certain workers within a given region and then picking them off one at a time.

Second, the board upheld the CPR's practice of leasing out porters to other railway companies without any consent required from its workers. Article 5 of this proposed contract confirmed that during periods of reduced service the CPR reserved the right to "loan" employees to other railway companies in the United States or Canada. Article 8 mandated that porters laid off for more than one year lost all seniority rights; such an employee, upon rehire, returned "to all intents and purposes a new employee."[154] This clause virtually guaranteed that black railroaders would never enjoy any meaningful seniority or job security, since the CPR relied heavily on seasonal immigrant contract workers from the United States and the West Indies. Moreover, it placed a strain on black families who could see their fathers—and chief wage earners—shipped off across the country or to the United States for work. Porters, already denied their right to unionization and forced into yellow dog agreements, now grappled with railway executives sanctioned to treat them like easily transferable rolling stock. Given that the Board of Conciliation served as the federal government's instrument for intervening in labor relations, the proposed 1920 ruling set a disquieting blueprint for a racially stratified policy designed to both nip black unionism in the bud and arm employers with greater control over their workforce.

That control by employers extended into workers' personal lives and had a measurable impact on the composition of black families during the interwar period. For one thing, the federal Board of Conciliation determined that unwed porters and those without children should be fired first and promised preference on rehire when men were once again needed, a protective measure popular since the war that favored veteran family men for employment. Additionally, article 10 robbed African Canadian sleeping car porters of seniority if they requested and accepted transfers to other districts, forcing workers to remain on the job regardless of the strained working climate in that region.[155] Moreover, it made family reunification that much harder and added financial pressure on black families who then had to maintain two households. Adding insult to injury, the board protected the CPR's right to fire sleeping car porters at will, though it conceded to a toothless bureaucratic appeal process.

Accordingly, the Board of Conciliation's damaging plan endorsed the CPR's existing approach to black railwaymen as a disposable class of workers. CPR executives trusted that curtailing the spread of black trade unionism would be much easier under these new guidelines. If the CPR could still fire African Canadian sleeping car porters without ever accounting for its actions, CPR executives surmised that it would not be long before all black unionists were purged from the rails.

Horrified by the proposed contract, Board of Conciliation member Fred Bancroft stood out as the only dissenter. Bancroft's minority report denounced the CPR's actions, citing the ruling as a disturbing and blatant violation of black railroaders' rights to collective bargaining, fair working conditions, due process, and the freedom to work and live wherever they wanted. Likewise, Bancroft condemned the CPR's unreasonable demands on black railroaders. Already burdened by low wages and tenuous job security, the CPR required that sleeping car porters pay for their own uniforms, meals, and accommodations while on the road. Exacerbating matters, Canadian Pacific Railway executives held porters fiscally responsible for all the equipment on sleepers. If passengers helped themselves to sleeping car keepsakes during their trip, as they so often did, porters defrayed the cost of stolen sheets, ashtrays, napkins, pillowcases, cutlery, dishes, and towels.[156] The company also taxed black railroaders' labor by deadheading porters and not paying them when on call or preparing their cars for a run.[157] Bancroft maintained that such deductions and penalties were all the more egregious for men— some of whom were Great War veterans—earning less than a living wage.

Bancroft pointed out that the Board of Conciliation's report had remained silent on paid holidays, maximum monthly hours for sleeping car workers, and mandatory time off at the end of runs and offered a poorly constructed seniority rights scheme. Worst of all, Bancroft rejected the CPR's resolution against recognizing collective bargaining rights for black railroaders and their union. In Bancroft's opinion, the company's insistence that it reserved exclusive right to handpick a "welfare committee," a group of porters' representatives, violated black railwaymen's choice of the OSCP as their selected negotiators. The CPR's purported welfare committee remained the only puppet employee bargaining unit ostensibly permitted by management.[158]

Bancroft castigated the Board of Conciliation for desperately failing the dismissed porters. He pointed out that, if the majority report's aim had been to equalize sleeping car porters' wages across Canadian lines by applying CNR rates to the CPR, the ruling had also missed the mark. Other stark discrepancies singled out CPR porters from those working for the Canadian National Railways. For instance, the CNR did not sequester black railroaders in its sleeping car service; African Canadian railwaymen also worked as cooks and dining car attendants, higher-wage positions not accessible on the CPR after World War I. Moreover, porters on the Canadian National Railways had their meals substantially subsidized by the company, while Bancroft concluded that "at a most conservative estimate, it costs the porters on the C. P. R. at least $16 per month more for meals than the porters on the C. N. R."[159] Most important, the CNR did not coerce black railwaymen into yellow dog contracts. Why, then, asked Bancroft, was the board not concerned with abolishing that CPR practice in the spirit of uniform industrial standards?

Judge Snider and Fred Bancroft submitted their reports to Minister of Labour Gideon Robertson in February 1920. The minister rejected the board's findings, ordering the three-man panel to "state in plain terms what in their opinion ought or ought not to be done by the Canadian Pacific Railway Company in regard to the dismissal of its porters." Although the board heard no additional evidence from the CPR or the OSCP, its new majority decision, handed down one month later, sided firmly with railway management. The Board of Conciliation's majority decision gave federal assent to the CPR's racist employment policies, concluding that "in our opinion the Canadian Pacific Railway acted within its rights under the Contracts of hiring and dismissing the seven porters" and recommended "that such action be approved."[160]

Once again, Fred Bancroft objected to the board's majority ruling, accusing that "the recommendation is illogical, and according to the evidence unfair to the men." In effect, the board's decision amounted to a dizzying display of circular reasoning that left Bancroft frustrated with the duplicitous partnership between the federal government and railway management. How, asked Bancroft, could the board definitively determine that "the men were not dismissed for being members of the Order or Union" without any corporate reasoning given for the dismissals?[161] After all, the CPR maintained that its yellow dog covenant with sleeping car porters empowered it to fire workers without ever justifying its actions.

The OSCP's 1920 Board of Conciliation hearings laid bare the scope of black railroaders' strained labor-management relations. Ever since its creation in 1917, the OSCP had been wrestling trade unionists and employers intent on upholding a segregationist workforce structure ten years in the making. By protesting racialized employment policies in the Canadian railroad industry, however, African Canadian railway unionists displayed determined grit against corporate intimidation. Emboldened by racial and working-class pride, the dismissed union men—and the others testifying on their behalf— affirmed that they were prepared to lose their jobs in defense of their rights both as workers and as citizens. By bringing Canadian railway executives before the federal government's Board of Conciliation, African Canadian railwaymen demonstrated a keen understanding of Canadian labor law and federal machinery, as well as the savoir faire to make them work on their behalf.

Although the OSCP secured few gains during the 1920 IDIA proceedings, John A. Robinson celebrated what he saw as a more meaningful triumph for the union. Despite CPR managers' stubborn opposition to recognizing black railwaymen's collective bargaining rights, Robinson and the Order of Sleeping Car Porters had successfully forced the company's hand. Insofar as the minister of labour had ordered CPR executives into negotiations with African Canadian unionists by requiring them to attend hearings, the OSCP had in fact bargained with the Canadian Pacific Railway. A keen political broker, Robinson knew that with such a precedent established with the largest employer of black workers in Canada, the OSCP could do battle with all other Canadian railway companies. Until that time, no other coalition of black railroaders in North America had accomplished such a bargaining feat.[162]

The 1920 IDIA Board of Conciliation proceedings with its sleeping car porters must have made clear for CPR management just how its stealthy traffic in black immigrant workers could backfire. If Robinson stood before them, what others among their imported ranks could galvanize African Canadian railwaymen to their defense? John A. Robinson, sitting across the table from CPR managers during the board's hearings, must have seemed like the company's worst nightmare. The CPR had recruited Robinson from St. Kitts; within just a decade, he faced down his former supervisors and exposed the CPR's exploitation of immigrant black workers before the federal government.

Against that background, the OSCP's 1920 Board of Conciliation challenge was in effect a success for a union with only three years of experience. The OSCP committed its resources to such battles, though fully aware of postwar corporate and federal antiunion sentiment. Robinson wagered that continued federal attention to black workers' plights would eventually undermine Jim Crow in the Canadian railway industry. Consequently, he spent the 1920s dueling Jim Crow in Canada's workforce, laws, and trade unions; he repeatedly fought for African Canadian railwaymen on other Canadian lines, arguing their cases before the Industrial Disputes Investigation Board in 1923, 1926, and again in 1927.[163] Thus the OSCP's leadership dedicated the 1920s to giving meaning to its status as the only active union for black railroaders in Canada. Within six years of its inauguration, the OSCP had successfully negotiated contracts for all African Canadian railwaymen on every major Canadian line.[164] Viewed from a global perspective, Robinson's achievement takes on even greater significance because, as one of the largest corporations in the world, the CPR prized its reputation as a transportation juggernaut.

John A. Robinson epitomized African Canadian railroaders' indomitable courage. A powerful race and union advocate, he wisely promoted shared leadership of Canada's nascent black railway union movement. He emphasized that the movement could succeed only if it was firmly rooted across a national stage. Sustaining national railway unionism among African Canadian sleeping car porters depended on learning and sharing union leadership skills. By the 1920s, black railroaders in Halifax, Montreal, Toronto, Winnipeg, Calgary, Edmonton, and Vancouver had made national unionization a viable institution. Robinson hoped that with a nationwide network company executives could not target a handful of leaders, killing the movement at its source in Winnipeg. Since many of the OSCP's members were foreign-born, the CNR and CPR could also threaten black railroaders with deportation. A black railway union movement of national scope likewise ensured nationwide attention to African Canadian railroaders' needs and grievances. More significant, it pointed to an emerging national consciousness and alliance among African Canadians too long overlooked by historians.

WORLD WAR I RADICALLY transformed African Canadians' lives. The world's first industrialized war also gave way to unprecedented strife in Canada. White Canadians and their government went into the war defending a racially divided society carefully crafted over the course of several decades. Black Canadians marched into the Great War fighting Jim Crow, just as they had done in years leading up to the war. In 1914, African Canadians wanted to fight to save an imperiled British Empire but found by war's end that they were the ones fighting off brutish attacks from fellow white servicemen. White Canadians and their government persistently denied that disgruntled soldiers had in fact racialized their discontent. The Borden administration added insult to injury by disavowing black Canadian soldiers' contributions after spending years discouraging black enlistment in the first place.

Black Canadians walked into World War I determined to prove to white Canadians that they were meaningful citizens worthy of the full rewards of citizenship. They returned from the Great War believing it for themselves. They spent the next decades unrepentantly demanding their rights from those white Canadians most opposed to equal citizenship. During World War I, black Canadians created various institutions and infrastructures that made real, perhaps for the first time, that they were organized communities equipped with national and international ties. A national black press and railway union reinforced these new bonds, allowing for the rapid exchange of information, news, strategies, and political ideas. These same structures, initially conceived for mobilization, survived the war and helped African Canadians navigate the turbulent twenties and economically devastating thirties.

Insofar as World War I produced a tangible transnational race consciousness among black Canadians, the Winnipeg General Strike of 1919 affirmed African Canadians' equally powerful radicalized working-class consciousness. During the Great War, black Canadian railroaders came into greater contact with other workers—black and white, male and female, immigrant and Canadian—throughout the dominion. They learned that they shared not only the same concerns as white men but also a common plight with women, immigrants, and other workers of color.

John A. Robinson's Order of Sleeping Car Porters institutionalized black railroaders' working-class consciousness into a national black trade union movement that challenged Canada's largest railway companies—the CNR, CPR, and GTR—and made the otherwise unbendable white-only Canadian Brotherhood of Railway Employees bend indeed. Black workers struck down the CBRE's Jim Crow membership policy, embracing the outcome of their fight—segregated locals—as an imperfect first step in a long battle against segregation in Canadian trade unionism. And when workers in Winnipeg took to the streets in the spring of 1919, black railway unionists understood their ire and joined them not in rhetoric but in practice, thereby dotting the mobs marching outside city hall on Bloody Saturday. These actions cost this first wave of black Canadian race men and trade union advocates their jobs but never their determination. Instead, as we shall see, African Canadians spent the interwar years investing this resolve into racial uplift and self-help organizations, wedding transnational race consciousness with international trade union advocacy.

CHAPTER FOUR

Building an Empire, Uplifting a Race

Race, Uplift, and Transnational Alliances

Though still dazed by race riots, disruptive strikes, and a double-cross by white workers, African Canadian railroaders licked their war wounds and focused on rebuilding their communities during the 1920s. Having proven his mettle, John A. Robinson broadened his vision of working-class trade unionism after the war, worrying less about alliances with other white railwaymen and concentrating more on racial uplift programs within black communities. For those fortunate enough to know him, and others content to have heard his name whispered in railway cars, black-owned boarding-houses, and African Canadian diners, Robinson personified sleeping car porters' undaunted courage. Certainly Canadian sleeping car porters knew the man who had stared down his bosses before the federal government's Board of Conciliation, making clear that black railroaders would not stand for exploitative employment practices without putting up a fight even at the risk of reprisals. White railway unionists also recognized Robinson, who, after a three-year campaign for admission in the Canadian Brotherhood of Railway Employees, insisted that black railwaymen's membership would never be questioned again.

The Great War and labor's rebellion had reinforced the importance of national and international mobilization for African Canadians. Black soldiers returned from the war front armed with a sense of fellowship and racial pride that transcended state-bound nationalism. Sleeping car porters, with many veterans of the Winnipeg General Strike, also shared a feeling of cama-raderie as union men; in subsequent years, both groups—porters and soldiers

—invested that esprit de corps into sundry racial uplift institutions. Accordingly, blacks in postwar Canada cultivated new relationships that shaped their understanding of collective bargaining, their right to work, citizenship, and their sense of community. They employed sophisticated strategies in defense of these citizenship rights, skillfully blocking the full onslaught of Jim Crow ideology into Canadian life during the interwar years.

African Canadian organizations created in the aftermath of World War I deliberately gave meaning and structure to the emerging consciousness that people like John A. Robinson fostered. Racial uplift organizations mushroomed during the 1920s and 1930s and became increasingly pivotal to African Canadians' survival, especially once the full impact of the Great Depression hit black communities. These associations reflected the international political awakening of people of African descent to the promise of race pride ideology. African Americans, West Indians, black Britons, and African Canadians manifested that hope with the broad range of associations created for and by blacks in the Atlantic world between the wars.[1]

Like their counterparts in the United States, West Indies, and Great Britain, African Canadian bellwethers experimented with various organizational models. Their institutions addressed women's rights, workers' plights, education, immigration, decolonization, art, literature, racial uplift, manhood, economics, and politics. At times, Canadian race men and women adopted nationalist rhetoric as a political tactic for uniquely Canadian problems. At other times, international organizations like the Universal Negro Improvement Association or the National Association for the Advancement of Colored People seemed more fruitful avenues for political action, as in the international lynching case of Matthew Bullock, a North Carolina fugitive who sought political asylum in Canada in 1922. Likewise, organizational leaders readily wedded religious and secular institutions when they shared a common goal. In either case, African Canadian organizational leaders understood the value of weighing different approaches and ideologies when assessing their applicability to the Canadian political archetype.

Whether overtly framed as white supremacy or couched in nativist rhetoric, race dominated postwar Canadian political discourse and federal policy. Some white Canadians rationalized that restrictions on immigration, deportation of immigrants, and control of people of color would restore calm to a nation rocked by foreign turmoil, imported labor radicals, and race riots. Throughout the interwar period, white newsmen, judges, politicians, unionists, and citizens promoted white supremacy and pressed for institutionalized racism in employment policy, access to state services, and federal legislation.

By the 1920s, white Canadian fears increasingly crystallized into xenophobic policies and advocacy of legalized Jim Crow, be it segregated seating in theaters or redlining neighborhoods. Accordingly, white Canadians returned to a prewar racial ideal first seen in the aftermath of African American immigration to Western Canada during the early 1900s.

Given that attacks on African Canadians' citizenship rights soared after the Great War, African Canadian sleeping car porters and their families became the vanguard of local, national, and international organizations dedicated to the interests of blacks in Canada. Sleeping car porters' extensive mobility promoted national and transnational political activism insofar as work on the rails gave black Canadian railwaymen critical access to urban centers from Halifax to Vancouver, from Montreal to Los Angeles, and from Toronto to New Orleans. African Canadian railroaders' various social and political organizations provided fraternity, recreational options, and political news to men whose work made them temporary residents in countless North American cities.[2]

African Canadian railroaders traversed provincial and international boundaries, quickly learning how to negotiate each region's distinct political order. For instance, knowledge of French in Quebec improved access to social services, while operating runs to northern American cities required a different set of skills, since de facto segregation regimented the lives of African Americans in Boston, New York, Detroit, and Chicago. Working for the railroads also plunged African Canadian railwaymen in and out of a legally segregated American South.[3] To the extent that African Canadian railroaders cut across linguistic and racial barriers as a condition of their employment, their binary existence demanded a firm understanding of each region and country's political culture. African Canadian railroaders' very survival, in fact, depended on their rapid discernment of social and political cultures. This transnational employment-based cultural intersection reinforced the importance of creating organizations that provided African Canadian workers with the tools needed for culturally and nationally transgressive lifestyles.

Sleeping car porters and their wives dominated the leadership of African Canadian organizations. Twenty years of experience fighting employment displacement, immigration discrimination, and xenophobic trade unionists turned Canadian sleeping car porters into masterful political activists. Founded during the Great War, the Order of Sleeping Car Porters upheld its crusade for black workers' rights in subsequent years. J. A. Robinson, B. F. Jones, and V. I. Coward quickly became the leading supporters of national black trade unionism in Canada.

African Canadian women also joined the political scene and became vocal civil rights activists.[4] Through African Canadian churches and such organizations as Montreal's Coloured Women's Club and the Women's Charitable Benevolent Association, an African Canadian variant of the YWCA, black women contested the encroachment of Jim Crow in Canada as well as some white Canadians' postwar fascination with lynching. African Canadian women also applied continuous pressure on the federal government's antiblack immigration policies. During the twenties, sleeping car porters' wives and families became well versed in trade union culture, skillfully implementing church, press, education, and consumer advocacy as racial uplift and self-help mechanisms.[5] By World War II, they formed formidable continentwide trade union partnerships with the Brotherhood of Sleeping Car Porters' Ladies' Auxiliary.[6] Astute political strategists, African Canadian sleeping car porters and their families mastered the art of utilizing various approaches when articulating their political demands.

With their lives and livelihoods jeopardized by white supremacist rationalization, African Canadians vigorously contested racialized restrictions of their citizenship rights. African Canadian men and women diversified and intensified organized resistance to white supremacy in Canada throughout the interwar period. Their organizations served as crucial vehicles of political protest in trade unionism, immigration, employment, antilynching, and desegregation movements. African Canadian social and political organizations, however, were not strictly reactionary. African Canadian organizational leaders shrewdly anticipated their communities' economic, social, and political needs, satisfying them when federal and municipal agencies would not. During the interwar years, African Canadians upheld their civil rights demands for fair access to housing, education, financing, employment, and health care. Therefore, African Canadian social and political organizations also served an important purpose as community-building devices.

SLEEPING CAR PORTERS WHO assumed leadership of their communities after the war understood the importance of coalitions with other organizations—namely, the black church and the nascent black press. Both had proven formidable partners during the war and held great promise as advocates. Black labor leaders understood that the new black Canadian press, the *Dawn of Tomorrow* in particular, provided a vital platform for national information campaigns and introduced otherwise nonunionized men and women to union culture. For that reason, African Canadian sleeping car porters capitalized on their access to a black press as a critical weapon for political action.

The *Canadian Observer* had demonstrated its effectiveness during the Great War by encouraging blacks in Canada to join the war effort. The *Atlantic Advocate* had explained how African Canadian families could contribute to victory bonds, stretch out rations, and send their sons abroad in defense of their country. Most important, African Canadian newsmen emphasized virtuous citizenship. The *Atlantic Advocate*'s editors proclaimed that during the Great War African Canadian "men [had] learn[ed] lessons which piping times of peace cannot afford . . . discipline, duty before pleasure, obedience, patience under suffering, courage." These lessons taught in war, averred the black Haligonian newspaper, also made great citizens of black Canadians in times of peace. "In steadfastness and self-sacrifice they are finding opportunities to high and noble and unselfish deeds which not otherwise could they gain."[7]

African Canadian journalists insisted that a vibrant black press would foster a strong sense of community among blacks across Canada and pointed to the same work being carried out by a cadre of African American journalists. Owned and operated by Freemasons who were also sleeping car porters and mariners, the *Atlantic Advocate* avowed, "The intellectual progress of the Colored Americans may be emphasized by reference to that highly modern and civilized agent of education known as 'The Press.'" What's more, the black press played a critical role as watchdog against assaults on African Americans' civil rights, turning black journalists into "soldiers without swords," a moniker bestowed by W. E. B. Du Bois. African Canadian newsmen envisioned a similar radical potential in Canada for "many strong and vigorous writers who [would] be able to crystallize the energies of this race into a determined effort to maintain their position in the onward movement of the human race."[8] James F. Jenkins, the *Dawn of Tomorrow*'s chief editor, underscored that the "mission of race papers is to keep the world informed of our upward striving; to tell of the many good deeds we are doing and of the noble thoughts we are thinking."[9] Sharing these "noble thoughts" was often dangerous work for black intellectuals, who worried about censure, FBI harassment, and violent retaliation. J. Edgar Hoover trained the FBI on A. Philip Randolph, W. E. B. Du Bois, Monroe Trotter, Ida B. Wells, and Marcus Garvey during the interwar years precisely because of the thoughts they advanced in the black press.[10]

The mass migration of African Americans in the first half of the twentieth century, first within the South and then to points north and west, breathed new life into the black press. African American newspapers born during this period catered to an overtly urban population in the South, North, and West.

Moreover, black newspapers focused on teaching the stuff of citizenship during the interwar years: how to vote; how to register for school or other public services; who would host a piano recital; where to join a union meeting; where to worship. Most important, the black press coached its readers on how to negotiate social spaces, contested interracial terrains, emphasizing that African Americans should stand their ground, fight for their place. Articles on how to ride streetcars, visit the local swimming pool, or attend the theater point to the quotidian need to fight off displacement, to secure one's rights, however seeming modest, like holding one's seat on the bus. Black newspapers celebrated these small-scale victories, showcasing them to their national readership, uplifting their communities' spirits and sense of entitlement in the process. Put simply, for much of the interwar years the work of the black press in Canada, as in the United States, focused on uplift: dialing up black political demands, discussing workers' rights, raising educational expectations, and fostering a deeply rooted sense of pride. Perhaps no other black figure did it better at this time than Marcus Garvey, who over the course of only a few years amassed a huge international following for his Universal Negro Improvement Association, thanks in large part to his internationally circulated multilingual newspaper the *Negro World*.

For sleeping car porters and union men driven by racial uplift ideals, African Canadian newspapers became important sustenance as a tool for union work. Fully aware of this railway readership, African Canadian editors dedicated regular columns addressing life on the rails. The *Canadian Observer*'s column "Trainmen" proselytized on work ethics and proper comportment at work, as well as in the black community writ large. "Try each day to prove your intelligence by working hard and studying hard along some well-outlined course," proposed the *Canadian Observer*, because the "big man becomes so thru his own efforts and those of the co-workers whom he has the intelligence to appoint."[11] The *Dawn of Tomorrow* frequently editorialized "the colored men as railway employees" and promised readers within its first months in circulation: "Coming! Big Feature on Railroad Men's Issue."[12]

Canada's black newspapers supplied men and families on the move with a road map into every black Canadian community and were sold in businesses contingent on railway clientele. The *Atlantic Advocate* advertised that it could be purchased in eateries, barbershops, and boardinghouses in Halifax and encouraged readers to "Patronize the Stores that Advertise in the *Atlantic Advocate*. Mention this Paper when you make your purchases."[13] *Canadian Observer* readers bought their copies in Toronto's and Hamilton's railway stations. The Order of Sleeping Car Porters' headquarters in Winnipeg, porters knew well, always carried the *Dawn of Tomorrow*. The African Canadian press also instructed travelers, especially porters, on where they could eat, sleep, and pray in any given Canadian city. Appealing directly to southern African American railroaders, Toronto's Mrs. H. B. Murdock publicized that she provided southern fried chicken, room and board, and could be found just two blocks from the railway station.[14] In Halifax, porters found a reliable meal and warm bed at Mrs. Hattie Bushfan's Railroad Porters' Home, where she promised that her "Home Cooking is a Specialty."[15] In Toronto, wayfarers were encouraged to visit H. O. Rudd's Pool Parlor, while James Hughes advertised his Hamilton operation as a "First-Class Barber Shop [with] razor honing a specialty."[16] In addition, all African Canadian newspapers publicized worship services, Freemasons' meeting times, and social events across Canada.[17]

For black Canadians Jim Crowed out of hotels, restaurants, and leisure facilities, these advertisements worked as important insider information. News columns directed at black railroaders reported on legal matters, antisegregation challenges, deaths, and work-related injuries across the nation.[18] "Race discrimination, characteristic of the United States, received what might be called a 'black eye' here last week," proclaimed the *Dawn of Tomorrow* in August 1924. The newspaper reported that Edmonton's city ordinance barring blacks from public swimming pools had been struck down after black Edmontonians contested that such statutes violated their "rights and privileges [as] rate paying citizens."[19] Though a Toronto-based newspaper, the *Canadian Observer* sadly reported that Montreal's "Mr. A. Knight, who is [also] known . . . as the colored socialist," had died, suggesting that readers west of Quebec might also mourn his passing. In that same issue, editors praised "Our Women Workers W.C.T.U. Owen Sound Doing Good Work" and the "Eureka Friendly Club 1915" for its "good work among the poor and sick" in Toronto.[20]

This attention to the social and political needs of African Canadians indisputably establishes that their communities were organized with institutions inspired by a palpable national racial identity. African Canadian newsmen advanced this racially based national identity as an integral part of their reporting. Columns on the Woman's Christian Temperance Union, Eureka, Universal Negro Improvement Association, and other self-help organizations introduced the broad possibilities offered by racial uplift ideology to African Canadians in towns without such institutions. Moreover, news of how others excelled must have been very comforting for African Canadians spread out across an expansive country. *Dawn of Tomorrow* coeditor Robert Paris Edwards acknowledged, "We, whose lot has fallen within the confines of this great Dominion, need to know each other better . . . and it is for these reasons that this paper has been inaugurated."[21] Edwards also stressed that the purpose of Canada's black press was "to unite and keep our people in touch with each other, thereby maintaining a Race pride."[22]

Sleeping car porters—editing, owning, buying, selling, distributing, and reading black newspapers—became crucial social and political conduits because of their access and connections to that national black Canadian network. When sleeping car porters ate and slept in the black-owned businesses advertised in African Canadian newspapers, they also schooled other black Canadians on workers' rights, shared news of labor unrest, and debated various political solutions. Many of Winnipeg's old-timers remember one such porter, E. L. Philips, affectionately known as "Trotsky," who "preached about communism to anyone who would listen."[23]

Social and political reports in Canada's emerging black press also testify to African Canadians' awareness of postwar race relations throughout North America. African Canadian newspapers frequently reproduced articles from the American Associated Negro Press dealing with desegregation cases, successful African American scholars, and prominent black entrepreneurs. For example, in the fall of 1923, the *Dawn of Tomorrow* notified readers, "Mrs. Johnson Files Suit Re: 'Jim Crow' Car Law" and "High Death Rate among [American] Colored Infants Reported," informing Canadians on the legal and health risks facing their neighbors to the south.[24] Contrary to what earlier historians have posited, sleeping car porters' mobility accelerated— rather than impeded—African Canadian political mobilization and activism specifically because of their access to major North American urban centers.[25] As one former sleeping car porter and labor activist from the 1950s, Eddie Blackman, compellingly put it, "If you wanted to have something known, you always told a porter"—after all, railwaymen certainly cut across the country with news of social and political events with greater speed and efficiency than newspapers.[26] With national and international sleeping car service provided by black railroaders as early as the 1880s, porters could disseminate news without the same burdens met by printing presses, strained budgets, or censorship laws.

Bought and sold alongside black Canadian gazettes, African American newspapers armed African Canadian readers with an alternative account of race relations in North America. The *Messenger, Crisis, Negro World, Courier, Chicago Defender, Opportunity, Baltimore Afro-American,* and *Black*

Worker found a loyal readership throughout Canada, thanks in large part to sleeping car porters who carried them across the border.[27] African Canadian railroaders shuttled black newspapers across the country, often concealing their politically charged cargo from supervisors by storing newspapers in their shoe shine kits. By the 1920s, the *Detroit Informer* paid ever more attention to "Our Canadian Cousins," while the *Black Worker* and *Chicago Defender*'s "Canada News" emphasized the importance of transnational connections with burgeoning African Canadian communities.[28] In fact, economist Ida Greaves's Depression-era study of blacks in Canada confirmed that "race journals published in the United States circulate in Canada, and hence diffuse here the race consciousness and attitudes that are prevalent there."[29]

Most prominent among these race journals spreading "race consciousness and attitudes" in Canada were railway union activist A. Philip Randolph's *Messenger*, and later his *Black Worker*. Randolph and his friend Charles Owen launched the *Messenger* in 1917, a radical newspaper with a decidedly socialist leaning. Throughout its ten-year run, the *Messenger* shaped political and union goals, gave voice to urban black working-class concerns, criticized Jim Crow practices, condemned lynching, called for women's rights, and, most important, persistently advanced an antiwar stance. For this work, Randolph and Owen were briefly jailed and remained under J. Edgar Hoover's hawkish surveillance for the remainder of their lives.

When Randolph trained his attention on forming a union within the Pullman Palace Car Company's ranks, he steered the black working class into trade union radicalism using the pages of the *Black Worker*. Randolph welcomed testimonies from Pullman porters operating in Canada during the interwar years, as evidenced by a porter's glowing account of life in the "Harlem of the North," as Montreal was known to many Americans.[30] The American porter transplanted in Quebec promoted work and migration to Canada and stressed, "Mr. Randolph, the conditions in this district, Montreal, are different from most all of the various ways." For this porter who did not offer his name, alcohol also made Canada a profitable option to life in the United States. "First, we have an advantage here as a result of prohibition. You know, that has made most of us indifferent, to tell you the truth, about our wages." Supplementing their incomes, the porter explained, was of utmost concern, given that it "costs us more to live in Canada than it does in the States." He testified that relations with Pullman's Montreal management were cordial and "we can get all the Pullman Company has to dole out to the porters and possibly a trifle more." Though African Canadian sleeping car porters made good money through railroading and bootlegging, the porter admitted that they recognized that "your move[ment] is for our welfare as a whole. Your interest is our interest."[31]

Mastery of meaningful citizenship, whether from American or Canadian news sources, permeated the black press in Canada. Likewise, black newsmen shaped African Canadians' understanding of themselves as North American race men and empowered citizens. Historian Robin Winks argued that the black press in Canada "rallied Negro opinion on local issues, kept Negro voters in line, attracted modest political advertising in election years, bolstered the churches . . . and joined the chorus that insisted on education" as essential building blocks to citizenship.[32] Accordingly, African Canadian newspapers devoted considerable attention to the actual exercise of citizenship rights.

A material dimension of that citizenship training included being well versed on the hazards threatening blacks throughout North America. With that in mind, by the 1920s, *Dawn of Tomorrow* editors James F. Jenkins and later his wife, Christine Elizabeth Jenkins, regularly published reports on lynching and Klan terrorism.[33] Originally from Forsyth, Georgia, James F. Jenkins was well acquainted with the Klan's murderous work and brought that insight with him when he migrated to Canada in 1907. His *Dawn of Tomorrow* editorial "Warning" admonished that "membership in the Ku Klux Klan must be made a criminal offence in Canada, because if permitted to grow and spread, that organization will have the same cancerous affect in the Dominion as it has had in the United States." Jenkins implored the federal government to act promptly against "this pernicious body . . . before it has sunk its venomous fangs into our grand Dominion."[34] To be sure, African Canadians had cause to worry about the appeal of white supremacist demagoguery and racial violence given the rapid spread of the Klan in Western Canada during the 1920s. In fact, the Klan became an international organization when it opened a chapter in Saskatchewan in 1922.[35] The Jenkinses and other African Canadian journalists saw it as imperative that the Klan, along with its ideology, be stopped dead in its tracks. As citizens, they implied that African Canadians had the dual duty of halting the advancement of that horrible institution and supporting African Americans doing battle with murderous white supremacists south of the border.

By the 1920s, the African Canadian New Negro was an informed voter, a capable citizen, an artist, a Christian, a Mason, a UNIA member, and a union man all wrapped into one. For their part, black women exercised their citizenship by being dedicated union wives, educators, consumer advocates, shrewd voters, caregivers to the sick, and the guardians of their communities' histories.[36] Here again, sleeping car porters emerged as the leading promoters of a black middle-class citizenship ideal. By the end of the 1920s, John A. Robinson's rise to national recognition as a man of action reinforced his personification of the Canadian New Negro. Robinson's battles with the Department of Immigration, the Department of Labour's Board of Conciliation, railway executives, and white trade unionists helped him mold unionized sleeping car porters into seasoned political actors. In Halifax, sleeping car porters established the Coloured Political and Protective Association "to promote good government, protect its members," and help African Canadians "take part in political matters."[37] Montreal's Negro Conservative League, founded during the 1920s, pressured the Quebec government for fair employment and fair accommodation legislation.[38]

For black railroaders and their families, this New Negro racial pride proved a powerfully seductive philosophy.[39] The Canadian League for the Advancement of Coloured People, loosely fashioned after the American-based National Association for the Advancement of Colored People, championed African Canadian political participation and provided a stage for New Negro firebrands. The *Dawn of Tomorrow*, the CLACP's national newspaper for almost forty years, provided African Canadians with extensive analysis of pertinent political issues as well as the means for voicing their concerns.[40] In its 14 July 1923 inaugural issue, the *Dawn of Tomorrow* declared itself the national advocate "of and for the advancement of coloured people in Canada."[41] Its editors, James F. Jenkins, Robert Paris Edwards, John W. Montgomery, and Christine E. Jenkins, stressed that African Canadians should demand their citizenship rights as legal entitlements and patriotic heritage. Edwards told his readers, "We wish to state in no uncertain terms that we, the Colored people of the Dominion of Canada are 100 per cent Canadians . . . by patriotism, by culture, and training, and by a heritage of more than 200 years of unbroken, unblemished citizenship." He instructed readers to "look with pride and . . . patriotism [to] the fact that, excluding the Indian, our race has as long a period of occupancy upon Canadian soil as any other race of people." African Canadians should celebrate that in "the early days when Canada was in the making and when she was threatened by invasion [by Americans], our forefathers bore arms in her defense." African Canadians' ancestors, explained Edwards, had "suffered and blazed the way and helped clear the forests to build the railroads and bridges to build the cities and towns" in Canada. Consequently, "by every natural and God-given right, we are one hundred per cent Canadians and we resent any insinuation to the contrary. Any attempt to proscribe or to treat us otherwise than as full Canadian citizens," contended Edwards, would be met with organized resistance "not only by our own race but by fair and broad minded men of all races."[42]

Blacks in Canada modeled their political agency on their own terms, though they remained aware of what blacks in the transatlantic world faced as well.[43] Unlike in the United States, where the UNIA, NAACP, and other black organizations vied for power and wrestled over loyal members, African Canadians pooled their resources and wedded various organizations, mining them for their greater political potential. For example, Canada's black press advocated trade unionism but did not herald it as the only solution to African Canadians' various political obstacles. Although John A. Robinson was certainly a celebrated African Canadian leader, he shared that stage with other OSCP activists, clergymen, Garveyites, and CLACP advocates. This noncompetitive marriage of a black press, church, UNIA, and trade union ideology singles out African Canadians' own ideal of a New Negro from that of most African Americans, who too often saw competing organizations as their assured undoing.[44] Although Du Bois and Garvey viewed their organizations as fundamentally incompatible, blacks in Canada melded the best of many organizations into their own distinctly Canadian prototype. In Canada, Garveyites and CLACP advocates wore the same hat. Some Canadian historians have misinterpreted the absence of a dominant black male leader, or his cantankerous challenger—like the American model of Du Bois versus Washington, or Du Bois versus Garvey—as meaning that African Canadians "stood alone, without effective national organizations, social cohesion, dynamic church leadership, full education, protective legislation, or a medium for making known their achievements or grievances."[45] Quite to the contrary, black intellectual-activists welded together the best of various uplift philosophies and shared the stage when others' strengths prevailed.

Black newspapers were by no means the only institution cultivating New Negro race pride in Canada. During the 1920s, a battery of organizations shaped African Canadians' ideas of the New Negro as a political agent. Fraternal orders worked in conjunction with the African Canadian press, with Masons often owning and operating black Canadian gazettes. Black fraternal orders had been extremely popular with transportation workers for some time. Globetrotters by occupational necessity, mariners and sleeping car porters had a heightened need for recognizable social order, especially when working in foreign countries with alien laws governing interracial socialization. Moreover, given corporate attacks on union men, black fraternal orders, much like budding unions, demanded a culture of secrecy. Founded in

1866, Halifax's Unity Lodge #18, one of the oldest black fraternal orders in Canada, gave black transportation workers a sense of home while on the road.[46] During its interwar years heyday, Unity Lodge's membership included black railroaders and seamen from Australia, the Caribbean, Great Britain, the United States, and various parts of Canada.[47]

Black Masons were also deeply involved in black migration to Canada. As early as 1910, Prince Hall Masons and Oddfellows lodges distributed information to African Americans interested in migrating to Canada, using their connections and resources to promote immigration as a viable political option to Jim Crow rule.[48] Reinforcing that connection, fraternal lodges, along with churches, were often the first black organizations established once African American or West Indian migrants settled in Canada. John A. Robinson presided over Winnipeg's Melenik Lodge #528, a division of the American-based Improved Benevolent and Protective Order of Elks of the World. Winnipeg porters chartered Melenik Lodge in 1917, just months before the Order of Sleeping Car Porters, and likely used lodge meetings as cover for their union plotting.[49] Other African American sleeping car porters operating in Canada created and joined Canadian branches of the Oddfellows, the Knights of Pythias, and the Elks during the early twentieth century. West Indian migrants traditionally belonged to the British-based Caledonia Club, while African Canadians joined their own secret organization called the Maple Leaf Club.[50] For their part, African Canadian women became auxiliary Masonic members of the House of Ruth, the Queen Victoria Temple, the Beaver Temple, or the Eastern Star, upholding the practice of having separate clubs for women.[51]

Membership in secret societies provided members with capital for business ventures and confirmed a would-be member's New Negro leadership potential. Presidents of the Order of Sleeping Car Porters, UNIA leaders, black Canadian clergymen, and prominent African Canadian entrepreneurs were often well known Masons. For example, Georgia-born heavyweight prizefighter Joe "Dad" Cotton, an experienced traveler titled in England and Australia, settled in Edmonton in 1912, where he lived out the rest of his life. A Mason and an active member of Edmonton's AME church, Cotton also owned a prosperous Edmonton boxing club.[52] B. J. Spencer Pitt, Marcus Garvey's chief Canadian advocate and a successful Toronto attorney, balanced his obligations to the UNIA with those of the Elks.[53] Thus, during the interwar years Masonry became an unmistakable measure of an African Canadian man's acquisition of New Negro status and a confirmation of his social stature.

Many African Canadian sleeping car porters, newsmen, and Masons also embraced much of the UNIA's racial archetype. Marcus Garvey's first visit to Canada in 1917 introduced African Canadians to his mission; within just two years, UNIA chapters flourished in Nova Scotia, Quebec, Ontario, Manitoba, Alberta, and British Columbia.[54] Tellingly, sleeping car porters chartered the UNIA in Halifax, Montreal, Toronto and Winnipeg and shared their union lodges with the new organization.[55] The UNIA's emphasis on self-help found attentive audiences, especially among African Canadian farmers for whom self-sufficiency was a matter of survival, not recent vogue.[56] Likewise, self-reliance appealed to urban blacks locked out of many employment options and recreational facilities across Canada.

Thus, during the 1920s, Marcus Garvey's Universal Negro Improvement Association became a powerful presence in Canada, with Toronto's B. J. Spencer Pitt and Montreal's Israel Sealy the most prominent Canadian Garveyites. Canadian Garveyites stressed the importance of transnational racial uplift and self-help without concern for national boundaries or citizenship, making real the value of racial uplift and self-help for blacks throughout the Atlantic world. For example, the West Indies Trading Association of Canada, the UNIA's Canadian subsidiary, encouraged international ties with blacks in Great Britain, the West Indies, Central America, and the United States.[57] Moreover, Garvey's black nationalism struck a chord with African Canadians who, facing xenophobia and Jim Crow during the interwar years, shaped the UNIA into "the chief instrument of protest" for racial uplift activists in Canada.[58]

Social events sponsored by Universal Negro Improvement Association chapters strategically married political activism and entertainment. The UNIA's Sunday afternoon sessions attracted large sections of Montreal's black community and provided a range of recreational opportunities for men, women, and children too often excluded from other mainstream social venues.[59] In other words, when by the 1920s pools and parks began turning away black children and their families citing Jim Crow rules, the UNIA's emphasis on providing alternative leisure options for African Canadians won the association great favor, especially among younger blacks. In Winnipeg, the Porters' Music Band, a jazz ensemble made up of porters, Masons, and Garveyites, played dances and held weekend concerts for North End residents (see Figures 12–14). As of the 1920s, annual balls sponsored by the UNIA and OSCP drew hundreds, sometimes even thousands, of African Canadians and African Americans alike.[60] For many, these yearly dances and picnics served multiple purposes: they brought together the bulk of any black Canadian community and provided Garveyites and unionists with audiences ripe for

Fig. 12. Winnipeg's Railroad Porters' Minstrels, 1 May 1922 (Archives of Manitoba, A. M. Foote Collection, 291-N1891)

political indoctrination. Likewise, socials sponsored by black organizations like the UNIA or Elks encouraged family reunions and presented opportunities to meet future spouses. Often the biggest event of the year, the UNIA, OSCP, and Masonic lodge galas also became unofficial debutante balls for young black Canadian girls of marrying age.[61]

African Canadians adopted the UNIA's race pride dogma without feeling bound to its militaristic rituals or its other more absurd tenets. Unlike in the United States, back-to-Africa programs, military camps, and the prospect of worshipping a black God never gained pride of place with blacks in Canada.[62] The *Dawn of Tomorrow* denounced "Garvey's Black God" as "foolish, grotesque and idolatrous," though editor James F. Jenkins conceded that "the present color schemes of North America [were] calculated to humiliate and degrade the spirit of all black people. All things pure, grand and noble are attached to the white race; all standards of excellency are measured from the white race downward."[63] Whether or not Garvey's black model was correct, concluded Jenkins, African Canadians needed more robust social and cultural sustenance.

Fig. 13. Winnipeg's Ace Club Spring Fête, 28 April 1932. Arthur R. Blanchette is sixth from the left and John Arthur Robinson seventh from the left in the first row. (Author's collection)

Because Canadian Garveyites were most often porters, entrepreneurs, and clergymen, they capitalized on all of their communities' resources, including Canada's black churches. Montreal's Union United Church, and later the Negro Community Center, hosted most of the UNIA social and political events during the 1920s. Back in Edmonton, Garveyites maintained close ties with the city's Shiloh Baptist Church and the Emmanuel AME Church.[64] In Winnipeg, the UNIA, Elks, and Order of Sleeping Car Porters pooled their funds in order to build a diamond-shaped community center in the heart of the city's black neighborhood, but the Great Depression eventually cut short their plans.[65] Even after Garvey's fall from grace in the United States, African Canadians held fast to the organization's racial uplift model because of its appeal to a race-based nationalism that defied borders, giving them a sense of belonging against mounting attacks on their civil rights in Canada.

African Canadian women flocked to the UNIA and crafted meaningful leadership roles for themselves within the organization's ranks. The Universal Negro Improvement Association promoted self-help roles that women embraced while thinly veiling their own reformer political agendas. UNIA women lectured on the value of strong work ethics, temperance, racial uplift, health care, thrift, self-sufficiency, and education. Given poor sanitary conditions and limited access to health care for Canada's urban blacks, UNIA women's public health awareness campaigns likely saved several young African Canadian lives. The Willing Workers, Montreal's Coloured Women's Club, and the Black Cross Nurses were at times the only reliable health care providers in Montreal's black St. Antoine district and other African Canadian urban communities.[66]

Fig. 14. The porter and the queen. *Top*: CPR porters in summer uniform, June 1928 (Canadian Pacific Archives, CPA# A-20174 and NS-1052). *Bottom*: Royal Tour Train, 1951. Queen Elizabeth and sleeping car porter on the platform of her private car (Library and Archives of Canada, PA# A-7334).

Likewise, the UNIA advanced higher education and better-wage professional work for black women when few other black organizations paid attention to black women's labor and financial needs. Even John A. Robinson had
not envisioned a meaningful role for working women in the railway industry.[67] Between 1922 and 1924, Ella Burns served as Winnipeg's OSCP secretary,
although black women were not made members of the railway union. With
the exception of at least one woman who portered out of Vancouver during
the 1920s, railway women worked for much lower wages than their male
counterparts.[68] Thus, race and gender discrimination thwarted black wom-
en's access to a living wage, increasing the likelihood of poverty in homes
reliant on their incomes and making destitution an even greater threat during hard economic times.[69]

Believing that higher education would secure better wages for young African Canadian women, the UNIA's Black Cross Nurses program moved many
black women away from domestic and factory work into historically black
colleges in the United States. Since the majority of Canadian universities and
hospitals refused residencies to black medical and nursing students during
the interwar years, the women of the UNIA coordinated scholarships and
internships at Howard University and in New York, Detroit, and Chicago
hospitals.[70]

Indeed, the UNIA's popularity among African Canadian men and women
peaked during the 1920s. Marcus Garvey's frequent visits to Canada became
great moments of race pride and community affirmation for African Canadians. In fact, UNIA, religious, Masonic, and labor union conventions were
important sites of transnational organizing and racial uplift.[71] Such conventions brought together blacks from the United States, the West Indies, Central America, Great Britain, and various parts of Canada, affording delegates
a chance for socialization, discussion, fellowship, and, most pertinent, the
opportunity to compare notes on their experiences. When the American
Federation of Labor held its meeting in Toronto in 1929, African Canadian
railway unionists capitalized on the occasion by approaching the Brotherhood of Sleeping Car Porters' A. Philip Randolph and Milton P. Webster as
potential trade union allies.[72]

The church, among various other African Canadian institutions, similarly
promoted meaningful citizenship and political savoir faire during the interwar years. African Canadian race men and women cultivated powerful religious alliances, since the black church formed the backbone of many black
Canadian communities. The church also anchored recent migrants to their
new host cities. In July 1907, twenty-six CPR porters and their families estab-

lished Montreal's Union Congregation Church.[73] Later renamed the Union United Church, and with a charismatic pastor, Rev. Charles H. Este, at its helm, Montreal's "Coloured Church" rallied St. Antoine's black population in defense of their right to proper housing, education, social services, and due process with the Department of Immigration. Historian Robin Winks confirmed that Este, who had come to Canada from the West Indies in 1913 with Canadian Pacific Railway recruiters, transformed Montreal's Union United Church into the "most vigorous of all the major church groups in promoting equal rights for blacks" in Canada.[74]

Other black clergymen paired off with secular black leaders seeking solutions to African Canadians' social and political problems. In Halifax, Rev. William Andrew White, official chaplain for the No. 2 Construction Battalion during World War I, led a radicalized congregation at the Cornwallis Street Baptist Church. In 1922, Rev. J. D. Howell of Hamilton's St. Paul's African Methodist Episcopalian Church organized protests against Jim Crow and the Ku Klux Klan in Canada with Walter White of the NAACP.[75] In Winnipeg, the Blairs, Burns, Howes, Jacksons, Lewseys, Nealys, Porters, and Williams— sleeping car porters and their wives—financed the Pilgrim Baptist Church, the oldest black church in Western Canada.[76] Pilgrim's founder and first pastor, Rev. Joseph Tyler Hill, an itinerant African American Baptist minister from Hot Springs, Arkansas, pulled together Winnipeg's black community. Thereafter, Hill spent summers traveling across the Canadian and American Midwest, establishing other black churches in Moose Jaw, Saskatchewan; Medicine Hat, Alberta; and Minneapolis, Minnesota.[77] John A. Robinson and his wife, Lena, founded Winnipeg's other black church, Bethel AME Mission.[78] Alberta's black congregations consisted of Edmonton's Shiloh Baptist Church and the Emmanuel AME Church and Calgary's Standard Church of Christ, with its strong revivalist tradition.[79]

African Canadian women made wise use of their black churches just as they did other institutions in their black communities. Rev. Charles H. Este's most reliable allies were often black Canadian club women, namely, Montreal's Coloured Women's Club, still in existence a century later. Anne Greenup and Matilda "Tilly" Mays, southern African American women married to sleeping car porters, organized the Coloured Women's Club in 1902, making it the first women's organization in Canada.[80] These race women served their communities' multiple needs by tending to sick veterans returning from the Boer War, counseling new mothers, clothing West Indian and American newcomers, serving as visiting nurses, running soup kitchens, operating a small black history library, and managing a burial plot at the

Mount Royal Cemetery for deceased itinerant or poor African Canadians.[81] In Winnipeg, Lena Robinson, wife of John A. Robinson, anchored her community and served as one of Bethel AME's pastors by 1934.[82]

Throughout the interwar years, black club women across Canada lectured on proper nutrition, sanitation, education, finance, and racial uplift through self-help and Masonic organizations (see Figure 15). Winnipeg's powerful matriarchs Phillis Briscoe, Beatrice Brown, Mabel Brown, Ella Burns, Daisy Burns, Inez Colbert, Thelma Johnson, Sarah Lewsey, Narcissia Nealy, Lena Robinson, and Edith Simmons—all porters' wives or relatives—kept their community safe, healthy, and politically active.[83] These Canadian New Negro women were business owners, UNIA activists, church deaconesses, and members of various Masonic orders.

Leadership of Canada's black communities required financial acumen, especially given limited resources during the Great Depression. Most often, porters, Masons, and UNIA men provided capital for black businesses and other community organizations like consumer cooperatives. In 1924 black entrepreneurs formed Toronto's Negro Business League; fashioned after Booker T. Washington's hugely popular business league, it was established for the stated "good of the entire race and the community at large." In Windsor, J. T. Bishop's Co-operative Company held capital stock worth forty thousand dollars at the time of its incorporation in 1924. The *Dawn of Tomorrow* explained that "the policy of this company is to establish a chain of businesses throughout the province, dealing in real estate, groceries and dry goods . . . [for the] benefit [of] the race by creating responsible positions for the young men and women."[84] In other words, as the business leaders of their communities, these black men and women saw entrepreneurial expertise as an important exercise of responsible citizenship. Montreal's Eureka Association, founded in 1917, helped African Canadians build and finance their first homes, since "neither the government nor the colonisation authorities seem interested in our racial development [and] landlords were not over particular in renting their houses to persons of colour."[85]

Also created in 1917, Winnipeg's Sleeping Car Porters Business Association, and later the Essceepee Limited, served as the black community's most active and accessible credit unions. Sleeping car porters Amos Williams, Thomas Donaldson, John Clemens, Charles Highgate, and John A. Robinson owned and operated the Essceepee Limited, as well as the barber shop, pool room, and boardinghouse financed by the corporation. According to the Essceepee Limited title issued by the province of Manitoba, the organization's chief purpose was to "carry on the business of an investment company and to

Fig. 15. Members of Young Women's Christian Association in front of their Toronto headquarters at 698 Ontario Street, circa 1900 (Library and Archives of Canada, PA# 126-710)

invest in any stocks, bonds, debentures, shares, or securities." The province empowered the Essceepee to "lease, construct, erect, purchase or otherwise acquire and to maintain and operate a residence, lodging house, meeting place, and rooms." Finally, the porters' enterprise permitted them "to buy, sell, and deal in real and personal estate . . . [and] advance and lend money."[86] These types of race-based credit unions run by porters and Masons provided an important service to blacks locked out of other sources of financing. In fact, but for access to Essceepee funds, many black Manitobans could not have secured capital for their business ventures or home purchases. Such community banking schemes demonstrate that sleeping car porters were guardians of their communities and provided urgently needed services to Canadians too often ignored by the mainstream banking establishment.

Extensive postwar urbanization and mounting xenophobia hastened the formation of local, provincial, national, and international organizations among African Canadians. To be sure, railroad corporations were singularly responsible for the dramatic increase in Canada's urban black population in the years leading up to World War II. Quebec's black population increased 3.7 times between 1901 and 1921, while Manitoba's grew eightfold. During that same period, Canadian cities serviced by railroads noted the largest influx in their black population: Montreal, Toronto, and Winnipeg experienced a growth of 49 percent, 21 percent, and 96 percent, respectively, in their black citizenry.[87] The arrival of so many blacks into cities, most of whom were African American men, rekindled white Canadian alarm about their influence over white women and their impact on public morality.

White Canadians worried that urbanization increased the threat of racial contamination and charged Chinese and blacks with introducing drug trafficking, gambling, jazz, and miscegenation into the dominion. Edmonton Juvenile Court judge Emily Murphy hyperbolically attributed Canada's drug and prostitution problems to the presence of black railwaymen. The author of Canada's 1922 *Opium Drug Act*, Judge Murphy insisted "that this nefarious traffic [in opium] has been partially carried on by Pullman-car porters. . . . Indeed, we know of a certain blackmoor—an erstwhile porter—who, at the present moment, is languishing in prison." Judge Murphy also warned that white women were in serious danger of moral turpitude as evidenced by the fact that "educated gentlewom[e]n, reared in a refined atmosphere," were increasingly found "consorting with the lowest class of yellow and black men" in Canadian cities.[88]

As of the 1920s, reports surfaced that white women were seen prowling in "jungle rooms," jazz clubs flourishing in major Canadian city centers, on the hunt for booze, blues, and black men.[89] Ragtime and jazz speakeasies began operating in Montreal, Toronto, and Winnipeg shortly after the Great War. Juke joints and gambling houses typically bordered railway stations and spread into nearby black communities. Montreal's hottest jazz clubs—the Nemderoloc Club, the Terminal Club, the Boston Café, and Rockhead's Paradise—attracted some of the finest jazz entertainers of the day, like Louis Armstrong, Fats Waller, Duke Ellington, and Cab Calloway.[90] Like postwar Parisians enraptured with Négritude and Joséphine Baker's *La Revue Nègre*, Montreal too lit up with black entertainers and became an important stop on the international jazz circuit.[91] Some Montreal hotels and theaters overlooked African Canadian musicians altogether, competing instead for the most "authentic" American jazz ensembles. They often boasted that their jazz acts were imported "directly from the Cotton Club in Harlem" (see Figure 16). Connies Inn, a white-owned jazz club in Montreal's St. Antoine district, advertised that it was "bringing Harlem to Montreal" by featuring topless black women and blackfaced minstrels on its posters and invitations bills.[92] Canadian ragtime and jazz establishments vied for the "highest caliber of colored divertissement direct from the world Famous Harlem" by offering up an array of lampooned images of black people for public consumption.

Colorful "divertissement" is exactly what unnerved most white Canadians. In 1921, Canada's leading newsmagazine, *Maclean's*, cautioned "Where Does Jazz Lead?" and concluded for its readers that "It Arouses Undesirable Instincts." *Maclean's* admonished white Canadian women to guard against jazz's health hazards. "It is merely an irritation of the nerves of hearing, a sensual teasing of the strings of physical passion, . . . a willful ugliness and a deliberate vulgarity."[93] According to the author, Anne Faulkner, jazz's musical roots reached as far back as Africa, making its pagan roots all the more sinister. "Jazz originally was the accompaniment of the voodoo dancer stimulating the half-crazed barbarian to the vilest deeds . . . brutality and sensuality." It also accounted for "the worst passions . . . barbarism and modern Bolshevism." John R. McMahon, who reported regularly on jazz for *Maclean's*, sounded the trumpet of doom when he warned that "the road to hell is paved with jazz steps." Judging from the "mental and physical harm which jazz, late hours, and cigarette-smoking [were] doing to college youth," McMahon denounced the musical form and "the Afro-American dance" as a "moral smallpox" and an "unholy invention [that] . . . mingles the civilized with the savage."[94] Indeed, jazz's detrimental effect so worried some white Canadians in Hamilton that in 1919 they petitioned the newly formed Department of Health to have the musical form declared a health nuisance.[95] In the summer of 1922, the *Montreal Herald* hoped that "Jazz's Day Is Done and White People Will Become Sensible" again.[96]

Just as the Canadian press feared, jazz's melodious seduction had entranced many young white women. Historian Wilfred Israel supplied an offbeat description of the frenzied pace of life in Montreal's jazz quarter, describing youthful white women, flappers their generation would be called, roving through black neighborhoods and swinging with abandon in underground jazz bars. According to Israel, jazz musicians "grind out the sensuous blue harmonies with a syncopation that sets the body in ready motion with sympathetic vibrations." He also testified that "lady patrons of these cabarets are largely white . . . of the teen age and early twenties, some of whom are never seen in this district, except at night." These impressionable white women "enjoy the freedom and abandonment of their new contacts. There is an emotional excitement to these girls from the fact of being in strange

Fig. 16. "Harlem of the North": Montreal jazz scenes (John Gilmore, *Swinging in Paradise*, 1989)

MONTREAL'S BIGGEST NEW YEAR'S EVE FROLIC AND DANCE ......!

Sat. Dec. 31st at 10 p.m.

THE LIONS CLUB PRESENTS

DUKE
ELLINGTON
"HARLEM'S ARISTOCRAT OF JAZZ"

Come and
Enjoy An
Outstanding
Vaudeville
Show and
Dance To
Your Heart's
Content

Form a Party
NOW —
Get Your Seats
In Advance
And Avoid
Disappointment

AND HIS WORLD FAMOUS
ORCHESTRA
Through Arrangement with MILLS ARTISTS INC., N.Y.

Plus VAUDEVILLE SHOW

SEATS ON SALE THURS. DEC. 15th AT FORUM
Tickets can now be obtained from members of the LIONS CLUB —
SARRAZIN and CHOQUETTE PHARMACY—STATION CHLP—
All seats are reserved. — Net proceeds to Lions Welfare Work.

GENERAL
ADMISSION **$1**50
PLUS TAX

FORUM

BOX
SEATS **$2**00
PLUS TAX

surroundings; the musical rhythm is most penetrating; the eating and drinking with the dark, soft-skinned male, supply that thrill and emotional release of unsatisfied wishes which she has sought for so long."[97] For Israel then, jazz and proximity to blacks—especially soft-skinned men—became the conduit for white women's precocious sexual awakening. Accordingly, Israel's account reveals that many white Canadians feared that jazz and interracial dating posed the same threat to white women's chastity.

If white Canadians felt defenseless against black migration, jazz music, and interracial dating, ridiculing portrayals of blacks on screen and stage helped soothe seething resentments. After the Great War, white Canadians displayed an insatiable appetite for shows featuring degrading depictions of black people. *The Birth of a Nation* toured Canadian theaters for more than five years, with many movie houses guaranteeing around-the-clock presentations of the film. According to the *Winnipeg Free Press, The Birth of a Nation*'s initial release in 1915 had sparked public outcry "by delegations of colored citizens" denouncing its racist content.[98] Vaudeville shows promising "blackface singers" packed Canadian theaters, while some white Masonic lodges raised funds for veterans with minstrel shows.[99] The *Hamilton Spectator* reported that the St. Thomas Church's Young Men's Club "presented The Tennessee Minstrels of 1922 . . . [to] a Sunday school room . . . crowded to capacity." The minstrel show was lauded as "one of the most successful entertainments . . . held in the Sunday school," with proceeds "which amounted to a godly sum [being] used entirely in connection with Sunday school work." Even when praising René Maran in 1921 for winning France's prestigious Goncourt Prize for his novel *Batouala*, the white newsmen at the *Hamilton Spectator* informed readers, "Maran is almost a pure negro. . . . He has wooly hair, dilated nostrils, and thick lips."[100]

Unnerved by what seemed like major shifts in social mores and perceived intimacies across racial lines, many white Canadians during the 1920s mused that immigrants and people of color required stricter regulation. After World War I, white supremacist ideology and restrictions of citizenship rights, like those proposed by Henry Bannan, increasingly proscribed the lives of immigrants and people of color in Canada and revealed a growing fascination with segregationist policies already popular in the American South and Southern Africa. Bannan, a white Nova Scotian, wrote an editorial column, "Canadian View," advocating more exacting legislative restrictions of African Canadians' civil rights. "I am very much interested in the race question and believe that these should become laws between the white and black races," stated Bannan. He then proposed that the "races shall not intermarry. No colored race shall vote for any member of Parliament and no member of a colored race shall become a member of Parliament." Disfranchisement and legislating against interracial union were not enough for Bannan, whose plan required that "no colored race be eligible for the office of mayor or member of the council of any town or city" and that "no colored person shall sit against any white woman." Bannan also suggested that African Canadians be forbidden to "carry firearms, knives or daggers or any such weapon," thereby ensuring that blacks could not defend themselves against violent assaults.[101]

The codification and institutionalization of segregationist ideology in Canada increasingly moved from rhetoric to practice during the 1920s. Reports in Canadian and British newspapers exposed that restaurants in Windsor were refusing service to uniformed black veterans.[102] Black Nova Scotian veterans were subjected to a final humiliation: burial in segregated lots in Halifax's Camp Hill Cemetery.[103] Even black orphans were housed separately from white ones; Nova Scotia's Home for Colored Children, founded by James A. R. Kinney in 1921, cared for orphaned black children overlooked by white social workers until the 1960s.[104]

For those living in other parts of Canada, conditions were equally troubling. In 1920, Calgary city officials institutionalized restrictive housing covenants and redlining to keep African Canadians from purchasing homes outside the boundaries of the railway yards.[105] Meanwhile, an Edmonton municipal ordinance barred black patrons from all public swimming pools.[106] After the Great War, white Canadian retailers brazenly posted white-only notices in restaurants, hotels, shops, theaters, and sport arenas. W. V. Franklin, an African Canadian watchmaker from Kitchener, sued the Cave Restaurant in 1923 for the "ignominy and shame" caused by its white-only service policy.[107] Black Londoners organized financial assistance to offset Franklin's legal expenses and support his claim to "what he believes is his right as a Canadian citizen," declared the *Dawn of Tomorrow*.[108] In Toronto, black children were turned away from public skating rinks, while Canadian hotels and hospitals rejected black clients, each citing their Jim Crow policies to protesters.[109] And in 1928, the Ku Klux Klan of Kanada underwrote a ward at the Moose Jaw Hospital in Saskatchewan; a special plaque posted at the entrance professed "Law and Order, Separation of Church and State, Freedom of Speech and Press, [and] White Supremacy."[110]

By the 1920s, Jim Crow also locked African Canadians out of theaters, hockey rinks, and concert halls. The Palace Theatre in Windsor sat black ticket holders in a segregated section they called the "Crow's Nest."[111] In 1921, Montreal's Loew's Theatre publicized that African Canadian patrons would be segregated in "Monkey Cages," the opera house's upper balcony. When the Coloured Political and Protective Association of Montreal sued the Loew's Theatre for violating black patrons' citizenship rights, the Supreme Court of Quebec ruled in *Loew's Theatre Ltd. v. Reynolds* that "when a coloured man . . . wants to take a seat in a part of the House which he knows is by rule of the manager prohibited to a coloured person, he cannot complain if he is refused admission."[112] In other words, the Quebec Supreme Court's ruling made law of designating segregated public spaces in Canada and holding those who challenged Canadian-style Jim Crow responsible for creating a nuisance for business owners and white patrons alike. Throughout the interwar years, black theatergoers in Toronto, Winnipeg, and Vancouver were subjected to the same humiliation without a different outcome when they raised grievances with the courts.[113]

Even French Canadians, who frequently bemoaned racism at the hands of Anglophones, invested in white supremacy and joined the chorus for segregation in Canada during the interwar years. Quebec's francophone independence movement openly espoused nativist rhetoric, especially with regard to Jews and African Canadians.[114] Blacks in Montreal spent much of the interwar period wrestling hostile city councilmen, fighting police harassment, and fending off deportation. Justice Louis-Philippe Pelletier of the Quebec Supreme Court offered interesting French Canadian insight on race relations during the Loew's Theatre case by insisting that white patrons' racism had forced the Loew's Theatre's Jim Crow seating policy; the proprietors should not, therefore, be penalized for meeting their white clients' expectations. In fact, almost all the legal challenges to Jim Crow in the public service sector were launched in Quebec courts between the two world wars. Canadian judges consistently gave legal sanction to Jim Crow policies and maintained that without explicit laws forbidding racial discrimination, business owners, recreational facilities, and public agencies could violate African Canadians' citizenship rights with impunity.[115]

African Canadians who did not take heed of white-only trade notices mounted on Canadian businesses and public services found white Canadians prepared to impose segregation by force. By 1922, the Ku Klux Klan had crept past the Canadian border and taken root in Saskatchewan, Alberta, British Columbia, Ontario, and Quebec.[116] The Klan carted more than eight thousand spectators to its inaugural celebration in Moose Jaw on a train specially commissioned for the event. The *Kourier Magazine* and the *American Standard* polluted white Canadian minds, while Klaverns defiled city streets.[117] The American and Canadian press took immediate notice of the Klan's Canadian campaigns and reported that in St. Catharines, Ontario, "a mob in riotous work" set the town hall ablaze while "crowds f[ou]ght to Lynch [an] alleged slayer of child."[118] The *Montreal Gazette* headlined the story "Crowd Clamors for Blood," while for its part the *New York Times* advised readers "Canadians Burn Jail to Lynch Ex-Soldier."[119]

African Canadians carried on their fight against Jim Crow, undaunted by segregationist judges, apathetic elected statesmen, or the Klan. They worried less about the successful outcome of their battles, focusing instead on unmasking escalating white supremacist practices in public policy and federal law. The suffusion of Jim Crow in Canada during the 1920s evoked the most rigorous protest from leaders of African Canadian racial uplift institutions like porters, club women, clergymen, Freemasons, and journalists. The case of Matthew Bullock, an African American émigré on the run from southern lawmen, serves as an insightful example of black Canadian insurgency and showcases the cooperative alliances created by national racial uplift organizations since the Great War.

Matthew Bullock's saga began in a sleepy North Carolina town one thousand miles from the Canadian border. On 24 January 1921, Norlina residents awoke to news of a race riot and lynching on the outskirts of town. The late-night row between a local white gang and teenaged black veterans had landed five men in hospital (with one white man shot in the stomach), left two adolescent African Americans dead, and sent another man, Matthew Bullock, on a two-year run for his life.[120] The son of a prominent local Baptist minister, Bullock had served in France during the Great War. He returned frustrated with North Carolina's white supremacist regime and with the white men determined to keep it in place.[121] That winter, his patience ran out.

Nestled along the North Carolina–Virginia border, Norlina in Warren County was home to primarily enfranchised African American tobacco, cotton, and mixed-grain farmers during the nineteenth century. Warren County had successfully elected a black representative after 1878, in what historians call the "Black Second," a rare, predominantly African American congressional district south of the Mason-Dixon line. During the Gilded Age, many African American families in the region had enjoyed a level of prosperity unmatched elsewhere in the state, as evidenced, for example, by the Bullocks, who owned more than 800 acres of farmland, a large church, and a car in 1921. In fact, by the end of the nineteenth century, most whites had abandoned the region to African Americans and their white Republican allies, focusing instead on securing Democratic control over the more affluent southern half of North Carolina. But after World War I, Tar Heel Democrats turned their attention once again to Warren County, owing in part to the Airline Seabord Railway's decision to build a train station in Norlina, where goods and soldiers regularly cut through the small town. According to several reports, even the Carolina Klan, resuscitated from its slumber during the Wilmington race riots in 1898, had moved into the region, intent on wresting land and the vote from blacks determined to defend their standing. Thus even before the Bullock lynchings occurred in 1921, tensions in Warren County had been slowly simmering throughout the Great War; when Matthew Bullock and other black soldiers returned from service abroad, those racial tensions had reached a boiling point.

Trouble began for Matthew Bullock when he and his teenaged brother Plummer crossed paths with Brady Taylor, manager of a local general store. The Bullocks purchased ten cents' worth of apples from Taylor on the afternoon of 23 January 1921. When they complained that the fruit was not fresh and requested a refund, white men loitering near the shop took offense with the young black shoppers' perceived impertinence. The *Raleigh News and Observer* claimed that the Bullocks had "cursed Tailor . . . and threatened him."[122] Word of the Bullocks' conduct spread quickly through town. By sundown, a team of armed white men vowed retaliation for the perceived insolence.

Taylor's gang cornered the Bullocks and their friends near the city's railway tracks, a favorite hangout with local black teens. A race riot ensued with reports of gunfire exchanged in what the *News and Observer* described as a "clash between races."[123] It is certainly well documented that, particularly in the years following the Great War, racial skirmishes erupted over seemingly insignificant infractions. In fact, in 1919 alone, there were thirty-seven racially driven altercations reported in the United States and hundreds more in Europe, the Caribbean, and Africa, making events unfolding in Norlina part of a broader and more international wave of violence. On that particular winter night back in Norlina, fighting raged for more than an hour before Warren County police ended the brawl, rounded up fourteen African American rioters, including Plummer Bullock, and charged them with inciting a riot. The boys were taken to the county jail in nearby Warrenton, where a crowd of white Norlinians clamored for speedy retribution. John Green, the black jail guard on duty that night, appealed for calm.

Matthew Bullock, the alleged ringleader, had slipped away from the melee before police arrived on the scene. Bullock eluded harm that night thanks to his father's insistence that he head for Canada in the family car. The young Bullock heeded his father's advice, stopping briefly in Batavia, New York, a suburb of Buffalo where the family had once lived and where Rev. William Bullock had pastored, before pressing on to the Canadian border.[124] Sensing the danger to his other son's life, William Bullock set off for the jail, hoping to rescue Plummer from the mob's ire. Tragically, only one Bullock brother would survive the night.

While Matthew raced north, his brother Plummer and longtime friend Alfred Williams faced a posse of white vigilantes. Black Norlinians who had been meeting in the nearby Oak Chapel AME Church ran for their guns and headed to the jail intent on defending their imprisoned young brethren. The *News and Observer* confirmed that "eight fire arms of various sorts were taken from the negroes who had gathered at a negro restaurant and in the basement of a negro church. The negroes are now believed to have gathered for the purpose of protecting the negroes in the jail."[125] One hundred and fifty enraged whites, however, had outpaced those African Americans, broken into the county jail, held the muzzle of a large-caliber pistol to the jail guard's head, and demanded Plummer's and Alfred's release.[126] Forced into a waiting vehicle, Williams and Bullock left Norlina in what some black residents described as a Klan caravan.[127]

Their torture at the hands of North Carolinian white supremacists would be long and lethal. First, the terrorists dragged the boys down the main road out of Warrenton. Then the men set Bullock and Williams free before hunting them down in nearby woods. Gunshots, if not the boys' cries, echoed from Norlina to Warrenton, more than four miles away.[128] The next morning, residents found Williams and Bullock hanging from a tree, their bodies charred, "riddled with bullets," and their genitals sliced off, the spoils of their captors' midnight rampage. Local newspapers reported that onlookers lined the highway as a "number of white people visited the scene" and approximately fifty black men and women staged a vigil, "quietly resentful of what had been done" to their young.[129] After what according to newspaper reports may have been as much as several days, state troopers eventually took down the corpses and returned the young boys' lynched remains to the county coroner. Reporters for the *Raleigh News and Observer* and the *Charlotte Observer* celebrated that "very little disorder [had] accompanied the lynching."[130]

Matthew Bullock, speeding northward along the well-worn path known to African American freedom seekers as the Underground Railroad, knew nothing of his brother's violent demise. He drove all night, stopping only for food and fuel once he crossed the Mason-Dixon line. The Great War veteran set his sights on Canada—the erstwhile haven for African Americans on the run from the South. There, he hoped to seek asylum as so many others had nearly a century ago. Unaware of Canada's ban on black immigration imposed by the federal government a decade earlier because of concern over southern African American migration into Western Canada, Matthew reached the border in early March only to be sent back to an uncertain destiny in the United States.[131]

Bullock painstakingly plotted his next move. He waited out the day along the shore of Lake Erie, studying its icy waters and wondering how he would get to its opposite shore. The nineteen-year-old Bullock resolved to literally jump for his life. Under cover of night, the veteran leapt across Lake Erie, just south of Niagara Falls' rushing waters, skipping from one ice islet to another, and eventually landed safely on Canadian soil. In an alternative account of Bullock's crossing, he is said to have entered Canada in the same dramatic way but this time with the help of a group heading north for worship. Even though the Canadian government did its best to erect barriers to black immigration, those intent on forming religious communities not only ignored such laws but had well-worn paths, even dangerous ones, that they traveled regularly. Still, in both versions of Bullock's entry into Canada, his dramatic and desperate escape conjures up powerful images of an endangered soul, crossing thunderous waters into the Promised Land, led by God's children singing his gospel, as the church-bound version alleges. Bullock is then absolved and cleansed in the transformative process of becoming Canadian. His tale is rich with the imagery of a flight from Egypt or even a flight from slavery. Not coincidentally, Matthew Bullock then made his way to Hamilton, home to many former African American freedom seekers, where he adopted the alias James Jones, took up work as a plasterer at the Pigott-Healey Company, and melted into the city's black community.[132]

Back in North Carolina, state troopers kept up their hunt for Matthew Bullock. They might never have learned of Bullock's daring escape had Canadian immigration officials not arrested the young man one year later on vagrancy charges and prepared for his deportation for violating the Immigration Act by unlawfully entering the country. Raiding rooming houses in black neighborhoods had become a common practice during the 1920s as Canadian authorities anxious about urban black populations singled out black men as purveyors of drugs and even worse—sinful jazz music. An anonymous Canadian, perhaps a bounty hunter, rekindled the Bullock matter by sending Norlina's chief of police a letter spelling out the young refugee's whereabouts. Chief O. B. Cook opened the envelope and found Matthew staring back from a yellowed newspaper clipping.[133] With Bullock in Canadian custody, North

Carolina governor Cameron Morrison, a self-proclaimed white supremacist and advocate of lynch law, set his sights on Canada.[134]

In a complete turnaround on its policy against black migration, the Canadian government denied North Carolina's initial habeas corpus request by declaring that Bullock's return would mean sure death at the hands of a lynch mob. The case developed into an international tug-of-war, pitting the Canadian government's antilynching stance against the state of North Carolina's determination to deal with Matthew Bullock on its own terms. The Bullock case dominated Canadian and American newspapers for almost four months, as courts, citizens, and elected statesmen wrestled over Matthew's fate. Politicians, black political organizations, and newsmen on both sides of the border joined the chorus for or against Bullock's extradition, citing the consequences of failed Reconstruction politics, southern segregation, and lynching. They argued that the outcome of Matthew Bullock's case would establish the legitimacy of Jim Crow practices or undermine them on an international stage.

African Canadians, especially clergymen, sleeping car porters, race men, and World War I veterans, instantly mobilized in defense of Matthew Bullock's life in what the *Toronto Globe* described as a "Resolute Fight to Hold [the] Negro under Our Flag."[135] Coordinating Bullock's trial showcased African Canadians' political sophistication as their campaign to save Matthew from the hawser of a southern mob demanded a mastery of the press, command of Canadian federal law, and diplomatic ingenuity. Because of their work, Bullock's extradition case became an international cause célèbre debated in the British, American, and Canadian press.[136] The *Savannah Tribune* announced that there were "ample funds to fight the case and while the Colored people of the United States and Canada have subscribed the greater amounts, organizations of Britishers are aiding substantially."[137] By the end of Bullock's ordeal, African Canadians had done battle with North Carolina's Governor Morrison, the Ku Klux Klan, the U.S. State Department, the American ambassador to Canada, the minister of immigration, the minister of justice, and Prime Minister King.

Rev. J. D. Howell of Hamilton's St. Paul's African Methodist Episcopal Church orchestrated Bullock's defense. He immediately contacted Toronto's *Globe*, Hamilton's *Herald* and *Spectator*, and the most influential African American newspaper of the day, the *Chicago Defender*. Headlines like "Bullock Fighter in France but South Would 'Get' Him" reminded readers that, despite having fought for democracy abroad, Matthew could not enjoy its reward in his own country.[138] African Canadians demanded that their government accord Bullock "British fair play," emphasizing that the young man's life depended on more levelheaded British justice given the southern alternative.[139] For its part, the *Chicago Defender* kept African American audiences informed of Bullock's fight and remarked that "the honor of Canada is at stake in this case."[140]

Some white Canadians, like former Toronto mayor Tommy Church, concurred with the *Chicago Defender*'s assessment. In a letter to Prime Minister King published in the *Herald* and *Globe*, Church warned that he would "hold him [King] personally responsible in the house of commons for the consequences that may be visited upon Bullock as a result of his deportation."[141] Even some Orangemen's lodges and the Army and Navy Veterans Associations telegrammed Prime Minister King in "protest against extradition [of] Matthew Bullock . . . [without a] trial in accordance with principles of British justice."[142]

British, American, and Canadian newspapers hotly debated the honor of saving Bullock's life because it resuscitated unresolved tensions between Canada and the United States, with the *New York Times* positing that "the situation thus created endangers the preservation of amicable relations between" the two countries.[143] Accordingly, race and immigration—whether by runaway slaves, southern homesteaders, or industrial workers—came up against an uneasy line for Americans and Canadians alike. On the one hand, for many white southerners, it revived contempt over Canada's protection of fugitive African Americans before the Civil War, just a little more than half a century earlier. North Carolina's Governor Morrison griped that "Negro societies for the protection of criminals," what he and other southern white supremacists called the NAACP, "have again proved successful in defense work [putting the] honor and integrity of the state" on trial on an international stage.[144]

White Canadians, on the other hand, saw the Bullock matter through rose-colored glasses. Matthew's trial rekindled fantasies about their abolitionist legacy, their sense of fair play inherited from the British, and confirmed, at least in white minds, that they were not racists—at least not ones capable of the southern horrors publicized in the Canadian press that winter. Many Canadian journalists emphasized that southern Ontario had been "the mecca for Southern slaves fleeing from cruel masters in the days before . . . the abolition of legalized slavery. Will Canada refuse to harbor descendants of these same slaves, now terrorized by descendants of these slave holders who murder them on sight on flimsy excuses and boast that the law never is permitted to intervene?"[145] An editorial published in the *Toronto Globe* declared that "whether the victim is innocent or guilty, lynching is anarchy, the negation of law and order. . . . The lyncher is as much an anarchist as any disciple of Lenin and Trotsky."[146] In short, Canadians saw themselves as indebted to Bullock's ancestors and by extension to him. They did not admonish against lynching so much as they witnessed it as an outcome and outgrowth of slavery itself.

Canadians used the Bullock case as a measure of their own record on race. Saving Bullock from southerners reassured white Canadians that despite increasing Jim Crow practices in the federal bureaucracy, housing, employment, education, service sector, and entertainment, their system still paled in comparison with American lynch law. Inasmuch as some white Canadians resented sharing schools, pools, cemeteries, concert halls, hotels, orphanages, and jobs with African Canadians, they relished the thought of waving a southern lamb into the lion's lair. Headlines self-righteously proclaimed that Bullock's fate "may be up to Canadian Courts" but that a "Canadian jail is better than [a] Carolina pole."[147] In other words, so long as Canada delivered Bullock from violent southerners, white Canadians felt exonerated from their own white supremacy.

Black Canadians stroked white Canadian egos and advanced their cause by playing up the dominion's abolitionist reveries. They provided the press with "lurid tales from [the] South" and offered Matthew's account of life under Jim Crow rule as a representative example of African Americans' plights.[148] Bullock's mother, exiled in Washington, D.C., since her son Plummer's assassination, sent a telegram beseeching Prime Minister King, "For God's sake save my son."[149] Rev. William Bullock, who traveled to Canada to support his son during the trial, awed Canadian newsmen with explicit accounts of conditions in the South, making clear that extradition would result in Matthew's murder.[150] Each day, sources close to the case spoke with reporters and explained their next plan of action, all the while reminding white Canadians of their duty to imperiled black southerners.[151]

African Canadian leaders skillfully avoided calling attention to Canada's hand in Matthew Bullock's problems. Were it not for the federal government's restriction of black immigration, Bullock would not have risked his life crossing Lake Erie. Had immigration officials not initiated deportation proceedings and publicized his hideaway to North Carolinian authorities, he could have lived out a peaceful life in Canada. Instead, Reverend J. D. Howell emphasized, "We are not opposed to law and order. We do not want to see a criminal go unpunished. But we do feel that, in the case of Matthew Bullock, sufficient evidence has already been brought to light to show that the whites of Norlina are deeply prejudiced. . . . We believe he is eminently worth saving."[152]

African Canadian leaders astutely sidestepped condemning Canadian segregationist practices, capitalizing instead on the costly international outcome of white supremacy and lynch law. Ever since southern African American and West Indian immigrants had forced their way west at the turn of the twentieth century, some white Canadians pointed to lynching as a viable solution to their problems and flaunted their views in the press and in letters to the federal government.[153] Free from public scorn, some white Canadians touted lynching with greater zeal after World War I.[154] Against that background, the Matthew Bullock case served as African Canadians' own campaign against the adoption of lynching as a messy, embarrassing scourge on British law and fair play. Most important, it shamed white Canadians back from a color line twenty years in the making.

African Canadians picked their battles very strategically. They made the case for Matthew's safeguarding by galvanizing their community, mobilizing their resources, tapping into transnational networks, rallying against lynching, and steering their consternation into the best defense for Matthew Bullock. The *Toronto Globe* confirmed that the "colored people of the city are considerably agitated over the case."[155] Concerts, town hall meetings, and church assemblies took up "Bullock Defense Funds" in London, Buffalo, Chicago, New York, Philadelphia, Baltimore, and Washington, D.C. In saving Matthew, African Canadians were saving themselves by proving that they were citizens capable of voicing their political concerns and improving conditions for blacks in the dominion. Black Canadian leaders welcomed alliances with other racial uplift organizations, given the international scope of the Bullock affair. For example, the NAACP's leading lynching investigator, Walter White, joined Canadian operations at the request of the Canadian League for the Advancement of Coloured People.[156]

Walter White had staked his career on studying lynching, often traveling to southern and midwestern states in the aftermath of unrest and interviewing witnesses involved in lynchings. White skinned, blond haired, and blue eyed, the NAACP investigator easily passed for white but explained in his autobiography, *A Man Called White*, that he still always feared for his life. Walter White was born in Atlanta in 1893, just as the South entrenched segregation into law. In September 1906, when he was just thirteen years old, White witnessed Atlanta erupt in riot over allegations that black men had taken license with white women. In his memoir, White recalled that his racial consciousness had been forged right then and there when his father, an otherwise mild-mannered postal carrier who enjoyed some prominence among both blacks and whites in the city, positioned his son at the living room window, slapped a revolver in his hands, and instructed him: "Son don't shoot until the first man puts his foot on the lawn and then—don't you miss!"[157] Nearly twenty years later, White traveled to Canada, he told awaiting reporters, because "whenever a colored man is accused of a crime against a white man in the South all law breaks down."[158] He committed the NAACP's expertise on lynching, its financial support, and a mass of documentary evidence to Bullock's legal team.[159]

A longtime antilynching advocate, the NAACP saw the Bullock case —and the international attention garnered by African Canadian organizations—as an effective weapon in its battle for federal legislation back in the United States, in this case, the Dyer antilynching bill before Congress in the winter of 1922. Like Ida B. Wells, who had used England as the platform for her antilynching awareness crusade and won critical support from Europe, Walter White staged his battlefield in Canada.[160] White explained, "There is pending before Congress at present a bill to make lynching a Federal offense, since individual States have been unable to prevent lynchings or punish lynchers." Southern Democrats, he added, opposed the law, with North Carolina congressmen leading the charge.[161] White also reminded Canadian audiences that racialized terror haunted African Americans, as evidenced by Chicago's Red Summer and the massacre in Tulsa just months before, where as many as 10,000 whites ransacked the black neighborhood, murdering more than 200 African Americans in the process. Thus, North Carolina was but one part of a broader problem in which Canadians could play an important role. Upon his return to New York to deal with both the Dyer bill and the aftermath of Tulsa's race riot, White told reporters, "Canada is aroused over the attempted extradition of Matthew Bullock as never before since the pre–Civil War days when fugitive slaves fled there for refuge."[162] White trusted that "North Carolina's record of 63 lynchings in 32 years proves that State incapable of protecting Bullock in case he should be returned. To prevent further shame to America, we sincerely hope that Bullock will remain in Canada."[163]

Other American race organizations did their part for Bullock south of the line, working in conjunction with Canadians. Buffalo's NAACP office coordinated church meetings and public lectures on Bullock's plight, offering their African Canadian neighbors organizational and financial support.[164] Meanwhile, Washington, D.C.'s National Race Congress, headed by prominent black Baptists, filed a petition with the U.S. State Department protesting North Carolina's extradition request.[165] The National Progressive Association assured African Canadians "that neither influence nor money shall be lacking to have Matthew Bullock remain in Canada as a free man."[166]

The press became the most passionate battleground over the Bullock affair. Advocates for Bullock's release in Canada juxtaposed stories of American violence with laudatory ones about Canadian/British fair play.[167] The *Globe*, *Spectator*, and *Herald* became the most outspoken defenders of Bullock's right to remain in Canada, thanks to constant pressure from many African Canadians. Editorial columns and daily articles outlined the implications of the case, the legal questions at hand, and the precedents strengthening Bullock's defense.[168]

Fugitive slave cases—Dred Scott, Jesse Happy, and John Anderson—provided fodder for Bullock's defense.[169] "There is . . . a possibility that the name of Matthew Bullock . . . will have the sort of immortality that was conferred on the name of Dred Scott," advised the *New York Times*.[170] Of these, the Anderson case most mirrored Bullock's plight. In 1853, John Anderson had allegedly stabbed and killed a white man during his escape from bondage. Fearing murder if he remained in the South, Anderson, like Bullock, sought asylum in Canada. Both men, young, black, and on the run—one from slavers, the other lynchers—crossed into Canada and ignited a firestorm of legal protest. Likewise, the pair provided white Canadians with a platform for criticizing American racism, and southern law in particular.[171] Both cases also called into question whether Canadians would respect the Webster-Ashburton Treaty of 1842 outlining conditions for extradition—murder, attempted murder, piracy, arson, robbery, and forgery—when slavery and the threat of lynching forced African Americans into committing crimes.

North Carolinian statesmen and journalists took offense at the constant Canadian reprimand and insisted that Matthew Bullock was theirs for the handling. Perhaps the *Raleigh News and Observer* said it best: "Who Made Canada a Ruler over North Carolina?"[172] Southern newsmen echoed escalating indignation over Canada's haughty directives on the proper exercise of American justice. Meanwhile, Governor Cameron Morrison reassured white southerners that he would not step down from his petition for extradition. He stressed, "People in some sections of the country do not seem to understand that so-called lynchings in the south are nothing more than the killing of criminals."[173] Morrison expressed complete disregard for Bullock's safety, adding that "lynching is just our way of dealing with criminals." The governor skirted criticism of Plummer Bullock's and Alfred Williams's murders, emphasizing instead, "It is true that Bullock's brother was lynched, but it was done quickly," as though expediency somehow softened the horror of racial terrorism.[174]

If Canadian sanctimony frustrated white southern bureaucrats and reporters, the *New York Times* raged over what it construed as Canada's violation of American sovereignty. The newspaper took issue with the Canadian government's demand that the State Department and the governor of North Carolina assure Bullock's safekeeping if he was sent back.[175] Anticipating Canada's refusal to "give him up to what might be a death by violence at the hands of a mob," the *New York Times* warned, "Should the Canadian Government in effect tell ours that it lacks confidence in our courts, the affront would be serious—[and] would constitute an 'international episode' of no little gravity."[176] Canada's likely repudiation of southern Jim Crow and its lethal application, the "affront" the *New York Times* so worried about, saw the United States' most powerful newspaper teaming up with southern white supremacists.

The *New York Times* accurately evaluated the legal questions at issue in the Bullock case. It did boil down to American legal sovereignty and whether the Canadian government would sanction a system of violence that it rebuked. Governor Morrison, whose southern roots ran deep, would not let a foreign government dictate his courts any more than he would let northerners do so. With the Dyer antilynching bill in Congress and white supremacists looking to him for unwavering leadership, Governor Morrison could not be seen bending to foreign will. Try though he did to warm white Canadians to his state's method of "dealing with criminals," his extradition petition crumbled in Canadian federal court.[177]

While Governor Morrison desperately canvassed support with the Harding administration in Washington and with North Carolina senators Furnifold Simmons and Lee Overman, African Canadians pushed Prime Minister King and the House of Commons for a resounding condemnation of lynching by granting Bullock permanent residence in the country.[178] Judge Snider, selected to rule on the case, felt the squeeze from both sides. President Warren G. Harding threw his government's weight behind Governor Cameron Morrison by signing North Carolina's writ of extradition on 18 February 1922. Hearings on the Bullock matter, however, rolled into March as the U.S. State Department shuttled lawyers and extradition papers to Ottawa on North Carolina's behalf.[179]

Canadian and American lawmakers cast their votes on lynching during the winter of 1922. For months, congressmen had been debating an antilynching bill spearheaded by Leonidas C. Dyer of St. Louis. The controversial Dyer antilynching statute gained approval in the House of Representatives that January, winning by a margin that sufficiently rattled southern Democrats, who then vowed to kill it in the Senate.[180] North Carolinians in favor of Bullock's return suffered a double blow that winter as Canada's Department of Immigration voted against Matthew's deportation on 3 March, citing a lack of faith in southern courts.[181] The *Raleigh News and Observer* fumed over the ruling. Its article "Too Much Coddling" griped that the "refusal of Canadian authorities to return Matthew Bullock for trial . . . shows that this coddling of the negro has gone over the border into Canada."[182] Joining the southern chorus denouncing Canada's decision, the *New York Times* belittled Bullock's win, describing his African Canadian supporters as "mawkish over Bulloch."[183]

African Canadians ignored American browbeating and celebrated their success, praising the Canadian press and federal government for taking the British moral high road. "British Justice Decrees He Is Not to Be Victim of Mob Vengeance," headlined the *Globe*.[184] Black Hamiltonians cheered as Bullock—"wrapped in the folds of a big Union Jack [flag] draped over his shoulders like a mantle"—was released, reported the *Herald*.[185] Disgusted by the display, a reporter for the *Charlotte Observer* informed readers that Bullock "permitted himself to be photographed by a bevy of female admirers of his own race. . . . They've made a Hero in Canada of a Negro who shot down a [white] man."[186] Skeptical of Morrison's surrender and alarmed by threats made by white supremacists to "kidnap the negro and take him back South," African Canadian political leaders canceled a public feast planned in Bullock's honor.[187] Within days of his release Matthew went into hiding, and within a month American and Canadian newspapers reported that Matthew Bullock was once again on the move, this time headed for Europe, "put[ting] himself well beyond [the] reach of the Ku Klux Klan."[188]

Matthew Bullock's fight showcased the very best of what the 1920s had taught African Canadians. Their unified, organized, and politically shrewd maneuverings saved a man's life. Mudslinging by white journalists and southern Democrats only strengthened their resolve to have the Canadian government take a stance on lynching. Reports of southern horrors reproduced in the Canadian press during the winter of 1922 made clear for white Canadians that any further adoption of Jim Crow practices or lynching brought them perilously close to their southern neighbors and betrayed their abolitionist legacy in the process. The international tug-of-war over Matthew Bullock, involving the Klan in its final stages, exposed that the implications of Jim Crow rule and lynch law extended well beyond the boundaries of North Carolina or even the South. It debunked white southerners' claims that "North Carolina is doing more than any other Southern State for the protection and care of its colored population. . . . And a negro tried for a crime is given as fair a trial as a white man."[189] African Americans knew this to be a lie; African Canadians would not gamble Bullock's life to find out otherwise.

THE INTERWAR YEARS PROVED a taxing time for people of color in Canada, as evidenced by one African Canadian's insightful description of Nova Scotia as "Little Mississippi."[190] In many parts of Canada, African Canadians discovered that if they wanted a cold beer, a hot meal, or a clean room, white-only trade signs reminded them of their place. Despite affirming their support for labor during the Winnipeg General Strike and creating a union of their own, the Order of Sleeping Car Porters, black workers spent the first half of the twentieth century under siege by railway executives and white trade unionists alike. Campaigns for disfranchisement, deportation of black immigrants, segregated public spaces, and quarantine in "Nigger Towns" demonstrate that some white Canadians were weighing the same concerns as white southerners tormented by their own insurgent black citizenry.[191]

African Canadians learned that if white Canadians took offense to their presence in hospitals, schools, suburbs, and cemeteries, they welcomed mockery of blacks on stage and screen. White Canadian audiences consumed minstrel shows like *Amos 'n' Andy* and films like *The Birth of a Nation* because they offered images of black people that reinforced white Canadians' beliefs of what black people ought to be and how their presence should be curtailed. With some white Canadians advocating the criminalization of interracial unions, many African Canadians feared that courting a white woman in some parts of Canada during the 1920s could end in violent retribution. Black veterans found that though they had fought for democracy in Europe, their citizenship rights were no more secure than before. The Great War had unveiled a wedge between white and black Canadians that only promised to deepen in times of peace and during economic turmoil.

Economic depression, rapid urbanization, and the uncertainty of postwar social order bolstered white Canadian xenophobia during the interwar years. Contrary to what most Canadian historians have alleged and what most white Canadians believe, this racist knee-jerk response was neither new nor imported from the United States. Rather, the resurrection and intensification of Canadian white supremacist ideology after the Great War represents a return to a prewar racial ideal upheld by white Canadians since the mass migration of African Americans at the turn of the twentieth century. If white Canadians looked to Americans for cues on race relations—be it minstrel ridicule, Jim Crow laws, or Klan violence—they also designed their own rationales for a distinctly Canadian racialized social order.

During the 1920s, the scope, intensity, and sophistication of African Canadians' defense of their citizenship rights took on national proportions. Blacks in Canada exercised an indefatigable determination to fight white supremacy and spent the decade fostering national coalitions that made their battles, especially legal ones later on, ever more effective, as evidenced by Matthew Bullock's case. Porters featured prominently among both organizational leaders and advocates of citizenship rights because twenty years of fighting off railway managers and racist white trade unionists shaped them into powerful political actors. Their mobility and connections to every urban center in North America helped nurture partnerships that defied borders and reinforced the non-state-bound benefits of racial uplift ideology. African Canadian women were also stalwart allies who made skillful use of the black church, the press, and the club movement for political action.

Unlike during the 1890s when they were without a press or political organizations of national scope, postwar African Canadians mounted an impressive offensive against Jim Crow wherever it reared its ugly head. Black workers spent the interwar years entangled with their employers in the Department of Labour's Board of Conciliation. African Canadian political activists—namely, porters—financed legal challenges to white-only practices in housing, restaurants, hotels, and theaters. Canadian race men and women juggled church, Freemasonry, business, unionism, and racial uplift work, all the while promoting the arts, education, nutrition, sanitation, women's rights, fair legislation, immigration, and entrepreneurial endeavors. The Canadian New Negro understood that these social and political infrastructures helped create a tangible sense of community for blacks scattered across the dominion that could then be tapped for national political action. During the 1930s, African Canadians maintained their national campaigns for equitable rights and were joined by African American political leaders eager to make racial uplift an international movement incorporating all people of African descent in North America.

CHAPTER FIVE

Bonds of Steel

Depression, War, and International Brotherhood

Arthur Robinson Blanchette felt the sting of the Great Depression. Born in St. Vincent in 1910, the son of a prominent dentist, Blanchette lost his father in childhood, the victim of the Spanish influenza epidemic sweeping the globe during the Great War era.[1] In 1927, he boarded a steamship for the United States, bound for medical studies at Howard University, then a crucial training ground for North America's burgeoning caste of civil rights activists. Wide eyed and eager, Blanchette enjoyed campus life, as well as the prosperity and prestige that it promised, particularly for young black men.[2] Regrettably, Blanchette's funds dried up well before his thirst for knowledge ever did. Forced out of Howard before completing his intended degree, the frustrated Blanchette cut short his experiment with black campus life and did what thousands of other men and women did during the Great Depression: he got his first job.

Blanchette set off for Winnipeg in 1931 to join his namesake and uncle John Arthur Robinson, the most prominent black railway unionist in Canada. Despite being ousted from the rails because of his tenacious unionization efforts, Robinson still held enough clout to secure a summer portering position for his nephew on the Canadian Pacific Railway.[3] The two Kittitians formed an immediately powerful bond. One a scholar and the other an activist, they exchanged ideas and strategies, wedded philosophy and pragmatism, and breathed new life into Winnipeg's Depression-beaten black community. Robinson, by then also president of the Porter's Social and Charitable Association, a racial uplift organization created to help blacks in

Winnipeg navigate the Great Depression, taught the young Blanchette the meaning of leadership, its daily exercise, and the indomitable spirit needed to exert it against irascible bosses, dispassionate white union leaders, and, at times, even furtive black co-workers.[4]

During his time in Winnipeg, Blanchette witnessed Robinson's unstinting campaigns within—and sometimes against—the Canadian Brotherhood of Railway Employees. Robinson accused the CBRE's leadership of being infuriatingly unmoved by the scale of unemployment ripping black men from the rails during the 1930s, leaving these otherwise proud men clustering around railway stations, hoping for day labor, struggling for survival when none was doled out. Though still in his early twenties, Blanchette apprenticed with the most experienced black trade unionist in Canada, learning by Robinson's side what no classroom could ever offer.[5]

Winnipeg, like all Canadian cities, buckled under the weight of the Great Depression, with African Canadians braving the same adversities—unemployment, hunger, destitution and despair—as other Canadians. In many respects, African Canadians' singular dependence on the railroads hastened and exacerbated their descent into poverty: when portering jobs dried up, as they did at arresting rates during the 1930s, black railwaymen could not simply turn to other employment options. As a result, blacks in Winnipeg, much like those elsewhere in Canada, banded together, shared meager resources, and cooked up creative survival strategies against often overwhelming circumstances. Robinson, Blanchette, and other sleeping car porters across Canada ultimately saved their communities from total penury through sheer determination and a willingness to test out a range of new approaches, namely, national and transnational ones. Winnipeg then, with its small though tightly knit black community, makes for a fascinating profile in labor and race relations from the 1930s to the 1950s. Moreover, as the seat of labor in Canada and the birthplace of black railway unionism, Winnipeg emerged as a captivating site of protest politics during the interwar years.

John A. Robinson and Arthur R. Blanchette spent the years leading up to World War II persuading black workers of the continued value of labor radicalism. At the same time, they focused ever more on social unionism, the practice of melding social justice struggles and community-building efforts with conventional union workplace concerns. In other words, social unionism sold black railwaymen on the profit of union membership and wedded race-based collective action campaigns with the work of shielding blacks from the full onslaught of the era's socioeconomic tumult. Put differently, Robinson and other black railway unionists broadened the scope of workers' demands from the railway station to full-scale desegregation, shifting African Canadians' requests from the workplace to the courts, the press, and other arenas of racialized conflict. In so doing, sleeping car porters renewed their community's esprit de corps precisely when the economic rewards of union membership seemed lagging. For example, while Robinson and the OSCP could do little to break the fall of wages or slow the pace of unemployment during the Great Depression, he and his band of union brothers could march down in lockstep and picket the local department store that still refused to hire black workers.

Porters' wives, daughters, and sisters also carried on the work of protecting black Canadians from mass misery during the Great Depression. Whether in Winnipeg, Montreal, or Halifax, porters' wives regularly organized food drives for unemployed black families. Likewise, these African Canadian women coordinated tuition fund-raisers, thereby limiting the number of black students who would have their educational dreams derailed by the Great Depression.[6] Working through their churches and race women's clubs, African Canadian porters' wives tended to the sick, helped bury the dead, and kept the healthy's hopes alive. Most often, this, more than securing higher wages or more lucrative contracts, became the real work of Canada's railway race men and race women during the turbulent interwar years.

It is precisely because sleeping car porters spent decades doing battle with white supremacy in the workplace that these men and their families were perfectly poised to shape new forms of protest politics by the 1930s. Even during the particularly oppressive early days of the Great Depression, when voicing seemingly benign calls for reform landed scores of labor activists in prison, Robinson's belief in radical railway unionism never faltered. In other words, sleeping car porters who challenged exploitative labor practices did so despite the potential risk of repression and spent the 1930s steadfastly trying to expand the Order of Sleeping Car Porters and having it join forces with A. Philip Randolph's Brotherhood of Sleeping Car Porters.

While Robinson, Blanchette, and other Winnipeg porters focused on growing the OSCP, they also poured critical resources into social unionism programs. Winnipeg porters, as well as those in other major Canadian cities, ultimately understood that if black railroaders' commitment to unionism wavered, the impact of the Great Depression would be worse still, since railway companies would pit desperately underemployed workers against each other. The challenge, then, was to impress upon African Canadians the importance of social unionism as an urgent racial uplift movement, especially given the dual impact of intensifying Jim Crow practices and local governments' apathy toward African Canadians' socioeconomic needs. Put differently, black railway unionists made it clear that whereas the OSCP might not always be able to protect its members' jobs during the 1930s, union membership locked porters into a more powerful and important compact: as a national, seasoned team of activists, they could quickly mobilize—locally, regionally, nationally, and even internationally—in defense of their communities' rights and interests.

Against that background, Robinson, Blanchette, and their Toronto and Montreal counterparts, Stanley Grizzle and Charles E. Russell, respectively, broadened the scope of protest politics for African Canadians during the interwar years, moving their cause from employment-driven issues to an array of multifaceted sociopolitical demands. To be sure, race-based social and political organizations were by no means new to blacks in Canada. In fact, racial uplift, as both an ideology and a practice, had successfully safeguarded blacks in the United States and Canada from various forms of socioeconomic crises long before the Great Depression delivered its own blow.[7] Overlooked by many social relief agencies or barred outright from them because of Jim Crow or xenophobic policies, blacks in Canada did what other African-descended people across North America did during the interwar years: they created self-help organizations and programs to save themselves. Institutions like the OSCP grew to encompass a larger range of issues pertinent to black communities—jobs, health, housing, education—in large part because municipal and provincial governments effectively left blacks in Canada to fend for themselves during the Great Depression.

Whatever the challenges they faced, blacks in Canada understood that they were not alone. While it is true that large distances separated blacks in Canada from one another, sleeping car porters and the organizations that they created throughout the twentieth century served as the critical connective tissue between outlying African Canadian communities. Moreover, the social and political issues that they tackled, such as restrictive housing covenants, shaped and reinforced African Canadians' sense of belonging to, and being connected by, a shared moral and political economy. For instance, sleeping car porters saw the rise of Jim Crow that accompanied the Great Depression as sufficiently alarming as to warrant their immediate nationally coordinated action. When African Canadians reported having been Jim Crowed out of social spaces or public services, as in the case of Fred Christie's exclusion from Montreal's York Tavern in 1934 or the McKay's Café's refusal to serve Bromley Armstrong in 1949, porters focused their organizations and resources on eradicating all forms of segregation in Canada.[8] Thus, forging regional, national, and even transnational alliances remained at the core of sleeping car porters' work, particularly when it came to uprooting segregationist practices. As experienced activists who had spent the Great War struggling for a place and voice on the rails, porters took their fight to Canadian streets by the 1930s, calling to task those white Canadians who embraced Jim Crow as a racial beau ideal. In so doing, porters modeled a new form of radicalism for their constituencies, one in which they stood their ground on workers' rights just as they also extended their demands to include civil and human rights reform.

The call for civil rights took on a fresh urgency for blacks in Canada during the mid-twentieth century because they witnessed three disquieting patterns of events: first, the encroachment of segregationist and xenophobic practices into ever more aspects of Canadian life; second, the devastation of the Holocaust and the real political awakening that it inspired among even the most apathetic on racial matters; and finally, the birth of the American civil rights movement, which heartened African Canadians because it coincided with their efforts at securing their own human rights in Canada.

Already the vanguard of their race both in Canada and in the United States, sleeping car porters in 1939 ignored their employers' browbeating, reached across the international boundary, locked arms, and through unflinching valor launched a civil rights movement—headed by A. Philip Randolph in the United States and Arthur R. Blanchette in Canada—that defied borders. In the United States, African Americans marshaled the language of civil rights, whereas in Canada, a human rights movement defined the crusades spearheaded by African Canadians who worked with—or against when called for—Canada's leading trade unionists and politicians. Black railway union men like Stanley Grizzle, a World War II veteran who invested his fighting spirit into the BSCP and the Joint Labour Committee to Combat Racial Intolerance, and Arthur R. Blanchette, vice president of the Canadian Labour Congress's Human Rights Committee and the BSCP international field organizer, anchored antidiscrimination campaigns at the center of mid-twentieth-century Canadian labor union and human rights movements. In so doing, Blanchette and his coterie of sleeping car porters made possible an impressive legacy of post–World War II human rights work in Canada.

THE GREAT DEPRESSION BLEW into Canada like an ill wind, throwing scores of workers into a state of panic and forcing millions to wonder just how bad things would get before they really improved. Before Canada's hungry decade ended, more than 1.3 million Canadians had lost their jobs and many more had been robbed of their dignity.[9] During the Great Depression's worst years, 50 percent of adults of working age could not secure jobs; those who could took home less than $500 per year, well below the Department of Labour's 1929 minimum calculation of $1,430 needed to sustain "an average Canadian family at a minimum standard of health and decency."[10] Prime Ministers Richard B. Bennett's and William Lyon Mackenzie King's infuriating insouciance for impoverished Canadians only worsened an already disastrous situation.[11] Relief came late to most Canadians because politicians either downplayed the scale of devastation wrought by the Great Depression or wasted years dodging responsibility to destitute Canadians. Despite ample evidence proving the contrary, municipal, provincial, and federal administrations insisted that laziness accounted for rising unemployment; distributing alms, they concluded, would simply reward shirkers.[12] That prevailing view—that certain groups were already predisposed to laziness—complicated how African Canadians navigated the Great Depression and accessed limited relief programs.

The refusal of both Bennett and King to authorize and subsidize aid for the poor literally resulted in Canadians of all stripes starving just as they were sometimes surrounded by rotting crops. Indeed, the Great Depression moved Canadians to new levels of misery as nearly a decade of failed harvests drove desperate farmers off their land and into cities where they hoped to get into factories or at the very least onto relief rosters. One such African Canadian homesteader turned city dweller, Robert Jamerson, abandoned Alberta farm life during the thirties, and after satiating his wanderlust riding freight cars, he hopped off a train in Winnipeg and took up work as a porter.[13] Jamerson would later rise to the rank of OSCP president and play an instrumental part in bringing the BSCP to Canada during World War II.

Most who headed for cities did not experience Jamerson's success. Instead, waves of jobless men traded in going hungry back home for starving in the city. Industrial workers, who had trusted that unionization would provide some measure of protection against wholesale unemployment, instead found employers eager to exploit the surplus of men now hard up for work. Even the railroads, an otherwise resilient industry, ordered major workforce reductions as fewer passengers traveled and companies dramatically cut back on the number of men needed to run their railcars.[14] Having zealously overspent on construction, expansion, and service since the 1870s, Canadian railway companies also faced huge debts that they could not support, forcing even deeper cuts in their workforce precisely during the worst of times for railroaders in need of jobs.

For black railwaymen, this reduction in service had staggering consequences, particularly in cities like Windsor in southwestern Ontario, where
portering effectively accounted for the only work available to black men. To
be clear, African Canadians working out of larger cities like Toronto or
Montreal did not enjoy much safer footing. There too men donned porters'
uniforms and turned up for work only to be sent home without pay or future
prospect of employment. According to the Canadian census of 1931, 30 percent of Saint John, New Brunswick's porters and 35 percent of those in
Winnipeg were already out of work at the dawn of the Great Depression.[15]
Hamilton's rate of unemployment was all the more jarring: an astounding 60
percent of the city's black porters were out of work with no chance of finding
a job elsewhere, since the three main railway companies with porters on their
rosters—the Canadian Pacific Railway, the Northern Alberta Railway, and the
Canadian National Railways—halted all hiring.

Porters' fears of widespread unemployment intensified even more once
out-of-work white railwaymen began coveting black railroaders' jobs. African Canadian railwaymen on the CNR had long accused that though blacks
had held positions as dining car cooks and stewards ever since the nineteenth
century, company managers began replacing them with white workers.[16]
Once the Great Depression hit, the CNR actively favored white men for these
higher-wage dining car jobs, further locking black railwaymen into competition for a limited number of portering positions.[17] Not until the Great Depression made stomachs grumble did destitute white men finally take up
sleeping car portering, symbolically connecting their economic fall from
grace with portering, long considered by whites as the exclusive province of
black men and degrading women's work.

Afraid that if black railwaymen lost their foothold on the rails they might
never win it back, John A. Robinson and Arthur R. Blanchette formed a tag
team offensive against Canadian railway companies ousting black railroaders
in favor of white men. Robinson appealed to the CBRE, the OSCP's parent
organization, for some measure of support and protection. He found none.
Even though Aaron Mosher conceded that "there is no doubt whatever regarding the policy of the Railway to discriminate against coloured persons,
by its refusal to employ any more of them in the Dining Car kitchen positions
anywhere on the CNR," the CBRE president persistently echoed the railway
company's stance that having once worked dining cars did not guarantee
black railwaymen continued access to those jobs.[18] The CNR could—and
would—replace retired black cooks with younger white workers, with the
CBRE condoning white railroaders' preferred treatment. Frustrated by the

CNR and the CBRE's torpor, black railroaders protested the railway company's decision to Jim Crow them out of higher-paying dining car jobs for more than a decade, with John A. Robinson holding the CBRE president Aaron Mosher personally responsible for failing black union members.[19] Mosher and the CBRE's culture of indifference ultimately fueled Robinson's resolve to find an alternative union for black railway workers by the late 1930s.

While surely shaken by the Great Depression's impact on workers and the government's crackdown on so-called dissidents, Aaron Mosher, as president of the CBRE, still had the duty to defend all his members' interests.[20] In truth, Mosher had never shared Robinson's and other sleeping car porters' dedication to interracial railway unionism, viewing black railroaders as rivals best controlled if held close to the vest. Though he initially rejected their bid for membership, Mosher later supported retiring the CBRE's white-only clause in favor of a firmly entrenched segregated hierarchy within his trade union. Even after more than a decade of formal membership, Canadian sleeping car porters remained Jim Crowed in separate all-black locals, and what is worse, Mosher and the CBRE's leadership adamantly refused to integrate railway workers' negotiating contracts, with the resulting effect that white workers squeezed regular, if sometimes small, dispensations from their employers while black railwaymen's demands got consistently swept under the carpet.[21] This so vexed John A. Robinson that he pointed to Mosher's negligence on contract negotiation matters as the chief reason for seeking alternative representation with the American-based Brotherhood of Sleeping Car Porters. After nearly two decades of irritation with Mosher, Montreal, Toronto, and Winnipeg porters bypassed the CBRE machinery altogether and took matters in their own hands by contacting A. Philip Randolph and the Brotherhood of Sleeping Car Porters.

Until CNR porters could jettison Mosher and vote the BSCP their new union representatives, Robinson, Blanchette, and other black Canadian union leaders waged a calculated assault on the CBRE's Jim Crow organizational culture, and its segregationist contract-negotiating scheme in particular. Even though white workers could work any division of running trades—as a conductor, server, bartender, porter, cook—black railroaders could be classified only as porters without any possibility of promotion to higher-paid positions within sleeping and dining service cars.[22] Despite blatant racially driven inequities within the CBRE and the workforce that it represented, Mosher belittled black union members' calls for fair treatment. Porters argued that the CBRE's inveterate Jim Crow hierarchy came at a tremendous cost—in terms of present salary, future earning potential, and, by the 1930s, their very livelihood. Instead of addressing the CBRE's Jim Crow structure and his particular role in keeping it in place, Mosher insisted that by drawing attention to their separate and unequal treatment black railroaders undermined union solidarity.[23]

The simple truth remains that the CBRE's organizational structure indisputably kowtowed to Jim Crow. Even when black and white members worked the same jobs, as for instance in the case of black cooks hired before 1924 and white cooks hired after that date, they belonged to racially segregated locals and had their contracts negotiated separately. Whereas white running tradesmen's contracts were renegotiated at regular intervals during the interwar years, with measurable improvements secured like raises, free uniforms, statutory holidays, and rate reductions on meals, sleeping car porters' contracts received less vigorous advocacy from CBRE executives. Long before the Great Depression's full onslaught, porters' wages stagnated, while white railroaders' incomes slowly inched toward a living wage. In 1927, full-time porters earned eighty dollars per month; by 1941, their monthly income had grown by merely eight dollars. In both cases, the porter's salary still hovered well below the poverty line.[24] Adding insult to injury, porters still had to buy their uniforms, pay full fare for meals while on the road, and reimburse the company for any missing linens, pillows, ashtrays, or other mementos pocketed by enthusiastic passengers.

In the end, regardless of Mosher's lip service, CNR sleeping car porters could not ignore that after twenty years of CBRE membership their victories were few; what's more, their gains overwhelmingly grew out of John A. Robinson's travails, not Aaron Mosher's.[25] In spite of years of fighting, porters still had not won their demands for the same statutory holidays as other railwaymen, longer rest periods between cross-country runs, or reduced rates on meals purchased from the dining car or railway stations. Moreover, protection of seniority rights and guaranteed rest during runs, issues of greatest importance to all porters, remained unresolved major points of contention.[26] Not until the BSCP successfully negotiated its first Canadian contract in 1945 would porters be given sleeping quarters and three hours of rest for every twenty-four hours worked.[27]

Sleeping car porters on the Canadian Pacific Railway and Northern Alberta Railway faced a different set of hazards given that they did not even have the safety net, however weak it may ultimately have been, of a contract or independent union representation. Ever since the Great War, the Canadian Pacific Railway and the Northern Alberta Railway strong-armed their porters into signing yellow dog contracts promising not to join a union, with the understanding that black workers could be fired without any due process or formal reason offered. Yellow dog contracts particularly roiled Robinson because of his failure to end the practice in 1920 when he brought the CPR before the Industrial Disputes Investigation Board of Conciliation on allegations that the company's policy amounted to Jim Crow because black railroaders were the only ones made to sign these agreements as a condition for employment. The CPR shook off accusations that it bullied porters by appointing a toothless Welfare Committee as its black workers' bargaining instrument.[28] Whereas other CPR workers had long since secured the right to elect their own representatives and negotiate their own contracts, black railwaymen who wanted to avoid swelling the ranks of the unemployed during the Great Depression simply had to accept the Welfare Committee and the company-controlled contracts forbidding them from ever electing their own union representatives.

Robinson raged over the Welfare Committee and stressed that it amounted to a puppet union designed to distract porters from their right to independent representation. Worse still for Robinson, the Welfare Committee served no practical purpose, since porters appointed to the group could not negotiate or oppose the company's proposals. The CPR ensured the Welfare Committee's compliance by having local managers handpick the most seemingly tractable porters for its negotiating body. In the case of Montreal, however, those managers' screening failed miserably because the titular head of the Welfare Committee, Charles E. Russell, was in fact clandestinely courting A. Philip Randolph and the Brotherhood of Sleeping Car Porters.[29]

Whether they ultimately sided with management or not, Robinson adamantly maintained that Welfare Committee members were in an untenable position. In a circular sent to all CPR porters in October 1938, Robinson castigated the Welfare Committee's actions, asking readers, "Are you satisfied not to be organized and without contracting powers? [And] can your representatives so elected do justice to your cause when they know that there is no organization from whence they came and none to report on their successes or to instruct them as to further endeavors?"[30] Their good intentions notwithstanding, Robinson emphasized that the Welfare Committee proved doubly ineffective because it was unaccountable to black railwaymen and it could not pressure the CPR for meaningful compensations. Therefore, Robinson insisted on a simple solution: eradicate the Welfare Committee and replace it with a real union, one that the CPR could neither ignore nor intimidate.

Canadian sleeping car porters agreed that the only man who could not be coerced or corrupted was A. Philip Randolph. The son of a Florida minister,

Randolph was raised on a solid southern biblical diet, which may account in part for his commitment to social justice causes and his irrepressible attraction to David-versus-Goliath battles like the one he took on with the Pullman Palace Car Company during the 1930s. Likewise, his relentless pursuit of equal status within the American Federation of Labor (AFL)—and his reports of that fight in the pages of the *Black Worker*—convinced black railroaders in Canada that he was the right man to advance their interests. Canadian porters were well aware of Randolph's work, with many having met him during his 1929 visit to Toronto for the AFL annual convention. What's more, Randolph already understood the value of black transnationalism, having been chosen—along with two other radical journalists, Ida B. Wells and Haitian Eliézer Cadet—to speak on behalf of African Americans during 1919's Paris peace talks. His publication the *Black Worker* also ran regular features on blacks in Europe and Africa, and by 1935 he set aside a whole page for reports on African Canadian life. Randolph's background as a seasoned trade unionist, unrepentant Socialist, and devout advocate of racial uplift and his reputation as a stalwart union man and civil rights activist proved powerfully seductive for African Canadians living with the daily affront of de facto segregation.

Inspired by A. Philip Randolph's victory against the Pullman Palace Car Company in 1937, Canadian porters trained their attention on bringing the BSCP—an organization they celebrated both for its labor radicalism and civil rights activism—to Canada.[31] Canadian porters carefully avoided making direct reference to each other in letters to Randolph, alluding instead to Canada's interest in the BSCP as a national sentiment, since the New York–based organization could serve dual duty by protecting African Canadians' labor and civil rights. The two men most responsible for convincing Randolph of Canadian porters' urgent cause were John A. Robinson and Charles E. Russell. Whether Robinson and Russell knew of each other's recruiting efforts is unknown, but both men agreed that the future of African Canadian railway unionism depended on two things: stronger national coalitions and new transnational alliances.

Robinson first contacted Randolph in 1937, the same year the Congress of Industrial Organizations' attempt to unionize Canadian coal miners ended in crushing defeat.[32] Just as the OSCP had been Robinson's brainchild during the Great War, Robinson once again advanced an innovative approach to black railroaders' needs by proposing incorporation with the BSCP.[33] In a series of letters exchanged with A. Philip Randolph over the course of three years, Robinson shared details of the OSCP's dogfight with CPR management and explained that he had launched a covert unionization drive among all CPR porters, with slow but measurable progress. Reaching out to Randolph may have seemed less daunting for Robinson, since he had lived in New York at the turn of the twentieth century and was well acquainted with Harlem as a hotbed of race radicalism.[34] Moreover, Randolph acknowledged having met Robinson "some time ago" and invited the Canadian labor leader to meet with him in New York in September 1939.[35] For more than two years, Robinson produced a series of circulars informing Canadian porters of his twofold plan to unionize all CPR porters under the OSCP and his campaign to attract the BSCP to Canada. These circulars, at times strained from Robinson's exasperation with the slow pace of advancement, charted his efforts for Randolph and provided the BSCP president with a very clear sense of working and union conditions on Canadian rails.[36]

Next to John A. Robinson, Charles E. Russell did the most to make real a union with the BSCP. Far less is known about Russell except that he was a Montreal-based CPR porter with enough muscle among his peers to chair the Welfare Committee since at least 1932. He was also instrumental in the creation of Montreal's Porters Mutual Benefit Association in 1925; the organization provided death, sickness, and accident insurance to black railroaders across Canada.[37] Russell repeatedly expressed his irritation with company managers tying his hands, though he was certainly smart enough to play the role of obedient porter and act out the part of the dutiful worker even as he plotted Randolph's visit to Canada in the summer of 1939. Randolph frequently wrote Russell thanking him for his recruitment work among Montreal porters and assured the Welfare Committee chair that his hand in the BSCP's Canadian mission would be kept confidential.[38] Over the course of several months, Russell scheduled secret meetings for Randolph and made sure that he and Bennie Smith, also along for the first canvassing of Canadian locals, were shown the best of Montreal hospitality.

Although Robinson made a career of being CPR managers' bête noire, even he could not escape the heightened climate of coercion on the rails during the Great Depression. Rallying CPR porters to the BSCP's cause and coordinating Randolph's Canadian lecture tour in 1939 could easily have resulted in black railwaymen losing their jobs. In letters to Randolph, porters continually described a spike in intimidation on the rails, with one porter reporting that in Winnipeg black railroaders had become "timid" with fear because of company reprisals.[39] For Robinson and Russell in particular, the first because of his long-standing union activities and the latter because of his position on the Welfare Committee, courting Randolph's support would surely have resulted in the gravest of punishments. In fact, prior to his arrival in Montreal in July 1939, Russell warned Randolph, "Again I must remind you that myself and my co-workers will not be present at any of the meetings you may hold, but, I shall arrange to meet you somewhere strictly private, when we shall be able to discuss any plans that you may have in mind." Russell explained that the "danger to myself and my co-workers" warranted this added measure of caution.[40]

The work of infusing much-needed brawn into Canada's bruised porters' union movement became the crux of Robinson and Russell's work. To be clear, African Canadian porters did not see their organization as defunct so much as they valued the strength in numbers promised by the BSCP. Also, like other black railwaymen across North America throwing the weight of their support behind A. Philip Randolph during the 1930s, Canadian porters were deeply moved by the civil rights work inherent in the Brotherhood of Sleeping Car Porters' vision. Thus Robinson and Russell viewed a partnership between American and Canadian railwaymen as mutually beneficial: with Canadian incorporation, the BSCP would become the world's largest black union and one spread across three countries—Canada, the United States, and Mexico—instantly maturing the organization into a transnational powerhouse. It should be recalled that the tremendously influential NAACP, the next largest organization at the time, never achieved this transnational goal.

Canadian sleeping car porters saw their decades of union experience as an especially useful asset for Randolph's BSCP. African Canadian railroaders had been unmasking white supremacy in railway unionism since before the Great War, with most feeling that the CBRE leadership was more invested in segregation than the bosses, the supposed enemy of all workers, black or white. But white union men, who had condemned black workers in 1918 for allegedly stealing their jobs, came full circle within one year, thanks to Robinson and other porters' inexorable campaigns. A. Philip Randolph never knew so swift an outcome with the American Federation of Labor, arguably larger then the CBRE but no less committed to white supremacy.

Whatever their setbacks with the CPR and CBRE, Canadian porters had nonetheless successfully managed to bring iconic corporate giants to the bargaining table as early as 1920. For its part, the Brotherhood of Sleeping Car Porters, certainly facing a formidable foe in the Pullman Palace Car Company, would need an extra fifteen years before winning a union contract. What's more, Canadian porters were already operating from a union infrastructure: they owned real estate, including in many cases their own union halls, and they had several nationally established self-help organizations. In addition, African Canadians had at least two black presses in circulation during the interwar years, Toronto's *Dawn of Tomorrow* and Montreal's *Free Lance*.[41] In other words, even before joining the BSCP, blacks in Canada were already sold on the value of railway unionism, making the work of the merger between Canadian and American sleeping car porters that much more seamless. In the end, African Canadian and African American sleeping car porters teamed up under the BSCP's banner at the start of World War II, driven to each other by common needs, shared obstacles, and a belief in transnational solutions. Though still in its infancy during the Great Depression, the BSCP found a ready-made following of experienced black unionists in Canada: veterans of a general strike, former Great War soldiers, intrepid race men, shrewd political actors.

In many respects, for most African Canadians the BSCP's civil rights work was as appealing as its organized labor platform. During all of Randolph's Canadian tours, blacks in Canada flocked to his town hall meetings, eager to see the man they immediately embraced as a seminal civil rights leader. Just as Randolph received letters on when and how the OSCP and BSCP would join forces, he also got letters from rank-and-file African Canadians asking for his counsel on how to join the NAACP or draw from his experience fighting Jim Crow in the United States. Velmer I. Coward, a Montreal porter's wife and member of the BSCP Ladies' Auxiliary, informed Randolph that black Canadian women were "determined to do everything in our power to stop and stamp out . . . several specific cases of open discrimination in this City [and] feel that if we became members of an International organized group such as the N.A.A.C.P. that could command greater respect, accomplish more and learn ways and means whereby we can combat these common forces of evil."[42] In other words, African Canadians hoped to learn how best to roll back the line on Jim Crow in Canada from Randolph, the BSCP's cadre of leaders, and other American civil rights groups.

After months of requests, Randolph eventually agreed to his first Canadian tour in the summer of 1939. In his early letters to Robinson and Russell, Randolph seemed very enthusiastic about Canadian porters' accomplishments and encouraged them to ramp up their CPR unionization drive in advance of his trip. Records do not indicate what A. Philip Randolph and Bennie Smith expected to discover once in Canada, but reports from the road published in the *Black Worker* confirmed that both men quickly found more than an eager network of railway union men and their families.[43] What they encountered, time and again, in every city visited were black communities bound by a shared racial and moral economy, held afloat by various racial uplift organizations headed by porters. In short, Randolph and Smith witnessed African Canadian communities galvanized in their own defense through a complex set of social unionism programs.

Winnipeg porters showcased the best of this social unionism work. Most black Winnipeggers lived within a six-block radius of the train station, with Sutherland Court housing several of the city's porters and their families. Two churches rooted blacks in Winnipeg: Pilgrim Baptist Church, still on Maple Avenue and the oldest black church in Western Canada, and Bethel AME Mission, which boasted in 1934 of having the extremely rare privilege of a black woman pastor, Lena Lucy Robinson, John A. Robinson's wife.[44] As in other black communities, the church provided crucial succor for African Canadians; by the Great Depression, it became their chief sustenance. On almost any given night, the church served as a safe harbor for families who within Pilgrim Baptist or Bethel AME's doors could find what they needed most: fellowship, food, hope, joy, God, and a touch of politics for good measure.

The Robinsons made Bethel AME their second home. Lena ran the choir, ministered on Sundays, raised funds, fed the poor, taught the youth, and helped hope float for black Winnipeggers. John A. Robinson and other porters who regularly gathered at Bethel, like the Reverend W. T. Romain, a sleeping car porter who later headed Edmonton's AME church, did their union plotting in Bethel's narthex, as Arthur R. Blanchette's vivacious organ music cloaked the men's work from suspicion. Over at the Pilgrim Baptist Church, the same hidden transcript went on several nights per week as OSCP leaders roused the congregation to the call for justice and labor's cause.

Lead by Robinson and Blanchette, Winnipeg porters were dogged in their belief in radical unionism, which for the era included placing race squarely at the center of the labor debate. Winnipeg porters astutely understood that fostering race pride through social unionism projects would keep railway unionism issues alive as well. Accordingly, at Robinson's insistence, Winnipeg's OSCP spun off a host of creative and urgently needed racial uplift organizations during the 1930s, with perhaps the Porters' Social and Charitable Association the most important one, since it explicitly catered to African Canadians weathered from the Great Depression. That porters could finance racial uplift and self-help organizations during the Great Depression's nadir, 1932–35, makes evident that there was still extra capital circulating in Winnipeg's black community. Even against major economic devastation, black Winnipeggers continued to rally around each other, held together by the realization that as a small, geographically isolated community they simply had to support each other, especially during hard times.

Black Winnipeggers' entire livelihood remained inextricably tied to the rails. The overwhelming majority of black men in Winnipeg worked the railroads, and those who did not depended on porters' wages to keep their businesses churning. Yet for so small a community, Winnipeg still had a full range of social organizations and found imaginative ways of funding them, pointing to a hearty local black economy, fueled in large part by Freemason institutions, the Universal Negro Improvement Association, the Porters Mutual Benefit Association, and other small capital ventures launched by sleeping car porters. At Sutherland Avenue and Main Street, the heart of Winnipeg's black community, there were two women-owned restaurants, two barbershops, a tailor, several rooming houses, and a pool hall. Even at the height of the Great Depression, black Winnipeggers kept two churches' coffers stocked, and in turn those churches served up a steady diet of social events: concerts, picnics, ice skating socials, Girl Guide and Boy Scout troops, baseball tournaments, piano recitals, bid whist championships, public health lectures, poetry competitions, and dances. The annual ball sponsored by Winnipeg's Menelik Elks lodge drew sizable crowds from across the Midwest, with some guests traveling from as far as Minneapolis, Duluth, Vancouver, Calgary, and Toronto.[45] Most notably, each spring the OSCP played host to the community's largest fête, attended by the province's premier, the lieutenant governor of Manitoba, the city's mayor, labor activists, and some feminist organizations.[46] Events of these kinds raised the community's spirits, generated much-needed funds, and promulgated the best of what black Winnipeggers had to offer. Most important, public celebrations offset the sense of desperation occasioned by the Great Depression and reminded all involved of better times past and even better ones still to come.

Like most other Canadians during the Great Depression, African Canadians made ends meet by any means necessary. George Beckford, a Winnipeg porter, Great War veteran, and hard-nosed OSCP president, drove a taxi when furloughed from the rails. John A. Robinson, whose career as a sleeping car porter never fully recovered after his involvement with the Winnipeg General Strike in 1919, took work whenever and wherever it became available, even working for a time as an insurance salesman and manager of the Main Street Sanitary Barbershop.[47] Robinson is even rumored to have joined others fattening their pockets through bootlegging; as a city well serviced by American and Canadian railway companies, Winnipeg made for a lucrative crossroads for rumrunners. A quick run to Minneapolis or Chicago could produce more riches than several lawful months of portering. Bootlegging also paid handsomely for Rufus Rockhead back in Montreal, a onetime porter whose assets from running grog provided all the venture capital needed to open the city's famed jazz club Rockhead's Paradise. The Jamaican-born Rockhead reinvested some of his profits into the black community by buying up a residential building so that, he explained, African Canadians Jim Crowed by landlords could finally have a place to live.[48] For proud men, with many a Great War veteran now in porters' uniforms, the prospect of queuing up in a soup kitchen or relief agency line must have seemed especially disconcerting, making the distinction between lawful and unlawful work far less compelling.

Blacks in Canada craved a sense of belonging. Hence, porters crafted organizations, businesses, and social clubs explicitly geared toward satiating that lacuna. Winnipeg's Order of Sleeping Car Porters' headquarters at 795 Main Street, also known as Unity Hall, served as the North End's nerve center, the black community's very epicenter, particularly during the decade of chaos leading up to World War II. Since it first opened its doors in 1917, the OSCP became a vibrant black men's social club. Its proximity to the railway station, just a few blocks away, made it a favorite haunt for all porters, even those briefly cutting through town. At the OSCP house, one could eat a cheap meal, catch up on local gossip, shoot pool, and buy, read, and hotly debate the *Chicago Defender*, the *Dawn of Tomorrow*, the *Negro Citizen*, or the *Amsterdam News*. If you had a coin to win or lose, you could gamble it on a round of poker or better still bid whist the day away. On weekends, Unity Hall transformed into a makeshift jazz club and hosted Ace Club or Menelik Lodge Elks parties. Several evenings a week, men traded their porters' uniforms for their fraternal-club attire; some were Elks, others Prince Hall Masons, Oddfellows, or Knights of Pythias. Even as late as the 1940s, anyone walking into Unity Hall on a Sunday afternoon would run into Garveyites discussing the value of black economic nationalism and promoting black cultural nationalism.[49] And just a few doors down from the OSCP office, a furloughed porter could get a trim at Charles Wilson's Pullman Barbershop, or he could have a suit fitted at Brower's tailor shop. He could jitterbug the night away at the Rumboogie Inn, then come sunrise be the first to breakfast at Busy Bee's famed diner.[50]

To be sure, black church women scoffed at the booze and brawls on Main Street, but everyone also knew that those men, proud even when unemployed, shouldered the weight of their community's worries. As the North End's chief income earners, sleeping car porters were acutely aware that their lives—and those of their families—were inescapably tied to the rails. Though they were certainly capable of doing any type of work, because they were black men, their labor was neither needed nor wanted elsewhere. Thus each day, the men returned to Winnipeg's railway station in crisp uniforms; empty pockets meant that no work had come and things would get harder still, as they invariably did for Yvonne Bouldin's family, one of many who during the Great Depression survived on relief issue food and fuel. Bouldin's father had for years run the rails for the CNR, but as with scores of other porters, the Great Depression sidelined him.[51] Whether the experience of watching her father struggle for work and food inspired her later racial uplift work among blacks in Winnipeg and Montreal is unclear, but as the wife of Arthur R. Blanchette by 1942, Yvonne had decidedly cast her ballot on the side of labor.

Getting onto relief rolls, especially in the Canadian West, was no easy task and opened up families to heightened levels of state scrutiny. In the case of blacks in Canada, however, relief policies also presented a twin racialized and xenophobic menace. Many Canadian cities responded to the rising toll of the unemployed by excluding all foreign-born residents from receiving public assistance, a particularly odd xenophobic policy given Canada's aggressive courtship of immigrants in preceding decades.[52] But for African Canadians, already presumed a troublesome population, exclusionary relief policies marginalized them even more. According to historian Pierre Berton, if someone seeking aid had a foreign accent, a non-Anglo name, or was not white, relief agents impetuously slapped him or her with deportation warrants.[53] Thus relief seekers' fears were well grounded, as in the case of a black porter with a Texas accent, for example, logically worrying that, instead of receiving relief rations, he could be arrested when applying for the dole. In the case of Winnipeg, where by 1936, 75 percent of porters were born abroad, this deportation concern beset the whole community, with hearsay of coercion keeping many from actually seeking the help they so desperately needed.[54] Some black families undoubtedly teetered on the brink of starvation during the Great Depression but were careful not to call attention to themselves—or to their community writ large—by pointing out this apparent crack in the relief system.

Despite the risk of being branded a malcontent, an agitator, or even worse a "Red," many black railway unionists still had the temerity to question the status quo. Back in Toronto, Leo Chevalier, B. J. Spencer Pitt, and Stanley Grizzle kept up the pressure on provincial and federal officers responsible for discriminatory immigration practices.[55] For his part, Rev. Charles Este, a Montreal sleeping car porter and minister at United Church of Canada, worked closely with African Canadian women's organizations fighting department stores that would not hire black store clerks.[56] But Winnipeg, with its reputation as a tough union town where old-time Wobblies and irascible Socialists kept politicians' feet to the fire, housed the most determined black unionists. Records do not indicate that any African Canadians rose within the ranks of the radical Left, though Robinson's OSCP lent its financial support to Cooperative Commonwealth Federation candidates, including James Woodsworth, who by 1935 became leader of what amounted to Canada's Socialist Party. In turn, Woodsworth, a champion of the working class and celebrated human rights advocate, proved a great ally in the House of Commons.[57]

Even though black Winnipeg porters were not known Communists, they hailed from pretty tough stock. Most OSCP members were descendants of African American homesteaders who had made their way west before World War I only to suffer through several seasons of backbreaking Prairie farming in Manitoba, Saskatchewan, and Alberta.[58] Lee Williams and Robert Jamerson, both eventual OSCP leaders, had left their farms for the railroads in the early thirties. Many of the OSCP's members had also seen battle in Europe, including George Beckford, whose refusal to stomach one more moment of ridicule had resulted in days of race rioting outside Liverpool during the spring of 1919. And after surviving Vimy Ridge, taking on the CPR seemed perfectly bearable for Robert Jamerson.[59] Then, of course, there were those who did battle on the home front, like John A. Robinson, whose approach to labor unionism included dogged determination matched by celebration of all victories, however ostensibly small. All told, these were not men who backed downed easily in the face of combat, whether at war or at work. Accordingly, that the OSCP could last twenty years operating in the shadow of what all Canadian porters acknowledged as the most coercive city for labor is no minor accomplishment. Moreover, that the Order of Sleeping Car Porters should stay on the rails, continue to press for railway unionism, and thrive enough to finance ancillary organizations is proof of an impressive tour de force on behalf of Winnipeg's black railway unionists.

But in the end, the Great Depression era tested even those most committed to unionization. Robinson, longer at the task than his protégé Blanchette, felt the stress of waging war on two fronts, facing down two foes wedded to the same color line. To be sure, the interwar years had not been easy on Robinson, who spent that time tilting his lance at both white labor leaders and recalcitrant employers, with a record of as many successes as disappointments. Though he was certainly proud of his twenty-year legacy of civil rights work in Canada, by the early forties the veteran unionist showed the signs of a man worn from constant struggle. The passing of Lena, his wife of thirty-seven years, hastened Robinson's decision to draw down from the OSCP's daily operations.[60] In all, the interwar years had for Robinson been consistently frustrating and invariably taxing. Having proved his mettle and completed his last greatest mission of bringing Randolph's BSCP to Canada, Robinson by 1942 passed the mantle onto his nephew Arthur R. Blanchette, who was younger, bolder, and less weary.

A new crew of black railwaymen moved into leadership during World War II. Whereas Robinson's generation had pushed their way past border guards, gradually worn down white unionists until they gave in, and secretly mapped out their union vision, Blanchette's peers were overwhelmingly raised in Canada, made no apologies for demanding their citizenship rights, and set aside white unionism for a transnational race-based model of organized labor. Before the Great War, the Order of Sleeping Car Porters focused on connecting black Canadian communities, building national partnerships, and creating a sustainable foundation for those alliances—a national press, union, churches, self-help organizations. By the 1940s, African Canadian union men, heirs to this infrastructure, forged new coalitions—ones that looked past borders and affirmed racial connections across North America. In so doing, they joined the resounding chorus of people of color around the world calling for the full rewards of citizenship. This politicized vision of transnational racial uplift also reflected postwar concerns over decolonization, desegregation, and the pursuit of human rights.

By the time Arthur R. Blanchette moved into a position of leadership in the early forties, he had already spent a decade earning his stripes as a trade unionist and organizational leader. Within just a few years of his arrival in Winnipeg, he had served multiple duty as the *Chicago Defender*'s official reporter, the OSCP's secretary, the Elks' Exalted Ruler, and Bethel AME's choir director.[61] Most important, Blanchette had earned the respect and admiration of his peers because of his firm but fair managerial style. Blanchette's leadership skills likewise impressed A. Philip Randolph, who selected him as the person best suited to incorporate all Canadian porters into the Brotherhood of Sleeping Car Porters. Blanchette spent the entire World War II era tirelessly cutting across Canada, recording sleeping car porters' hopes and grievances, reminding them of the import of their union membership, and convincing them that a union with the BSCP was pending and profitable.

No man hedged his bets on A. Philip Randolph more wholeheartedly than Arthur R. Blanchette. In fact, Blanchette paved the way for Randolph's success by virtually doing all the ground work that made possible the BSCP's

quick expansion into Canada. Blanchette built up rosters of all porters operating in Canada and held locals accountable for all dues collected, thereby
establishing important operating standards for the BSCP's Canadian chapters.
During Randolph's 1945 visit, Blanchette helped inaugurate the BSCP's civil
rights wing, the Canadian League for the Advancement of Coloured People.
CLACP chapters spread across Canada and included "liberal whites," Indian,
Chinese, and Japanese Canadians who were "dedicated to the struggle and
liberations of the darker races."[62] In addition, Blanchette found time to serve
on a bevy of committees, including sitting on several CNR and CPR grievance
committees and, most important, on emerging coalitions between human
rights and labor union groups.

As Randolph's right-hand man in Canada and the international field organizer, Arthur R. Blanchette essentially conducted all Canadian BSCP business,
including wrestling with CPR managers and CBRE union leaders. For nearly
two years, the CPR found surreptitious ways of avoiding meeting with the
BSCP or addressing new War Labour Board regulations making it possible for
all workers to elect their unions of choice. Unable to outpace the forces of
change, the CPR by 1943 reluctantly agreed to call a vote among its sleeping car
porters on the matter of BSCP representation. With all but ten of the five
hundred porters in its employ voting the BSCP their official bargaining agent,
Randolph and Blanchette capitalized on the élan created by their victory and
moved swiftly into contract negotiations with the Canadian Pacific Railway.[63]
Within a year, Blanchette and Randolph signed the largest and most lucrative
CPR contract that black railroaders had ever seen in Canada and delivered
with the stroke of their pens the most substantive improvements for CPR
porters. By war's end, sleeping car porters' starting salaries leaped up to at
least $113.50 for a 210-hour month. They also finally received pay for set up
and dead time at stations; guaranteed sleep time on runs lasting more than
twelve hours; credit for standby and time away from home due to deadheading; two weeks of paid vacations after one year of service; half-price meals
while on the road; due process when being reprimanded or fired; and of
course recognition of the BSCP as solely empowered to negotiate on their
behalf.[64] By 1951, porters' starting salaries climbed to $188.57, making sid-
ing with the BSCP an obviously profitable gamble for CPR railwaymen. (See
Figure 17.)

While Canadian BSCP porters celebrated their win against the CPR's long-
standing intransigence, black railroaders on the CNR plotted how they too
could join Randolph's union. Despite having claimed in 1942 that "if Sleeper
Car porters feel that they can safely leave the C.B.R.E. which has supported

Fig. 17. Brotherhood of Sleeping Car Porters, Winnipeg Division, 1942. *Left to right*: Jack Wilson (president), Archibald Archer, Robert "Buddy" Jamerson, Arthur R. Blanchette (national field organizer), and John M. "Doc" Sledd (Manitoba Museum, Neg #14002)

them all down through the years, to join another organization, I shall be the last one to question their right to do so," Mosher responded to the Brotherhood of Sleeping Car Porters' presence with hostility and vitriol because he saw Randolph's arrival as an affront to his organization.[65] Quite simply, Blanchette's and Randolph's work made the CBRE's inertia on black workers' concerns all the more glaring and in some respects forced Mosher's hand. But instead of taking seriously the extent of black railroaders' dissatisfaction with his leadership, Mosher wrote off CNR porters' complaints about his culture of Jim Crow rule within the CBRE as a question of morale, rather than a pressing civil rights matter.

In order to appear as though the CBRE were finally moved to action, and as a transparent preemptive strike in advance of Randolph's summer of 1945 tour of Canadian BSCP chapters, Mosher sent Winnipeg porter Earl Swift on a fact-finding mission across Canada. Throughout his travels and in all his meetings, Swift found that African Canadian railwaymen's grievances centered more on Jim Crow at work and within the CBRE than with direct working conditions.[66] Perhaps most worrisome of all, Mosher and other CBRE leaders missed the gravity of conditions for porters and their intense disgruntlement with Mosher's leadership in particular. In the end, all black divisions echoed the conviction that local grievance committees did not take objections filed by porters seriously, especially when they involved claims of racial discrimination. Instead of moving those complaints up the CBRE's chain of command, Swift informed Mosher that porters believed that "the majority of the men [porters] . . . are obsessed with the idea that there is a pernicious system of divide and rule in operation in their district. They claim that most of their local officers are made incompetent to represent their grievances by being recipients of personal favors from the management."[67]

Of all sleeping car porters' locals, Halifax had it the worse and voiced the most urgent calls for getting out of the CBRE. Working conditions were especially horrid there, where the lone restroom available for porters worked only part of the time and where CNR managers forced black railroaders into janitorial tasks instead of assigning them to the roads. Most telling, all sleeping car porters' locals reported not feeling any real protection from the CBRE machinery and therefore saw no point in keeping up with union dues. Swift's report to CBRE leaders admonished that "the men working on the CNR are no longer isolated. They come in daily contact on the job, in the public meeting places, and even on the streets with their fellow workman of other railways." And according to Swift, "they discuss the merits and demerits of the various labour organizations which represent them, and take pride in belonging to the organization which offers them the best working conditions or guarantees the maximum protection."[68] In that respect, then, Mosher and his CBRE were a resounding failure compared with what Arthur R. Blanchette, A. Philip Randolph, and the BSCP promised as champions of labor and civil rights.

Mosher displayed a baffling bewilderment after receiving Swift's assessment of the CBRE's black divisions. Instead of understanding Randolph's and the BSCP's appeal as a powerful rebuke of decades of Jim Crow on the rails, Mosher charged that African Canadian railwaymen were being seduced by foreign black agitators stoking racial tensions within the Canadian house of labor. In yet another example of his condescending and infantilizing handling of black CBRE members, Mosher sent a circular to all black locals chastising them for "unwittingly or deliberately lending themselves to a movement which, if successful, will result in race distinction in Canadian labour organizations and retard, if not completely break down, the efforts of the C.B.R.E. . . . during the past thirty-five years."[69] In other words, in a classic display of squaring the circle, Mosher and the CBRE accused black railroaders of being harbingers of "racist unionism" for trying to improve their working conditions by seeking stronger representation than he and the CBRE were prepared to offer.

In a completely disingenuous recasting of both his actions and the CBRE's history, Mosher insisted that from "the very inception of the Brotherhood, its policy has been to accord equal status to all workers in the transportation industry without regard to race, creed, or colour. . . . It is difficult, therefore, to understand why any [black] members would even consider abandoning the principles of industrial unionism to become not only craft unionists but race unionists." Mosher added insult to injury by indicting A. Philip Randolph for doing a terrible disservice to African Canadian porters by "mislead[ing] them into taking action[s] detrimental to their own cause."[70]

John A. Robinson, who by then had effectively retired from union work, fumed over Mosher's hubris and made hash of his unctuous pretensions. Robinson denounced Mosher's hypocrisy, reminding him that the CBRE's racialized hierarchy, as evidenced by segregated locals and a policy of brokering employee contracts along firm racial lines, was the true testament to racist unionism. Robinson concluded that for black railwaymen "being considered as advocates of race unionism is a compliment because in unity is strength, and with the darker races united, we can look forward to this being a better world to live in."[71] More important, Robinson gave the lie to most of Mosher's claims and pressed for incorporation in the BSCP by stressing that black railroaders' twenty-year experiment with the CBRE had been a persistent failure that CNR porters could now correct. He emphasized that, "contrary to your tirade against it," the BSCP had always been a fully integrated union and added that African Canadian porters were "well advised to place their future in the hands of the Brotherhood of Sleeping Car Porters," since at least Randolph valued black labor and dedicated his life's work to protecting black railwaymen' rights. Put differently, in the view of Robinson, Blanchette, and so many other porters, black railroaders' future rested with the Brotherhood of Sleeping Car Porters, not in Mosher's archaic model of Jim Crow industrial unionism.[72]

If Mosher proved completely out of touch with the changing nature of postwar racial politics, even within the ranks of the Canadian labor movement, Arthur R. Blanchette was incredibly smart at forging new partnerships, especially with Jewish Labour Committee leaders galvanized to action after World War II. A whole cast of Canadians horrified by the chaos and carnage of the Holocaust threw down the gauntlet on racism during the 1950s. Not until World War II and Canada's unflinching focus on the implications of the Holocaust and other forms of human rights violations did Canadian labor leaders demand a real turnaround on Jim Crow in organized labor and in Canadian public services more broadly. Canadian sleeping car porters, who clearly understood the connections between discrimination in the workplace and Jim Crow practices in other aspects of Canadian life, partnered with like-minded reformers such as Kalmen Kaplansky, director of the Jewish Labour Committee, and Sid Blum, executive secretary of the Joint Labour Committee for Human Rights. A. Philip Randolph also shared African Canadians' civil rights concerns and hoped that they would make good use of CLACP chapters when keeping up the pressure on de facto segregation. He and Blanchette strongly encouraged BSCP members to join labor committees and other social organizations dedicated to antidiscrimination work after World War II.

Throughout his time in Canada, A. Philip Randolph was consistently surprised by the extent to which African Canadians were frustrated by the same sociopolitical problems haunting many African Americans. At first blush, he, like most Americans, could have presumed that without outright Jim Crow laws race relations in Canada would be less strained, more amicable. In later years, even Malcolm X repeated that same erroneous assumption when he declared that "Mississippi is anywhere south of the Canadian border."[73] But in truth, most African Canadians could not disagree more strongly with that point of view. In "I Am a Canadian: Negro," an article published in *New Liberty* magazine, African Canadian Dorothy Sylvia captured the painful paradox of black life in Canada during the twentieth century. As "far as jobs are concerned," she opined, "the Negro is better off in the much-maligned Southern United States than in Canada." At least there, blacks could "get on the police force. In any American city Negroes can find jobs as hotel bellhops, or elevator boys, but this hasn't been so in Canada."[74] A decade later, black residents corroborated Sylvia's sentiment in the Canadian Broadcasting Corporation's special investigative report *Eye to Eye: The Negro in Winnipeg*. Mrs. Gerri Sylvia, a Winnipeg hospital aide, captured so many African Canadians' resentments when she told reporters that at least "in the Southern states, the Negro knows where he stands. I see all those Negro girls working in just about every department store in Minneapolis; they work in offices in Minneapolis. And yet they talk about the States. But you show me one Negro sales girl here in Winnipeg!"[75] In other words, African Canadians consistently felt that, despite the existence of segregation, African Americans enjoyed freedoms unparalleled among people of African descent elsewhere. They owned or operated their own businesses, hospitals, and historically black colleges and universities, and whatever Jim Crow's constraints, in the United States blacks could be accountants, surgeons, railway conductors, bankers, or college professors. Not so in Canada.

In truth, Canadians shared many common threads with the de facto segregation model of the American North and West, but with the added pernicious element of denying that racism could ever thrive in Canada in the first place. In other words, at least in the American North and West, de facto Jim Crow relied on separation of the races as the social ideal, and if that ideal was respected, the types of extralegal violence seen in the South and Midwest could be avoided. Of course it was not, as lynching, banishment, and other forms of racial terrorism found willing participants in both the American North and West. By the interwar years, many white Canadians wanted it both ways: they wanted loosely articulated and applied segregation policies, like redlining, but they also wanted to avoid embracing what such practices ultimately meant about them as a nation and a people. After all, the simple fact remained that Jim Crow laws and social conventions had salience only in societies propped up on white supremacist ideology.

To be sure, there were no shortages of segregationist practices in Canada from the 1930s to the 1950s. Virtually all forms of American Jim Crow policies thrived in Canada, with Canadians bringing their own views and fears—like xenophobia—to segregationist schemes. For example, restrictive housing covenants prevented most people of color—and in some cases even southern and eastern Europeans—from renting or buying property in certain cities. Clayton Mosher explains how, in the case of Great Depression–era Hamilton, neither blacks, Asians, Bulgarians, Serbs, Turks, Greeks, Italians, nor Jews could purchase land in selected parts of town. This pattern was repeated across Canada, as evidenced by a 1959 Toronto and District Committee for Human Rights study that found 60 percent of surveyed landlords unwilling or uncomfortable with renting to black residents.[76]

Even Winnipeg, with its small cluster of North Enders, was a city that could not escape the trappings of segregation, which is of course why most black Winnipeggers resided within blocks of each other. There too Jim Crow conventions dictated housing patterns and set distressing limitations on African Canadians' other social, political, and economic options. Many black Winnipeggers reported hassles when trying to rent an apartment or even worse when buying a home. Though armed with college degrees and specialized skills, they often still could not secure jobs in their fields; being pointed to the CPR railway station for men, or domestic work for women, passed for problem solving from well-meaning white Canadians.[77] Just as in the United States—but especially in the North and Midwest—blacks were also barred from leisure options like ice skating rinks, swimming pools, clubs, dance halls, and dining in certain restaurants.

African Canadians faced discrimination in other sectors as well and found it increasingly difficult to escape mocking public depiction of blackness during the interwar years. For one thing, from its introduction to Canadian audiences in 1929, *Amos 'n' Andy*, the radio equivalent of the blackface minstrel comedic genre, topped Canadians' list of favorite shows, so much so, in fact, that during the critical 1930 federal election season both candidates, Bennett and King, "carefully . . . steered away from competing with the Amos 'n' Andy Show" in order not to upset potential supporters.[78] Even after World War II, many white Canadians still operated from a set of assumptions about blacks that harkened back to early debates about black immigration to Canada and African Canadians' suitability for the full rewards of citizenship. For example, when discussing the revised 1952 Immigration Act, Minister of Citizenship and Immigration Jack Pickersgill reiterated a view long held by most Canadians: that discrimination against certain classes of migrants was perfectly appropriate when in the service of preserving a distinctly Canadian way of life.[79] For that reason, Pickersgill rationalized his department's continued exclusion of black and Asian would-be migrants as being for the nation's long-term good. Accordingly, the Canadian federal government, just as it had nearly a half century before, showed the most obdurate attachment to Jim Crow laws and practices, seemingly oblivious to its role as a moral measure of the nation.

Minister Pickersgill's stance on Canada's 1952 federal immigration law seemed woefully out of step with the spirit of reform—largely inspired and advanced by black and white labor activists—sweeping through provincial courts and legislatures. As early as 1944, Ontario had adopted its Racial Discrimination Act, prohibiting the use of white-only trade signs and other public postings singling out ethnic groups for separate and unequal treatment. For the countless Jews and African Canadians subjected to degrading signs like "No Jews, No Dogs Allowed," the ban could not have come fast enough.[80] Six years later, the Ontario Conveyancing and Law of Property Act and the Fair Employment Act rounded out legislation designed to halt Jim Crow in access to housing and jobs. Four more provinces joined the chorus against discrimination between 1953 and 1956; Quebec, long suspicious of those it perceived as outsiders, shamefully dragged its feet on antidiscrimination legislation until 1964. For its part, Saskatchewan had, in April 1947, been the first province to pass a Bill of Rights Act outlawing all exercises of segregation based on race or religion.[81]

Canadian provincial courts likewise registered the new postwar distaste for Jim Crow. Cases like *Franklin v. Evans* (1924), *Rogers v. Clarence Hotel Co. Ltd.*

(1940), *Christie v. York Tavern* (1940), and *Regina v. Emerson* (1950) demonstrate that Canadians victimized by segregationist practices, whether overt or de facto, had reached a saturation point and were prepared to challenge their displacement in court. It is also pertinent that legal challenges to Canadian Jim Crow made their way through the courts during the same decades when African Americans targeted their legislatures and courts for a more exacting defense of their civil rights.

If the 1950s gave birth to the civil rights movement in the United States and inspired young African Americans to tear down Jim Crow, the same was true in Canada with the exception that there young Canadians of all races framed the call for reform as a human rights movement. Once again, Asian Canadian, African Canadian, Jewish, and white labor activists teamed up to eradicate segregation in Canada, with Kalmen Kaplansky and Sid Blum working closely with sleeping car porters from Toronto's Road Roamers, the CBRE's local #175. Kaplansky and Blum also turned to Arthur R. Blanchette for counsel and insight into African Canadians' most urgent sociopolitical needs. As vice president of the Canadian Labour Congress's Human Rights Committee, Blanchette spent the better part of his career as a union man also being a pertinacious human rights exponent, sharing A. Philip Randolph's belief that the cause of labor and civil rights were different sides of the same sword.

Sid Blum also shared Blanchette's vision and understood white supremacy's destructive nature. He resolved to uproot it in Ontario by turning university students on restaurants that boasted their refusal to serve people of color. Blum is best known for working with University of Toronto students staging lunch counter sit-ins at Dresden's McKay's Café, Fitzgerald's Grill, and Emerson Restaurant in 1949. Restaurant owners in this small Ontario town were adamant about not serving black patrons and cited the right to decide with whom to conduct business as their reason for holding the line on Jim Crow. Despite the unforgiving media attention and sounding very much like white Americans who shared his racial beliefs, Dresden's mayor insisted that "you can't force anyone to serve Negroes. Perhaps you can get away with that sort of thing under Communism" but not here in Canada.[82] Even if most white Canadians might not have wanted to share a table with African Canadians, they were scandalized by white Dresden residents' raw and unapologetic resistance to integration. Like so many white Americans in favor of segregation, many white Canadians blamed blacks' calls for civil and human rights as the work of foreign agitators, namely, Communists, conveniently ignoring the reality that opposition to Jim Crow was not new and in fact strictly inspired by continued violations of blacks' citizenship rights. Writing for *Maclean's* exposé on events in Dresden, journalist Sid Katz opined, "Jim Crow Lives! The Canadian who looks down on the Southern United States for 'Jim Crow' racial segregation will suffer a rude shock on visiting [this] sleepy agricultural center"—and what a century earlier had been home to scores of American freedom seekers.[83]

Whereas during the 1950s African Americans focused on a range of civil rights causes, African Canadians' postwar concerns centered on discriminatory federal laws, most important Canada's 1952 Immigration Act. Given that so many blacks in Canada were foreign-born and viewed immigration restriction as a twofold violation—as an exercise of racism and xenophobia—African Canadian human rights activists wed immigration reform and dismantling segregation into a single pursuit, with sleeping car porter Stanley Grizzle perhaps its most vocal proponent. Born in Toronto in 1918 to Jamaican parents, Grizzle made human rights pursuits his life's work, first as a railway union man and then as a political agitator.[84] After serving in World War II, Grizzle, like most black men at the time, found work on the railroad. More important, as president of Toronto's Road Roamers and an active member of the Negro Citizenship Association, he became part of an outspoken group of black railway unionists dedicated to human rights advocacy.

If Montreal had the largest and most vociferous group of porters, and Winnipeg the most courageous ones, Toronto was, without a doubt, home to the most politically astute black railroaders in Canada. Toronto porters worked closely with other human rights organizations and Kalmen Kaplansky's Jewish Labour Committee in particular. Canada's discriminatory immigration laws roused Grizzle's and Kaplansky's ire because of how they had effectively barred European Jews from safe harbor in Canada during World War II.[85] And for blacks who had once braved passage into Canada or who were now separated from their families because the Immigration Act raised the bar on admission requirements, the time had come for reform. In April 1954, Grizzle and other Road Roamers traveled to Ottawa to petition the minister of citizenship and immigration, Walter Harris, to reconsider Canada's nearly fifty-year stance on race and immigration.

With the support of Arthur R. Blanchette back in Montreal, and working through Toronto's Negro Citizenship Association, an organization created by porters, Stanley Grizzle delivered a brief attacking the minister of immigration's continued restrictions on black migration to Canada. Grizzle took very seriously that he shouldered the hopes and disappointments of many blacks in Canada fatigued from decades of fighting Jim Crow immigration policies. Given the scope of the federal government's reach and the Ministry of Citizenship and Immigration's particular impact on African Canadians' lives, Grizzle stressed that, whether black or white, "we [as human rights advocates] take the uncompromising position that what appears to be premeditated discrimination in Canada's Immigration laws and policy is utterly inconsistent with democratic principles and Christian ethics."[86]

Grizzle—as well as the BSCP and other labor organizations that fully backed his actions—framed his critique of Canadian immigration law as morally bankrupt, especially against the background of the Holocaust. Jim Crow federal policy, Grizzle insisted, should be immediately abandoned given what investment in racism and white supremacy wrought in Nazi Germany. By defining as desirable only whites of British and northern European heritage, and excluding nonwhite British subjects, which of course included West Indians, South Asians, and Africans, Canada had created a two-tiered, race-based definition of citizenship that, as Grizzle reminded the minister, worked directly against the 1948 United Nations' Declaration of Human Rights and Queen Elizabeth's 1953 pronouncement of equal partnership within the Commonwealth.[87] Grizzle called on Canadians—with the federal government leading the way—to move away from white supremacy by finally rejecting as false the belief that people of color and non-Christian Canadians warranted separate and unequal treatment. Refusing to do so, Grizzle cautioned, would reinforce the notion "that there are superior and inferior races [which] has the tendency to raise animosity between people."

Stanley Grizzle, Minister Harris, and all others gathered for these immigration meetings could not ignore the political chaos and collective call for civil rights and human rights happening around the world. In 1954 alone, Laos and Vietnam won their independence, with Ho Chi Minh becoming the unrepentant face of French postcolonial defiance. That same year, France hoped that by turning over its South Asian possessions it could avoid the kind of rebellion erupting in Algeria. Meanwhile in Africa, four countries— Egypt, Tunisia, Tanzania, and South Africa—embraced new administrations in 1954, with the last electing Johannes Gerhardus Strijom, an aberrant apartheid advocate. Within months, François Duvalier took Haiti, and just across the Caribbean Sea, the CIA seized Guatemala from Jacobo Arbenz.

Destruction came to North America in various forms as well that year. President Eisenhower finally admitted to years of nuclear testing, more recently in the Bikini Islands. Meanwhile, Hurricane Edna struck New York, causing more than fifty million dollars in damage, only to have Hazel a few months later repeat the carnage. Most important, especially for Grizzle's greater point before the Ministry of Immigration, 1954 sounded Jim Crow's death knell, with *Brown v. Board of Education* making clear that sanction of segregation had lost its legal and moral legitimacy.

The federal government had already adopted the Fair Employment Act of 1953 outlawing discrimination in the workplace, making the minister of immigration's recalcitrance on Jim Crow matters all the more obstinately outmoded. By refusing to amend its immigration policy, Canada—and its Ministry of Immigration in particular—risked being seen as upholding white supremacy and siding with the likes of South Africa's Johannes Gerhardus Strijom and Georgia's Herman Talmadge. Grizzle contended that "the Western races hold the predominance in material wealth and power. They evince in a hundred ways a determination to assert their superiority, and to keep other races in a position of subordination and inferiority. It is against this very attitude [that] peoples the world over are in revolt.[88] Canada's BSCP and the Negro Citizenship Association demonstrated their keen understanding of global Cold War racial politics when Grizzle concluded that "it is our sincere belief that we cannot expect to win friends and allies among the free nations when we discriminate against their peoples, and so in the interest of national and international welfare and security, this 'Jim Crow Iron Curtain' which exists in Canada's Immigration policy must be eradicated immediately." Aware that he might never again have the opportunity to affect such radical legal reform in Canada, Grizzle minced no words in his closing, exhorting Harris: "Honourable Minister, do not be recreant in facing your responsibility."[89]

THE POSTWAR ERA BROUGHT a season of major changes in North America. In the United States, African Americans and their allies rallied around civil rights causes, while in Canada, activists focused their attention on human rights and reformulating the nation's place in the British Commonwealth. In each arena, sleeping car porters fueled the spirit of reform, bringing to their respective political campaigns what they had learned first on the railroads. The 1950s were also a decade in which people of color—in Canada and around the world—held their countries up to their own democratic ideals, and in particular to the rhetoric of equality. Thus young radicals doing so in Saigon, Cairo, Algiers, Montgomery, and Montreal raised comparable debates about the meaning of citizenship in a post–World War II era.

For blacks in Canada, the 1950s represented an important changing of the guards. The first caste of African Canadian activists, the most notable among them John A. Robinson and his band of brothers on the rails, fought for the right to be heard, for a place in the Canadian house of labor, for the right to defend their country, and for fair access to the full range of citizenship privileges afforded to Canadians. Throughout his career as a railway man and early Canadian industrial unionist, Robinson remained indefatigable, never backing down from exploitation at the hands of employers or other white Canadians, even those like Aaron Mosher of the CBRE, who claimed to be working on black railroaders' behalf. Over the course of nearly three decades, Robinson gave birth to a black railway union movement that lasted more than seventy years. In the process, he taught other African Canadians the importance of weeding out Jim Crow wherever it set root and plant in its place a robust social unionism vision that gave the lie to assumptions about black inferiority.

Arthur R. Blanchette could not have learned his trade from a more dedicated man. From the Great Depression's early days, Blanchette reinvigorated black communities in Canada, serving for decades as the nation's most important black political leader. Blanchette always seemed two steps ahead of his peers and strategically positioned himself as the vanguard of both labor radicalism and human rights activism. The Brotherhood of Sleeping Car Porters that he almost single-handedly shepherded grew into the largest national civil rights organization operating in Canada after World War II. To this tour de force he added A. Philip Randolph's wisdom, partnership, strategies, and friendship. As in the United States, where porters shaped the civil rights movement, so too in Canada did porters do this work. There, they trained their attention on legal reform, especially at the federal level, where Jim Crow proved more deeply entrenched. The 1953 Fair Employment Practices Act and at least the start of a debate in 1954 about the Immigration Act pointed Canadians in the right direction.

The fifties transformed the Canadian rails as well. The Fair Employment Practices Act meant that employers could no longer lawfully avoid hiring workers of color. Canadian railway managers quickly interpreted that to mean that they did not have to hire black people at all, especially if they had to pay them the same wage as a white man. Accordingly, when black sleeping car porters retired, they were increasingly replaced by younger and less politically seasoned white ones. But the juggernauts that were for nearly a century the icons of modernity—the Canadian Pacific Railway and the Canadian National Railways—had passed their zenith. Bus, private car, and air transportation pushed railway travel to the margins as a romantic *passe-temps*. In the second half of the twentieth century, younger, eager, going-somewhere Canadians hopped a flight or raced off in their new cars if they wanted to make a statement about their social mobility.

The sleeping car porter too became a thing of the past. Some younger African Canadians repudiated portering as a job for the weak and yielding, a pursuit for Uncle Toms when times called for Martin Luther King's and Robert F. Williams's models of upheaval. What those younger African Canadians could not know is that the older porter's silence or his smile hid what for so many had been decades of steadfast resistance. Many of Canada's black old-timers retired or moved on to other professional options once Jim Crow had become outlawed in the workplace. Some porters returned to university in order to complete degrees interrupted by years of travel. In other cases, former porters headed to the United States to take up the sword in the burgeoning civil rights movement. Growing anticolonialism in the West Indies promised substantive political reform and attracted former Canadian sleeping car porters who wanted to take part in casting off the yoke of imperial rule. St. Vincent and the Grenadines' second prime minister, the Honorable James F. Mitchell, had for years been a Montreal sleeping car porter.

Whether they remained in Canada, like Stanley Grizzle, who in 1978 became the first African Canadian citizenship judge, or hit the road for points abroad, the fifty-year legacy of labor activism and antidiscrimination advocacy made real by sleeping car porters in Canada is one that lives on in the laws that they transformed, the communities that they brought to life, and the human rights work that they inspired.

Notes

Abbreviations

In addition to the abbreviations found in the text, the following source abbreviations are used in the notes.

AAG   Acting Adjutant General
AG   Adjutant General
AM   Archives of Manitoba, Winnipeg
BW   *Black Worker* (New York)
CPA   Canadian Pacific Archives, Montreal, Quebec
DND   Department of National Defence
DT   *Dawn of Tomorrow* (Hamilton, Ont.)
EEJ   *Edmonton (Alta.) Evening Journal*
HCD   *House of Commons Debates*
IBR   Immigration Branch Records, Library and Archives of Canada, Ottawa, Ontario
LAC   Library and Archives of Canada, Ottawa, Ontario
LG   Department of Labour, *Labour Gazette*
LH   *Lethbridge (Alta.) Herald*
LC   Library of Congress
MD   Militia and Defence Collection, Library and Archives of Canada, Ottawa, Ontario
MFP   *Manitoba Free Press* (Winnipeg)
NYT   *New York Times*
PANS   Public Archives of Nova Scotia, Halifax

Introduction

1. *Manitoba Daily Free Press* (Winnipeg), 2 July 1886.

2. Bonar, *Montreal and the Inauguration of Trans-Canada Transportation*; *MFP*, 2 July 1886.

3. W. F. Salisbury to Mrs. Salisbury, 5 July 1886, RG31 CPA.

4. Mayor H. S. Wesbrook's speech as quoted in *Manitoba Daily Free Press*, 2 July 1886.

5. Ibid.

6. There has always been some controversy over the terms used to refer to people of African descent. Given that blacks in Canada were ethnically diverse, no single term accurately captures their nuanced identities. Here, all black people in Canada will be referred to as either "black" or "African Canadian," regardless of citizenship status. When making specific reference to those born elsewhere, I will refer to them ethnically—e.g., African Americans, West Indians, or Jamaicans.

7. *LH*, 22 March 1911; *MFP*, 27 March 1911.

8. Greaves, *National Problems in Canada*, 70–73; Murphy, *Black Candle*.

9. *Maclean's*, 15 May 1922, 13.

10. *Census of Canada*, 1931, 1:247.

11. See, for example, Shortt and Doughty, *Canada and Its Provinces*, vol. 1, *Immigration by Races*, by William D. Scott; *EEJ*, 8 April 1911; and *MFP*, 27 March 1911.

12. *Manitoba Daily Free Press*, 29 June 1886.

13. Sir John A. Macdonald as quoted in Den Otter, *Philosophy of Railways*, 6.

14. Berton, *National Dream: The Last Spike*.

15. Ibid., 9.

16. Balibar and Wallerstein, *Race, Nation, Class*, 71–103.

17. Trout and Trout, *Railways of Canada*, 72, 127.

18. Ibid., 58–59.

19. Ibid. The son of American Loyalists who immigrated to Nova Scotia, Howe served as editor of the *Nova Scotian* between 1828 and 1841 before leading the opposition to Confederation (1866–68). He was later elected to the House of Commons (1869–73) and then served as lieutenant governor-general for Nova Scotia (1873–74). *Canadian Encyclopedia*, 1109.

20. Dominion Bureau of Statistics, *Canada Yearbook*, 1906, 285.

21. Cruise and Griffiths, *Lords of the Line*. With the exception of George Stephen, who was born in Great Britain, all the other captains of the railway industry listed were born in the United States but made their name and career in Canada. Accordingly, I refer to them here as "Canadian" railway barons.

22. Celebrations of the first transcontinental train conveniently ignored that the Maritimes were amputated from Canada's transcontinental vision, this despite making up more than 50 percent of the Confederation's partnership. The *Pacific Express* departed for Port Moody, British Columbia, from Montreal on 28 June 1886.

23. Holt, *Grand Trunk in New England*, 83.

24. *Canadian Illustrated News* (Montreal), August 1870.

25. Agreement between Pullman Palace Company and Grand Trunk Railway of Canada, 1 August 1870, CNR, RG30-12680, LAC.

26. Vaughan, *Life and Work of Sir William Van Horne*, 50–55, 64–75.

27. F. C. Blair, Ottawa, to W. Gillan, Montreal, 11 July 1923, IBR, 816222, LAC.

28. J. Pierson, "William Van Horne and the Canadian Pacific Railway," pt. 1, n.d., Van Horne Papers, MG29-A60, LAC.

29. Bederman, *Manliness and Civilization*, 1–44.

30. Santino, "Miles of Smiles, Years of Struggle."

31. Sladen, *On the Cars and Off*, 216.

32. Ibid., 216–18.

33. Chateauvert, *Marching Together*, 1–19.

34. Sladen, *On the Cars and Off*, 218–19; Roper, *By Track and Trail*.

35. Katz, *Black West*.

36. Lee, *At America's Gates*, 44–45. There was no shortage of hysteria over the arrival of Chinese, Japanese, and East Indian migrants in Canada either, and those populations faced virulent racism, especially in the western provinces. See McKeown, *Melancholy Order*, and McGee, Laqian, and Aquan, *Silent Debate*.

37. Dan Williams, an irascible former Virginia or Georgia slave turned fur trader, came to Canada in the nineteenth century. Also known as the "Negro Bismarck," Williams is said to have taken part in the famed Palliser Expedition in 1857 that cut its way through the

Canadian Rockies and charted what would later become the CPR's chief lines to the West. Williams married Beaver Indian chief Komaxala's daughter, Thela, and lived near Peace River until the 1870s. Winks, *Blacks in Canada*, 302.

38. *Toronto Globe*, 25 September 1915.

39. Winks, *Blacks in Canada*, 327.

40. *Montreal Gazette*, 17 August 1920; *NYT*, 17 August 1920.

41. *Census of Canada*, 1921, 646–47, 828.

42. The neighborhood in Winnipeg where most black people lived is known by three interchangeable names: Point Douglas, New Jerusalem, and the North End.

43. Edward ("Eddie") Blackman, interview by author.

44. Commanding Officer 147th to AAG Toronto, 4 April 1916, DND, RG24-4387-34-7-141, LAC. Also see Walker, *"Race," Rights and the Law*.

Chapter 1

1. *MFP*, 27 March 1911.

2. *Ottawa Free Press*, 18 January 1911.

3. *MFP*, 22 March 1911; Painter, *Exodusters*.

4. Headline from *Port Arthur (Ont.) Evening Chronicle*, 21 January 1911.

5. *LH*, 22 March 1911; *MFP*, 27 March 1911.

6. Palmer and Palmer, *Peoples of Alberta*, 377.

7. *Winnipeg (Man.) Tribune*, 22 March 1911; *MFP*, 27 March 1911.

8. *Calgary (Alta.) Herald*, 25 March 1911; *MFP*, 27 March 1911.

9. *MFP*, 27 March 1911. W. H. Rogers to William D. Scott, 6 April 1911, IBR, RG76-192-7552-4, LAC. Rogers, a Canadian immigration official stationed in Oklahoma, reported to his supervisors that "several times recently, those people have brought with them both doctors and lawyers . . . all the way from Oklahoma" to Canada. One such group of migrants were said to have "drafts amounting to $9,000" and "declared they were physically fit as any white men."

10. *Ottawa Free Press*, 20 March 1911; *MFP*, 22 March 1911.

11. *MFP*, 27 March 1911.

12. Ibid.

13. Rev. Will H. Hurt to James S. Crawford, 6 October 1910, IBR, RG76-192-7552-1, LAC.

14. Shortt and Doughty, *Canada and Its Provinces*, vol. 1, *Immigration by Races*, by William D. Scott, 531.

15. Ibid. Scott began his career with the Canadian Pacific Railway before joining the immigration branch in 1903. By 1922, Scott had become the chief controller of Chinese immigration and made keeping blacks and Asians out of Canada his life's work.

16. *EEJ*, 8 April 1911.

17. Ibid., 7 April 1911.

18. Edmonton Police Department, 15 April 1911, IBR, RG76-192-7552-1, LAC.

19. Daughters of the Empire to Frank Oliver, 31 March 1911, IBR, RG76-192-7552-3, LAC.

20. Fritz V. Freidrichs to Frank Oliver, April 1911, IBR, RG76-192-7552-3, LAC.

21. *Toronto Globe*, 28 March 1911.

22. *EEJ*, 27 March 1911.

23. *Order in Council* 1–2 Geo. 5, 1911.

24. *Winnipeg Tribune*, 12 April 1911.

25. Winks, *Blacks in Canada*, 288–336; Walker, *"Race," Rights and the Law*, 24–136.

26. *EEJ*, 11 April 1911.

27. I do not suggest that all African American southerners bolted out of Dixie. The advent of segregation certainly forced millions into northern states. Canada, Mexico, Europe, and Africa were also important destinations. Millions more, though, stayed in the South and defended their land and their rights. See Woodward, *Origins of the New South*, vol. 9; Gilmore, *Gender and Jim Crow*; Grossman, *Land of Hope*; and Kelley, *Hammer and Hoe*.

28. Sneed as quoted in *Edmonton (Alta.) Capital*, 13 April 1911. Department of Immigration officials frequently complained that the monetary requirements for entry to Canada presented no problems for African Americans, who usually carried at least $300. Each of the Sneed party's families carried $3,000 with them upon arrival. Another group coming in April 1911 brought $9,000 per family. James S. Crawford to William D. Scott, 6 April 1911, IBR, RG76-192-7552-4.

29. Gilmore, *Gender and Jim Crow*, xv–xxii; Kelley, *Hammer and Hoe*, 1–12.

30. *Calgary Herald*, 28 March 1911.

31. Laurier's other early projects included forming a Canadian navy and negotiating a broader free trade agreement with the United States, also known as reciprocity agreements. Both endeavors were utter failures and eventually cost the Liberals control of the Canadian government in 1911. See "Sir Wilfrid Laurier" in *Canadian Encyclopedia*, 1302–3.

32. See "Arthur Lewis Sifton" and "Clifford Sifton" in *Canadian Encyclopedia*, 2161. Interestingly, Arthur Sifton became the premier of Alberta during the peak of the movement against black immigration to the province, thereby inheriting the outcome of his brother's immigration policy.

33. Avery, *Reluctant Host*; Troper, *Only Farmers Need Apply*.

34. Troper, *Only Farmers Need Apply*, 30, 62.

35. Ministry of the Interior, *Immigration Facts and Figures*, 1919, 2.

36. Ibid., 10. It is difficult to assess the exact number of returning Canadians, as the Dominion Bureau of Statistics only recorded entries of Canadians returning via ocean ports. Between 1896 and 1911, the bureau reported that 135,391 Canadians returned to the land of their birth.

37. Ibid., 2–7.

38. Canadian Sessional Papers, 1911, n. 25, xxix.

39. Woodsworth, *Strangers within Our Gates*, 221.

40. Ministry of the Interior, *Report on Immigration*, 1912, 91.

41. *HCD*, 17 April 1902, 2991.

42. Athabasca Landing Board of Trade to Frank Oliver, 17 April 1911, IBR, RG76-192-7552-3, LAC.

43. Shortt and Doughty, *Canada and Its Provinces*, 531.

44. Woodward, *Origins of the New South*, 350–53.

45. Smith, *Civic Ideals*; *Plessy v. Ferguson*, 163 U.S. 537 (1896).

46. See IBR, RG76-192-7552-1, LAC.

47. Barney McKay to commissioner of immigration, 27 October 1901, IBR, RG76-192-7552-1, LAC.

48. James A. Strachan to Clifford Sifton, 21 July 1902, IBR, RG76-192-7552-1, LAC.

49. Rev. Will H. Hurt to James S. Crawford, 6 October 1910, IBR, RG76-192-7552-1, LAC.

50. *Regina (Sask.) Leader*, 25 August 1908. Some of the men were hired in a coal mine at Roche Percée. See Alexander McGregor to mayor of Estevan, 22 August 1908, Royal Canadian Mounted Police Papers, 469, LAC.

51. George Clingan to J. Bruce Walker, 21 August 1908, IBR, RG76-192-7552-1, LAC.

52. J. B. Williams to William D. Scott, 29 June 1909, IBR, RG76-566-810666-1, LAC.

53. W. L. Barnstead to L. M. Fortier, 30 June 1914, IBR, RG76-566-810666-1, LAC. For more on West Indian immigration to Canada during this period, see Schultz, " 'White Man's Country,' " and Calliste, "Race, Gender, and Canadian Immigration Policy."

54. Lyndwode Pereira to James S. Crawford, 23 January 1899, IBR, RG76-192-7552-1, LAC.

55. Mathieu, "Under the Lion's Paw," 15–38; Winks, *Blacks in Canada*, 272–87.

56. *Census of Canada*, 1901, 392–405, 446–47.

57. For additional information on African Americans in British Columbia, see Pilton, "Negro Settlement in British Columbia"; Kilian, *Go Do Some Great Thing*; Edwards, "War of Complexional Distinction"; and Irby, "Black Settlers on Saltspring Island."

58. *Immigration Act*, 6 Edw. 7, c. 19, and *Revised Statutes of Canada*, c. 93.

59. Knowles, *Strangers at Our Gates*, 93.

60. Immigration records for that period indicate that 317 African Americans and 527 West Indians entered Canada via ocean ports. Data were not collected at border entries. See Ministry of the Interior, *Immigration Facts and Figures*, 1919, 6–9.

61. *Ottawa Free Press*, 20 April 1908.

62. *MFP*, 30 May 1908. The *MFP* frequently published inaccurate accounts; 1,500 migrants never arrived in Alberta during 1907 or 1908. In fact, immigration branch records show that between 1900 and 1916 a total of 1,234 African Americans immigrated to Canada. See Ministry of the Interior, *Immigration Facts and Figures*, 6–9.

63. Border Entry Records for Emerson, Manitoba, March 1910, IBR, RG76, LAC.

64. Ibid., June 1910, RG76, LAC.

65. *Immigration Act*, 9–10 Edw. 7 c. 27.

66. Ibid.

67. Shepard, *Deemed Unsuitable*, 34–49.

68. Painter, *Exodusters*, 137–45; Shepard, *Deemed Unsuitable*, 50–65.

69. Painter, *Exodusters*, 108–17, 184–201.

70. Grossman, *Land of Hope*, 23–27.

71. Gilmore, *Gender and Jim Crow*, 1–30.

72. Winks, *Blacks in Canada*, 178–232.

73. Horne, *Black and Brown*, 12–24; Winks, *Blacks in Canada*, 142–78.

74. Black migrants from Oklahoma and Kansas established black townships modeled after their U.S. homeland throughout the Canadian West. Western Canadian communities with black settlers included Maidstone, North Battleford, Amber Valley, and Breton; as of the Great Depression, second-generation Canadian "Exodusters" increasingly abandoned farming for urban careers. See Winks, *Blacks in Canada*, 303–6, and Shepard, "Diplomatic Racism."

75. Constitution and By-Laws for the Alberta Negro Colonization and Settlement Society as cited in *EEJ*, 11 April 1911.

76. *MFP*, 30 May 1908.

77. Oklahoma City newspaper, title unknown, 26 March 1911, clipping included in IBR, RG76-192-7551-1, LAC.

78. *Calgary Herald*, 25 March 1911.

79. Rev. W. A. Lamb-Campbell to Department of Immigration, 6 September 1906, IBR, RG76-192-7551-1, LAC.

80. *Edmonton (Alta.) Daily Capital*, 13 April 1911.

81. Frank Powell to Frank Oliver, 2 March 1910, IBR, RG76-192-7551-1, LAC.

82. Ibid.

83. Oklahoma City newspaper, title unknown, 26 March 1911, clipping included in IBR, RG76-192-7551-1, LAC.

84. For additional information on American-Canadian diplomatic relations pertaining to black immigration, see Thomson, "Dark Spots in Alberta," and Troper, "Creek Negroes of Oklahoma."

85. W. H. Rogers to William D. Scott, 2 February 1912, IBR, RG76-192-7551-3, LAC.

86. *Lethbridge (Alta.) Morning Leader Post*, 24 March 1911.

87. *MFP*, 27 February 1911.

88. *NYT*, 2 April 1911.

89. J. Bruce Walker to Frank Oliver, 23 May 1911, IBR, RG76-192-7551-3, LAC.

90. *Chicago Record Herald*, 28 April 1911.

91. W. E. B. Du Bois, New York, to Department of Immigration, 4 March 1911, IBR, RG76-192-7552-2, LAC. Du Bois's letter and the Canadian government's response were printed in *Crisis*. Subsequent articles also dealt with black immigration to Canada; see *Crisis*, April through June 1911.

92. F. C. Blair to W. E. B. Du Bois, 7 March 1911, IBR, RG76-192-7552-2, LAC.

93. By 1915, the immigration branch noted a marked increase in requests for information from African Americans in the Northeast. See IBR, RG76-192-7552-5, LAC.

94. Many white settlers frequently contacted immigration branch offices for confirmation that African Americans were indeed barred from Western Canada. See James S. Crawford to William D. Scott, 31 December 1910, IBR, RG76-192-7552-2, LAC.

95. *Crisis*, May 1911.

96. John T. Richards to Frank Oliver, 27 March 1911, IBR, RG76-192-7552-3, LAC.

97. *HCD*, 2 March 1911, 4471.

98. *HCD*, 22 March 1911, 5912.

99. *HCD*, 23 March 1911, 5943.

100. *HCD*, 22 March 1911, 5912.

101. William D. Scott to Frank Oliver, 23 March 1911, IBR, RG76-192-7551-2, LAC.

102. The inspector of U.S. agencies was the Canadian government bureaucrat in charge of field agents working in the United States. William J. White to Frank Oliver, 14 September 1909, IBR, RG76-192 f. 7552-1, LAC.

103. William J. White to W. O. Callaway, 22 February 1912, IBR, RG76-192-7552-3, LAC.

104. Hill, "Alberta's Black Settlers," 86.

105. McLaren, *Our Own Master Race*, 46–67.

106. Some immigration medical inspectors really capitalized on Canada's negrophobia. In 1915, a lull year in African American immigration, Emerson's Dr. Maxwell Wallace earned almost one thousand dollars from border examinations bonuses alone. The Department of Immigration paid out bonuses only for rejected black migrants at that time, though Asians would soon follow. See IBR, RG76-192-7552-5, LAC.

107. William D. Scott to J. Bruce Walker, 2 November 1911, IBR, RG76-192-7552-5, LAC.

108. These figures reflect only immigrants denied entry at ocean ports, as the immigration branch did not include data from border entries in its annual report at that time.

109. In its annual report on immigration, the Ministry of the Interior documented that twenty women had been rejected at ocean ports between 1902 and 1914 on the grounds of pregnancy; an additional thirteen had been deported for the same reason. Ministry of the Interior, *Report on Immigration*, 1912, 74–75. For reference to the rejection of African

Americans on the basis of hookworms, see G. L. Milne to William D. Scott, 13 December 1913, IBR, RG76-820636, and William D. Scott to J. Bruce Walker, 11 November 1915, IBR, RG76-192-7552-5, LAC.

110. Ministry of the Interior, *Immigration Facts and Figures*, 1919, 6–9.

111. William D. Scott to W. J. Webster, 5 January 1911, IBR, RG76-192-7552-2, LAC.

112. M. C. Baltrip to commissioner of immigration, 29 May 1911, IBR, RG76-192-7552-2, LAC.

113. William D. Scott to commissioner of immigration, 9 June 1911, IBR, RG76-192-7552-2, LAC.

114. Charles Speers to William White, 8 May 1911, IBR, RG76-192-7552-4, LAC. J. B. Buckett and C. W. Miller were the two African American physicians employed by the immigration branch. See IBR, RG76-192-7552-4, LAC.

115. Charles Speers to William White, 17 May 1911, IBR, RG76-192-7552-3, LAC.

116. Charles Speers to Rev. W. H. Jernegin, 24 May 1911, IBR, RG76-192-7552-4, LAC.

117. Jones was also president of the Muskogee Fruit and Bottling Company and a successful preacher who led Oklahoma's wealthiest black church. William White to William D. Scott, 20 February 1912, and W. H. Rogers to William D. Scott, 15 February 1912, IBR, RG76-192-7552-5.

118. Charles Speers to Rev. S. S. Jones, 24 May 1911, IBR, RG76-192-7552-4, LAC.

119. *Baptist Informer*, n.d., in IBR, RG76-192-7552-3, LAC.

120. In 1936, Department of Immigration bureaucrats still boasted of the department's Miller campaign, recounting that "one of the stories he [Miller] used to tell was he had seen the coloured people frozen along the roadside." Gilmore to assistant deputy minister, 27 October 1936, IBR, RG76-192-7552-7, LAC.

121. *Oklahoma Guide* (Oklahoma City), 6 July 1911.

122. Ibid.

123. Ibid.

124. Miller claimed that he visited Western Canada, but after examining border entry records for British Columbia, Saskatchewan, and Manitoba, I could find no record of his entry. He never tells his readers how long he stayed in Canada or, more important, how he survived through such harrowing experiences.

125. For Oklahoma and Kansas field agent reports, see IBR, RG76-192-7552-5, LAC.

126. W. H. Rogers to William D. Scott, 6 April 1911, IBR, RG76-192-7552-4, LAC.

127. Washington, *Up from Slavery*, 158–61.

128. *Times* (London), 10–13 April 1911.

129. *Chicago Tribune*, 1 June 1911.

130. *MFP*, 3 January 1911.

131. Edmonton Board of Trade to Sir Wilfrid Laurier, 3 May 1911, IBR, RG76-192-7552-3, LAC.

132. See various telegrams, wires, and petitions from western boards of trade in IBR, RG76-192-7552-3, LAC.

133. F. D. Fisher to Frank Oliver, 8 April 1911, IBR, RG76-192-7552-3, LAC.

134. Edmonton Board of Trade to Sir Wilfrid Laurier, 8 April 1911, IBR, RG76-192-7552-3, LAC.

135. Frank Oliver, the minister of immigration, owned Edmonton's *Bulletin*—the most vehemently antiblack newspaper in the West.

136. Knowles, *Strangers at Our Gates*, 91.

137. F. D. Fisher to Frank Oliver, late March 1911, IBR, RG76-192-7552-3, LAC.

138. Athabasca Landing Board of Trade to Frank Oliver, 17 April 1911, IBR, RG76-192-7552-3, LAC. Battleford's, Red Deer's, and Saskatoon's Boards of Trade specifically asked that black settlers already in the West be sequestered in one part of the Plains.

139. *Edmonton Capital*, 27 April 1911.

140. *Lethbridge (Alta.) Daily Herald*, 11 April 1911.

141. Hill, "Alberta's Black Settlers," 92.

142. *Calgary Herald*, 25 March 1911; *LH*, 22 March 1911.

143. *EEJ*, 27 March 1911.

144. *Lethbridge Daily Herald*, 7 April 1911.

145. Ibid.

146. *LH*, 15 April 1911.

147. *Winnipeg Tribune*, 6 April 1911.

148. *EEJ*, 13 April 1911; *LH*, 15 April 1911; *MFP*, 12 April 1911.

149. *Lethbridge (Alta.) Daily News*, 8 April 1911.

150. *Calgary (Alta.) Albertan*, as quoted in McKague, *Racism in Canada*, 23.

151. *Lethbridge Daily News*, 8 April 1911.

152. *EEJ*, 5 April 1911.

153. *Edmonton (Alta.) Daily Bulletin*, 7 April 1911.

154. Walker, *"Race," Rights and the Law*, 122–81.

155. *EEJ*, 13 April 1911.

156. Bederman, *Manliness and Civilization*, 1–44.

157. *LH*, 11 April 1911.

158. Ibid.

159. Ibid. Based in Montreal, the Victor Gramophone Company created Canada's only race label, Ajax, and distributed jazz and blues records throughout the dominion. See Gilmore, *Swinging in Paradise*, 36–41.

160. *Winnipeg Tribune*, 12 April 1911; *Lethbridge Morning Leader Post*, 13 April 1911; *Calgary (Alta.) Daily Herald*, 13–15 April 1911; *EEJ*, 4 and 12 April 1911.

161. *Winnipeg Tribune*, 12 April 1911.

162. *EEJ*, 8 April 1911.

163. *HCD*, 3 April 1911, 6524.

164. Ibid., 6525–26.

165. *Orders in Council* 1–2 Geo. 5, 1911.

166. P.C. 1324, 12 August 1911, *Orders in Council*, RG2-769-370, LAC.

167. To be sure, Asian and South Asian migrants faced impossible odds when coming to Canada, including the continuous journey requirement and predatory head taxes. Loopholes for students and diplomats allowed for some Asian migrants' entry into Canada, but the 1911 order in council targeting black immigrants did not include provisions for students or other special set-aside classes of black migrants.

168. *HCD*, 23 March 1911, 5947. Also see Dr. J. J. Chandler to U.S. Consul General Jones, 27 June 1912, and George B. Kelley to William D. Scott, 22 March 1917 (and reply), IBR, RG76-192-72552-6, LAC.

169. Winks, "Canadian–West Indian Union," 39.

170. Hoerder, *Creating Societies*, 237–278.

Chapter 2

1. *Provincial Freeman* (Chatham, Ont.), 16 September 1854.

2. William W. Overton to J. E. McGuire, 11 March 1943, CBRE, MG28-I215, LAC.

3. Quoted in Cameron, " 'Wheat from the Chaff,'" 4.

4. Mika and Mika, *Illustrated History of Canadian Railways*, 97, 208.

5. Van Horne and Hays, both American-born, transformed Canadian railways during their tenure as general managers for the CPR and GTR, respectively. Hays died on the *Titanic* in April 1914, never having witnessed the GTR's national service. See "Charles Melville Hays," *Canadian Encyclopedia*, 1052, and "William Cornelius Van Horne," *Canadian Encyclopedia*, 2437.

6. Canadian Pacific Railway, *Annual Report of the Canadian Pacific Railway Company*, April 1896, 28. According to its May 1886 report, the CPR spent $24,098.99 on the parlor and sleeping car department during fiscal year 1885. See Canadian Pacific Railway, *Annual Report of the Canadian Pacific Railway Company*, May 1886, 27.

7. Vaughan, *Life and Work of Sir William Van Horne*, 50–52, 141–43.

8. Canadian Pacific Railway, *Annual Report of the Canadian Pacific Railway Company*, May 1884, 27, and August 1904, 26.

9. "Canada Atlantic Railway Contract with Pullman Palace Car Company, 1898," CNR, RG30-12619-508, LAC.

10. Department of Railways and Canals, *Auditor General's Report, 1898–99*, 1900, R-29. Also see "William S. Webb," *Biographical Directory of Railway Officials*, 638.

11. Brazeal, *Brotherhood of Sleeping Car Porters*, 1–5.

12. *Census of Canada*, 1911, 372–73.

13. Winks, *Blacks in Canada*, 24–95; Whitfield, *Blacks on the Border*.

14. Fingard, "From Sea to Rail." For a discussion of West Indian mariners, see James, *Holding Aloft the Banner of Ethiopia*, and Fryer, *Staying Power*.

15. Fingard, "From Sea to Rail," 52.

16. Ibid., 53.

17. Department of Railways and Canals, *Auditor General's Report 1898–99*, 1900, R-242.

18. "Grand Trunk Railway Payrolls for 1902," CNR, RG30-2035, LAC.

19. Department of Railways and Canals, *Auditor General's Report 1898–99*, 1900, R-207–8. Canadian census reports do not list porters as a classification on the rails before 1921 and probably included their numbers under "labourers" or "other workers."

20. Ibid., R-38. Also see Fingard, "From Sea to Rail," 52–53.

21. "May 1909 Payroll Records for Canadian Northern Railway, Western Region," CNR, RG30-7075, LAC.

22. Arnesen contends that while southern African American railwaymen worked as firemen and porter-brakemen, virtually none could be found on northern lines, thanks to relentless protest by the Big Four brotherhoods. See Arnesen, *Brotherhoods of Color*, 5–41.

23. Department of Railways and Canals, *Auditor General's Report 1900*, R-196–97.

24. Ibid., R-196–98.

25. Ibid., R-195–99.

26. Fingard, "From Sea to Rail," 54.

27. H. F. Matthews to Thomas Gelley, 20 April 1920, IBR, RG76-576-816222, LAC. Also see Arnesen, *Brotherhoods of Color*, 19–21.

28. Santino, "Miles of Smiles, Years of Struggle"; Grizzle, *My Name's Not George*.

29. "Good Morning with Avril Benoit," CBC Radio interview with Stanley Grizzle, Herb Carvery, and Saje Mathieu.

30. Halliday, *Wreck!*; Lamb, *History of the Canadian Pacific Railway*, 117–19, 432.

31. Kempton, *Part of Our Time*, 240.

32. Grizzle, *My Name's Not George*, 67.

33. Scott, *Domination and the Arts of Resistance*, 17–45.

34. Fingard, "From Sea to Rail," 53.

35. Ibid., 54; Gilmore, *Swinging in Paradise*, 163–67, 193–95.

36. *Halifax (N.S.) Herald*, 28 March 1898.

37. Union Lodge Records, PANS, MG20-2012 and MG20-2218. Pursuant to an agreement with Mr. Robert Northup, grand secretary of the Grand Lodge of Nova Scotia, I am unable to release the names of Union Lodge members. Also see Fingard, "From Sea to Rail," 49–64.

38. *Halifax Herald*, 25 March 1898.

39. Ibid., 6 April 1898.

40. Ibid.

41. Ibid.

42. Ibid. The dismissed porters were eventually rehired by the ICR or accepted positions with the CPR once they became available. See Fingard, "From Sea to Rail," 57–59.

43. *Halifax Herald*, 6 April 1898.

44. *Toronto Globe*, 7 April 1898; *Halifax Herald*, 25–28 March and 8–15 April 1898. Also see *HCD*, 31 March–14 April 1898.

45. *Chatham (Ont.) Planet*, as cited in *HCD*, 6 April 1898, 3167.

46. *Halifax Herald*, 6 April 1898.

47. *HCD*, 31 March 1898, 2852.

48. Ibid.

49. *HCD*, 6 April 1898, 3167–69.

50. Beaton, "African-American Community in Cape Breton." For additional information on West Indian immigration to Canada, see Schultz, " 'White Man's Country.'"

51. John Means to Thomas Goodwin, 9 August 1901, as quoted in Beaton, "African-American Community in Cape Breton," 76. Beaton reproduced several letters exchanged between DISCO managers and southern workers.

52. John Means to George Strong, 29 August 1901, as quoted in Beaton, "African-American Community in Cape Breton," 75–76.

53. John Means to James Jackson, 2 September 1901, as quoted in Beaton, "African-American Community in Cape Breton," 78.

54. Ibid., 75.

55. Ibid., 76.

56. *Sydney (N.S.) Daily Post*, 16 October 1901.

57. John Means as quoted in Beaton, "African-American Community in Cape Breton," 79.

58. *Bangor (Maine) Daily News*, 13 January 1903.

59. Beaton, "African-American Community in Cape Breton," 79.

60. Ibid., 81–91.

61. *Bangor Daily News*, 13 January 1903.

62. Ibid.

63. Grossman, *Land of Hope*; Lemann, *Promised Land*.

64. On shuttle industrial migration among southern African Americans, see Letwin, *Challenge of Interracial Unionism*; Dickerson, *Out of the Crucible*; Honey, *Southern Labor and Black Civil Rights*; Jones, *Labor of Love, Labor of Sorrow*; and Hunter, *To 'Joy My Freedom*.

65. Hoerder, *Creating Societies*. For immigration to the United States, see Archdeacon, *Becoming American*; Bodnar, *Transplanted*; Daniels, *Coming to America*; Glazer, *Clamor at the Gates*; Miller, *Emigrants and Exiles*; Nugent, *Crossings*; Vecoli and Sinke, *Century of European Migrations*; and Yans-McLaughlin, *Immigration Reconsidered*.

66. Hale, *Making Whiteness*; Williamson, *Crucible of Race*.

67. Williams, *Story of Unions in Canada*, 75.

68. Babcock, *Gompers in Canada*; Steedman, *Angels of the Workplace*; Leier, *Where the Fraser Flows*; McCormack, *Reformers, Rebels, and Revolutionaries*; Craven, *"Impartial Umpire"*; Palmer, *Working Class Experience*, 135–42, 155–210.

69. Williams, *Story of Unions in Canada*, 77.

70. Morton, "Aid to the Civil Power."

71. Jamieson, as quoted in Williams, *Story of Unions in Canada*, 79.

72. Department of Labour, *LG* (April 1906–7), 1108. "An Act to Aid in the Prevention and Settlement of Strikes and Lockouts in Coal Mines and Industries Connect with Public Utilities" received royal assent on 23 April 1907.

73. Ibid.

74. Quoted in Greening, *It Was Never Easy*, 7–14.

75. Charter of the Canadian Brotherhood of Railroad Employees, 12 October 1908, as reprinted in Greening, *It Was Never Easy*.

76. Ibid., 9; *LG* (December 1908), 606.

77. Greening, *It Was Never Easy*, 59–60.

78. "CBRE Annual Convention Minutes 1908 and 1919," CBRE, MG28-I215, LAC.

79. Arnesen, " 'Like Banquo's Ghost' "; Nelson, *Iron Confederacies*; Jacobson, *Whiteness of a Different Color*, 1–136; Roediger, *Wages of Whiteness*; Ignatiev, *How the Irish Became White*; Nelson, *Divided We Stand*.

80. Arnesen, " 'Like Banquo's Ghost,' " 1602; Arnesen, *Brotherhoods of Color*, 24–27. On international brotherhoods in Canada, see Tuck, "Canadian Railways and the International Brotherhoods."

81. Arnesen, " 'Like Banquo's Ghost,' " 1606–9; Nelson, *Iron Confederacies*, 1–11. Arnesen posits that black porter-brakemen operated on many railway lines in the South.

82. *LG* (December 1909); Greening, *It Was Never Easy*, 17–19.

83. *LG* (October 1913), 466–74.

84. Calliste, "Blacks on Canadian Railways," 44–47.

85. All new wage agreements were reproduced in the *Labour Gazette*, pursuant to federal labor law.

86. The CPR owned and operated 60 percent of first-class sleeping and dining cars during the second decade of the twentieth century. Canadian Pacific Railway, *Annual Report of the Canadian Pacific Railway Company*, 1910–19; Urquhart and Buckley, *Historical Statistics of Canada*, 532.

87. Aaron Mosher to J. E. McGuire, 11 March 1943, CBRE, MG28-I215, LAC. Also see Aaron Mosher to William D. Scott, 28 May 1919, and Thomas J. Murray to assistant commissioner of immigration, 4 June 1919, IBR, RG76-576-816222, LAC; Israel, "Montreal Negro Community."

88. Arnesen, " 'Like Banquo's Ghost' "; Foner, *Organized Labor and the Black Worker*.

89. Aaron Mosher to William D. Scott, 28 May 1919, IBR, RG76-576-81622, LAC.

90. Adelaide-Merlande, *Histoire générale des Antilles et des Guyannes*, 221–35; Dookhan, *Post-Emancipation History of the West Indies*, 9–105; Palmer, *Pilgrims from the Sun*, 1–8.

91. See *St. Vincent Times*, 12 June 1919, 19 June 1919, 26 June 1919; *St. Kitts–Nevis Daily Express* (Basseterre), 15 June 1919.

92. Innis, *Historic Basseterre*, 30–31.

93. Innis, *Whither Bound*, 49.

94. Innis, *Historic Basseterre*, 32–33.

95. For a list of Canadian businesses operating in the Caribbean, see Winks, "Canadian–West Indian Union," 30–35.

96. Bertley, "Role of the Black Community in Educating Blacks in Montreal," 10, 16. Este, only seventeen years old when he came to Canada, worked as a bootblack and bellhop before attending the Congregational College of Canada in 1918.

97. William D. Scott to A. W. Macdonald, 12 September 1915, IBR, RG76-566-810666, LAC. Also see Schultz, " 'White Man's Country,'" 57–59.

98. *Toronto Globe*, 8 April 1911, *Saturday Night Magazine Edition*, and 12 April 1911. Also see *By-Water Magazine* (October 1916); Sawh, *Canadian Caribbean Connection*, 103–19; and Gagnon, "Canadian Soldiers in Bermuda."

99. Winks, "Canadian–West Indian Union," 35.

100. Quoted in ibid., 32.

101. Ibid., 7–9, 36.

102. Ibid., 12.

103. *Toronto Globe*, 27 October 1911.

104. Ibid.

105. Quoted in Winks, "Canadian–West Indian Union," 38.

106. *MFP*, 5 April 1911.

107. *Alien Labour Act*, 6061 Victoria, c. 11.

108. *Alien Labour Act, Revised Statutes of Canada* 1906, c.97, s. 12.

109. *Immigration Act*, 6 Edward vii, c.19, s.32.

110. Minister Blair to W. Y. Gillian, 11 July 1923, IBR, RG76-576-816222, LAC.

111. T. Gelley to F. C. Blair, 22 April 1920, IBR, RG76-576-816222, LAC.

112. Testimony of George Hepburn in *LG* (August 1918), 593, 598.

113. Canadian Pacific Railway, *Annual Report of the Canadian Pacific Railway Company*, August 1913, 29, and March 1920, 29.

114. "Contract for Colonist Sleeping Cars, Canadian Foundry Car & Foundry Co. Ltd. and Canadian Northern Rolling Stock Ltd.," CNR, RG30-9575, LAC.

115. A. Caminetti to W. W. Cory, 11 January 1919, IBR, RG76-576-816222, LAC.

116. H. F. Matthews to Thomas Gelley, 20 April 1920, IBR, RG76-576-816222, LAC.

117. *LG* (June 1918), 396.

118. *LG* (August 1918), 597–604.

119. Testimony of George Hepburn in *LG* (August 1918), 603.

120. Ibid., 597, 593, 598. CPR headquarters approved using women on the rails, but Winnipeg officials vetoed the plan in favor of African Americans.

121. Ibid., 593, 598.

122. Ibid., 593, 598, 601.

123. Ibid., 597, 603, 600.

124. Ibid., 600, 604.

125. Ibid., 604, 601, 603.

126. Aaron Mosher to William D. Scott, 28 May 1919, IBR, RG76-576-816222, LAC.

127. Thomas Murray to commissioner of immigration, 4 June 1919, IBR, RG76-576-816222, LAC.

128. William D. Scott to Aaron Mosher, 23 May 1919, IBR, RG76-576-816222, LAC.

129. Knowles, *Strangers at Our Gates*, 86–90. Scott worked for the CPR in Manitoba between 1881 and 1887.

130. See William D. Scott directives in IBR, RG76-576-816222, IBR, RG76-566-810666, and IBR, RG76-7552-3, LAC.

131. Ibid.

132. IBR, RG76-816222, LAC.

133. "Circular to All Border Inspectors of Western District," 2 July 1920, IBR, RG76-7552-6, LAC.

134. Report submitted by William D. Scott to Thomas Gelley, Commissioner of Immigration, Western District, 10 June 1919, IBR, RG76-576-816222, LAC. In his report, Scott describes his recent correspondence with Aaron Mosher.

135. Brazeal, *Brotherhood of Sleeping Car Porters*, 6–14. See also F. Boyd's article "Previous Struggles of the Pullman Porters to Organize," in the *Messenger* (September 1926), 283–84. Boyd describes how twenty African American sleeping car porters on runs from Seattle to Chicago began discussing the possibility of forming a black railway union in 1909. No records indicate that these men considered Canadian porters for their union or that Robinson's group knew of their American counterparts' deliberations. Also see Arnesen, *Brotherhoods of Color*, 42–44.

136. The social center for black railwaymen in Winnipeg, 175 Main Street, became the official headquarters for the Order of Sleeping Car Porters, Universal Negro Improvement Association, Porters' Charitable Association, and the Imperial Order of the Benevolent and Protective Elks. The building also housed a barbershop, pool hall, and café. Robinson and his colleagues likely held their meetings on the upper floor, where the Elks also gathered, and used the organization as a cover in case of harassment by company officials. Frances Atwell, Helen and Eddie Bailey, and Eddie Blackman, interviews by author. See also *Henderson's Directory* (Winnipeg), 1917, 353, and Manitoba Certificate of Title, 175 Main Street, Certificate #579059, Manitoba Land Titles Office.

137. John A. Robinson to J. E. McGuire, 27 March 1941, CBRE, MG28-I215, LAC.

138. *Canadian Railroad Employee Monthly*, Convention Number 1929, 33, CPA. Also see "CBRE Convention Proceedings, 1918," CBRE, MG28-I215, LAC, and Greening, *It Was Never Easy*, 59.

139. "CBRE Convention Proceedings," Port Arthur, 24 September 1918, 60, 61, CBRE, MG28-I215, LAC.

140. Ibid., 64.

141. Ibid. Also see *Port Arthur (Ont.) Daily-News Chronicle*, 24 and 28 September 1918.

Chapter 3

1. Arthur Alexander to Prime Minister Borden, 11 June 1914, DND, RG24-1206-HQ-297-1-21, LAC.

2. John T. Richards to Governor-General Duke of Connaught, 10 April 1915, DND, RG2-1206-HQ-297-1-21, LAC.

3. George Morton to General Sam Hughes, 7 September 1915 and 29 November 1915, DND, RG24-1206-HQ 297-1-21, LAC.

4. Ibid.

5. *Canadian Observer* (Toronto), 8 January 1916.

6. Lieutenant colonel military secretary at Headquarters to Arthur Alexander, 20 November 1914, DND, RG24-1206-HQ 297-1-21, LAC.

7. *Ottawa Citizen*, 20 November 1915; *Halifax (N.S.) Morning Chronicle*, 20 November 1915.

8. Chateauvert, *Marching Together*, 7.

9. *Washington (D.C.) Bee*, 4 August 1917; Johnson, *Along This Way*, 320–22.

10. Greaves, *National Problems in Canada*, 70–73.

11. A. G. Gayfer to GOC MD #13, 16 September 1916, DND, RG24-4739-448-14-259, LAC.

The War Measures Act forbade undermining the war effort or speaking against recruitment in the Canadian Expeditionary Force.

12. *Atlantic Advocate* (Halifax, N.S.), 7 January 1917.

13. Lieutenant colonel, officer commanding 119th, to AG Toronto, 5 April 1916; Lieutenant Colonel H. Cockshutt, officer commanding 215th, to AAG Toronto, 4 April 1916; and Lieutenant Colonel A. A. Cockburn to AAG Toronto, 5 April 1916, DND, RG24-4387-34-7-141, LAC.

14. Officer commanding 173rd to AAG Toronto, 4 April 1916, DND, RG24-4387-34-7-141, LAC.

15. Commanding officer 95th to AAG Toronto, 3 April 1916, DND, RG24-4387-34-7-141, LAC.

16. See Department of National Defence file "Organization of Colored Platoons" for circular to all commanding officers dated 3 April 1916 in RG24-4387-34-7-141, LAC. Lieutenant Colonel Dundas informed his supervisor that when one of his commanding officers had suggested recruiting black soldiers, "he was dismissed for making the suggestion." One commanding officer proposed that black recruits should be rerouted to the French Canadian 22nd Battalion, as he suspected that they might not object as strongly to a racially integrated platoon.

17. Commanding officer 147th to AAG Toronto, 4 April 1916, DND, RG24-4387-34-7-141, LAC.

18. For Department of Militia and Defence recruitment of black enlistees, see "Co. 2 Construction Battalion CEF Composed of Negroes," DND, RG24-4680-18-24-1, LAC, and "Coloured Battalion for Alberta," DND, RG24-4739-448-14-259, LAC.

19. Major Private Secretary Bristol to Major W. R. Creighton, 26 August 1918, DND, RG24-1469-HQ-600-10-35, LAC.

20. Commanding officer military district #1 to secretary militia council, 10 May 1918, DND, RG24-1469-HQ-600-10-35, LAC.

21. Lieutenant Colonel Young to Lieutenant Colonel H. L. Milligan, 13 March 1918, DND, RG24-1469-HQ-600-10-35, LAC.

22. Major Private Secretary Bristol to Major W. R. Creighton, 26 August 1918, DND, RG24-1469-HQ-600-10-35, LAC.

23. Lieutenant Colonel Young to Lieutenant Colonel H. L. Milligan, 13 March 1918, DND, RG24-1469-HQ-600-10-35, LAC.

24. Telegram from the British-Canadian Recruiting Mission in New York to Headquarters, 1 May 1918, DND, RG24-1469-HQ-600-10-35, LAC. The British-Canadian Recruiting Mission was established in several American cities to recruit British and Canadian citizens living in the United States. Minister of Militia Sam Hughes courted white American soldiers for a separate unit called the American Legion. The plot ended in disaster and strained American-Canadian relations, given that Americans advocated neutrality prior to 1917. See Haycock, "American Legion in the Canadian Expeditionary Force," 115–19.

25. Ruck, *Black Battalion*, 18.

26. Captain W. A. White to Sir Robert Borden, 11 August 1918, DND, RG24-1469-HQ-600-10-35; Ruck, *Black Battalion*, 20; Walker, "Race and Recruitment in World War I."

27. Quoted in Ruck, *Black Battalion*, 20.

28. Ibid., 19–20; Walker, *"Race," Rights and the Law*, 134.

29. Brigadier General E. A. Cruikshank, "History of the Great War, 1914–1918," in Dominion Bureau of Statistics, *Canada Yearbook*, 1920, 14–61.

30. Morton, "Kicking and Complaining," 342.

31. Morton, *Peculiar Kind of Politics*, 180–95.

32. Ibid., 178.

33. *Halifax Morning Chronicle*, 10 March 1919; *Montreal Gazette*, 8–11 March 1919; *Ottawa Citizen*, 8–10 March 1919; *Toronto Daily Star*, 8 March 1919. See also Morton, "Kicking and Complaining," 333–38.

34. Morton, *Peculiar Kind of Politics*, 169–80; Morton, *When Your Number's Up*, 253–76. See also Gagnon, *Le vingt-deuxième bataillon Canadien-français*. In "Indians and World War One," Dempsey posits that Native Canadians joined the Canadian Expeditionary Force during World War I believing that service would inspire citizenship, franchise, and respect.

35. *Halifax Morning Chronicle*, 8 March 1919; *Toronto Daily Star*, 8 March 1919.

36. General Currie as quoted in Morton, "Kicking and Complaining," 337.

37. Morton, "Kicking and Complaining," 341.

38. Ibid., 334–37; *Halifax Morning Chronicle*, 10 March 1919.

39. Minister Kemp to Prime Minister Borden, 8 March 1919, Borden Papers, MG26-H-55847, LAC.

40. Major G. V. Collier to Officer Commanding Canadian Troops, 10 January 1919, MD, RG9-III-1709 D-3-13-6, LAC.

41. Ibid.; Morton, *Peculiar Kind of Politics*, 180–85; Walker, *"Race," Rights and the Law*, 135.

42. *Times* (London), 7–14 March 1919; *Halifax Morning Chronicle*, 8 March 1919; *Montreal Gazette*, 8–11 March 1919; *Ottawa Citizen*, 8–13 March 1919.

43. *Toronto Daily Star*, 8 March 1919; *Halifax Morning Chronicle*, 10 March 1919.

44. *Toronto Daily Star*, 8 March 1919.

45. See MD, RG9-III-1709-D-3-13-6, for court-martial records and MD, RG9-III-1709-D-13-3-4, for trial records from Kinmel Camp riots. Also see Morton, *Peculiar Kind of Politics*, 169–90, and Morton, "Supreme Penalty."

46. Morton, "Kicking and Complaining," 342.

47. *Montreal Gazette*, 15 May 1919.

48. George Hutchinson Beckford (Regimental #2378966), Ministry of Overseas Forces, RG150-1992-93-166-577-2, LAC; *Times* (London), 12 May 1919.

49. *Times* (London), 12 May 1919.

50. Colonel J. G. Rattray to Lieutenant General Sir Richard E. W. Turner, 13 May 1919, Turner Papers, MG30-E46-5624 and secret circular MG30-E46-5627, LAC.

51. *NYT*, 8 March 1919; *Times* (London), 8–12 March 1919; *Guardian* (Manchester), 3–11 May 1919; *Liverpool Post and Mercury*, 8 May 1919.

52. Morton, "Kicking and Complaining," 346.

53. *Times* (London), 20 March 1919.

54. *Halifax Morning Chronicle*, 8 and 10 March 1919.

55. Morton, *When Your Number's Up*, 242–45; Morton and Wright, *Winning the Second Battle*, 105–15.

56. *Halifax Morning Chronicle*, 10 March 1919.

57. *HCD*, 17 March 1919, 512–13.

58. *Times* (London), 8–11 March 1919; *Guardian*, 8 March 1919; *NYT*, 8 March 1919.

59. *Times* (London), 28 March 1919.

60. Kemp Papers, MG27-IID9-138-D-2, LAC; Morton, "Kicking and Complaining," 350–57.

61. Morton, *Peculiar Kind of Politics*, 183; Morton, "Kicking and Complaining," 340; Walker, *"Race," Rights and the Law*, 130–35.

62. Fryer, *Staying Power*, 295–315.

63. *Liverpool Courier*, 6–10 June 1919; *Liverpool Echo*, 6–10 June 1919; *Liverpool Post and Mercury*, 6–10 June 1919; *Western Mail* (Cardiff), 7–12 June 1919; *Times and South Wales Weekly News* (Cardiff), 14–21 June 1919.

64. Fryer, *Staying Power*, 301; Jenkinson, *Black 1919*, 80–83.

65. *Liverpool Echo*, 6 and 10 June 1919. Despite eyewitness accounts of the affray, the local magistrate acquitted the men involved in Wooton's murder, reasoning that there existed no proof of "how he [Wooton] got into the water." Wooton is also referred to as Charles Wotten in some newspaper accounts and is reported as being from Bermuda or Trinidad.

66. *South Wales News*, 14 June 1919.

67. *Times* (London), 13 June 1919; *Liverpool Echo*, 17 June 1919.

68. *Liverpool Echo*, 11 June 1919.

69. Ibid., 14 June 1919.

70. *Times* (London), 13–14 June 1919.

71. *Liverpool Echo*, 18 June 1919; *Times* (London), 13–14 June 1919.

72. *Guardian*, 17 June 1919; *Times* (London), 13 June 1919.

73. *Times* (London), 14 June 1919.

74. *Times* (London), 13 June 1919.

75. *African Telegraph* (London), April 1919. Also see January–February 1919.

76. *Liverpool Courier*, 12 June 1919.

77. *Times and South Wales Weekly News*, 14 June 1919; Fryer, *Staying Power*, 306.

78. Fryer, *Staying Power*, 311–16.

79. *Sunday Times* (London), 12 June 1919; *Crisis*, June 1919. The *African Telegraph* reproduced Du Bois's *Crisis* essay "The Black Man in the Revolution of 1914–1918." Also see the *African Telegraph*, March and April 1919.

80. Tuttle, *Race Riot*.

81. Greaves, *National Problems in Canada*, 72–73.

82. Barbeau and Henri, *Unknown Soldiers*, 111–63; Fryer, *Staying Power*, 295–97.

83. *HCD*, 20 June 1919, 3741.

84. Bercuson, *Confrontation at Winnipeg*, 103–14; Palmer, *Working Class Experience*, 167–98; Heron, *Workers' Revolt in Canada*, 11–42, 176–232; Morton and Wright, *Winning the Second Battle*, 62–104; Knowles, *Strangers at Our Gates*, 99–112.

85. Resina Asals as quoted in Kealey, *Workers and Canadian History*, 293.

86. Ibid., 288–92; Bercuson, *Confrontation at Winnipeg*, 107. The Royal Commission on Industrial Relations is also known as the Mathers Commission, so named after Chief Justice T. G. Mathers.

87. *Canadian Railway and Marine World*, April 1917, 131. Also see Lamb, *History of the Canadian Pacific Railway*, 279–87, and Gibbon, *Steel of Empire*, 374–83.

88. Hopkin and Kealey, *Class, Community, and the Labour Movement*, 134–59; L. Kealey, "Canadian Socialism and the Woman Question"; Kealy and Cherinski, *Lectures in Canadian Labour and Working-Class History*, 59–88; Steedman, *Angels of the Workplace*; Heron, *Workers' Revolt in Canada*, 162, 185–222.

89. Bumsted, *Winnipeg General Strike of 1919*, 55; Kealey, *Workers and Canadian History*, 315–17. Also see *NYT*, 18 June 1919.

90. *Canadian Observer*, 26 February 1915.

91. *Atlantic Advocate*, April 1915.

92. *Canadian Railway and Marine World*, March 1918, 92, and August 1918, 332. CPR employees Yochi Kamakura and Yasogiro Tanaka, Calgarian red caps killed in action in Europe, received mention in the company's war honor rolls.

93. Hopkin and Kealey, *Class, Community, and the Labour Movement*, 134–59; Palmer, *Working Class Experience*, 192–96.

94. *Henderson's Directory* (Winnipeg), 1917, 1109. Winnipeg's directory reveals that Robinson worked as a porter on the CPR from 1909 until 1916. After a year of work as a stable hand, he moved to the CNR.

95. Bercuson, *Confrontation at Winnipeg*, 119–28; Knowles, *Strangers at Our Gates*, 104–6.

96. Dominion Bureau of Statistics, *Canada Yearbook*, 1920, 533.

97. Kealey, *Workers and Canadian History*, 295–302.

98. *HCD*, 2 June 1919, 3009.

99. *La Presse* (Montreal), 21 May 1919.

100. *Regina (Sask.) Morning Leader*, 30 May 1919.

101. *Chicago Tribune*, 3 June 1919. Also see Frank, *Purchasing Power*, 34–39, 94–101.

102. *Toronto Daily Star*, 2 May 1919.

103. Alex T. Mackay, steelworker, as quoted in Kealey, *Workers and Canadian History*, 292.

104. Quoted in Balawyder, *Winnipeg General Strike*, 13.

105. Bercuson, *Confrontation at Winnipeg*, 113–19, 150–57; Bumsted, *Winnipeg General Strike of 1919*, 27–30; *Western Labor News* (Winnipeg, Man.), special edition #3, 20 May 1919.

106. Bercuson, *Confrontation at Winnipeg*, 78–89; Heron, *Workers' Revolt in Canada*, 177–222; Babcock, *Gompers in Canada*.

107. *Henderson's Directory* (Winnipeg), 1919, 1109, and *Henderson's Directory*, 1909, 1141. Robinson first appears in the Winnipeg city directory in 1909 and is listed as a CPR porter. On 20 May 1919, the *Winnipeg Free Press* reported that CNR running tradesmen had joined the general strike, bringing railway service into the city to a standstill. In June 1919, the Canadian government amalgamated the GTR, CNR, and ICR into the Canadian National Railways. The merger was finally completed in 1924. Thereafter, there were only two national lines in Canada—the Canadian Pacific Railway and the Canadian National Railways. See Dorin, *Canadian National Railways's Story*, 9–13; MacKay, *People's Railway*, 127–50; and Stevens, *History of the Canadian National Railways*, 265–71.

108. Frances Atwell, interview by author.

109. Howard R. Blanchette, interview by author.

110. Knowles, *Strangers at Our Gates*, 99–112; Kelley and Trebilcock, *Making of the Mosaic*, 164–215; Heron, *Canadian Labour Movement*, 56–57.

111. Lamb, *History of the Canadian Pacific Railway*, 279–87; MacKinnon, "Canadian Railway Workers and World War I Military Service"; Sharpe, "Enlistment in the Canadian Expeditionary Force."

112. Sharpe, "Enlistment in the Canadian Expeditionary Force," 86–89; Morton and Wright, *Winning the Second Battle*, 120–21; Bumsted, *Winnipeg General Strike of 1919*, 22.

113. John A. Robinson to J. E. McGuire, 27 March 1941, CBRE, MG28-I215, LAC.

114. *Western Labor News*, special edition #5, 22 May 1919.

115. Ibid., special edition #10, 28 May 1919.

116. Ibid., special edition #11, 29 May 1919.

117. Ibid., special edition #13, 31 May 1919; Bercuson, *Confrontation at Winnipeg*, 123–28. The Citizens' Committee of One Thousand, the group that was opposed to the strike, also headlined "I.W.W. Ideals Don't Appeal to White Men," *Winnipeg (Man.) Citizen*, 21 May 1919.

118. *Western Labor News*, special edition #24, 13 June 1919.

119. Ibid., special edition #26, 15 June 1919; Aaron Mosher to William D. Scott, 28 May 1919, and Thomas J. Murray to assistant commissioner of immigration, 4 June 1919, IBR, RG76-576-816222, LAC; Bumsted, *Winnipeg General Strike of 1919*, 22.

120. Bumsted, *Winnipeg General Strike of 1919*, 39–40.

121. *Winnipeg Citizen*, 26 May 1919.

122. Bumsted, *Winnipeg General Strike of 1919*, 22–42; *Winnipeg (Man.) Tribune*, 13 May 1919.

123. *Report of the Royal North-West Mounted Police*, 11 June 1919, Borden Papers, MG26-H-62036, LAC.

124. Bercuson, *Confrontation at Winnipeg*, 155–56, 132–35.

125. Ibid. Making matters worse, Robertson strong-armed federal postal workers back to their jobs, enforcing a twenty-four-hour back-to-work ultimatum or threatening permanent unemployment.

126. Ibid., 147–48.

127. Ibid., 146–49.

128. Ibid., 117–19; Heron, *Workers' Revolt in Canada*, 207–10.

129. Bercuson, *Confrontation at Winnipeg*, 152–55.

130. Ibid., 170–75.

131. Ibid.; Bumsted, *Winnipeg General Strike of 1919*, 52.

132. Bercuson, *Confrontation at Winnipeg*, 176–95; Kealey, *Workers and Canadian History*, 317–19.

133. *LG* (March 1920), 239–49.

134. *LG* (June/September/October 1918), 432–39, 759–60, 857–66. The Canadian government adopted the American McAdoo award in 1918 and applied that salary scale to Canadian industries.

135. *LG* (June 1919), 679.

136. Ibid., 679, 1036–49.

137. *LG* (September 1919), 1039.

138. *LG* (October 1913), 466–74.

139. CBRE Convention Record, 1919, 17, CBRE, MG28-I215, LAC.

140. CBRE Convention Record, 1918, CBRE, MG28-I215, LAC.

141. CBRE Convention Record, 1919, Resolution #7, 62, CBRE, MG28-I215, LAC.

142. Ibid.

143. Calliste, "Struggle for Employment Equity by Blacks on American and Canadian Railroads"; Arnesen, " 'Like Banquo's Ghost.' "

144. CBRE Convention Records, CBRE, MG28-I215, LAC.

145. The OSCP wasted no time getting involved in the CBRE machinery. Members of the OSCP sat on the CBRE's Atlantic, Central, and Western Grievance Committees from the 1920s to the 1950s. See CBRE, MG28-I215-12, LAC.

146. See the "Race Issues" file in CBRE, MG28-I215-81, LAC, and the "Sleeping Car Department Correspondences" file MG28-I215-84, LAC.

147. Greening, *It Was Never Easy*, 60.

148. John A. Robinson to Aaron Mosher, 1 August 1945, CBRE, MG28-I215-81, LAC.

149. Ibid.

150. *LG* (January/March 1920), 28–29, 239–49.

151. Ibid., 240–44.

152. Ibid., 240.

153. Ibid., 241.

154. Ibid., 242.

155. Ibid.

156. Ibid.; Santino, "Miles of Smiles, Years of Struggle."

157. Deadheading meant doubling out without enough time for rest after a long run. Railroad companies did not consider this overtime; therefore, a porter could work two runs but only be paid for one. For example, a train arriving in Vancouver at 5 P.M. heading back out for Winnipeg at 10 P.M. would be considered one day of work, despite the previous four days' trek out from Winnipeg.

158. *LG* (March 1920), 239–49.

159. Ibid., 247.

160. Ibid., 248.

161. Ibid., 249.

162. The Railway Men's International Benevolent Industrial Association, a predominantly black union, won important concessions for its members but had not yet successfully negotiated contracts by 1920. See Arnesen, *Brotherhoods of Color*, 60–65.

163. *LG* (August 1923), 838–45; *LG* (March/July 1926), 230, 647; *LG* (January/December 1927), 17, 1284–90.

164. John A. Robinson to J. E. McGuire, 27 March 1941, CBRE, MG28-I215-81, LAC.

Chapter 4

1. Fryer, *Staying Power*, 298–375; Pfeffer, *A. Philip Randolph*; Wintz, *African American Political Thought*; Carby, *Race Men*, 9–44.

2. Fingard, "From Sea to Rail."

3. Eddie Bailey remembered that during runs to Louisiana he and other porters were unnerved by Jim Crow restaurant and depot laws. "It's a big difference down there in . . . Louisiana than Canada. And the treatment! You go around the back to eat. If you want a sandwich, you go 'round back!" Eddie Bailey, interview by author.

4. Brand, *No Burden to Carry*; Bristow, *"We're Rooted Here and They Can't Pull Us Up"*; Williams, *Road to Now*, 50–60, 140–44.

5. Chateauvert, *Marching Together*; Higginbotham, *Righteous Discontent*; Gilmore, *Gender and Jim Crow*, 31–60, 147–76. For a study on union women and consumer advocacy, see Frank, *Purchasing Power*. African Canadian women were the main reporters for African American newspapers and were overwhelmingly responsible for Canadian submissions to the *Black Worker*.

6. Chateauvert, *Marching Together*, 36–52.

7. *Atlantic Advocate* (Halifax, N.S.), January 1917.

8. Ibid.

9. *DT*, 23 February 1924.

10. Kornweibel, *Seeing Red*.

11. *Canadian Observer* (Toronto), 8 January 1916.

12. *DT*, 7 June 1924 and 28 July 1923.

13. *Atlantic Advocate*, January and April 1917.

14. *DT*, 16 February 1924.

15. *Atlantic Advocate*, January 1917.

16. *Canadian Observer*, 8 January 1916.

17. Ibid., 8 January 1916 and 18 March 1916; *DT*, 19 January 1924, 2 February 1924, and 26 July 1924.

18. *Atlantic Advocate*, January 1917, announced the death of James McCutcheon, ICR porter, and the injury of A. Wright during a derailment. Also see *DT*, 2 February 1924.

19. *DT*, 9 August 1924.

20. *Canadian Observer*, 18 March 1916. Critics of Canada's black press stress that publications were often short lived, largely advertisements and reports on social events. They undervalue the importance of birth, marriage, illness, and death announcements for a population separated by great distances and living in small pockets across the country. Yet a cursory study of mainstream newspapers like the *Ottawa Citizen*, *Windsor (Ont.) Star*, or *Calgary (Alta.) Albertan* reveals that they too reported heavily on social events, art, sports, automobiles, and household maintenance. Advertisements accounted for nearly 40 percent of the *Windsor Star*'s issues in winter 1922. See Winks, *Blacks in Canada*, 390–413, and Henry, *Black Politics in Toronto since World War I*, 4–7.

21. First editorial published in the *DT*, 14 July 1923.

22. *DT*, 18 August 1923.

23. Frances Atwell, Lee Williams, and Eddie Blackman, interviews by author. Also see Grizzle, *My Name's Not George*, 63.

24. *DT*, 1 September 1923.

25. Winks, *Blacks in Canada*, 390–412; Henry, *Black Politics in Toronto since World War I*.

26. Eddie Blackman, interview by author.

27. Winks, *Blacks in Canada*, 392–95, 407.

28. Ibid., 392. Reports from blacks in Canada began appearing in the *Black Worker* in 1929. By 1935, the *Black Worker* and the *Chicago Defender* were dedicating almost a whole page to Canadian activities. See *BW*, 25 November 1929, 2 October 1935, August 1935, and June 1939.

29. Greaves, *National Problems in Canada*, 72–73.

30. Gilmore, *Swinging in Paradise*; Winks, *Blacks in Canada*, 332–35; Williams, *Road to Now*, 44; Israel, "Montreal Negro Community," 189–95.

31. *Messenger* (New York), April 1926. The Pullman porter's unsigned letter was dated 27 February 1926.

32. Winks, *Blacks in Canada*, 391.

33. See *DT*, 27 December 1924. For a biography of Christine E. Jenkins, see Braithwaite, *Black Woman in Canada*, 6.

34. *DT*, 9 August 1924.

35. Winks, *Blacks in Canada*, 320–25.

36. Myrtle Carrington of Toronto and H. Sheffield of Montreal submitted regular reports to the *Black Worker*, especially with regard to women's auxiliaries.

37. Israel, "Montreal Negro Community."

38. Winks, *Blacks in Canada*, 458.

39. Locke, *New Negro*.

40. The *DT* took particular interest in municipal elections during the 1930s; see "Using Our Franchise" in November 1934.

41. Inaugural issue of *DT*, 14 July 1923.

42. *DT*, 1 September 1923.

43. Articles like *DT*'s "Negroes in France Found Magazine 'Voice of the Negro'" and other articles on lynching in the United States and West Indian incorporation kept Canadians abreast of international race issues. See *DT*, 4 December 1926.

44. Bates, "New Crowd Challenges the Agenda of the Old Guard in the NAACP"; Gaines, "Rethinking Race and Class in African-American Struggles for Equality"; Meier and Rudwick, *Black Detroit and the Rise of the UAW*, 3–33.

45. Winks, *Blacks in Canada*, 413–14. In *Black Politics in Toronto since World War I*, Henry is most critical of African Canadian leaders and often misreads their objectives.

46. Unity Lodge received its charter on 20 May 1866. See Grand Lodge of Nova Scotia, Halifax #18 Union Lodge, Union Lodge Records, MG20-2130-34, PANS. For material on black Freemasonry, consult Carnes, *Secret Rituals of Manhood in Victorian America*; Cass, *Negro Freemasonry and Segregation*; Davis, *History of Freemasonry among Negroes in America*; Muraskin, *Middle Class Blacks in a White Society*; and Williams, *Black Freemasonry and Middle-Class Realities*. I would like to thank Paul Gilroy for his insight into black Freemasonry in the black Atlantic world.

47. In exchange for permission to view the Unity Lodge and Equity Lodge Papers held at PANS, the Grand Lodge of Nova Scotia Ancient Free and Accepted Masons required that I not use any members' names. For a thorough study of African Canadian Freemasonry and Unity and Equity Lodge that includes members' biographical data, see Fingard, "From Sea to Rail," and Israel, "Montreal Negro Community," 167–76.

48. Palmer and Palmer, *Peoples of Alberta*, 377; Winks, *Blacks in Canada*, 300–313.

49. Improved Benevolent and Protective Order of Elks of the World, Menelik Lodge #528, charter in possession of the author.

50. Israel, "Montreal Negro Community," 170–71.

51. Frances Atwell and Helen Bailey, interviews by author. Also see *Pilgrim Baptist Church 40th Anniversary Bulletin, 1964*, 22, Black Community in Manitoba Collection, AM.

52. Palmer and Palmer, "Urban Blacks in Alberta," 11.

53. Winks, *Blacks in Canada*, 416; Bertley, "Universal Negro Improvement Association of Montreal," 73–88.

54. The last UNIA offices in Nova Scotia and Alberta finally closed in the late 1940s. See Winks, *Blacks in Canada*, 414–16, and Walker, *"Race," Rights and the Law*, 142–43.

55. Bertley, "Universal Negro Improvement Association of Montreal," 40–88.

56. Palmer and Palmer, *Peoples of Alberta*, 365–93.

57. Bertley, "Universal Negro Improvement Association of Montreal," 305–69; Winks, *Blacks in Canada*, 414.

58. Winks, *Blacks in Canada*, 413–14.

59. Williams, *Road to Now*, 58–94.

60. Ibid., 62–63; *DT*, 8 March 1924.

61. Frances Atwell, interview by author. Also see advertisements in *DT*, 8 March 1924.

62. Winks, *Blacks in Canada*, 414–18.

63. *DT*, 20 September 1924.

64. Palmer and Palmer, *Peoples of Alberta*, 372–87.

65. Porters' Social and Charitable Association By-Laws, revised 1937, in possession of the author. Also see Correspondence Papers, Porters' Social and Charitable Association, Black Community in Manitoba Collection, 1–12, AM.

66. Williams, *Road to Now*, 50–55.

67. Though I have not found evidence that black women worked as laundresses and cleaners of sleeping cars, as they did in the United States, they did work in Montreal's Angus shops and as seamstresses in Winnipeg and Calgary.

68. *Census of Canada*, 1921, 646–47, 828. Also see Chateauvert, *Marching Together*, 36–53.

69. For a discussion of the split labor market theory, see Bonacich, "Theory of Ethnic Antagonism."

70. Brand, *No Burden to Carry*; Bristow, *"We're Rooted Here and They Can't Pull Us Up"*; Williams, *Road to Now*; Walker, *"Race," Rights and the Law*, 142–43; Winks, *Blacks in Canada*, 414–17.

71. *DT*, 18 August 1923.

72. *BW*, 25 November 1929.

73. Bertley, "Role of the Black Community in Educating Blacks in Montreal"; Riley, " 'Colored Church' of Montreal," 24–26. Riley claims that pianist Oscar Peterson was born in the church rectory in 1925.

74. Winks, *Blacks in Canada*, 358; Bertley, "Role of the Black Community in Educating Blacks in Montreal."

75. *Hamilton (Ont.) Spectator*, 18 January 1922.

76. Records indicate that in 1939 all of Pilgrim Baptist Church's trustees were sleeping car porters and their wives. Jerry R. Brisco, Ernest B. Branch, Raymond Harris, Mabel and Mervin Brown, Hettie and Thomas Shores were active community leaders in Winnipeg's North End. See Manitoba Certificate of Title, 46 Maple Street, Certificate #A1222, Manitoba Land Titles Office. Many thanks to Gerry Atwell for introducing me to the wealth of information housed at Manitoba's Land Titles Office.

77. Hill toured his ministries annually during the 1920s. Born in Port Royal, Virginia, in 1877, Hill studied medicine at the University of Southern California. He eventually settled in Baltimore, where his Second Street Church still thrives to this day. *Black Biographical Dictionaries, 1750–1950*, 253. The *DT* reported that in August 1923 Hill's sermon at Toronto's Knox Presbyterian Church delighted the congregation, suggesting that he was well known to black churchgoers in the East as well. Also see *Pilgrim Baptist Church 40th Anniversary Souvenir Bulletin*, 1964, 5 and 22. Hill's Memorial Baptist Church, as it was originally called, was founded on 24 October 1924. During the 1930s Pilgrim moved to 41 Maple Street, where it remains an active part of Winnipeg's black community to this day.

78. Frances Atwell and Yvonne Blanchette, interviews by author. Bethel AME Church is listed under "negro church" in the *Henderson's Directory* (Winnipeg) for the years 1916 and 1917, 153 and 162.

79. Palmer and Palmer, "Urban Blacks in Alberta," 12; Winks, *Blacks in Canada*, 362–89.

80. Bud Jones, telephone interview by author. Mr. Jones confirmed that many of the Coloured Women's Club's members were also members of various Masonic auxiliaries. Williams, *Road to Now*, 50–52.

81. Braithwaite, *Black Woman in Canada*, 7, 59.

82. *Chicago Defender*, 13 September 1941.

83. Frances Atwell, interview by author.

84. *DT*, 19 January 1924.

85. Greaves, *National Problems in Canada*, 66.

86. The Essceepee Limited was incorporated on 29 January 1937 as an amalgamation of the "Order of Sleeping Car Porters, Menelik Lodge of Elks, the U.N.I.A., and the [other] members of the Race." These three Winnipeg black organizations had previously formed the Sleeping Car Porters Business Association. See circular entitled "Coordination versus Separation," a type of Essceepee manifesto submitted to the Province of Manitoba with application for title, in possession of the author.

87. *Census of Canada*, 1911, 370–71, and *Census of Canada*, 1921, 722–36. Black residential neighborhoods in these cities were usually concentrated around railway stations.

88. Murphy, *Black Candle*, 35–36, 17.

89. Winks, *Blacks in Canada*, 332.

90. Rufus Rockhead financed his Paradise with wages earned as a porter; lore has it that he also subsidized his meager railway wages by running booze for Al Capone. The Nemderoloc Club, "coloredmen" spelled backward, was particularly popular with sleeping car porters. See Winks, *Blacks in Canada*, 333, and Gilmore, *Swinging in Paradise*, 23.

91. Stovall, *Paris Noir*; Shack, *Harlem in Montmartre*; Fabre, *From Harlem to Paris*; Archer-Straw, *Negrophilia*.

92. Gilmore, *Swinging in Paradise*, 48, 61–62.

93. Anne Shaw Faulkner, *Maclean's*, 1 October 1921, 27. The article was reproduced from the American publication *Ladies' Home Journal*.

94. John R. McMahon, *Maclean's*, 15 April 1922, 34–36.

95. *Hamilton Spectator*, 1 February 1922.

96. *Montreal Herald*, 17 June 1922.

97. Israel, "Montreal Negro Community," 189–91.

98. *Winnipeg (Man.) Free Press*, 20 November 1920; *Windsor Star*, 8 February 1919.

99. *Windsor Star*, 10 February 1919.

100. *Hamilton Spectator*, 1 February 1922.

101. Copy of Bannan article in "Suggested Legislation against Coloured Persons," Department of External Affairs, RG25-1322-673, LAC.

102. *Times* (London), 10 February 1919; *Windsor Star*, 17 February 1919.

103. Walker, *"Race," Rights and the Law*, 132.

104. Ibid.; Winks, *Blacks in Canada*, 349.

105. *Calgary Albertan*, 29–30 April 1920 and 1 May 1920. Black neighborhoods almost always horseshoed railway stations, demonstrating the interconnection between African Canadians and the rails. Also see Williams, *Blacks in Montreal*, and Walker, *"Race," Rights and the Law*, 130.

106. *DT*, 9 August 1924.

107. *DT*, 2 February 1924.

108. *Franklin v. Evans*, 55 Ontario Law Reports 139 (1924); *DT*, 2 February 1924; Winks, *Blacks in Canada*, 432.

109. Walker, *"Race," Rights and the Law*, 130–32.

110. Winks, *Blacks in Canada*, 324.

111. Walker, *"Race," Rights and the Law*, 131.

112. Winks, *Blacks in Canada*, 431–32; Walker, *"Race," Rights and the Law*, 148–49.

113. Kilian, *Go Do Some Great Thing*, 116–72; Walker, *"Race," Rights and the Law*, 122–81.

114. Walker, *"Race," Rights and the Law*, 147–51.

115. Ibid., 144–51.

116. Calderwood, "Rise and Fall of the Ku Klux Klan in Saskatchewan"; Shepherd, "Night Riders Come to Canada." For newspaper articles on the Klan in Canada, see *Montreal Star*, 1 and 20 October 1921; *Victoria (B.C.) Daily Times*, 21 November 1922; and *DT*, 9 and 29 August 1924.

117. Winks, *Blacks in Canada*, 322–23.

118. *Toronto Globe*, 17 August 1920. *New York Tribune*, 17 August 1920; *New York World*, 17 August 1920; *Toronto Daily Star*; 17 August 1920. Also see NAACP Collection, Lynching in Canada file C-348, LC.

119. *Montreal Gazette*, 17 August 1920; *NYT*, 17 August 1920.

120. *Charlotte Observer*, 24 January 1921; *Raleigh News and Observer*, 24 January 1924. I would also like to thank Vann Newkirk for being such a great help during my research in North Carolina.

121. Gilmore, *Gender and Jim Crow*, 1–31; Tindall, *Emergence of the New South*, 186–96; Jones, *Southern Horrors and Other Writings*; Blee, *Women of the Klan*; Trelease, *White Terror*; Wade, *Fiery Cross*.

122. *Raleigh News and Observer*, 24 January 1921.

123. Ibid.

124. *Toronto Globe*, 17 January 1922.

125. *Raleigh News and Observer*, 25 January 1921.

126. *Charlotte Observer*, 24 January 1921.

127. *Raleigh News and Observer*, 24 January 1921.

128. Ibid.

129. Ibid., 25 January 1921.

130. Ibid., 24 January 1921; *Charlotte Observer*, 24 January 1921. Accounts of the lynching vary widely. Canadian newspapers claimed that the boys were also hung from a telephone pole, while Buffalo newspapers alleged that they were also burned. See *Buffalo (N.Y.) American*, 26 January 1922.

131. *Hamilton Spectator*, 16 January 1922; *Toronto Globe*, 19 January 1922.

132. *Hamilton Spectator*, 16 January 1922; *Toronto Globe*, 19 January 1922. Also see Hill, *Freedom Seekers*.

133. *Raleigh News and Observer*, 15 January 1922.

134. *Charlotte Observer*, 21 January 1922.

135. *Toronto Globe*, 19 January 1922; *Hamilton Spectator*, 14–19 January 1922; *Hamilton Herald*, 12–21 January 1922.

136. *NYT*, 18 January 1922; *Chicago Defender*, 28 January 1922; *Times* (London), 21 February 1922 and 6 March 1922; *Toronto Globe*, 16 January 1922.

137. *Savannah Tribune*, 26 January 1922; *Raleigh News and Observer*, 19 January 1922; *Charlotte Observer*, 19 January 1922.

138. *Toronto Globe*, 17 January 1922.

139. Ibid., 16–19 January 1922.

140. *Chicago Defender*, 28 January 1922.

141. Ibid.; *Hamilton Herald*, 14–16 January 1922.

142. *Toronto Globe*, 18–19 January 1922; *Hamilton Spectator*, 19 January 1922.

143. *NYT*, 28 January 1922; *Hamilton Herald*, 18 January 1922.

144. *Charlotte Observer*, 4 March 1922.

145. *Windsor Star* editorial reprinted in *Raleigh News and Observer*, 25 January 1922.

146. *Toronto Globe*, 21 February 1922.

147. Ibid., 19 January 1922 and 26 January 1922.

148. Ibid., 26–28 January 1922; *Hamilton Spectator*, 14–18 and 28 January 1922; *Hamilton Herald*, 26 and 31 January 1922.

149. *Toronto Globe*, 16 January 1922; *Hamilton Spectator*, 16 January 1922.

150. *Toronto Globe*, 26 January 1922; *Hamilton Spectator*, 22 January and 22 February 1922.

151. *Toronto Globe*, 19–20 January 1922.

152. Ibid., 16 January 1922.

153. Daughters of the Empire to Frank Oliver, 31 March 1911, IBR, RG76-192-7552-3, LAC; *Toronto Globe*, 28 March 1911; *Edmonton (Alta.) Daily Bulletin*, 7 April 1911; *EEJ*, 7 April 1911.

154. *Toronto Globe*, 1–5 March 1930.

155. Ibid., 16 January 1922.

156. Ibid., 20–23 January 1922; *Hamilton Spectator*, 14 and 20 January 1922; *Hamilton Herald*, 24 January 1922; White, *Man Called White*.

157. White, *Man Called White*, 11.

158. *Toronto Globe*, 20 January 1922.

159. *Hamilton Herald*, 21 February 1922; *Hamilton Spectator*, 20 January 1922; *Toronto Globe*, 20 January 1922; *Charlotte Observer*, 21 February 1922.

160. Jones, *Southern Horrors and Other Writings*; Bederman, *Manliness and Civilization*, 45–76; Bay, *To Tell the Truth Freely*; Giddings, *Ida*; Tindall, *Emergence of the New South*, 173–78.

161. *Toronto Globe*, 20 January 1922; *Hamilton Spectator*, 24 February 1922; *Raleigh News and Observer*, 23 January 1922.

162. *Chicago Tribune*, 2 February 1922.

163. *Toronto Globe*, 21 February 1922.

164. Ibid., 19 January 1922; *Charlotte Observer*, 27 January 1922; and *Hamilton Herald*, 26 January 1922. Although the account of the Bullock case here is mostly erroneous, see Williams, *Strangers in the Land of Paradise*, 163–65.

165. *Raleigh News and Observer*, 22 January 1922; *Charlotte Observer*, 22 January 1922; *NYT*, 22 January 1922.

166. *Toronto Globe*, 20 February 1922.

167. Ibid., 27 January 1922.

168. *Hamilton Spectator*, 20–25 January 1922; *Hamilton Herald*, 16–18 January 1922.

169. *Raleigh News and Observer*, 18 January 1922; *Hamilton Spectator*, 16 January 1922.

170. *NYT*, 18 January 1922; *Toronto Globe*, 19 January 1922.

171. Finkelman, *Dred Scott v. Sandford*; Reinders, "John Anderson Case"; and Silverman, "Kentucky, Canada, and Extradition."

172. *Raleigh News and Observer*, 25 February 1922.

173. Ibid., 19 February 1922; *Toronto Globe*, 20 February 1922; *NYT*, 19 February 1922; *Charlotte Observer*, 19 February 1922.

174. *Charlotte Observer*, 19 February 1922.

175. *Herald*, 27 January and 24–25 February 1922.

176. *NYT*, 18 January 1922; *Toronto Globe*, 19 January 1922.

177. *Hamilton Herald*, 24 February 1922.

178. *Toronto Globe*, 21 and 28 January 1922; *Raleigh News and Observer*, 3 March 1922; *Charlotte Observer*, 21 January and 3 March 1922. Charles Evans Hughes of the State Department directed the U.S. consul in Ottawa, Jose De Olivares, to represent North Carolina during Bullock's hearings. Hughes, a onetime New York governor and unsuccessful presidential candidate, would become chief justice of the Supreme Court in 1930.

179. *Toronto Globe*, 18 February 1922; *Hamilton Herald*, 17 February 1922; *Hamilton Spectator*, 17 February 1922. Also see Extradition to U.S.A. of Matthew Bullock, Department of Justice, RG13-C1-993-1922, LAC.

180. Tindall, *Emergence of the New South*, 174–76. The House of Representatives passed the Dyer antilynching bill by 230-119 votes, but southern Democrats in the Senate eventually killed the bill.

181. *Raleigh News and Observer*, 25–26 February and 3 March 1922.

182. Ibid., 28 January 1922. The Department of Immigration first ruled on Bullock in late January, but after an appeal by Governor Morrison, a final decision on the matter was handed down in March.

183. *NYT*, 5 March 1922 and 30 April 1922.

184. *Toronto Globe*, 28 January 1922.

185. *Hamilton Herald*, 4 March 1922.

186. *Charlotte Observer*, 4 March 1922. It was never proven that Bullock shot a white man during the Norlina fracas, but the mere accusation would have stirred up even greater ire and presumably strengthened North Carolina's petition to Canada.

187. *Hamilton Herald*, 3 March 1922.

188. *Hamilton Spectator*, 28 March 1922; *Hamilton Herald*, 18 March and 29 April 1922; *NYT*, 19–20 March 1922. It is rumored that Bullock settled in Great Britain.

189. *NYT*, 5 March 1922.

190. Winks, *Blacks in Canada*, 420.

191. Ibid.

Chapter 5

1. Charles Bernard Blanchette, Death Certificate, 8 January 1917, Registrar General's Office, Department of Health, Government of St. Kitts–Nevis, Basseterre, St. Kitts–Nevis. Also see *St. Kitts–Nevis Daily Bulletin* (Basseterre), 13 January 1917 and 14 February 1917.

2. Howard R. Blanchette, interview by author. Also see Arthur R. Blanchette to W. C. Hueston, 27 February 1939, Black Community in Manitoba P6895/4, AM.

3. Obituary for Arthur Robinson Blanchette, *Montreal Gazette*, 10 August 1977.

4. The Porters' Social and Charitable Association was created by OSCP members in 1932. See Porters' Social and Charitable Association Papers, Order of Sleeping Car Porters, AM.

5. Winks, *Blacks in Canada*, 425–74.

6. *Chicago Defender*, 18 June 1938.

7. Gaines, *Uplifting the Race*.

8. *Maclean's*, 1 November 1949; *Toronto Daily Star*, 30 October 1954; Lambertson, "Dresden Story."

9. Berton, *Great Depression*, 87–107; Thompson and Seager, *Canada*, 138–44.

10. Thompson and Seager, *Canada*, 138.

11. Richard B. Bennett, Conservative, served as prime minister from 1930 to 1935, while William Lyon Mackenzie King, Liberal, was reelected in 1935 and remained in office until 1948.

12. Berton, *Great Depression*, 142–51.

13. Robert Jamerson funeral service program, 18 October 1993, and transcript of Robert "Buddy" Jamerson interview conducted by Patricia Clements, Black Community in Manitoba P6899/1, AM.

14. Canadian railways earned $31.9 million in passenger traffic revenue in 1933, the Great Depression's nadir, compared with $83.8 million in 1927; not until 1942 would passenger traffic revenue return to pre-Depression standards. See Urquhart and Buckley, *Historical Statistics of Canada*, 537.

15. *Census of Canada*, 1931, Bulletin No. 1, 14; Bulletin No. 2, 22; Bulletin No. 6, 22.

16. See "Race Issue—Canadian National Railways Employees," CBRE MG28-I-215, LAC.

17. Gendered divisions in the Canadian workforce exacerbated the economic squeeze felt by blacks during the Great Depression. Since railway managers reserved sleeping car portering exclusively for black men, black women and the families they cared for shouldered the brunt of even greater poverty, since they could not even access higher-wage portering jobs. See Calliste, "Sleeping Car Porters in Canada."

18. Aaron Mosher to W. W. Overton, chair of the Road Roamers, Toronto's local 175 of the CBRE, 6 November 1942, MG28-I 215, LAC.

19. Robinson and Mosher exchanged a number of letters regarding the CBRE's treatment of black members. See "Race Issue—Canadian National Railways Employees," CBRE MG28-I-215, LAC.

20. By 1940, Aaron Mosher also served as president of the Canadian Labour Congress,

which had been known as the Canadian Congress of Labour from 1927 to 1940. Both organizations were the largest national industrial unions and functioned in Canada much like the AFL in the United States.

21. Mosher delayed the renegotiation of porters' contracts by more than three years, this despite all black locals' requests that he bring their contracts before CNR managers.

22. See Calliste, "Blacks on Canadian Railways," and Calliste, "Sleeping Car Porters in Canada."

23. Aaron Mosher, Circular #248-NP-45, 17 July 1945, CBRE MG28-I-215, LAC.

24. A. Philip Randolph to Arthur R. Blanchette, 12 July 1950, BSCP, pt. 1, General Correspondence, Arthur R. Blanchette, container 6, LC.

25. Robinson had launched IDIA proceedings on behalf of CNR porters in 1919, 1920, and again in 1927, winning important concessions for black workers, with Mosher and the CBRE doing very little to support his campaigns.

26. Porters were particularly worried that, because of dramatic reductions on the lines, many were not able to work full-time for six months, thus forfeiting their seniority rights accordingly to company managers. Porters argued instead that seniority rights were secured so long as they worked six months per year. Without seniority wage scales, porters' wages were driven down, and most lost access to their pensions throughout the 1930s. See BSCP, pt. 1, CPR General Correspondence, 1940–68, container 39, LC.

27. Ibid.

28. Circular #3 by John A. Robinson, 20 November 1937, BSCP, pt. 1, Canadian Porters, 1940–68, container 68, LC.

29. Charles E. Russell to A. Philip Randolph, 4 May 1939, BSCP, pt. 1, Canadian Porters, 1940–68, container 68, LC.

30. Circular #6 by John A. Robinson, 24 October 1938, BSCP, pt. 1, Canadian Porters, 1940–68, container 68, LC.

31. John A. Robinson to A. Philip Randolph, 25 July 1939, BSCP, pt. 1, Canadian Porters, 1940–68, container 68, LC.

32. Berton, *Great Depression*, 482–96.

33. John A. Robinson to A. Phillip Randolph, 29 May 1937, BSCP, pt. 1, Canadian Porters, 1940–68, container 68, LC.

34. Lena Lucy Robinson obituary, *Chicago Defender*, 13 September 1941. John A. Robinson also traveled regularly to Chicago and New York, narrowly missing Randolph in September 1939, though he held a meeting with BSCP secretary Ashley Totten.

35. A. Philip Randolph to John A. Robinson, 14 September 1939, BSCP, pt. 1, Canadian Porters, 1940–68, container 68, LC.

36. John A. Robinson, "Circular to all Canadian Sleeping Car Porters," 20 May 1938, BSCP, pt. 1, Canadian Porters, 1940–68, container 68, LC.

37. Russell served as chair of Montreal's Porters Mutual Benefit Association during the 1930s. See file memo, 31 October 1942, BSCP, pt. 1, Canadian Porters, 1940–68, container 39, LC.

38. A. Philip Randolph to Charles E. Russell, 10 May 1939, BSCP, pt. 1, Canadian Porters, 1940–68, container 68, LC.

39. Roy L. Lewis to A. Philip Randolph, 24 August 1939, and Arthur R. Blanchette to A. Philip Randolph, 29 October 1939, BSCP, pt. 1, Canadian Porters, 1940–68, container 68, LC.

40. Charles E. Russell to A. Philip Randolph, June 1939, BSCP, pt. 1, Canadian Porters, 1940–68, container 68, LC.

41. Winks, *Blacks in Canada*, 404–6.

42. Velmer I. Coward to A. Philip Randolph, 23 November 1942, BSCP Ladies' Auxiliary Montreal, container 75, LC.

43. *BW*, August 1939. The extensive national network of Canadian porters facilitated the BSCP's organizing efforts in Canada throughout the 1940s and 1950s. African Canadian sleeping car porters supplied Randolph with the halls and audiences he needed and held open meetings in Montreal's UNIA Hall, Toronto's Oddfellows Temple, Winnipeg's Lithuanian Hall, and Vancouver's Croatian Hall and AME Church; also see *BW*, November 1944, July 1945, and October 1945.

44. Lena Lucy Robinson obituary, *Chicago Defender*, 13 September 1941.

45. Black Community in Manitoba P6900/1, AM. The annual balls sponsored by Montreal porters and Elks regularly attracted four hundred guests, with many coming from as far as Washington, D.C. See Israel, "Montreal Negro Community," 175.

46. *BW*, July 1945.

47. *Henderson's Directory*, 1931, 1507; *Henderson's Directory*, 1936, 1113.

48. Winks, *Blacks in Canada*, 320–26.

49. The UNIA headquarters is listed at 795 Main Street in the OSCP building. See *Henderson's Directory*, 1923, 1174.

50. *Henderson's Directory*, 1945, 184. Eddie Blackman and Frances Atwell, interviews by author.

51. Yvonne Blanchette, interview by author. Born in Sedalia, Missouri, Harvey B. Bouldin arrived in Winnipeg around 1927 with his French Canadian wife, Marie Lemieux, and their twin daughters, Elaine and Yvonne.

52. Within the first five years of the Great Depression alone, nearly thirty thousand foreign-born Canadians were deported. See Berton, *Great Depression*, 106–10.

53. Ibid., 150–62. Berton explains that in many instances relief agencies were posted in railway stations in order to deport applicants with even greater expediency.

54. Dominion Bureau of Statistics, *Census of the Prairie Provinces*, 1936, 46–47, 58–59.

55. BSCP, pt. 2, A. Philip Randolph Papers, 1953–68, container 106, LC.

56. Williams, *Road to Now*, 74–83; Winks, *Blacks in Canada*, 358–60, 413–70.

57. Established in Calgary in 1932, the Co-operative Commonwealth Federation quickly emerged as a progressive political party working on behalf of labor and Canadians most adversely affected by the Great Depression. Woodsworth served as the party's first president and became Canada's best-known and most vocal mid-twentieth-century Socialist. See E. D. Collins memo to CBRE Division 130, 8 March 1940, Black Community in Manitoba P6893/6, AM.

58. Transcripts of interviews with retired Winnipeg porters Lee Williams and Robert Jamerson, Black Community in Manitoba P6899/1, AM.

59. Robert Jamerson funeral program, Black Community in Manitoba P6898/19, AM. Great War veterans peppered other porters' locals as well. Montreal CPR porter Sam Morgan served in both world wars and spent nearly a year at the hands of Nazis as a prisoner of war. See "Veterans of Two Wars Aid on Hospital Cars," Sleeping Car Porters Employee Files B-20, CPA.

60. *Chicago Defender*, 13 September 1941. Yvonne Blanchette recalled that Robinson retired to the Caribbean, most likely St. Kitts, shortly after World War II. Yvonne Blanchette, interview by author.

61. Menelik Lodge #528 Minutes and By-Laws, 1939–47, Blacks in Manitoba, P6893/6, AM. Also see Arthur R. Blanchette to Rev. J. L. Davis, 17 February 1938, Blacks in Manitoba, P6895/4, AM; *Chicago Defender* 29 October 1932; and *Labour Organisations in Canada*, 1931, 134.

62. *BW*, September 1945. It is interesting to note that although the CLACP was established in 1925 by James F. Jenkins, J. W. Montgomery, and African Canadian history enthusiasts Fred Landon and Judge William Riddell, in a peculiar display of Americocentrism, Randolph claimed to have "inaugurated" the CLACP during his visit to Canada in 1945. See *DT*, 16 August 1924.

63. 9 November 1943, BSCP, General Correspondence, 1940–68, container 39, LC.

64. 1 June 1945, New CPR Agreement (1945), BSCP, General Correspondence, 1940–68, container 39, LC.

65. Aaron Mosher to W. W. Overton, 6 November 1942, CBRE, MG28-I-215, LAC.

66. Earl Swift report submitted to S. H. Eighteen, 2 November 1942, CBRE, MG28-I-215, LAC.

67. Earl Swift to Aaron Mosher, 26 June 1945, CBRE, MG28-I-215, LAC.

68. Ibid.

69. Aaron Mosher circular to CNR locals #132 (Halifax), #128 (Montreal), #175 (Toronto), and #130 (Winnipeg), 17 July 1945, CBRE, MG28-I-215, LAC.

70. Ibid.

71. John A. Robinson to Aaron Mosher, 1 August 1945, CBRE, MG28-I-215, LAC.

72. Despite trying for years to get out of the CBRE, A. Philip Randolph never succeeded at bringing CNR porters into the BSCP's fold, thanks to Mosher's unyielding blockade and his refusal to release black workers from CBRE representation.

73. Borstelmann, *Cold War and the Color Line*, 4.

74. Sylvia, "I'm a Canadian: Negro," 72–73.

75. *Eye to Eye*, CBC Television Winnipeg, 1961.

76. Mosher, *Discrimination and Denial*, 95–98.

77. *Eye to Eye*, CBC Television Winnipeg, 1961.

78. Berton, *Great Depression*, 65.

79. Pickersgill, who became the minister of citizenship and immigration in the summer of 1954, was a career civil servant who first served as Prime Minister King's speech writer during the Great Depression before becoming a member of Parliament in 1953. Negotiating Newfoundland's incorporation into Canada stands out as one of Pickersgill's most important accomplishments. Renowned for his straight talk and stubbornness, Pickersgill made his presence felt in the House of Commons, with Prime Minister John Diefenbaker declaring, "Parliament without Pickersgill would be like hell without the devil." *Maclean's*, 24 November 1997.

80. Berton, *Great Depression*, 568–77.

81. Backhouse, *Colour-Coded*, 251–52; Winks, *Blacks in Canada*, 425–30.

82. *Maclean's*, 1 November 1949.

83. Ibid., 8.

84. Grizzle, *My Name's Not George*, 31.

85. Berton, *Great Depression*, 568–77.

86. Negro Citizenship Association Brief, 27 April 1954, BSCP, pt. 2, A. Philip Randolph Papers, 1953–68, container 106, LC.

87. Ibid.

88. Ibid.

89. Ibid. Stanley Grizzle eventually joined Toronto's Committee for Human Rights and in 1959 ran for election to the Ontario legislature as a Co-operative Commonwealth Federation candidate. In 1978, Grizzle became Canada's first black citizenship judge.

Sources

Primary Sources

Manuscripts

Basseterre, St. Kitts–Nevis
  Department of Health
    Registers of Births, Marriages, and Deaths
  National Archives
    National Newspaper Collection
  St. Christopher Heritage Society
    National Church Papers
Calgary, Alberta
  Glenbow-Alberta Institute
    Blacks in Alberta Papers and Photograph Collection
    Ware/Lewis Family Papers
Chicago, Illinois
  Chicago Historical Society
    Brotherhood of Sleeping Car Porters Chicago Division Papers
  Newberry Library
    Pullman Papers
Halifax, Nova Scotia
  Public Archives of Nova Scotia
    Unity Lodge/Equity Lodge Collection
Montreal, Quebec
  Archives municipale de la ville de Montréal
    Quartier St-Antoine Papers
  Bibliothèque et archives nationales du Québec
    Judicial Reports and Probate Records
  Canadian Pacific Archives
    Thomas G. Shaughnessy Papers
    Sleeping Car Porters and Red Caps Papers
    Sleeping, Dining and Parlor Car Department Papers
    William Van Horne Papers
  McGill University
    Roy States Collection
New York, New York
  Schomburg Center for Research in Black Culture, New York Public Library
    Afro-American Labor Archives
    Blacks and the Railroad Industry Papers
    Brotherhood of Sleeping Car Porters Collection
    A. Philip Randolph Papers

Ottawa, Ontario
  Library and Archives of Canada
    Sir Robert Borden Papers
    Canada Labour Relations Board
    Canadian Brotherhood of Railway Employees Collection
    Canadian Congress of Labour Papers
    Canadian National Railways Collection
    Canadian Sessional Papers, 1900–1915
    Department of External Affairs
    Department of Justice
    Department of National Defence
    Governor-General's Office
    Immigration Branch Records
    Sir Edward Kemp Papers
    William Lyon Mackenzie King Papers
    Labour Canada
    Sir Wilfrid Laurier Papers
    Militia and Defence
    Ministry of Overseas Forces of Canada
    National Health and Welfare
    Privy Council Office
    Railways and Canals
    Royal Canadian Mounted Police Papers
    Sir Richard Turner Papers
    Sir William Van Horne Papers
    War Labour Board
Toronto, Ontario
  Archives of Ontario
    Black History Research Collection
    Daniel G. Hill Fonds
  City of Toronto Archives
    City Directories and Criminal Records
    Judicial Reports and Probate Records
  Ontario Black History Society
    General Collection
Washington, D.C.
  Library of Congress
    General Records of the Department of Labor
    National Association for the Advancement of Colored People Papers
    Records of the Brotherhood of Sleeping Car Porters
    Records of the Foreign Service Posts of the Department of State
    Records of the U.S. State Department
Winnipeg, Manitoba
  Archives of Manitoba
    Black Community in Manitoba Collection
  Government of Manitoba
    Land Titles Office
  Provincial Museum of Manitoba
    Sleeping Car Porters Photo Collection

Documents and Reports

Bonar, James C. *Montreal and the Inauguration of Trans-Canada Transportation.* Montreal: La ligue du progrès civique, 1936.

Brazeal, Brailsford R. *The Brotherhood of Sleeping Car Porters: Its Origin and Development.* New York: Harper and Brothers, 1946.

Burdon, Katharine J. S. *A Handbook of St. Kitts–Nevis.* London: West India Committee, 1920.

Canadian National Railways. *Annual Report.* 1926–60.

Canadian Pacific Railway. *Annual Report of the Canadian Pacific Railway Company.* 1884–1955.

——. *Proceedings at Annual Meeting of the Shareholders.* 1884–1960.

——. *Staff Bulletin.* 1925–60.

Canadian Railway and Marine World. 1914–19.

Carter, Charles F. *When Railroads Were New.* New York: Henry Holt and Co., 1909.

Davis, Harry E. *A History of Freemasonry among Negroes in America.* Cleveland: n.p., 1946.

Department of Labour. *Annual Report.* 1902–60.

——. *Labour Gazette.* 1900–1960.

——. *Labour Organisations in Canada.* 1911–68.

——. *Report on Strikes and Lockouts in Canada.* 1901–60.

——. *Wages, Rates, Salaries and Hours of Labour Report.* 1901–44.

Department of Railways and Canals. *Auditor General's Report.* 1880–1955.

Dominion Bureau of Statistics. *Canada Yearbook.* 1900–1960.

——. *Census of Canada.* 1881, 1901–61.

——. *Census of the Prairie Provinces*, 1936.

——. *Statistical Year-Book of Canada.* 1900–1960.

——. *Statistics of Steam Railways of Canada.* 1926–60.

Gibbon, John Murray. *Steel of Empire: The Romantic History of the Canadian Pacific, the Northwest Passage of Today.* London: Rich and Cowan, 1935.

Greaves, Ida C. *National Problems in Canada: The Negro in Canada.* Orillia, Ont.: Packet-Times Press, 1929.

House of Commons of Canada. *House of Commons Debates.* 1880–1955.

Innis, Harold A. *A History of the Canadian Pacific Railway.* Toronto: McClelland and Stewart, 1923.

Kempton, Murray. *Part of Our Time: Some Ruins and Monuments of the Thirties.* New York: Simon and Schuster, 1955.

LeBourdais, I. "Canada's First Community House for Negroes Represents a Forward Step in Social Services." *Saturday Night*, 25 July 1942.

Ministry of the Interior. *Immigration Facts and Figures.* 1916–55.

——. *Report on Immigration.* 1910–60.

Murphy, Emily F. *The Black Candle: Canada's First Book on Drug Abuse.* Toronto: Thomas Allen, 1922.

Porter, M. "Three Thousand Nights on Wheels." *Maclean's*, 15 March 1949.

Report of Hours of Work and Regular and Sufficient Time for Sleep to the Health of Pullman Porters, Waiters and Cooks on Railways. New York: Workers's Health Bureau, 1927.

Sessing, Trevor. "A Single Barbarian." Seminar paper presented at the Lakeshore Unitarian Church for the Study Group in Canadian History, Montreal, 1971.

Shepherd, William G. "Night Riders Come to Canada." *Maclean's*, 15 October 1921.

Shortt, Adam, and Arthur Doughty, eds. *Canada and Its Provinces: A History of the*

Canadian People and Their Institutions by One Hundred Associates. Vol. 1, *Immigration by Races,* by William D. Scott. Toronto: Publisher's Association of Canada, 1914.

Sylvia, Dorothy. "I'm a Canadian Negro." *New Liberty* (September 1952).

Thompson, Norman, and Major J. H. Edgar. *Canadian Railway Development from the Earliest Times.* Toronto: Macmillan Company of Canada, 1933.

Trout, John Malcolm, and Edward Trout. *The Railways of Canada for 1870–1, Showing the Progress, Mileage, Cost of Construction, the Stocks, Bonds, Traffic, Earnings, Expenses, and Organization of the Railways of the Dominion.* Toronto: Office of the Monetary Times, 1871.

Wells, Ida B., et al. *The Reason Why the Colored American Is Not in the World's Columbian Exposition.* N.p., 1893. Reprint, Chicago: University of Illinois Press, 1999.

Winks, Robin W. "Canada and Racial Exclusion: Two Case Studies." Postgraduate seminar paper presented at the University of London Institute of Commonwealth Studies, London, 13 November 1969.

——. *Canadian–West Indian Union: A Forty-Year Minuet.* Institute of Commonwealth Studies. London: Athlone Press, 1968.

Woodsworth, James S. *Strangers within Our Gates.* 3d ed. Toronto: Tenth Thousand, 1911.

Autobiographies, Memoirs, and Narratives

Grizzle, Stanley G. *My Name's Not George: The Story of the Brotherhood of Sleeping Car Porters in Canada.* Toronto: Umbrella Press, 1998.

Johnson, James. *Along This Way: The Autobiography of James Weldon Johnson.* New York: Viking Press, 1961.

Riley, Betty. "The 'Coloured Church' of Montreal: An Intimate Thumbnail Historical Account." *Spear: Canadian Magazine of Truth and Soul* 3, no. 10 (1974).

Roper, Edward. *By Track and Trail: A Journey through Canada.* London: W. H. Allen and Co., 1891.

Sladen, Douglas. *On the Cars and Off: Being the Journal of a Pilgrimage along the Queen's Highway, from Halifax in Nova Scotia to Victoria in Vancouver's Island.* London: Ward, Lock, and Co., 1895.

Vaughan, Walter. *The Life and Work of Sir William Van Horne.* New York: Century Company, 1920.

Washington, Booker T. *Up from Slavery: An Autobiography.* 1901. Reprint, Garden City, N.Y.: Doubleday and Co., 1963.

White, Walter. *A Man Called White: The Autobiography of Walter White.* New York: Viking Press, 1948. Reprint, Athens: University of Georgia Press, 1995.

Newspapers and Magazines

UNITED STATES

Baltimore Afro-American
Bangor (Maine) Daily News
Baptist Informer (Muskogee, Okla.)
Black Worker (New York)
Buffalo (N.Y.) American
Charlotte (N.C.) Observer

Chicago Defender
Chicago Record Herald
Chicago Tribune
Chicago Whip
Crisis (New York)
Detroit Informer
Messenger (New York)
Minneapolis Star
National Advocate (Minneapolis)
Negro World (New York)
New York Times
New York Tribune
New York World
Oklahoma Guide (Oklahoma City)
Opportunity (New York)
Pittsburgh Courier
Railway Age (Chicago)
Raleigh (N.C.) News and Observer
Savannah (Ga.) Tribune
Twin City American (Minneapolis)
Washington (D.C.) Bee

CANADA

Atlantic Advocate (Halifax, N.S.)
By-Water Magazine (Montreal)
Calgary (Alta.) Albertan
Calgary (Alta.) Daily Herald
Calgary (Alta.) Eye-Opener
Calgary (Alta.) Herald
Canadian Illustrated News (Montreal)
Canadian Observer (Toronto)
Chatham (Ont.) Planet
Dawn of Tomorrow (Hamilton, Ont.)
Edmonton (Alta.) Bulletin
Edmonton (Alta.) Capital
Edmonton (Alta.) Daily Bulletin
Edmonton (Alta.) Daily Capital
Edmonton (Alta.) Evening Journal
Edmonton (Alta.) Journal
Free Lance (Montreal)
Halifax (N.S.) Herald
Halifax (N.S.) Mail Star
Halifax (N.S.) Morning Chronicle
Halifax (N.S.) Morning Chronicle Herald
Hamilton (Ont.) Herald
Hamilton (Ont.) Spectator
La Presse (Montreal)
Lethbridge (Alta.) Daily Herald

Lethbridge (Alta.) Daily News
Lethbridge (Alta.) Herald
Lethbridge (Alta.) Morning Leader Post
Maclean's
Manitoba Daily Free Press (Winnipeg)
Manitoba Free Press (Winnipeg)
Montreal Gazette
Montreal Herald
Montreal Star
Ottawa Citizen
Ottawa Free Press
Port Arthur (Ont.) Chronicle
Port Arthur (Ont.) Daily-News Chronicle
Port Arthur (Ont.) Daily Times Journal
Port Arthur (Ont.) Evening Chronicle
Provincial Freeman (Chatham, Ont.)
Regina (Sask.) Leader
Regina (Sask.) Morning Leader
Saskatchewan Herald (Battleford)
Sydney (N.S.) Daily Post
Toronto Daily Star
Toronto Globe
Toronto Globe and Mail
Toronto Star
Victoria (B.C.) Daily Times
Western Labor News (Winnipeg, Man.)
Windsor (Ont.) Star
Winnipeg (Man.) Citizen
Winnipeg (Man.) Free Press
Winnipeg (Man.) Tribune

CARIBBEAN

Kingston (Jamaica) Daily Gleaner
St. Kitts–Nevis Daily Bulletin (Basseterre)
St. Kitts–Nevis Daily Express (Basseterre)
St. Kitts–Nevis Union Messenger (Basseterre)
St. Vincent Times (Kingstown)

UNITED KINGDOM

African Telegraph (London)
Guardian (Manchester)
Liverpool Courier
Liverpool Echo
Liverpool Post and Mercury
Sunday Times (London)
Times (London)
Times and South Wales Weekly News (Cardiff)
Western Mail (Cardiff)

Interviews and Video Recordings

Atwell, Frances. Interview by author. 26 June 1997 and 14 March 1998, Winnipeg. Tape recording. In possession of the author.

Atwell, Gerald ("Gerry"). Telephone interview by author. 1 February 1998, Winnipeg.

Bailey, Edward ("Eddie") and Helen. Interview by author. 16 March 1998, Winnipeg. Tape recording. In possession of the author.

Blackman, Edward ("Eddie"). Interview by author. 17 March 1998, Winnipeg. Tape recording. In possession of the author.

Blanchette, Howard R. Interview by author. 22 February 1999, Framingham, Mass. Tape recording. In possession of the author.

Blanchette, Yvonne. Interview by author. 16 November 1998, Montreal. Tape recording. In possession of the author.

"Good Morning with Avril Benoit." CBC Radio interview with Stanley Grizzle, Herb Carvery, and Saje Mathieu (Toronto), 11 August 1998.

Jones, Bud. Telephone interview by author. 18 May 2000, Brockville, Ontario.

Lewsey, Lawrence and Ethel. Interview by the author. 16 March 1998, Winnipeg. Tape recording. In possession of the author.

"Some of the Best Minds of Our Times." Peter Gzowski, CBC Radio interview with Saje Mathieu, 2 July 2001.

Williams, Lee and Alice. Interview by the author. 16 March 1998, Winnipeg. Tape recording. In possession of the author.

Legal Citations

Alien Labour Act, 60–61 Victoria c. 11
Alien Labour Act, Revised Statutes of Canada, c. 97, 1906
Dred Scott v. Sandford 60 U.S. (19 How.) 393, 1857
Immigration Act, 6 Edw. 7 c. 19
Immigration Act, 9–10 Edw. 7 c. 27
Immigration Act, Revised Statutes of Canada, c. 93, 1919
Industrial Disputes Investigation Act, 1907
Order in Council, 1–2 Geo. 5, 1911
Plessy v. Ferguson, 163 U.S. 537, 1896

Secondary Sources

Books

Adelaide-Merlande, Jacques. *Histoire générale des Antilles et des Guyannes: Des Précolombiens à nos jours*. Paris: Édition L'Harmattan, 1994.

Anderson, Benedict. *Imagined Communities: Reflections on the Origin and Spread of Nationalism*. 2d ed. London: Verso Press, 1991.

Anderson, Jervis. *A. Philip Randolph: A Biographical Portrait*. New York: Harcourt Brace Jovanovich, 1973.

Archdeacon, Thomas J. *Becoming American: An Ethnic History*. New York: Free Press, 1983.

Archer-Straw, Petrine. *Negrophilia: Avant-Garde Paris and Black Culture in the 1920s*. London: Thames and Hudson, 2000.

Arnesen, Eric. *Brotherhoods of Color: Black Railroad Workers and the Struggle for Equality.* Cambridge: Harvard University Press, 2001.

Arnesen, Eric, Julie Greene, and Bruce Laurie, eds. *Labor Histories: Class, Politics, and the Working-Class Experience.* Chicago: University of Illinois Press, 1998.

Avery, Donald H. *"Dangerous Foreigners": European Immigrant Workers and Labour Radicalism in Canada, 1896–1932.* Toronto: McClelland and Stewart, 1979.

——. *Reluctant Host: Canada's Response to Immigrant Workers, 1896–1994.* Toronto: McClelland and Stewart, 1995.

Babcock, Robert H. *Gompers in Canada: A Study in American Continentalism before the First World War.* Toronto: University of Toronto Press, 1974.

Backhouse, Constance. *Colour-Coded: A Legal History of Racism in Canada, 1900–1950.* Toronto: Osgoode Society for Canadian Legal History, Toronto University Press, 1999.

Baker, E. C. *A Guide to Records in the Leeward Islands.* Oxford: University of the West Indies, 1965.

Balawyder, Aloysius. *The Winnipeg General Strike.* Vancouver: Copp Publishing Co., 1967.

Balibar, Etienne, and Immanuel Wallerstein. *Race, Nation, Class: Ambiguous Identities.* London: Verso Press, 1991.

Barbeau, Arthur, and Florette Henri. *The Unknown Soldiers: African-American Troops in World War I.* Philadelphia: Temple University Press, 1974. Reprint, New York: Da Capo Press, 1996.

Bates, Beth Tompkins. *Pullman Porters and the Rise of Protest Politics in Black America, 1925–1945.* Chapel Hill: University of North Carolina Press, 2001.

Bay, Mia. *To Tell the Truth Freely: The Life of Ida B. Wells.* New York: Hill and Wang, 2009.

Bederman, Gail. *Manliness and Civilization: A Cultural History of Gender and Race in the United States, 1880–1917.* Chicago: University of Chicago Press, 1995.

Bercuson, David J. *Confrontation at Winnipeg: Labour, Industrial Relations, and the General Strike.* Montreal: McGill-Queen's University Press, 1974.

Berton, Pierre. *The Great Depression, 1929–1939.* Toronto: Penguin Books, 1991.

——. *The Great Railway: Illustrated.* Toronto: McClelland and Stewart, 1972.

——. *The National Dream: The Great Railway, 1871–1881.* Toronto: McClelland and Stewart, 1971.

——. *The National Dream: The Last Spike.* Toronto: McClelland and Stewart, 1974.

——. *The Promised Land: Settling the West, 1896–1914.* Toronto: McClelland and Stewart, 1984.

Blee, Kathleen M. *Women of the Klan: Racism and Gender in the 1920s.* Berkeley: University of California Press, 1991.

Bodnar, John E. *The Transplanted: A History of Immigrants in Urban America.* Bloomington: Indiana University Press, 1985.

Borstelmann, Thomas. *The Cold War and the Color Line: American Race Relations in the Global Arena.* Cambridge: Harvard University Press, 2001.

Braithwaite, Rella, ed. *The Black Woman in Canada.* N.p., 1976.

Brand, Dionne. *No Burden to Carry: Narratives of Black Working Women in Ontario, 1920s to 1950s.* Toronto: Women's Press, 1991.

Brault, Jean-Rémi, ed. *Montréal au XIXème siècle: Des gens, des idées, des arts, une ville.* Quebec: Lémac, 1990.

Bristow, Peggy, et al. *"We're Rooted Here and They Can't Pull Us Up": Essays in African Canadian Women's History.* Toronto: University of Toronto Press, 1994.

Brody, Jennifer DeVere. *Impossible Purities: Blackness, Femininity, and Victorian Culture.* Durham, N.C.: Duke University Press, 1998.

Brown, Jacqueline Nassy. *Dropping Anchor, Setting Sail: Geographies of Race in Black Liverpool*. Princeton, N.J.: Princeton University Press, 2005.

Brundage, W. Fitzhugh, ed. *Under Sentence of Death: Lynching in the South*. Chapel Hill: University of North Carolina Press, 1997.

Bumsted, J. M. *The Winnipeg General Strike of 1919: An Illustrated History*. Winnipeg: Watson and Dwyer Publishing, 1994.

Carby, Hazel. *Race Men*. Cambridge: Harvard University Press, 2000.

Carnes, Mark C. *Secret Rituals and Manhood in Victorian America*. New Haven, Conn.: Yale University Press, 1989.

Cass, Donn A. *Negro Freemasonry and Segregation: An Historical Study of Prejudice against American Negroes as Freemasons and the Position of Negro Freemasonry in the Masonic Fraternity*. Chicago: Ezra A. Cook Publications, 1957.

Chateauvert, Melinda. *Marching Together: Women of the Brotherhood of Sleeping Car Porters*. Chicago: University of Illinois Press, 1998.

Collins, Sydney. *Coloured Minorities in Britain: Studies in British Race Relations Based on African, West Indian, and Asiatic Immigrants*. London: Lutterworth Press, 1957.

Copp, Terry. *The Anatomy of Poverty: The Condition of the Working Class in Montreal, 1897–1929*. Toronto: McClelland and Stewart, 1974.

Craven, Paul. *"An Impartial Umpire": Industrial Relations and the Canadian State, 1900–1911*. Toronto: University of Toronto Press, 1980.

Cruise, David, and Alison Griffiths. *Lords of the Line*. Markham, Ont.: Penguin Books of Canada, 1988.

Daniels, Roger. *Coming to America: A History of Immigration and Ethnicity in American Life*. New York: Harper Collins, 1990.

Dempsey, Hugh A., ed. *The CPR West: The Iron Road and the Making of a Nation*. Vancouver: Douglas and McIntyre, 1984.

Den Otter, Andy A. *The Philosophy of Railways: The Transcontinental Railway Idea in British North America*. Toronto: University of Toronto Press, 1997.

Dickerson, Dennis. *Out of the Crucible: Black Steelworkers in Western Pennsylvania, 1875–1980*. Albany: State University of New York Press, 1986.

Dookhan, Isaac. *A Post-Emancipation History of the West Indies*. Essex, England: Longman Caribbean, 1975.

Dorin, Patrick C. *The Canadian National Railways's Story*. Seattle: Superior Publishing Co., 1975.

Edwards, Brent Hayes. *The Practice of Diaspora: Literature, Translation, and the Rise of Black Internationalism*. Cambridge: Harvard University Press, 2003.

Fabre, Michel. *From Harlem to Paris: Black American Writers in France, 1840–1980*. Chicago: University of Illinois Press, 1991.

Finkelman, Paul. *Dred Scott v. Sandford: A Brief History with Documents*. Boston: Bedford Books, 1997.

Foner, Philip S. *First Facts of American Labor: A Comprehensive Collection of Labor Firsts in the United States Arranged by Subject*. New York: Holmes and Meier, 1984.

——. *Organized Labor and the Black Worker*. New York: Praeger, 1974.

Foner, Philip S., and Ronald Lewis, eds. *The Black Worker: A Documentary History from Colonial Times to the Present*. Vols. 4 and 5. Philadelphia: Temple University Press, 1979.

Frank, Dana. *Purchasing Power: Consumer Organizing, Gender, and the Seattle Labor Movement, 1919–1929*. Cambridge: Cambridge University Press, 1994.

Fryer, Peter. *Staying Power: The History of Black People in Britain*. 6th ed. London: Pluto Press, 1992.

Gagnon, Jean-Pierre. *Le vingt-deuxième bataillon Canadien-français, 1914–1919: Étude socio-militaire.* Quebec: Les Presses de l'université Laval, 1986.

Gaines, Kevin. *Uplifting the Race: Black Leadership, Politics, and Culture in the Twentieth Century.* Chapel Hill: University of North Carolina Press, 1996.

Giddings, Paula. *Ida: A Sword among Lions: Ida B. Wells and the Campaign against Lynching.* New York: Harper, 2009.

Gilmore, Glenda E. *Defying Dixie: The Radical Roots of Civil Rights, 1919–1950.* New York: W. W. Norton and Co., 2009.

———. *Gender and Jim Crow: Women and the Politics of White Supremacy in North Carolina, 1896–1920.* Chapel Hill: University of North Carolina Press, 1996.

Gilmore, John. *Swinging in Paradise: The Story of Jazz in Montreal.* Montreal: Véhicule Press, 1989.

Gilroy, Paul. *The Black Atlantic: Modernity and Double Consciousness.* Cambridge: Harvard University Press, 1993.

Glazer, Nathan, ed. *Clamor at the Gates: The New American Immigration.* San Francisco: ICS Press, 1985.

Gordon, Joyce. *Nevis: Queen of the Caribees.* London: Macmillan, 1985.

Greenberg, Cheryl Lynn. *"Or Does It Explode?": Black Harlem in the Great Depression.* New York: Oxford University Press, 1991.

Greening, William E. *It Was Never Easy, 1908–1958: A History of the Canadian Brotherhood of Railway, Transport and General Workers.* Ottawa: Mutual Press, 1961.

Grossman, James R. *Land of Hope: Chicago, Black Southerners, and the Great Migration.* Chicago: University of Chicago Press, 1989.

Hahn, Steven. *A Nation under Our Feet: Black Political Struggles in the Rural South from Slavery to the Great Migration.* Cambridge: Harvard University Press, Belknap Press, 2003.

Hale, Grace Elizabeth. *Making Whiteness: The Culture of Segregation in the South, 1890–1940.* New York: Pantheon Books, 1998.

Halli, Shiva, Frank Trovato, and Leo Driedger, eds. *Ethnic Demography: Canadian Immigrant, Racial and Cultural Variations.* Ottawa: Carleton University Press, 1990.

Halliday, Hugh A. *Wreck!: Canada's Worst Railway Accidents.* Toronto: Robin Brass, 1999.

Harris, William H. *Keeping the Faith: A. Philip Randolph, Milton P. Webster, and the Brotherhood of Sleeping Car Porters, 1925–37.* Chicago: University of Illinois Press, 1991.

Hart, E. J. *The Selling of Canada: The CPR and the Beginnings of Canadian Tourism.* Banff, Alta.: Altitude Publishing, 1983.

Haynes, Sam W., and Christopher Morris, eds. *Manifest Destiny and Empire: American Antebellum Expansionism.* Arlington: University of Texas, 1997.

Henry, Keith S. *Black Politics in Toronto since World War I.* Toronto: Multicultural History Society of Ontario, 1981.

Heron, Craig. *The Canadian Labour Movement: A Brief History.* 2nd ed. Toronto: Lorimer and Co., 1996.

———, ed. *The Workers' Revolt in Canada, 1917–1925.* Toronto: University of Toronto Press, 1998.

Higginbotham, Evelyn Brooks. *Righteous Discontent: The Women's Movement in the Black Baptist Church, 1880–1920.* Cambridge: Harvard University Press, 1993.

Higham, John. *Strangers in the Land: Patterns of American Nativism, 1860–1925.* 3rd ed. New Brunswick, N.J.: Rutgers University Press, 1988.

Hill, Daniel G. *The Freedom Seekers: Blacks in Early Canada.* Agincourt, Ont.: Book Society of Canada, 1981.

Hill, Herbert. *Black Labor and the American Legal System: Race, Work, and the Law.* Madison: University of Wisconsin Press, 1985.

Hoerder, Dirk. *Creating Societies: Immigrant Lives in Canada.* Montreal: McGill-Queen's University Press, 1999.

Holt, Jeff. *The Grand Trunk in New England.* West Hill, Ont.: Railfare Books, 1986.

Honey, Michael. *Southern Labor and Black Civil Rights: Organizing Memphis Workers.* Chicago: University of Illinois Press, 1993.

Hopkin, Deian R., and Gregory S. Kealey, eds. *Class, Community, and the Labour Movement: Wales and Canada, 1850–1930.* St. John's, N.F.: Llafur/CCLH, 1989.

Horne, Gerald. *Black and Brown: African Americans and the Mexican Revolution, 1910–1920.* New York: New York University Press, 2005.

Horsman, Reginald. *Race and Manifest Destiny: The Origins of American Racial Anglo-Saxonism.* Cambridge: Harvard University Press, 1981.

Hunter, Tera. *To 'Joy My Freedom: Southern Black Women's Lives and Labors after the Civil War.* Cambridge: Harvard University Press, 1997.

Ignatiev, Noel. *How the Irish Became White.* New York: Routledge, 1995.

Inniss, Sir Probyn. *Historic Basseterre: The Story of a West Indian Town.* St. John's, West Indies: n.p., 1985.

———. *Whither Bound: St. Kitts–Nevis?* St. John's, West Indies: Antigua Printing and Publishing, 1983.

Jacobson, Matthew F. *Whiteness of a Different Color: European Immigrants and the Alchemy of Race.* Cambridge: Harvard University Press, 1998.

James, Winston. *Holding Aloft the Banner of Ethiopia: Caribbean Radicalism in Early Twentieth-Century America.* New York: Verso Press, 1998.

Janken, Kenneth R. *White: The Biography of Walter White, Mr. NAACP.* New York: New Press, 2003.

Jenkinson, Jacqueline. *Black 1919: Riots, Racism, and Resistance in Imperial Britain.* Chicago: University of Chicago Press, 2009.

Jones, Jacqueline. *American Work: Four Centuries of Black and White Labor.* New York: W. W. Norton and Co., 1998.

———. *Labor of Love, Labor of Sorrow: Black Women, Work, and the Family, from Slavery to the Present.* New York: Vintage Books, 1995.

———, ed. *Southern Horrors and Other Writings: The Anti-Lynching Campaign of Ida B. Wells.* Boston: Bedford Books, 1997.

Jordan, William G. *Black Newspapers and America's War for Democracy, 1914–1920.* Chapel Hill: University of North Carolina Press, 2000.

Kasinitz, Philip. *Caribbean New York: Black Immigrants and the Politics of Race.* Ithaca, N.Y.: Cornell University Press, 1992.

Katz, William Loren. *The Black West: A Documentary and Pictorial History of the African American Role in the Westward Expansion of the United States.* New York: Simon and Schuster, 1996.

Kealey, Gregory S. *Workers and Canadian History.* Montreal: McGill-Queen's University Press, 1995.

Kealey, Gregory S., and W. J. C. Cherinski, eds. *Lectures in Canadian Labour and Working-Class History.* St. John's, N.F.: Committee on Canadian Labour History, 1985.

Kealey, Gregory S., and Michael S. Cross, eds. *Modern Canada, 1930–1980's.* Vol. 5, *Readings in Canadian Social History.* Toronto: McClelland and Stewart, 1984.

Kealey, Gregory S., and Peter Warrian, eds. *Essays in Canadian Working Class History.* Toronto: McClelland and Stewart, 1976.

Kealey, Gregory S., and Reg Whitaker, eds. *R.C.M.P. Security Bulletins: The Early Years, 1919–1929*. St. John's, N.F.: Canadian Committee on Labour History, 1994.

Kealey, Linda, and Joan Sangster, eds. *Beyond the Vote: Canadian Women and Politics.* Toronto: University of Toronto Press, 1989.

Keene, Jennifer D. *Doughboys, the Great War, and the Remaking of America.* Baltimore: Johns Hopkins University Press, 2001.

Kelley, Ninette, and Michael Trebilcock. *The Making of the Mosaic: A History of Canadian Immigration Policy.* Toronto: University of Toronto Press, 1998.

Kelley, Robin D. G. *Hammer and Hoe: Alabama Communists during the Great Depression.* Chapel Hill: University of North Carolina Press, 1990.

Kersten, Andrew W. *A. Philip Randolph: A Life in the Vanguard.* New York: Rowan and Littlefield, 2006.

Kilian, Crawford. *Go Do Some Great Thing: The Black Pioneers of British Columbia.* Vancouver: Douglas and McIntyre, 1978.

Knowles, Valerie. *Strangers at Our Gates: Canadian Immigration and Immigration Policy, 1540–1997.* Rev. ed. Toronto: Dundurn Press, 1997.

Kornweibel, Theodore, Jr. *No Crystal Stair: Black Life and the Messenger, 1917–1928.* Westport, Conn.: Greenwood Press, 1975.

———. *"Seeing Red": Federal Campaigns against Black Militancy, 1919–1925.* Bloomington: Indiana University Press, 1999.

Lamb, W. Kaye. *History of the Canadian Pacific Railway.* New York: Macmillan, 1977.

Lavallée, Omer. *Van Horne's Road: An Illustrated Account of the Construction and First Years of Operations of the Canadian Pacific Transcontinental Railway.* Don Mills, Ont.: Railfare Enterprises, 1974. Reprint, 1977.

Lee, Erika. *At America's Gates: Chinese Immigration during the Exclusion Era, 1882–1943.* Chapel Hill: University of North Carolina Press, 2003.

Leier, Mark. *Where the Fraser River Flows: The Industrial Workers of the World in British Columbia.* Vancouver: New Star Books, 1990.

Lemann, Nicholas. *The Promised Land: The Great Black Migration and How It Changed America.* New York: Vintage Books, 1991.

Lentz-Smith, Adriane. *Freedom Struggles: African Americans and World War I.* Cambridge: Harvard University Press, 2009.

Letwin, Daniel. *The Challenge of Interracial Unionism: Alabama Coal Miners, 1878–1921.* Chapel Hill: University of North Carolina Press, 1998.

Lipsitz, George. *Rainbow at Midnight: Labor and Culture in the 1940s.* Chicago: University of Illinois Press, 1994.

Locke, Alain, ed. *New Negro: Voices of the Harlem Renaissance.* New York: Albert and Charles Boni, 1925. Reprint, New York: Atheneum, 1992.

Logan, H. A. *Trade Unions in Canada: Their Development and Functioning.* Toronto: Macmillan, 1948.

MacKay, Donald. *The People's Railway: A History of Canadian National.* Vancouver: Douglas and McIntyre, 1992.

MacKay, Donald, and Lorne Perry. *Train Country: An Illustrated History of Canadian National Railways.* Vancouver: Douglas and McIntyre, 1994.

McCormack, A. Ross. *Reformers, Rebels, and Revolutionaries: The Western Canadian Radical Movement, 1899–1919.* Toronto: University of Toronto Press, 1977.

McGee, Terry, Eleanor Laqian, and Aprobicio Aquan, eds. *The Silent Debate: Asian Immigration and Racism in Canada.* Vancouver: University of British Columbia, 1997.

McKague, Ormond, ed. *Racism in Canada.* Saskatoon: Fifth House Publishers, 1991.

McKee, Bill, and Georgeen Klassen. *Trail of Iron: The CPR and the Birth of the West, 1880–1930*. Vancouver: Douglas and McIntyre, 1983.

McKeown, Adam. *Melancholy Order: Asian Migration and the Globalization of Borders*. New York: Columbia University Press, 2008.

McLaren, Angus. *Our Own Master Race: Eugenics in Canada*. Toronto: McClelland and Stewart, 1990.

Meier, August, and Elliott Rudwick. *Black Detroit and the Rise of the UAW*. Oxford: Oxford University Press, 1979.

Michel, Marc. *L'appel à l'Afrique: Contributions et réactions à l'éffort de guerre en A.O.F. (1914–1919)*. Paris: Publications de la Sorbonne, 1982.

Mika, Nick, and Helma Mika. *An Illustrated History of Canadian Railways*. Belleville, Ont.: Mika Publishing Co., 1986.

——. *Railways of Canada: A Pictorial History*. Toronto: McGraw-Hill Ryerson, 1972.

Miller, Kerby. *Emigrants and Exiles: Ireland and the Irish Exodus to North America*. New York: Oxford University Press, 1985.

Montero, Gloria. *We Stood Together: First-Hand Accounts of Dramatic Events in Canada's Labour Past*. Toronto: James Lorimer and Co., 1979.

Morton, Desmond. *A Peculiar Kind of Politics: Canada's Overseas Ministry in the First World War*. Toronto: University of Toronto Press, 1982.

——. *When Your Number's Up: The Canadian Soldier in the First World War*. Toronto: Random House of Canada, 1993.

Morton, Desmond, and J. L. Granatstein. *Marching to Armageddon: Canadians and the Great War 1914–1919*. Toronto: Lester and Orpen Dennys Publishers, 1989.

Morton, Desmond, and Glenn Wright. *Winning the Second Battle: Canadian Veterans and the Return to Civilian Life, 1915–1930*. Toronto: University of Toronto Press, 1987.

Mosher, Clayton J. *Discrimination and Denial: Systemic Racism in Ontario's Legal and Criminal Justice System, 1892–1961*. Toronto: University of Toronto Press, 1998.

Muraskin, William A. *Middle Class Blacks in a White Society: Prince Hall Freemasonry in America*. Berkeley: University of California Press, 1975.

Nelson, Bruce. *Divided We Stand: American Workers and the Struggle for Black Equality*. Princeton, N.J.: Princeton University Press, 2001.

Nelson, Scott. *Iron Confederacies: South Railways, Klan Violence, and Reconstruction*. Chapel Hill: University of North Carolina Press, 1999.

Noiriel, Gérard. *The French Melting Pot: Immigration, Citizenship, and National Identity*. Minneapolis: University of Minnesota Press, 1996.

Northrup, Herbert N. *Negro Employment in Basic Industry: A Study of Racial Policies in Six Industries*. Philadelphia: Industrial Research Unit, Wharton School of Finance and Commerce, University of Pennsylvania, 1970.

——. *Organized Labor and the Negro*. New York: Harper and Brothers, 1944.

Nugent, Walter. *Crossings: The Great Transatlantic Migrations, 1870–1914*. Bloomington: Indiana University Press, 1992.

Painter, Nell Irvin. *Exodusters: Black Migration to Kansas after Reconstruction*. New York: Alfred A. Knopf, 1977.

Palmer, Bryan D., ed. *Working Class Experience: Rethinking the History of Canadian Labour, 1800–1991*. 2nd ed. Toronto: McClelland and Stewart, 1992.

Palmer, Howard, ed. *Immigration and the Rise of Multiculturalism*. Vancouver: Copp Clark Publishing, 1975.

——. *Land of the Second Chance: A History of Ethnic Groups in Southern Alberta*. Lethbridge, Alta.: Lethbridge Herald, 1972.

——. *Patterns of Prejudice: A History of Nativism in Alberta*. Toronto: McClelland and Stewart, 1982.

——, ed. *The Settlement of the West*. Calgary: Comprint Publishing Co., 1977.

Palmer, Howard, and Tamara Palmer. *Alberta: A New History*. Edmonton: Hurtig Publishers, 1990.

——, eds. *Peoples of Alberta: Portraits of Cultural Diversity*. Saskatoon: Western Producer Prairie Books, 1985.

Palmer, Howard, and Donald Smith, eds. *The New Provinces: Alberta and Saskatchewan, 1905–1980*. Vancouver: Tantalus Research, 1980.

Palmer, Ransford W., ed. *In Search of a Better Life: Perspectives on Migration from the Caribbean*. New York: Praeger, 1990.

——. *Pilgrims from the Sun: West Indian Migration to America*. New York: Twayne Publishers, 1995.

Parry, J. H., and P. M. Sherlock, eds. *A Short History of the West Indies*. London: Macmillan, St. Martin's Press, 1971.

Perata, David. *Those Pullman Blues: An Oral History of the African-American Railroad Attendant*. New York: Twayne Publishers, 1996.

Pfeffer, Paula F. *A. Philip Randolph, Pioneer of the Civil Rights Movement*. Baton Rouge: Louisiana State University Press, 1990.

Phillips, Sir Fred. *Caribbean Life and Culture: A Citizen Reflects*. Kingston, Jamaica: Heinemann Publishers Caribbean, 1991.

Roediger, David. *The Wages of Whiteness: Race and the Making of the American Working Class*. New York: Verso Press, 1991.

Rogozinski, Jan. *A Brief History of the Caribbean from the Arawak and the Carib to the Present*. New York: Facts on File, 1992.

Ruck, Calvin W. *The Black Battalion—1916–1920: Canada's Best Kept Military Secret*. Halifax: Nimbus Publishing, 1987.

Santino, Jack. *Miles of Smiles, Years of Struggle: Stories of Black Pullman Porters*. Chicago: University of Illinois Press, 1990.

Sawh, Gobin, ed. *The Canadian Caribbean Connection—Bridging North and South: History, Influences, Lifestyles*. Hansport, N.S.: Carindo Cultural Association, 1992.

Scott, James C. *Domination and the Arts of Resistance: Hidden Transcripts*. New Haven, Conn.: Yale University Press, 1990.

Shack, William A. *Harlem in Montmartre: A Paris Jazz Story between the Great Wars*. Berkeley: University of California Press, 2001.

Shepard, R. Bruce. *Deemed Unsuitable: Blacks from Oklahoma Move to the Canadian Prairies*. Toronto: Umbrella Press, 1997.

Silverman, Maxim, ed. *Race, Discourse, and Power in France*. Brookfield, Vt.: Gower Publishers, 1991.

Smith, Rogers. *Civic Ideals: Conflicting Visions of Citizenship in U.S. History*. New Haven, Conn.: Yale University Press, 1997.

Smucker, Joseph. *Industrialization in Canada*. Scarborough, Ont.: Prentice-Hall of Canada, 1980.

Steedman, Mercedes. *Angels of the Workplace: Women and the Construction of Gender Relations in the Canadian Clothing Industry, 1880–1940*. Toronto: Oxford University Press, 1997.

Stevens, George R. *The History of the Canadian National Railways*. New York: Macmillan, 1973.

Stovall, Tyler. *Paris Noir: African Americans in the City of Light*. Boston: Houghton Mifflin, 1996.

Thompson, John Herd, and Allen Seager. *Canada, 1922–1939: Decades of Discord*. Toronto: McClelland and Stewart, 1985.

Tindall, George Brown. *The Emergence of the New South*. Baton Rouge: Louisiana State University Press, 1967.

Trelease, Allen W. *White Terror: The Ku Klux Klan Conspiracy and Southern Reconstruction*. Baton Rouge: Louisiana State University Press, 1971.

Troper, Harold M. *Only Farmers Need Apply: Official Canadian Government Encouragement of Immigration, 1896–1911*. Toronto: Griffin House, 1972.

Tuttle, William. *Race Riot: Chicago in the Red Summer of 1919*. Chicago: University of Illinois Press, 1996.

Tye, Larry. *Rising from the Rails: Pullman Porters and the Making of the Black Middle Class*. New York: Henry Holt, 2004.

Vecoli, Rudolph, and Suzanne Sinke, eds. *A Century of European Migrations, 1830–1930*. Chicago: University of Illinois Press, 1991.

Wade, Wyn Craig. *The Fiery Cross: The Ku Klux Klan in America*. New York: Simon and Schuster, 1987.

Walker, James W. St. G. *"Race," Rights and the Law in the Supreme Court of Canada*. Waterloo, Ont.: Osgoode Society for Canadian Legal History and Wilfrid Laurier University Press, 1997.

Welles, Benjamin. *Sumner Welles: FDR's Global Strategist—A Biography*. New York: St. Martin's Press, 1997.

Whitaker, Reginald. *Canadian Immigration Policy since Confederation*. Ottawa: Canadian Historical Association, 1990.

Whitfield, Harvey Amani. *Blacks on the Border: Black Refugees in British North America, 1815–1860*. Burlington: University of Vermont Press, 2006.

Williams, Dorothy W. *Blacks in Montreal, 1628–1986: An Urban Demography*. Cowansville, Que.: Les Éditions Yvon Blais, 1989.

———. *The Road to Now: A History of Blacks in Montreal*. Montreal: Véhicule Press, 1997.

Williams, Jack. *The Story of Unions in Canada*. Toronto: J. M. Dent & Sons, 1975.

Williams, Lillian S. *Strangers in the Land of Paradise: The Creation of an African American Community, Buffalo, New York, 1900–1940*. Bloomington: Indiana University Press, 1999.

Williams, Loretta. *Black Freemasonry and Middle-Class Realities*. Columbia: University of Missouri Press, 1980.

Williamson, Joel. *The Crucible of Race: Black-White Relations in the American South since Emancipation*. New York: Oxford University Press, 1984.

Wilson, Barbara. *Ontario and the First World War, 1914–1918*. Toronto: Champlain Society, 1977.

Wilson, Norman. *Tearing Down the Color Bar: A Documentary History and Analysis of the Brotherhood of Sleeping Car Porters*. New York: Columbia University Press, 1989.

Winks, Robin W. *The Blacks in Canada: A History*. 2nd ed. Montreal: McGill-Queen's University Press, 1997.

Wintz, Cary D., ed. *African American Political Thought, 1890–1930: Washington, Du Bois, Garvey, and Randolph*. Armonk, N.Y.: M. E. Sharpe, 1996.

Woodward, C. Vann. *Origins of the New South, 1877–1913*. Vol. 9. Baton Rouge: Louisiana State University Press, 1971.

Yans-McLaughlin, Virginia, ed. *Immigration Reconsidered: History, Sociology, and Politics*. New York: Oxford University Press, 1990.

Articles

Arnesen, Eric. " 'Like Banquo's Ghost, It Will Not Down': The Race Question and the American Railroad Brotherhoods, 1880–1920." *American Historical Review* 99, no. 5 (1994): 1601–33.

Backhouse, Constance. " 'I Was Unable to Identify with Topsy': Carrie M. Best's Struggle against Racial Segregation in Nova Scotia, 1942." *Atlantis* 22, no. 2 (1998): 16–26.

Bates, Beth Tompkins. "A New Crowd Challenges the Agenda of the Old Guard in the NAACP, 1933–1941." *American Historical Review* 102, no. 2 (1997): 340–77.

Beaton, Elizabeth. "An African-American Community in Cape Breton, 1901–1904." *Acadiensis* 24, no. 2 (1995): 65–97.

Bonacich, Edna. "A Theory of Ethnic Antagonism: The Split Labor Market." *American Sociological Review* 37, no. 5 (1972): 547–59.

Bracey, John H. "Allies or Adversaries? The NAACP, A. Philip Randolph and the 1941 March on Washington." *Georgia Historical Quarterly* 75, no. 1 (1991): 1–17.

Calliste, Agnes. "Blacks on Canadian Railways." *Canadian Ethnic Studies* 20, no. 2 (1988): 36–52.

——. "Race, Gender, and Canadian Immigration Policy: Blacks from the Caribbean, 1900–1932." *Journal of Canadian Studies* 28, no. 4 (1993–94): 131–48.

——. "Sleeping Car Porters in Canada: An Ethnically Submerged Split Labour Market." *Canadian Ethnic Studies* 19, no. 1 (1987): 1–20.

——. "The Struggle For Employment Equity by Blacks on American and Canadian Railroads." *Journal of Black Studies* 25, no. 3 (1995): 297–317.

Carrigan, D. Owen. "The Immigrant Experience in Halifax, 1881–1931." *Canadian Ethnic Studies* 20, no. 3 (1988): 28–41.

Chapman, Terry. "Early Eugenics Movement in Western Canada." *Alberta History* 25, no. 4 (1977): 9–17.

Charland, Maurice. "Technological Nationalism." *Canadian Journal of Political and Social Theory/Revue canadienne de théorie politique et sociale* 10, no. 1–2 (1986): 196–220.

Dempsey, James. "The Indians and World War One." *Alberta History* 31, no. 3 (1983): 1–8.

Edwards, Malcolm. "The War of Complexional Distinction: Blacks in Gold Rush California and British Columbia." *California Historical Quarterly* 56, no. 1 (1977): 34–45.

Fingard, Judith. "From Sea to Rail: Black Transportation Workers and Their Families in Halifax, c. 1870–1916." *Acadiensis* 24, no. 2 (1995): 49–64.

——. "Race and Respectability in Victorian Halifax." *Journal of Imperial and Commonwealth History* 20, no. 2 (1992): 169–95.

Gagnon, Jean-Pierre. "Canadian Soldiers in Bermuda during World War One." *Histoire sociale–Social History* 23, no. 45 (1990): 9–36.

Gaines, Kevin. "Rethinking Race and Class in African-American Struggles for Equality, 1885–1941." *American Historical Review* 102, no. 2 (1997): 378–87.

Gullace, Nicoletta F. "Sexual Violence and Family Honor: British Propaganda and International Law during the First World War." *American Historical Review* 102, no. 3 (1997): 714–47.

Harris, William H. "A. Philip Randolph as a Charismatic Leader, 1925–1941." *Journal of Negro History* 64, no. 4 (1979): 301–15.

Haycock, Ronald G. "The American Legion in the Canadian Expeditionary Force, 1914–1917: A Study in Failure." *Military Affairs* 63, no. 3 (1979): 115–19.

Henson, Tom M. "Ku Klux Klan in Western Canada." *Alberta History* 25, no. 4 (1977): 1–8.

Heron, Craig. "The Great War and Nova Scotia Steelworkers." *Acadiensis* 16, no. 2 (1987): 3–34.

Irby, Charles. "The Black Settlers on Saltspring Island in the Nineteenth Century." *Phylon* 35, no. 4 (1974): 368–74.

Kealey, Linda. "Canadian Socialism and the Woman Question, 1900–1914." *Labour/Le Travail* 13 (Spring 1984): 77–100.

Kelley, Robin D. G. "'But a Local Phase of a World Problem': Black History's Global Vision." *Journal of American History* 86, no. 3 (1999): 1045–77.

Lambertson, Ross. "The Dresden Story: Racism, Human Rights, and the Jewish Labour Committee of Canada." *Labour/Le Travail* 47 (Spring 2001): 43–82.

LeRoy, Gregory. "The Founding Heart of A. Philip Randolph's Union: Milton P. Webster and Chicago's Pullman Porters Organize, 1925–1937." *Labor's Heritage* 3, no. 3 (1991): 22–43.

MacKinnon, Mary. "Canadian Railway Workers and World War I Military Service." *Labour/Le Travail* 40 (Fall 1997): 213–34.

McWatt, Arthur C. "A Great Victory: The Brotherhood of Sleeping Car Porters in St. Paul." *Minnesota History* 55, no. 5 (1997): 202–16.

Morton, Desmond. "Aid to the Civil Power: The Canadian Militia in Support of Social Order, 1867–1914." *Canadian Historical Review* 51, no. 4 (1970): 407–25.

——. "Kicking and Complaining: Demobilization Riots in the Canadian Expeditionary Force, 1918–1919." *Canadian Historical Review* 61, no. 3 (1980): 334–60.

——. "The Supreme Penalty: Canadian Deaths by Firing Squad in the First World War." *Queen's Quarterly* 79, no. 3 (1972): 345–52.

Mundende, Chongo D. "The Undesirable Oklahomans: Black Immigration to Western Canada." *Chronicles of Oklahoma* 76, no. 3 (1998): 282–97.

Palmer, Howard, and Tamara Palmer. "Urban Blacks in Alberta." *Alberta History* 29, no. 3 (1981): 8–18.

Pfeffer, Paula F. "The Women behind the Union: Halena Wilson, Rosina Tucker, and the Ladies' Auxiliary to the Brotherhood of Sleeping Car Porters." *Labor History* 36, no. 4 (1995): 557–78.

Ponting, J. Richard, and Richard A. Wanner. "Blacks in Calgary: A Social and Attitudinal Profile." *Canadian Ethnic Studies* 15, no. 2 (1983): 57–76.

Posadas, Barbara M. "The Hierarchy of Color and Psychological Adjustment in an Industrial Environment: Filipinos, the Pullman Company, and the Brotherhood of Sleeping Car Porters." *Labor History* 23, no. 3 (1982): 31–52.

Price, Charles. "White Restrictions on Coloured Immigration." *Race and Class* 7, no. 3 (1966): 217–34.

Reinders, Robert C. "The John Anderson Case, 1860–1: A Study in Anglo-Canadian Imperial Relations." *Canadian Historical Review* 56, no. 4 (1975): 393–415.

Santino, Jack. "Miles of Smiles, Years of Struggle: The Negotiation of Black Occupational Identity through Personal Experience Narratives." *Journal of American Folklore* 96, no. 382 (1983): 393–412.

Schultz, John. "'White Man's Country': Canada and the West Indian Immigrant, 1900–1965." *American Review of Canadian Studies* 12, no. 1 (1982): 53–64.

Shadd, Adrienne. "Dual Labour Markets in 'Core' and 'Periphery' Regions of Canada: The Position of Black Males in Ontario and Nova Scotia." *Canadian Ethnic Studies* 19, no. 2 (1987): 91–109.

Sharpe, C. A. "Enlistment in the Canadian Expeditionary Force 1914–1918: A Regional Analysis." *Journal of Canadian Studies* 18, no. 4 (1983–84): 15–29.

Shenk, Gerald E. "Race, Manhood, and Manpower: Mobilizing Rural Georgia for World War I." *Georgia Historical Quarterly* 81, no. 3 (1997): 622–62.

Shepard, R. Bruce. "Diplomatic Racism: Canadian Government and Black Migration from Oklahoma, 1905–1912." *Great Plains Quarterly* 3, no. 1 (1983): 5–16.

———. "Plain Racism: The Reaction against Oklahoma Black Immigration to the Canadian Plains." *Prairie Forum* 10, no. 2 (1985): 365–82.

Silverman, Jason H. "Kentucky, Canada, and Extradition: The Jesse Happy Case." *Filson Club History Quarterly* 54 (January 1980): 342–52.

Stephens, Michelle A. "Black Transnationalism and the Politics of National Identity: West Indian Intellectuals in Harlem in the Age of War and Revolution." *American Quarterly* 50, no. 3 (1998): 592–608.

Stovall, Tyler. "The Color Line behind the Lines: Racial Violence in France during the Great War." *American Historical Review* 103, no. 3 (1998): 737–69.

Thomson, Colin. "Dark Spots in Alberta." *Alberta History* 25, no. 4 (1977): 31–36.

Troper, Harold M. "The Creek Negroes of Oklahoma and Canadian Immigration, 1909–1911." *Canadian Historical Review* 53, no. 3 (1972): 272–88.

Tuck, J. Hugh. "The United Brotherhood of Railway Employees in Western Canada, 1898–1905." *Labour/Le Travail* 11 (Spring 1983): 63–88.

Van Der Linden, Marcel. "Transnationalizing American Labor History." *Journal of American History* 86, no. 3 (1999): 1078–92.

Walker, James W. St. G. "Race and Recruitment in World War I: Enlistment of Visible Minorities in the Canadian Expeditionary Force." *Canadian Historical Review* 70, no. 1 (1989): 1–26.

Winks, Robin W. "A History of Negro School Segregation in Ontario and Nova Scotia." *Canadian Historical Review* 52, no. 2 (1969): 164–91.

Master's Theses and Doctoral Dissertations

Austin, B. "The Social Status of Blacks in Toronto." Ph.D. diss., McMaster University, 1972.

Avery, Donald H. "Canadian Immigration Policy and the Alien Question, 1896–1919: The Anglo-Canadian Perspective." M.A. thesis, University of Western Ontario, 1973.

Bates, Beth Tompkins. "The Unfinished Task of Emancipation: Protest Politics Come of Age in Black Chicago, 1925–1943." Ph.D. diss., Columbia University, 1997.

Bertley, June A. "The Role of the Black Community in Educating Blacks in Montreal, from 1910 to 1940, with Special Reference to Reverend Dr. Charles Humphrey Este." M.A. thesis, McGill University, 1982.

Bertley, Leo W. "The Universal Negro Improvement Association of Montreal, 1917–1979." Ph.D. diss., Concordia University, 1983.

Calderwood, William. "The Rise and Fall of the Ku Klux Klan in Saskatchewan." M.A. thesis, University of Saskatchewan, 1968.

Cameron, Ruth. " 'The Wheat from the Chaff': Canadian Restrictive Immigration Policy, 1905–1911." M.A. thesis, Concordia University, 1976.

Handleman, Don. "West Indian Associations in Montreal." M.A. thesis, McGill University, 1964.

Hill, Daniel G. "Negroes in Toronto: A Sociological Study of a Minority Group." Ph.D. diss., University of Toronto, 1960.

Hill, Judith S. "Alberta's Black Settlers: A Study of Canadian Immigration Policy and Practice." M.A. thesis, University of Alberta, 1981.

Israel, Wilfred. "Montreal Negro Community." M.A. thesis, McGill University, 1928.

Kornweibel, Theodore. "The Messenger Magazine, 1917–1928." Ph.D. diss., Yale University, 1971.

Lawson, Hilary. "Black Immigration to Canada, 1763–1975." M.A. thesis, University of Waterloo, 1979.

Mathieu, Sarah-Jane. "Under the Lion's Paw: Black Migration to Canada and the Development of Canadian Immigration Policy, 1880–1914." M.A. thesis, Yale University, 1995.

Pilton, James W. "Negro Settlement in British Columbia, 1858–1971." M.A. thesis, University of British Columbia, 1951.

Tuck, Hugh. "Canadian Railways and the International Brotherhoods: Labour Organizations in the Railway Running Trades in Canada, 1865–1914." Ph.D. diss., University of Western Ontario, 1975.

Williams, Charles. "Canadian-American Trade Union Relations: A Study of the Development of Bi-National Unions." Ph.D. diss., Cornell University, 1964.

Encyclopedias, Dictionaries, and Directories

Bacote, Samuel William, ed. *Who's Who among the Colored Baptists of the United States.* Kansas City, Mo.: Franklin Hudson Publishing, 1913.

Biographical Directory of Railway Officials in America. Chicago: Railway Age, 1906.

Black Biographical Dictionaries, 1750–1950. Alexandria, Va.: Chadwyck-Healey, 1987.

Canadian Encyclopedia: Year 2000 Edition. Toronto: McClelland and Stewart, 1999.

Henderson's Directory (Winnipeg). 1900–1955.

Jeffreys, Thomas. *Chronology of Nevis Events.* N.p., 1985.

Urquhart, Malcolm, and Kenneth Buckley, eds. *Historical Statistics of Canada.* Toronto: Macmillan, 1965.

Who's Who in Railroading. Chicago: Railway's Age, 1940.

Index

Adams, Henry, 34
African Americans: Matthew Bullock affair and, 171–83, 184, 242 (n. 130), 243 (nn. 164, 178, 182, 186), 244 (n. 188); collaboration with Canadian anti-black immigration policy, 43–47, 225 (nn. 114, 117, 120, 124); deportation of immigrants from Canada, 43, 140, 224–25 (n. 109), 246 (nn. 52–53); fear of rape by, 15, 25, 52–54; as general railroad workers in Canada, 5, 13, 62, 120; as general railroad workers in United States, 81, 227 (n. 22), 229 (n. 81); homesteading in Canada, 13, 22–24, 28–30, 31–38, 48–51, 53, 54–56, 59–60, 108, 203, 223 (n. 74); immigration to Canada, 1870 to 1914, 12–14, 16–17, 18–19, 22–30, 31–60, 75–79, 222 (nn. 27–28), 223 (nn. 60, 62, 74), 224 (nn. 93–94, 106, 108), 224–25 (n. 109); as industrial workers in Canada, 62, 75–79; labor unions and, 151, 195, 197, 198; medical inspections for immigrants, 23, 32, 42–43, 47, 59, 221 (n. 9), 224 (n. 106), 224–25 (n. 109); mixed race Native American and, 12–13, 22; monetary requirements for, as immigrants, 32, 33, 59, 95, 221 (n. 9), 222 (n. 28); newspapers of, 39–40, 45, 47, 147–48, 150–51, 152; in North Carolina, after World War I, 171–72, 174, 179, 183; professional immigrants to Canada, 34–35, 37–38, 221 (n. 9); social and political organizations of, 154, 155; underground railroad and, 5, 16, 173; white Canadian view of, as immigrants, 6, 7, 12–14, 15, 22–27, 36–38, 41–42, 48–57, 60, 145, 224 (n. 94); World War I and, 104–5, 107–8, 114, 119, 173, 175. *See also* Lynching; Sleeping car porters
African Canadians: Matthew Bullock affair and, 175–83, 184, 242 (n. 130), 243 (nn. 164, 178, 182, 186); businesses of, 18, 71, 72, 149, 150, 162, 200, 201, 240 (nn. 86, 90); churches of, 86, 146, 155, 158, 160–62, 175, 178, 179, 187, 199, 200, 202, 204, 240 (nn. 76–78); citizenship and, 145, 152, 153–54, 219 (n. 6); farmers, 156, 190, 202; fraternal lodges and, 18, 20, 72, 147, 154–56, 163, 201, 239 (nn. 46–47); as general railroad workers, 61, 62; housing and, 169, 201, 210; industrial workers, 75, 105, 120, 190; journalists of influence, 152, 153–54, 237 (n. 5), 238 (n. 36); leadership, 154, 238 (n. 45); neighborhoods of, 18, 125, 161, 164–65, 200, 201–2, 210, 221 (n. 42), 240 (n. 87), 241 (n. 105); newspapers of, 61, 100, 105, 106, 120, 141, 146–47, 148–50, 152, 153–54, 184, 198, 201, 237 (n. 18), 238 (nn. 20, 28, 36, 43); population increase after World War I, 163–64; social and political organizations of, 142, 144, 146, 149–50, 154–55, 156–58, 160, 162; white Canadian view of, after World War I, 6–7, 164, 165, 168–69, 183; white Canadian view of, before World War I, 40, 41, 57; white stereotyping of, 5, 51, 54, 58, 168. *See also* Civil rights; Great Depression; Jim Crow era; Labor unions; Segregation; Sleeping car porters; World War I
African Telegraph, 117, 234 (n. 79)
Afro-American Literary Bureau, 30
Alabama, 75, 76, 78
Alberta, 79, 156, 170, 239 (n. 54); black churches of, 102, 161; black immigration and, 22, 24, 25, 26, 32–33, 34–35, 36–37, 38, 41, 49–57, 222 (n. 32), 223 (n. 62); homesteading in, 17, 22–24, 26–27, 28, 32–33, 34–35, 38, 190, 203; World War I and, 102, 105. *See also* Calgary; Edmonton